THE GUIN
WHO'S WHO OF

General Editor: Colin Larkin

GUINNESS PUBLISHING

Dedicated to Chris Blackwell, who made a lot of it happen

FIRST PUBLISHED IN 1994 BY
GUINNESS PUBLISHING LTD
33 LONDON ROAD, ENFIELD, MIDDLESEX EN2 6DJ, ENGLAND

GUINNESS IS A REGISTERED TRADEMARK OF GUINNESS PUBLISHING LTD

BRITISH LIBRARY CATALOGUING-IN-PUBLICATION DATA
A CATALOGUE RECORD FOR THIS BOOK IS AVAILABLE FROM THE BRITISH LIBRARY

ISBN 0-85112-734-7

CONCEIVED, DESIGNED, EDITED AND PRODUCED BY
SQUARE ONE BOOKS LTD
IRON BRIDGE HOUSE, 3 BRIDGE APPROACH, CHALK FARM, LONDON NW1 8BD

EDITOR AND DESIGNER: COLIN LARKIN
EDITORIAL AND PRODUCTION: ALEX OGG, SUSAN PIPE AND JOHN MARTLAND
SPECIAL THANKS: CATHY BROOKS, DIANA NECHANICKY, TONY GALE, MARK COHEN,
SIMON DUNCAN, DAVID ROBERTS, SARAH SILVÉ
LOGO CONCEPT: DARREN PERRY

IMAGE SET BY L & S COMMUNICATIONS LTD

PRINTED AND BOUND IN GREAT BRITAIN BY THE BATH PRESS

EDITORS NOTE

The Guinness Who's Who Of Reggae forms a part of the multi-volume Guinness Encyclopedia Of Popular Music. There are now 12 titles available in the series, with further volumes planned.

Already available:
The Guinness Who's Who Of Indie And New Wave Music.
The Guinness Who's Who Of Heavy Metal.
The Guinness Who's Who Of Fifties Music.
The Guinness Who's Who Of Sixties Music.
The Guinness Who's Who Of Seventies Music.
The Guinness Who's Who Of Jazz.
The Guinness Who's Who Of Country Music.
The Guinness Who's Who Of Blues.
The Guinness Who's Who Of Soul.
The Guinness Who's Who Of Folk Music.
The Guinness Who's Who Of Stage Musicals.

Since the publication of the first of the Who's Who series in 1992 the most requested item has been 'when are you going to do a reggae one?'

By a wonderful coincidence of lucky scheduling we find ourselves in the midst of the biggest reggae boom since 1973. My own interest started in the mid-60s as an obnoxious little Essex mod desperately trying to listen to Prince Buster, The Folks Brothers, the Ethiopians and the Skatalites. These artists were never heard on the BBC and it was left to the Pirate Radio ships on the east coast and the London club scene. We would wait for the interval between sets from bands such as Georgie Fame And The Blue Flames to hear the latest imports. Ska and Bluebeat gradually evolved into Reggae - the common bond for Jamaican music other than Calypso. The next golden age began in the early 70s and by another coincidence I found myself in Jamaica

during 1973. For me the creative leaders were artists such as Scotty, U Roy, I Roy, Burning Spear and my personal favourite, Big Youth. Clearly though, Bob Marley is the pivotal figure from the genre. The worldwide acceptance and popularity of Marley is unlikely to ever be challenged or beaten. As we progress through the 90s his catalogue continues to sell as newcomers are introduced to the man who really put reggae into people's hearts and mind.

Although many of us were involved in writing entries, the vast majority were carried out by a group of seriously dedicated reggae lovers. Contributions were received from Mike Atherton, Johnny Rogan and Steve Barrow, but it was the co-ordination and enthusiasm of Harry Hawke that led us to dog lover Ian McCann, Lol Bell-Brown, Jean Scrivener and John Masouri. Harry attempted to beat them into shape and must be profusely thanked for his patience and ability to answer countless questions from the assistant editor Alex Ogg. He joined us towards the end of the project but took on great responsibility with good humour and diplomacy in addition to writing many entries at short notice. Alex would like to thank in addition to the contributors, the press department of Trojan Records and to Kate at Greensleeves Records who proved unflinchingly helpful and generous with their time. Ray Hurford joined us at the end to put together an accurate discography under great pressure.

Readers complaining of the inevitable omissions should write (politely) to me and considerations will be given for the next edition.

Tim Barrow supplied most of the photographs in the book. The quality of his work is quite outstanding and he deserves our thanks and a wider recognition in the future. The remaining photographs were supplied by Pictorial Press; pages 16, 66, 121, 134, 162, 165, 187, 208, 252, 254, 271 and 278; Island Records pages 28 and 279; EMI Records page 30; Jean Scrivener page 123; On-U-Sound page 248.

Once again Susan Pipe co-ordinated the production, this time with Alex. Both succeeded with no fuss and ridiculously good tempers.
The past year has been a particularly frenetic and difficult time and I have been fortunate to have had loyal friendship, love, help and support from the following trusted people: Brian Hogg, Johnny Black, Simon Barnett, Ken Hatherley, John Reiss, Jason Bryant, Mark Cohen, John Orley, Ken Bolam, Kip Trevor, Jane Stobart, Mustapha Sidki, David Larkin, Sabra Elliott, Carolyne Bowler, Tom, Dan, Carmen, Nana, Leone, Joanna, Geoff, Rhian and Diana. Final thanks to Chris and the Lime Squash King. Had I not been in Jamaica in 1973 I most certainly would have missed out on some perennially inspiring music.

Colin Larkin, March 1994

Abyssinians

Formed in 1968 in Jamaica, the Abyssinians comprised; lead singer Bernard Collins, with brothers Lynford and Donald Manning, who had been members of brother Carlton's group, Carlton And His Shoes. The latter band's 1968 recording, 'Happy Land', proved something of a blueprint for the Abyssinians' first record, 'Satta Massa Gana', a Rastafarian hymn sung partly in the ancient Ethiopian Amharic language, recorded at Coxsone Dodd's Studio One in March 1969. 'Satta', which has been 'versioned' countless times and by dozens of artists since, is a classic reggae roots song, its plangent, understated rhythm and the group's cool harmonies providing the template for the roots music that dominated throughout the following decade. Dodd apparently saw little potential in the song at the time though, and 'parked' it. Eventually the group saved enough money to buy the tape and release it on their own Clinch label in 1971, after which their faith in the song was repaid when it became a huge Jamaican hit. In order to cash in on 'Satta's' popularity, Dodd was then obliged to re-record the rhythm himself, releasing his own DJ and instrumental cuts. The Abyssinians second hit record, 'Declaration Of Rights', which actually featured Leroy Sibbles and another unknown on the backing vocals rather than the Manning brothers, also recorded at Studio One later in 1969, is similarly notable. The combination of the group's militant lyrics, their intense close harmony vocals and hard, rootsy rhythms has been much imitated but seldom equalled. During 1972 the trio released two more singles on Clinch, 'Let My Days Be Long' and 'Poor Jason White', both recorded at Dynamic Studios, as well as a version of 'Satta', retitled 'Mabrak', which featured the group reciting from the Bible. Keen listeners can actually hear them leafing through the book, searching for the relevant verses. Their next release, 'Yim Mas Gan' (1973), was recorded for producer Lloyd 'Matador' Daley and was released in the UK on the Harry J label. The group continued releasing tunes on their own label through the 70s, including 'Leggo Beast', Bernard Collins' solo on the 'Satta' rhythm track 'Satta Me No Born Yah', Big Youth's DJ version of 'Satta' called 'I Pray Thee'/'Dreader Dan Dread', Dillinger's 'I Saw Esaw' and Bernard, solo again on 'Crashie Sweep Them Clean', backed with Dillinger's 'Crashie First Socialist'. Records for other producers during the same period included 'Reason Time' (c.1974) for Federal Records, 'Love Comes And Goes' (1975) for Tommy Cowan's Arab label and the Amharic 'Tenayistillin Wandimae' (1975) for Geoffrey Chung. Their first album, *Forward On To Zion* was released in 1976, after being pirated in the UK, and further singles appeared on Clinch, including 'Propehcy' (1977) and 'This Land Is For Everyone' (1979). However, internal rivalries threatened the group's stability, and their second album, *Arise*, was recorded in less than amicable conditions. Eventually relations worsened and the group went their separate ways. Little was heard from any of them throughout the next decade, although Donald Manning, as Donald Abyssinians, released an excellent single, 'Peculiar Number', in the early 80s on his own Dahna Dimps label, and an American record company, Alligator, released the *Forward* compilation. The 90s though saw renewed activity from the group who had by now settled their differences and released two excellent singles, 'African Princess' and 'Swing Low', as well as making much of their classic back catalogue available again. They also embarked on a few concert dates in the UK which were very well received, their beautiful harmonies undiminished by the years.

Albums: *Forward On To Zion* (Different 1976), *Arise* (Front Line 1978).

Compilations: *Forward* (Alligator/Clinch 1980), *Satta Massa Gana* (Heartbeat 1993).

Adams, Glen

b. c.1950, Jamaica. Reggae organist and vocalist Glen Adams first came to prominence in the late 60s as a solo singer and a member of the Reggae Boys/Hippy Boys, although he had spent time earlier in the decade as part of the Pioneers. His noisy, but varied organ style made him a favourite in the studio bands of Lee Perry and Bunny Lee, and Adams was first choice for Perry's band on the UK tour that followed his 1969 hit, 'Return Of Django'. Perry was unlucky when 'A Live Injection', the most likely follow-up to 'Django', failed to chart, as Adam's playing on the record was astonishingly exciting. As part of Perry's Upsetters, Adams backed the Wailers, and when Bob Marley took Perry's rhythm section, the Barrett Brothers, with him to Island Records, Adams stuck loyally with Perry. However, by 1973-74 a new life was beckoning Adams in the USA, and he began to spend more and more time in Brooklyn, issuing records on his own Capo label. Adams finally moved to New York permanently in 1975, working on the Clocktower and Bullwackie labels, his material betraying the new influences of soul and funk. In the early 80s he worked with rapper T Ski Valley, meeting limited success, and appears to have retired from the business at present.

Admiral Bailey

b. Glendon Bailey, Kingston, Jamaica. The good humoured Admiral, with his burly, hook-laden dancehall anthems and a taste for military uniforms, got his break in 1986 when fellow DJ Josey Wales took him from U Roy's King Sturgav Hi-Fi to King Jammys. With Steelie & Clevie building the new digital rhythms and a prodigious line-up of artists to cater for, the Waterhouse studio was a hub of activity; Bailey promptly broke through the ranks with a run of hit tunes beginning with 'One Scotch', duetted with Chaka Demus. Then came 'Politician', 'Chatty Chatty Mouth', 'Ballot Box' (with Josey Wales) and in 1987, 'Punany', which fell foul of an airplay ban and necessitated a 'clean' version re-titled 'Healthy Body'. Further singles 'Big Belly Man', 'Jump Up', 'Top Celebrity Man' and 'Cater For Woman' continued the winning sequence throughout that year as Jammys released his debut album, *Kill Them With It*. There was evidence of work for other producers too; 'Neighbourhood Living' and 'Newsflash Time' for DJ Papa Biggy, and in 1988 tunes for Donovan Germain and Jah Life. Still the hits flowed for King Jammys. 'No Way No Better Than Yard', 'Don't Have Me Up', 'Original Dela Move' and 'Science' maintained his presence but found him flagging in the wake of Shabba Ranks' success, prompting the assertive 'Think Me Did Done'. Sadly *Ram Up You Party* failed to live up to expectations and he slipped into a relative decline, despite the occasional flurry of activity for Penthouse ('Help') in 1990 and Bobby Digital ('Ah Nuh Sin') a year later. In 1993 he returned to King Jammy, the only producer with whom he has enjoyed a consistent run of success.
Selected albums: *Kill Them With It* (Jammys/Live & Love 1987), *Undisputed* (Dynamic 1988), *Ram Up You Party* (Powerhouse 1989), *Born Champion* (Jammys/Live & Love 1991).

Admiral Tibet

Among the more 'correct' or 'cultural' of new dancehall singers, Tibet enshrined his intentions via the title-track of his Bobby Digital-produced album, *Reality Time*: 'Reality time, culture time, We want no slackness'. In the process Tibet accomplished one of the happier compromises between the dancehall era and the Rasta/roots fundamentals inspired by Bob Marley, Burning Spear *et al*.
Selected albums: *Come Into The Light* (Live & Love 1987), *The Time Is Going To Come* (Greedy Puppy 1988), *War In A Babylon* (RAS 1988), *Reality Time* (Digital B 1991).

Bernard Collins of the Abyssinians

Aggrovators

This was the name given by Jamaican producer Bunny Lee to whichever team of session musicians he happened to be using at any given time. Bunny had named his reggae shop and record label 'Agro Sounds' in the late 60s after hearing about the UK skinheads' adoption of the word to indicate a fight or problem, and he passed the name on to his musicians. These included many artists of varying quality but on their few long playing releases the Aggrovators included: Robbie Shakespeare (bass), Carlton 'Santa' Davis (drums), Earl 'Chinna' Smith (lead guitar), Ansel Collins (piano), Bernard 'Touter' Harvey (organ), Tony Chin (guitar), Bobby Ellis (trumpet), Vin Gordon (trombone), Tommy McCook (tenor saxophone) and Lennox Brown (alto saxophone). Lee's work came to the fore during the rocksteady period but he achieved real prominence in the mid-70s when his 'flying cymbals' sound, originally a reaction to the then prominent American 'disco beat', was ubiquitous. Rivalling the popularity of the vocal sides of the flying cymbal-releases, were the instrumental b-side 'versions', credited to the Aggrovators and mixed by King Tubby, and it was through these Jackpot and Justice record label releases that the Aggrovators achieved their real notoriety/fame.

Albums: *Bunny Lee Presents The Roots of Dub*, *Bunny Lee Presents Dub From The Roots*, *Brass Rockers - Introducing - The Aggrovators*, *Meets The Revolutionaries* (Third World 1977), *Kaya Dub* (Third World 1978), *Jammies In Lion Dub Style* (Live & Love 1978), *Johnny In The Echo Chamber* (Attack 1989), *Dub Jackpot* (Attack 1990), *Dub Justice* (Attack 1990).

Aitken, Laurel

b. 1927, Cuba. Of mixed Cuban/Jamaican extraction, Laurel, with his five brothers (including the veteran guitarist Bobby Aitken) and sisters settled in his father's homeland, Jamaica, in 1938. In the 40s he earned a living singing calypso for the Jamaican Tourist Board, as visitors alighted on Kingston Harbour. By the age of 15 Aitken, like many of the early Jamaican R&B and ska singers, including Owen Gray and Jackie Edwards, entered Vere John's 'Opportunity Hour', an amateur talent contest held on Friday nights at Kingston's Ambassador Theatre. He won the show for several weeks running, and his success there led to his establishment as one of the island's most popular club entertainers.

His first sessions were for Stanley Motta's Caribbean Recording Company, where he cut some calypso sides, the spiritual 'Roll Jordan Roll' and 'Boogie Rock'. The latter was one of the first ever Jamaican R&B/shuffle recordings. In 1958 he recorded 'Little Sheila'/'Boogie In My Bones', one of the first records produced by future Island Records boss, Chris Blackwell, using a Jamaican saxophonist and a white Canadian backing band. It emerged on Blackwell's R&B imprint where it spent over 12 months in the Jamaican chart, and in the UK on Starlite and, some years later, Island. Between 1958 and 1960, Aitken made a number of recordings in the pre-ska shuffle mode, including 'Bartender' and 'Brother David' for Ken Khouri, 'Judgement Day', 'More Whisky', 'Mighty Redeemer' and 'Zion' for Duke Reid, and 'Remember My Darling', 'The Saint', 'I Shall Remove', 'What A Weeping'/'Zion City Wall' and 'In My Soul' for Leslie Kong. On the strength of the popularity of these records in the UK, Aitken came to London in 1960, where he linked up with entrepreneur Emile Shalett, owner of Melodisc Records, to record a number of songs including 'Sixty Days & Sixty Nights', 'Marylee' and 'Lucille'. These were released on Shalett's new Blue Beat label, created to handle Jamaican music exclusively in the UK, one of its first releases being Aitken's aforementioned 'Boogie Rock'. Aitken returned to Jamaica in 1963 and cut 'Weary Wanderer' and 'Zion' for Duke Reid, and these too emerged on Blue Beat, the label which gave its name to this new music in the UK.

Back in London, he linked up with Graeme

Dennis Alcapone

Goodall's Rio Records, upon which around 20 titles appeared between 1964 and 1966, including 'Adam & Eve', 'Bad Minded Woman', 'Leave Me Standing', and 'We Shall Overcome', other titles appearing on the Ska Beat and Dice labels. In 1969 he enjoyed great success on Nu Beat, a subsidiary of the Palmer brothers' Pama group of labels, writing songs for other artists' including 'Souls Of Africa' for the Classics. He also cut 'Guilty' by Tiger (which was Aitken under a different name), and enjoyed great success with his own exuberant reggae sides like 'Woppi King', 'Haile Selassie', 'Landlords & Tenants', 'Jesse James', 'Skinhead Train', 'Rise & Fall', 'Fire In Me Wire', and the notorious 'Pussy Price', in which he bemoans the rising cost of personal services. During this period Aitken's popularity among Britain's West Indian population was matched only by his patronage by white skinhead youths, and it is mainly with successive skinhead and mod revivals that his name and music have been preserved.

The emerging trend towards cultural and religious (ie Rasta) themes amongst a new generation of young British (and Jamaican) blacks in the early 70s sharply contrasted with Aitken's brand of simple knees–up style. It probably did not help either that he had spent so long away from Jamaica's rapidly changing music scene, where producers like Lee Perry and Bunny Lee were coming up with new rhythms and ideas in production almost monthly. Aitken spent the 70s in semi–retirement, more or less gave up recording and moved to Leicester performing the odd club date, his show–stopping act undiminished despite his advancing years. He has recorded intermittently since, almost scoring a Top 40 hit with 'Rudi Got Married' for Arista in 1981, and riding for all he was worth on the 2-Tone bandwagon. UB40's *Labour Of Love* featured a cover of 'Guilty', since when Aitken has largely disappeared from view.

Selected albums: *Ska With Laurel* (Rio 1965), *High Priest Of Reggae* (Nu Beat 1969), *Early Days Of Blue Beat, Ska And Reggae* (Bold Reprive 1988), *It's Too Late* (Unicorn 1989), *Rise And Fall* (Unicorn 1989), *Sally Brown* (Unicorn 1989). With Potato 5: *Potato 5 Meet Laurel Aitken* (Gaz's 1987).

Video: *Live At Gaz's Rockin' Blues London* (1989).

Alcapone, Dennis

b. Dennis Smith, 6 August 1947, Clarendon, Jamaica. Initially inspired by U Roy, Alcapone began DJing for El Paso Hi-Fi in 1969. He was the first DJ to enjoy success on record after U Roy, and likewise the first to challenge his dominance. His initial records were made for youth producer and sometime ghetto dentist Keith Hudson; titles including 'Shades Of Hudson' (1970), 'Spanish Omega' (1970), 'Revelation Version' (1970), 'Maca Version' (1970) and 'The Sky's The Limit' (1970). During 1970-72 Dennis had big hits with Duke Reid, toasting his witty, half-sung, half-spoken lyrics over classic Treasure Isle rhythms and coasting to the top of the Jamaican chart with regularity. Tunes like 'Number One Station' (1971), 'Mosquito One' (1971), 'Rock To The Beat' (1972), 'Love Is Not A Gamble' (1972), 'Wake Up Jamaica' (1972), 'The Great Woggie' (1972), 'Teach The Children' (1972) and 'Musical Alphabet' (1972), all of which were recorded at Treasure Isle, and 'Ripe Cherry' (1971) and 'Alcapone Guns Don't Argue' (1971) for producer Bunny Lee, put Alcapone in the front rank of Jamaican DJs.

In the period from 1970 until he left for the UK in 1973, Alcapone's services were continually in demand. He made over 100 singles in this time and released three albums, in the process working with such producers as Coxsone Dodd, Lee Perry, Sir J J, Winston Riley, Joe Gibbs, Prince Buster, Randy's and others. He toured Guyana in 1970 and the UK in 1972-73, after having won the cup presented to the best DJ by *Swing* magazine in Jamaica. He also began production work, issuing music by himself, Dennis Brown, Augustus Pablo and Delroy

Roland Alphonso

Bob Andy

Wilson. Since the mid-70s he has been less active, still finding time to record albums for Sidney Crooks, Bunny Lee and Count Shelly. In the late 80s he returned to live performance, appearing at the WOMAD festival in Cornwall and Helsinki in 1989. 1990 saw him make more club appearances in the UK. Later in the year he returned to Jamaica for three months and recorded over digital rhythms for Bunny Lee. Alcapone remains the classic Jamaican toaster, on his best form capable of transforming and adding to any song he DJs, in the great toasting tradition pioneered in Jamaican dancehalls.

Albums: *Forever Version* (Studio One 1971), *Guns Don't Argue* (Attack/Trojan 1971), *King Of The Track* (Magnet 1974), *Belch It Off* (Attack 1974), *Dread Capone* (Third World 1976), *Investigator Rock* (Third World 1977), *Six Million Dollar Man* (Third World 1977). With Lizzy: *Soul To Soul DJ's Choice* (Treasure Isle/Trojan 1972). Compilations: *My Voice Is Insured For Half A Million Dollars* (Trojan 1989), *Universal Rockers* (RAS 1992).

Alphonso, Roland

b. c.1936, Clarendon, Jamaica. Alphonso attended the Alpha Catholic School For Boys where he learned tenor saxophone, flute and music theory. In 1959, he joined the studio group Clue J And His Blues Blasters who recorded several instrumentals including 'Shuffling Jug', which many hail as the first ska record. Other members of the group included Cluett Johnson (bass), Ernest Ranglin (guitar), Theophilus Beckford (piano) and Rico Rodriguez (trombone). In 1963, he became a founding member of the Skatalites, and was featured on hits such as 'Phoenix City' and 'El Pussy Cat'. After the Skatalites split up, he became the leader of the newly-founded Soul Brothers, whose hits included 'Dr Ring A Ding' and 'Miss Ska-Culation', many of which were credited to Rolando Al and the Soul Brothers. In 1967 he became a member of the Soul Vendors, led by Jackie Mittoo (organ, piano and arrangements). Roland was a featured soloist on many of their instrumentals such as 'Death In The Arena' and 'Ringo Rock', and can be heard on many other recordings made at Coxsone Dodd's Studio One. Dodd also released two excellent solo albums by Alphonso, *The Best Of Roland Alphonso* (c.1973) and *King Of Sax* (1975). During the mid-to late 70s, he recorded as a session musician for Bunny Lee, and an album of solo recordings from this period, *Brighter Shade Of Roots*, was later issued. In the early 80s he spent some time in New York recording for Lloyd Barnes' Wackies label. In 1984, a solo album from these sessions, *Roll On*, was issued.

Albums: *The Best Of Roland Alphonso* (Studio One 1973), *King Of Sax* (Studio One 1975), *Brighter Shade Of Roots* (Imperial 1982, covers c.1977-78), *Roll On* (Wackies 1984). Various: *Plays Ska Strictly For You*. With Jerry Johnson: *Reggae Sax*. With Don Drummond: *I Cover The Waterfront*.

Althea And Donna

Jamaican schoolgirls Althea Forest and Donna Reid were 17 and 18 years old respectively when their catchy, novelty hit 'Uptown Top Ranking', hit the top of the charts in their home country. Their producer Joe Gibbs had supplied the tune for his own label (Lightning in the UK) and the girls were responsible for the patois lyrics, complete with girlish yelps in the background. The infectious tune and lyrics caught the attention of the British record buying public in 1978 and the record went to number 1. A highly unusual event, made doubly so by the fact that 'Uptown Top Ranking' was actually an answer record to Trinity's 'Three Piece Suit'. Despite the backing of major record company Virgin, the duo found it impossible to produce an equally effective follow-up and went into the annals of pop history as chart-topping one-hit wonders.

Album: *Uptown Top Ranking* (Front Line 1978).

Andy, Bob

b. Keith Anderson, 1944, Jamaica. A former

Horace Andy

member of the original Paragons, Andy's late 60s work with Coxsone Dodd has become almost common property in reggae, and his rhythms and lyrics are still recycled time after time. All of his legendary Studio One output is collected conveniently on *Bob Andy's Song Book*. He has continually maintained that he is neither a great singer nor a songwriter, and it is possibly this self-effacement that has led to his lack of recognition outside reggae circles, despite national chart success in the UK with Marcia Griffiths (later of the I Threes) in 1969. Two duets (versions of 'Young, Gifted And Black' and 'Pied Piper') made the charts in the UK and led to extensive touring but little financial reward. Best known for his intelligent, thoughtful lyrics set within memorable song structures, Bob continued to work through the 70s and 80s with varying degrees of success, at times returning to his acting career. He has, however, still produced more time-honoured tracks than many more prolific artists, and songs such as 'You Don't Know', 'Feel The Feeling', 'The Ghetto Stays In The Mind' and 'Sun Shines For Me' are rightly regarded as classics, and serve only to enhance his reputation as one of the most important figures in Jamaican music.

Albums: *Bob Andy's Songbook* (Studio One 1972), *The Music Inside Me* (Sound Tracks 1975), *Lots Of Love And I* (High Note 1978), *Friends* (I-Anka 1983), *Freely* (I-Anka 1988), *Bob Andy's Dub Book As Revealed To Mad Professor* (I-Anka 1989), *Bob Andy's Dub Rock* (I-Anka 1992). With Marcia Griffiths: *Young Gifted And Black* (Harry J 1971), *Pied Piper* (Harry J 1971), *Really Together* (I-Anka 1987). Compilations: *Retrospective* (I-Anka 1986).

Andy, Horace

b. Horace Hinds, 1951, Kingston, Jamaica. This artist was affectionately renamed Andy as a tribute to Bob Andy, in respect of their mutual songwriting abilities, by Coxsone Dodd. Horace, also known as Sleepy, has always been a favoured vocalist among reggae fans and his eerie, haunting style has

been imitated endlessly by scores of lesser talents over the years. It was his work with Dodd which would make his reputation. His career at Studio One began with the single 'Something On My Mind', and eventually resulted in the classic 'Skylarking', one of reggae's most popular songs. From the mid-70s onwards, after leaving Studio One, Andy has worked with many important reggae producers in Jamaica, America and England. In the process he has recorded literally hundreds of records, most of which are now only available on impossible to find 45s, although some of the highpoints of his work with Coxsone, Bunny Lee and Wackies are still available on the listed albums. In the late 70s Andy moved to his new home in Hartford, Connecticut. His influence on reggae music in general, and reggae singers in particular is incalculable, yet he remains a diffident figure amongst much brasher yet less talented reggae 'stars'.

Selected albums: *Skylarking* (Studio One 1972), *You Are My Angel* (Trojan 1973), *In The Light* (Hungry Town 1977), *Dance Hall Style* (Wackies 1983, released in the UK as *Exclusively* - Solid Groove 1982), *Showcase* (Vista Sounds 1983), *Sings For You And I* (Striker Lee 1985), *Confusion* (Music Hawk 1985), *Elementary* (Rough Trade 1985), *Big Bad Man* (Rockers Forever 1987), *Haul And Jack Up* (Live & Love 1987), *Fresh* (Island In The Sun 1988), *Shame And Scandal* (1988), *Everyday People* (Wackies 1988). With Patrick Andy: *Clash Of The Andys* (Thunderbolt 1985). Compilations: *Best Of Horace Andy* (Coxsone 1974), *Best Of Horace Andy* (Culture Press 1985; different track-listing).

Apache Indian

The 'Don Raja' of British Asian raggamuffin, Apache Indian (b. Steve Kapur, Birmingham, England, 11 May 1967) has come to represent a cross-cultural fusion of musics that has both baffled and excited pundits and punters alike in the mid-90s. Apache Indian grew up in Handsworth, Birmingham, in the 70s - an era when the

Apache Indian

city was being celebrated as a kind of UK reggae melting pot through the efforts of Steel Pulse and others, whose *Handsworth Revolution* (1976) first put it on the musical map. Although he was of Indian parentage, Apache hung out in the early 80s with reggae sound systems, sporting dreadlocks and an abiding love of Bob Marley. By the mid-80s, locks trimmed to a sharp fade, he was known locally on the mic as a dancehall rapper, and in 1990 he cut his first single, 'Movie Over India', as a white label, later picked up by British reggae distributors Jet Star. A compelling, catchy ragga tune, with a few elements of bhangra, the preferred music of many UK Asian kids, the record was a huge hit in both the reggae and bhangra markets. Two more cult hits followed, 'Chok There' and 'Don Raja', before the majors became interested in him.

Island Records finally lured him into a contract, and 1993's *No Reservations* was cut in Jamaica and included Sly Dunbar, Bobby Digital and Robert Livingstone in the producers' sofa. Critically acclaimed, it saw Apache move away from the frothier elements of his distinctive ragga-reggae and towards the role of social commentator and Anglo-Asian representative. This approach was exemplified in the three crossover hits, 'Arranged Marriage', 'Boom Shack A Lack' and 'Moving On (Special)', the latter a cry of resistance against the election of a BNP member to a council seat in Tower Hamlets, London. At the time of writing, Apache's assimilation into the mainstream music business continues apace (drawing a little flak from more traditional elements in the reggae business, perhaps miffed at the apparent ease with which Apache has conquered the pop charts as his ragga audience has dropped him). His propensity for winning baubles ('Best Newcomer' in the British Reggae Industry Awards 1990 was built upon by a short-list entry for the Mercury Prize in 1993 and a nomination for four BRIT awards in 1994) and his open, friendly personality made him a media favourite throughout 1993.

Album: *No Reservations* (Island 1993).

Ariwa Sounds

One of only two studio-owning reggae labels to survive in the UK for any length of time (the other is Fashion), the success of Ariwa Sounds can be put down to the determination of one man, Neil Fraser. Guyana-born Fraser started Ariwa as a four-track operation in his living room in Thornton Heath, South London in 1979, prompted by a lifelong love of electronics and reggae, plus an interest in the sweet sounds of lovers rock, which were close enough to the Philly soul he also loved to make Fraser want to get involved. Those first recordings, including the debut of the late lovers' legend Deborahe Glasgow, can be found on *The Early Sessions* LP. By 1982 Fraser had moved premises to Peckham, working on at first eight, and subsequently sixteen-track equipment. Styling himself as the Mad Professor, and calling his band The Sane Inmates, Fraser rapidly acquired a reputation for eccentric, attention-grabbing records. Though his influences could clearly be discerned, his mixes soon revealed a quality all of their own, to a point where an Ariwa recording could be easily differentiated from all others. His 'Dub Me Crazy' series, eventually running into double figures, won him a reputation on the alternative rock scene, and John Peel was an early champion, frequently spinning his productions. Early albums with Tony Benjamin, Sergeant Pepper and Ranking Ann did not sell especially well in the reggae market, but were always out-of-the-ordinary or worthy of note. By 1984 Fraser had teamed up with Sandra Cross, a lovers rock singer and sister of Victor Cross, an early Ariwa sessioneer. The siblings had worked together as The Wild Bunch, an Ariwa album act, before Sandra, a sweet-voiced, confident singer, proved capable of delivering Ariwa the hits it was seeking. Her *Country Life* (1985), built around a string of hits including a cover of The Stylistics' 'Country Living' (previously covered in the

18

Neil Frazer aka The Mad Professor (see Ariwa Sounds)

reggae idiom by the Diamonds) was something of a commercial breakthrough. Other albums from Jamaican singer Johnny Clarke, and DJs Peter Culture and Pato Banton brought further acclaim, and the open-minded Fraser began to work with acts as diverse as UK indie bands and sound system legend Jah Shaka.

Wolverhampton-based DJ Macka B's debut album, *Sign Of the Times* (1986), was the strongest Ariwa release yet, and remains perhaps the most effective roots statement ever recorded in the UK. A move to West Norwood found Fraser the boss of the largest black-owned studio complex in the UK, with two consoles, one a powerful, outboard-littered twenty-four track. It was here he fashioned some of his most wonderful lovers rock records, including John Mclean's 'If I Give My Heart To You' (actually produced by Captain Sinbad at Ariwa in 1988), Sandra Cross' 'Best Friend's Man' and Kofi's revival of her own earlier hit, 'I'm In Love With A Dreadlocks' (both 1989). Fraser also attracted some heavyweight Jamaican names to his premises, including Bob Andy, Lee Perry and Faybiene Miranda. He did not neglect his eccentric side though, cutting strange tunes such as Professor Doppler's 'Doppler Effect', and 'Echoes Of Deaf Journalists', an attack on the writers at *Echoes* newspaper. Although more recent times have not seen the Mad Professor dominating the UK reggae charts with quite such regularity (Fraser has always shied away from the guns'n'sex sound of ragga), he retains huge respect and a loyal following world-wide. Regular Ariwa jaunts from New York to Holland, Australia to Poland and elsewhere have ensured strong export sales for his unique talents.

Selected albums: *Dub Me Crazy* (Ariwa 1982), *Mad Professor: The African Connection* (Ariwa 1984), *Jah Shaka Meets Mad Professor At Ariwa Sounds* (Ariwa 1984), *Negus Roots Meets The Mad Professor* (Negus Roots 1984), *Dub Me Crazy Part 5* (Ariwa 1985), *Professor Captures Pato Banton* (Ariwa 1985), *Schizophrenic Dub* (Ariwa 1986), *Stepping In Dub Wise Country* (Ariwa 1987), *The Adventures Of A Dub Sampler* (Ariwa 1987), *Dub Me Crazy Party* (Ariwa 1987), *Roots Daughters* (Ariwa 1988). Productions: Macka B: *Sign Of The Times* (Ariwa 1986). Sandra Cross: *Comet In The Sky* (Ariwa 1988). Kofi: *Black With Sugar* (Ariwa 1989). Various: *Roots Daughters* (Ariwa 1988), *Ariwa Hits '89* (Ariwa 1989).

Aswad

Formed in west London, England, in 1975, this premier UK reggae group featured Brinsley Forde (b. 1952, Guyana, vocals/guitar), George Oban (bass), Angus Gaye (b. 1959, London; drums) and Donald Griffiths (b. 1954, Jamaica; vocals). Additional musicians include Vin Gordon, Courtney Hemmings, Bongo Levi, Karl Pitterson and Mike Rose. Taking their name from the Arabic word for black, they attempted a fusion of Rastafarianism with social issues more pertinent to their London climate. Their self-titled debut was well received, and highlighted the plight of the immigrant Jamaican in an unfamiliar and often hostile environment. A more ethnic approach was evident on the superior follow-up, *Hulet*, which placed the group squarely in the roots tradition only partially visited on their debut. Their instrumentation proved particularly impressive, with imaginative song structures filled out by a dextrous horn section. The departure of Oban, who was replaced by Tony 'Gad' Robinson (who had previously served as keyboard player) did little to diminish their fortunes. Forde, meanwhile, was featured in the film *Babylon,* which included Aswad's powerful 'Warrior Charge' on its soundtrack. A brief change of label saw them record two albums for CBS before they returned to Island for *Live And Direct*, recorded at London's Notting Hill Carnival in 1982. By early 1984 they were at last making a small impression on the UK charts with 'Chasing The Breeze', and a cover of Toots Hibbert's '54-46 (Was My Number)'. *To The Top* in 1986 represented arguably the definitive

Aswad

Aswad studio album, replete with a strength of composition which was by now an enviable trait. While they consolidated their reputation as a live act, they would use *Distant Thunder* as the launching pad for a significant stylistic overhaul. The shift to lightweight funk and soul, although their music maintained a strong reggae undertow, saw them become national chart stars. The album bore a 1988 UK number 1 hit in 'Don't Turn Around'. Since then, Aswad have remained a major draw in concert, though their attempts to plot a crossover path have come unstuck in more recent times, despite the appearance of such as Shabba Ranks on their 1990 set, *Too Wicked*. Although they have not always appealed to the purists, Aswad are one of the most successful reggae-influenced groups operating in the UK, thoroughly earning all the accolades that have come their way, particuarly via their riveting live act.

Albums: *Aswad* (Mango/Island 1975), *Hulet* (Grove Music 1978), *New Chapter* (CBS 1981), *Not Satisfied* (CBS 1982), *A New Chapter Of Dub* (Mango/Island 1982), *Live And Direct* (Mango/Island 1983), *Rebel Souls* (Mango/Island 1984), *Jah Shaka Meets Aswad In Addis Ababa Studio* (Jah Shaka 1985), *To The Top* (Simba 1986), *Distant Thunder* (Mango/Island 1988), *Too Wicked* (Mango/Island 1990). Compilations: *Showcase* (Grove Music 1981), *Renaissance* (Stylus 1988), *Crucial Tracks - The Best Of Aswad* (Mango/Island 1989), *Don't Turn Around* (Mango/Island 1993), *Firesticks* (Mango/Island 1993).

Videos: *Always Wicked* (1990), *Distant Thunder Concert Video* (1991).

B

Banton, Buju

b. Mark Myrie, 1973, Kingston, Jamaica. Raised in Denham Town, Buju began his DJ apprenticeship at the age of 13 with the Rambo Mango and Sweet Love sound systems. Fellow DJ Clement Irie took him to producer Robert French for his debut release, 'The Ruler', in 1986. The following year he voiced for Red Dragon, Bunny Lee and Winston Riley, who later remixed his tracks with a notable degree of success. By 1990 his voice had ripened to a warm, deep growl that drew comparisons with Shabba Ranks. He was then introduced to Dave Kelly, resident engineer at Donovan Germain's Penthouse Studio. Together they wrote many of the hits that established Buju as the most exciting newcomer of 1991: courting controversy with lyrics revealing his preference for light-skinned girls on 'Love Mi Browning', and defining dancehall fashions with tunes like 'Women Nuh Fret', 'Batty Rider', 'Bogle Dance' and 'Big It Up', the debut release on Kelly's own Mad House label.

Penthouse released the *Mr. Mention* album as a wave of hits for themselves, Soljie, Shocking Vibes, Bobby Digital and Exterminator began to underline his rapid rise to prominence. Most notorious of these projects was the violently homophobic 'Boom Bye Bye' for Shang. Given national TV exposure in the UK, it created a storm of media protest. By now his records were dominating the reggae charts; often in combination with fellow Penthouse artists like Wayne Wonder, Beres Hammond, Marcia Griffiths and Carol Gonzales. Mercury Records signed him to a major label US deal later that year. By 1993 his lyrics dealt increasingly with cultural issues. 'Tribal War', featuring an all-star ensemble - was voiced in response to Jamaica's warring political factions, 'Operation Ardent' railed against Kingston's curfew laws and 'Murderer' was provoked by the shooting of his friend and fellow DJ, Pan Head. It is this streak of hard-edged reality - offset by his typically coarse, melodic romancing of the ladies - that has established him as an artist of international repute, second only to Shabba in the DJ popularity stakes.

Selected albums: *Stamina Daddy* (Techniques 1991), *Mr. Mention* (Penthouse 1991), *Voice Of Jamaica* (Mercury 1993).

Banton, Pato

b. Patrick Murray, Birmingham, England. Banton first came to the public's attention in 1982 on the Beat's *Special Beat Service* album, duelling with Ranking Roger on 'Pato And Roger A Go Talk', before releases on the Fashion and Don Christie labels. His first long playing effort saw him paired with the wizardry of the Mad Professor, a combination that he would return to four years later for the *Recaptured* set. On his solo debut Banton was backed instead by the Birmingham-based Studio 2 house band. Throughout he coloured his Rasta toasting/dub with comic impersonations of those characters populating his songs. Since then his records have leaned progressively towards pop/soul, blurring the dividing lines between Jamaican toasting and American rap. For *Wize Up!*, which contained an unlikely alternative radio hit in his cover of the Police's 'Spirits In The Material World', Banton was joined by David Hinds of Steel Pulse.

Albums: *Mad Professor Captures Pato Banton* (Ariwa 1985), *Never Give In* (Greensleeves 1987), *Visions Of The World* (IRS 1989), *Recaptured* (Ariwa 1989), *Wize Up! (No Compromize)* (IRS 1990).

Barnes, Lloyd

b. c.1948, Jamaica. In the early 70s Barnes emigrated to New York where he commenced his career as a producer and recording engineer, having previously recorded as a singer for Prince Buster in the mid-60s. Originally working in partnership with Munchie Jackson, he established one of the first reggae studios in the USA, and developed his own roots sound. Using the Reckless Breed as his house band, his recordings with local and established talent were released on a bewildering array of labels including Hamma, Rawse, Bullwackie, City Line, Senrab (Barnes backwards), Senta (his mother's name) and Wackies, the latter becoming his main outlet. By the late 70s he had developed a magical and intoxicating sound and issued outstanding recordings by artists such as Horace Andy, Junior Delahaye, Jerry Harris, Milton Henry, Jah Batta, Wayne Jarrett, Jezzreel, the Lovejoys, Maxine Miller, Sugar Minott and Audley Rollins. He also issued his own vocal recordings as the Chosen Brothers, as well as a series of dub albums featuring his skills as an engineer. He issued streams of music until the mid-80s, after which his output became more erratic, but he was still capable of releasing such fine works as Chris Wayne's *Freedom Street* (1988), and Jackie Mittoo's *Wild Jockey* (1989).

Albums: As the Chosen Brothers: *Sing And Shout* (Wackies 1985). Dub albums: *Creation Dub* (Wackies 1977), *Tribesman Assault* (Wackies 1977), *African Roots Act I* (Wackies 1980), *African Roots Act 2* (Wackies 1980), *African Roots Act 3* (Wackies 1983), *Jamaica Super Dub* (Wackies 1983), *African Roots Act 4* (Wackies 1984), *African Roots Act 5* (Wackies 1985). Productions: Various: *Selective Showcase* (Wackies 1980), *Jah Son Invasion* (Wackies 1982), *Jah Children Invasion* (Wackies 1983), *Dance Hall Collection* (Tachyon 1987), *Free South Africa* (Wackies 1987), *Dance Hall Reality* (Wackies 1987). Roland Alphonso: *Roll On* (Wackies 1984). Horace Andy: *Dance Hall Style* (Wackies 1982), *Everyday People* (Wackies 1988). John Clarke: *Visions Of John Clarke* (Wackies 1979). Junior Delahaye: *Reggae* (Wackies 1982). Tyrone Evans: *Sings Bullwackie Style* (Wackies 1984). Jerry Harris: *I'm For You* (Wackies 1982). Milton Henry: *Who Do You Think I Am?* (Wackies 1985), *Babylon Loot* (Wackies 1988). Jah Batta: *Argument* (Wackies 1984). Wayne Jarrett: *Bubble Up* (Wackies 1982). Jezzreel: *Great Jah Jah Showcase* (Wackies 1980), *Rockers* (Wackies 1982). Jerry Johnson: *For All Seasons* (Wackies 1985), *The Score* (Wackies 1988). The Lovejoys: *Lovers Rock Showcase* (Wackies 1981). Maxine Miller: *Showcase* (Wackies 1980). Sugar Minott: *Wicked A Go Feel It* (Wackies 1984), *Jamming In The Street* (Wackies 1987). Jackie Mittoo: *Wild Jockey* (Wackies 1989). Audley Rollins: *Role Model* (Wackies 1985). Chris Wayne: *Freedom Street* (Wackies 1988).

Beckford, Theophilus

b. 1935, Kingston, Jamaica. One of the pioneers of indigenous Jamaican music, Theo Beckford's piano playing was one of the factors that determined and defined the feel and sound of ska music (as opposed to Jamaican rhythm and blues) in the late 50s and early 60s. Having purchased a piano in 1955 Beckford conquered the instrument and was playing professionally two years later. His 'Easy Snapping', on Coxsone Dodd's Worldisc label was a huge hit, and its 'oh so lazy' feel, and emphasis firmly on the off-beat, were widely imitated. Theo hit again for Coxsone with 'Jack & Jill Shuffle', and he formed his own label King Pioneer, but it is his session work with Clue J And His Blues Blasters, and countless other studio/session bands that form the bulk of his recorded work. He was employed by Coxsone in this capacity as well as by Duke Reid, Beverley's, Prince Buster and Clancy Eccles. Beckford reappeared in 1991 as part of Studio One's *The Beat Goes On: 35 Years In The Business* shows at Kingston's National Arena, and in 1992 'Easy Snapping' enjoyed something of a revival when it was used as background music for a television jeans advert - further proof of its timeless appeal.

Albums: Various: *Oldies But Goodies (Vol. 1)* (Studio One - includes 'Easy Snapping').

Bell, Nyanka

b. 1954, Touba, Cote d'Ivoire. Like her

fellow-Ivoirian vocalist Alpha Blondy, Bell has looked overseas for much of her inspiration. While Blondy turned to Jamaican reggae, Bell found a stylistic home in the faster and more effervescent rhythms of the Francophone Caribbean. Her 1984 debut album, *Amio*, embraced funk, disco and ballads. Two years later the follow-up, *If You Came To Go,* moved towards the Antilles with one track, 'Emotion', written by top Antillean band Kassav's Jacob Desarieux, and the Desarieux-arranged 'Chogologo'. Despite a strong international repertoire - she speaks French but sings in English - Bell remains largely viewed as a reggae artist.

Albums: *Amio* (1984), *If You Came To Go* (1986), *Djama* (1989).

Beverley's

(see Kong, Leslie)

Big Youth

b. Manley Augustus Buchanan, February 1955, Jamaica. A stylistic and artistic innovator of the highest order, Big Youth started life, following a youth of extreme poverty, as a cab driver. He subsequently found employment as a mechanic working in the Skyline and Sheraton hotels in Kingston. He practised while at work, listening to his voice echo around the empty rooms, and would sometimes be allowed to take the microphone at dances and thereby gain some experience. His popularity grew steadily until Big Youth became the resident DJ for the Lord Tippertone sound system (one of the top Kingston sounds in the early 70s), where he clashed regularly with other top DJs and gradually built an awesome reputation. It was not too long before he was approached by record producers eagerly looking for the next 'big thing'. Unfortunately his early attempts, notably the debut cut 'Movie Man', released on Gregory Isaacs and Errol Dunkley's African Museum label, failed to capture this live magic. Further sides such as 'The Best Big Youth', 'Tell It Black' and 'Phil Pratt Thing' helped to marginally enhance his reputation. But his first recording for Keith Hudson in 1972 changed everything. Hudson was a producer who understood DJs, knew how to present them properly and was one of the first to record U Roy and Dennis Alcapone. The memorable 'S.90 Skank' went straight to number 1 in Jamaica and stayed there for many weeks. Celebrating the West Kingston cult of the motorbike (the S.90 was a Japanese model), it opened with the sounds of an actual motorbike being revved up in the studio, and continued with Youth proclaiming 'Don't you ride like lightning or you'll crash like thunder'. For the next few years he really did ride like lightning and Bob Marley was the only artist to approach his popularity. Even the latter could not lay claim to Youth's unique distinguishing feature, front teeth inlaid with red green and gold jewels.

Representing the authentic sound of the ghetto, Big Youth set new standards for DJs to say something constructive on record as well as exhort dancers to greater heights. The stories he told gave penetrating insights into the downtown Kingston ghettoes and into the mind of Rastafarian youth. His debut set featured rhythms from previous Dennis Brown and Gregory Isaacs recordings, though by *Hit The Road Jack* Youth had moved on to covering soul standards in his distinctive style. Hit followed hit and while he always gave his best for other producers, his self-produced records were even better. He formed his Negusa Nagast (Amharic for King of Kings) and Agustus Buchanan labels in 1973 for greater artistic and financial control of his career and many of these records' stark, proud lyrics set against jagged, heavy rhythms still sound as stunning 20 years after their initial release. He held little appeal outside of the Jamaican market perhaps because he was too raw and uncompromising, but his innovations are still reverberating through reggae and rap. Though his records and live appearances are now few and far between, Youth has remained at the top for longer than any

Big Youth

other DJ apart from U Roy, and he is still respected and revered by the reggae cogniscenti.

Albums: *Screaming Target* (Trojan 1973), *Reggae Phenomenon* (Negusa Nagast 1974), *Dreadlocks Dread* (Klik 1975, Front Line 1978), *Natty Cultural Dread* (Trojan 1976), *Hit The Road Jack* (Trojan 1976), *Isaiah First Prophet Of Old* (Front Line 1978), *The Chanting Dread Inna Fine Style* (Heartbeat 1983), *Live At Reggae Sunsplash* (Sunsplash 1984), *A Luta Continua* (Heartbeat 1985), *Manifestation* (Heartbeat 1988). Compilations: *Everyday Skank - The Best Of Big Youth* (Trojan 1980), *Some Great Big Youth* (Heartbeat 1981), *Jamming In The House Of Dread* (ROIR 1991, cassette only).

Biggs, Barry

b. 1953, St Andrews, Jamaica. Biggs is a lovers rock specialist, who started his professional career in 1968 with a version of Stevie Wonder's 'My Cheri Amour' for his producer, Harry 'J' Johnson. Previously he had worked as a backing singer for mid-60s Coxsone Dodd productions at Studio One, and with Duke Reid at Treasure Isle. He also spent six months working with the Crystalites. Biggs subsequently made the local Jamaican charts with 'One Bad Apple' for the Dynamic Sounds label, where he also worked as a producer and engineer. However, it took a recording originally completed in 1972, 'Work All Day', to break him internationally. From then on he would be closely identified with the blend of sweet reggae and high pitched soul vocals the single introduced. Although he amassed a total of six UK chart entries between 1976 and 1981, he would only break the UK Top 20 once. The occasion was the release of 'Sideshow', distinguished by its low-key, distant production, which rose to number 3 in December 1976. There were also two albums cut with Bunny Lee which were destined never to see the light of day. However, both 'Wide Awake In A Dream' (1980) and 'A Promise Is A Comfort To A Fool' (1982) topped the Reggae listings.

Albums: *What's Your Sign Girl?* (Dynamic 1980), *Barry Biggs & The Inner Circle* (Trojan 1983), *Mr Biggs* (Trojan 1983), *So In Love* (Starlight 1989).

Black Slate

Large roots reggae ensemble comprising members drawn from both Jamaica and the UK. Black Slate originally comprised George Brightly (aka Sir George, b. 1960, London, England; keyboards), Desmond Mahoney (b. 1955, St Thomas, Jamaica; drums), Keith Drummond (b. 1955, Mandeville, Jamaica; lead vocals), Chris Hanson (b. 1956, Kingston, Jamaica; lead guitar), Cledwyn Rogers (b. 1955, Anguilla; rhythm guitar) and Ras Elroy (b. Elroy Bailey, 1958, London; bass and vocals). Subsequent members would include Henschell Holder, Rudy Holmes, Ray Carness and Nicky Ridguard. Formed in 1974, they found their first employment as backing band to Dennis Brown, Delroy Wilson, Ken Boothe and many other visiting Jamaican musicians. After gigging heavily on the London reggae circuit their first hit under their own steam arrived with the anti-mugging 'Sticks Man' in 1976. They embarked on their first nationwide tour in 1978, launching their own TCD label and going on to their debut chart appearance with 'Mind Your Motion'. 1980 was the band's watershed year. A simple Rastafarian rallying call, 'Amigo' was picked up by Ensign, and with the extra corporate muscle the single rose to number 7 in the UK charts. It would become their signature tune. Although follow-ups skirted with the charts, notably 'Boom Boom', the band's initial impact was never repeated.

Albums: *Black Slate* (TCD 1979, remixed and re-released by Ensign in 1980), *Sirens In The City* (Ensign 1981), *Six Plus One* (Top Ranking 1982), *Black Slate* (Sierra 1985).

Black Uhuru

Formed in Jamaica by Garth Dennis, Derrick 'Ducky' Simpson and Don McCarlos in the early 70s, Black Uhuru first recorded a version of Curtis Mayfield's 'Romancing To

The Folk Song' for Dynamic's Top Cat label as Uhuru (the Swahili word for 'Freedom'), which met with limited success. Garth Dennis joined the Wailing Souls and McCarlos (as Don Carlos) went on to a solo career. 'Ducky' then enlisted Michael Rose as lead singer, who himself had previously recorded as a solo artist for Vivian 'Yabby You' Jackson (on the excellent 'Born Free') and for Winston 'Niney' Holness, including the first recording of 'Guess Who's Coming To Dinner', inspired by the Sidney Poitier film. Errol Nelson, from the Jayes, was used for harmonies. This line-up voiced an album for Prince Jammy in 1977 entitled *Love Crisis*, later reissued and retitled *Black Sounds Of Freedom*, after the group had found success. Nelson returned to the Jayes soon afterwards and Puma Jones (b. Sandra Jones, 5 October 1953, Columbia, South Carolina, USA, d. 28 January 1990, New York) took over. Formerly a social worker, she had worked with Ras Michael And The Sons Of Negus as a dancer in a bid to retrace her African ancestry via Jamaica. This combination began work for Sly Dunbar and Robbie Shakespeare's Taxi label in 1980, and Black Uhuru mania gripped the Jamaican reggae audience. The solid bedrock of Sly And Robbie's rhythms with Puma and Duckie's eerie harmonies provided a perfect counterpoint to Rose's tortured vocals as his songs wove tales of the hardships of Jamaican life which managed to convey a far wider relevance. Their first album for Taxi, *Showcase*, later reissued as *Vital Selection*, gave equal prominence to the vocal and instrumental versions of songs such as 'General Penitentiary', 'Shine Eye Gal' and 'Abortion', and was a massive reggae seller.

Island Records signed the group and they became a hot property throughout the musical world over the next few years. Their albums for Mango/Island continued in the same militant vein, and *Anthem* was remixed for the American market and earned a Grammy for the band. They toured all over the globe with the powerhouse rhythm section of Sly And Robbie in addition to a full complement of top Jamaican session musicians. For a time they were widely touted as the only reggae band with the potential to achieve international superstar status, but, although their popularity never waned after their initial breakthrough, it sadly never seemed to grow either. Michael Rose left the band in the mid-80s for a solo career which has always promised more than it has delivered, although his 1990 album *Proud* was very strong. Junior Reid took over on lead vocals but, in retrospect, his approach was too deeply rooted in the Jamaican dancehalls at the time for Black Uhuru's international approach, and after a couple of moderately well-received albums he too left for a solo career, which to date has been remarkably successful. For *Now* Don Carlos returned to his former position as lead singer, reuniting the original triumvirate of Carlos, Duckie Simpson and Garth Dennis, and the group still tour and release records, which are particularly popular in America. Tragically Puma Jones died of cancer in 1990. She had left the band after *Brutal*, and been replaced by soundalike Olafunke. Black Uhuru will always remain one of *the* great reggae acts despite the fact that the international status that they deserved proved elusive.

Albums: *Love Crisis* (Prince Jammys/Third World 1977), *Showcase* (Taxi/Heartbeat 1979), *Sinsemilla* (Mango/Island 1980), *Black Sounds Of Freedom* (Greensleeves 1981, repackaging of *Love Crisis*), *Red* (Mango/Island 1981), *Black Uhuru* (Virgin 1981, repackaging of *Showcase*), *Guess Who's Coming To Dinner* (Heartbeat 1981, repackaging of *Showcase*), *Chill Out* (Mango/Island 1982), *Tear It Up - Live* (Mango/Island 1982), *The Dub Factor* (Mango/Island 1983), *Anthem* (Mango/Island 1984), (*Brutal* (RAS 1986), *Brutal Dub* (RAS 1986), *Positive* (RAS 1987), *Positive Dub* (RAS 1987), *Live In New York City* (Rohit 1988), *Now* (Mesa 1990), *Now Dub* (Mesa 1990), *Iron Storm* (Mesa 1991), *Mystical Touch* (Mesa 1993). With Johnny Osbourne: *Uhuru In Dub* (CSA 1985).

Chris Blackwell

Compilations: *Reggae Greats* (Mango/Island 1985), *Liberation: The Island Anthology* (Mango/Island 1993, 2 CD box set).

Blackwell, Chris

b. 22 June 1937, London, England, the son of Middleton Joseph Blackwell, a distant relative of the power behind the Crosse & Blackwell food empire. Chris moved to Jamaica at the age of six months with his family, who settled in the affluent area of Terra Nova. Three years later he returned to England to attend prep. school and subsequently enrolled at Harrow Public School. A mediocre scholar, he failed to get to university and spent the late 50s commuting between London and Kingston, uncertain of what to do with his life. During the summer of 1958 he was stranded on a coral reef near the Hellshire Beaches. Dehydrated and sunburnt, he was rescued by members of a small Rastafarian community. He never forgot that formative incident and, in later life, displayed every willingness to deal directly with Rasta musicians and introduce their philosophy and culture to European and American audiences. Blackwell was one of the first to record Jamaican rhythm and blues for his R&B and Island labels, and he achieved the very first number 1 hit in Jamaica with Laurel Aitken's 'Little Sheila'/'Boogie In My Bones'. Through his mother's friendship with writer Ian Fleming, Blackwell entered the film business during the early 60s, and worked with producer Harry Saltzman on the set of *Dr No*. Although he was offered the opportunity to work on further Bond films, Blackwell declined this invitation and instead returned to music. In May 1962 he founded Island Records in London, borrowing the name from Alec Waugh's 50s novel, *Island In the Sun*. After leasing master recordings from Jamaican producers such as Leslie Kong, Coxsone Dodd and King Edwards, he issued them in the UK through Island. The company boasted a number of subsidiaries, including Jump Up, Black Swan and, most notably, Sue, co-managed by producer Guy

Stevens. Blackwell bought and promoted his own records, delivering them in his Mini Cooper. Early signings included a host of Jamaican talent: Owen Gray, Jimmy Cliff, Derrick Morgan, Lord Creator and Bob Morley (aka Bob Marley). However, it was 14 year old Millie Small who provided Blackwell with his first UK breakthrough away from the West Indian and mod audiences. The infectious 'My Boy Lollipop' sold six million copies, and precipitated Blackwell's move into the mainstream UK pop/R&B market.

Blackwell continued to build up Island Records during the 60s and 70s simply by having a remarkably 'good ear'. He knew what he liked and chose well from a slew of 'progressive' groups and, it seemed, largely lost interest in Jamaican music - Island's catalogue was now handled by Trojan Records. However, he signed up and promoted Bob Marley & The Wailers in 1972 as if they were one of his rock bands and because of Island's huge influence (and the eye catching Zippo sleeve for *Catch A Fire*) the rock audience was forced to accept reggae on its own terms - and they liked what they heard. The story of Bob Marley and The Wailers has been well documented, and Island continued to promote reggae music throughout the 70s, 80s and 90s (as well as their rock catalogue, of course) always giving the music and its performers the type of promotion and profile that they so rarely received elsewhere. Such attention was almost invariably deserved and nearly all of the first division Jamaican (and UK) reggae artists have worked with Island Records at some time or another. Blackwell's reputation for nurturing talent and persevering with his artists has long been legendary and his contribution to exposing reggae music to a wider audience is inestimable.

Selected albums: Various: *Pressure Drop* (Mango/Island 1987, 4 LP box set), *Tougher Than Tough - The Story Of Jamaican Music* (Mango/Island 1993, 4 CD box set).

Alpha Blondy

Blondy, Alpha

b. 1953, Dimbokoro, Cote d'Ivoire. During the mid-80s, reggae vocalist Blondy, whose name translates as First Bandit, became one of West Africa's most successful bandleaders, his songs widely covered by other local reggae artists. Adopting not only the rhythms and instrumental arrangements of Jamaican reggae, Blondy also followed its tradition of militant, protest lyrics. After releasing his searing *Apartheid Is Nazism* album, he took the logical next step of flying to Jamaica to record the follow-up, *Jerusalem*, with the Wailers. Blondy's embrace of reggae and rasta was not without its problems: after he returned in 1981 from two years' study at Columbia University in the USA, his parents committed him to a psychiatric hospital for eighteen months because of his Rasta beliefs. There is certainly some evidence to support their view: though he dresses as a Rasta, Blondy travels everywhere with the Star of David, a copy of the bible, and one of the Koran. He also modulates his language according to his location, resolutely speaking Arabic in Israel, and Hebrew in the Arab world.

Albums: *Jah Glory* (Celluloid 1983), *Cocody Rock* (Shanachie 1984), *Apartheid Is Nazism* (Shanachie 1985), *Jerusalem* (Shanchie 1986), *Jah Jah Seh* (1989), *Masada* (EMI 1992).

Bob And Marcia

Bob Andy and Marcia Griffiths had two UK chart entries at the turn of the 70s - the first a version of Nina Simone's 'Young, Gifted And Black', was a UK Top 5 hit in 1970 on reggae producer Harry J's self-titled label and the follow-up, 'Pied Piper', which reached number 11 later on the Trojan label. Both Andy and Griffiths were hugely popular artists in Jamaica in their own right before and after their pop crossover success, but neither felt that this particular interlude was successful for them, especially in financial terms. It is sad that these two hits have become all that they are known for outside of reggae music circles. Sadder still, that their best duet of the period, the timeless 'Always

Together', which they recorded for Coxsone Dodd, failed to make any impression outside Jamaica.

Album: *Young, Gifted And Black* (Harry J 1970), *Pied Piper* (Harry J 1971), *Really Together* (I-Anka 1987).

Bolo, Yammie

b. Roland Maclean, 1970, Kingston, Jamaica. Bolo entered the music business as a youngster, singing on Sugar Minott's Youth Promotion sound system. He cut his first record 'When A Man's In Love' (1985), for producer Winston Riley. Several other 45s followed, including 'Jah Made Them All' (1986) for Riley, 'Roots Pon Mi Corner' (1986) for Minott, and 'Free Mandela' (1987) for Miami-based Skeng Don. Afterwards he linked up with Junior Delgado and Augustus Pablo to record a number of excellent singles exploring social and cultural issues, including 'Ransom Of A Man's Life' (1987), 'Tell Me Why Is This Fussing & Fighting' (1988), 'Love Me With Feeling' (1989), 'Poverty & Brutality' (1989), 'Poor Man's Cry' (1990) and 'Struggle In Babylon' (1990). In 1989 Junior Delgado produced *Ransom*, and later that year Pablo issued *Jah Made Them All*, a vocal/dub set. More singles for other producers followed: 'Turbo Charge' (1991) for Winston 'Niney' Holness, 'Blood A Run' and 'Iniquity Worker' (both 1991) for Trevor Douglas, 'Jah Jah Loving' (1991), a co-production between Bolo and Neville Thompson, 'It's Not Surprising' (1992) for Barry O'Hare, 'Joe The Boss', 'Be Still' (both 1992) and 'Revolution' for Tapper Zukie, and 'Bowl Must Full' for Augustus Pablo. In 1992 he made what most observers feel is his best album, *Up Life Street,* for Trevor Douglas' Leggo label, and *Who Knows It Feels It* for Niney. The same year also saw the inauguration of Bolo's own Yam Euphony label, with a version of Madonna's 'La Isla Bonita', not quite the disaster one might imagine, and the fiery anti-gunman title, 'The Glock War, Gun War'. Bolo's vocal delivery is similar to that of the so-called

Yammie Bolo

Waterhouse style of Junior Reid, Don Carlos, and Michael Rose (Black Uhuru). Nevertheless, Bolo is an exciting and original young artist in his own right.

Albums: *Ransom* (Greensleeves 1989), *Jah Made Them All* (Greensleeves 1989), *Who Knows It Feels It* (Heartbeat 1991), *Up Life Street* (Heartbeat 1992), *Cool And Easy* (Tappa 1993). With Lloyd Hemmings: *Meets Lloyd Hemmings* (1993).

Boom, Barry

Barry Boom is the pseudonym Paul Robinson first employed to mask his backroom duties. These activities were many; he helped write and produce Maxi Priest's debut album, and Phillip Papa Levi's groundbreaking 'Mi God Mi King' 45. He had also been part of the hotly-tipped One Blood with other family members until his brother and fellow band member, Errol, died. Robinson briefly worked with Sly And Robbie before electing to pursue a solo career under the name Barry Boom, which he had previously used in a production capacity. He kicked off his career on the Fashion subsidiary Fine Style in 1989, cutting a number of hit singles as Barry Boom, including the reggae number 1's 'Making Love and 'Number One Girl', and 'Hurry Over'. His debut album was a consistent, polished affair which mixed lovers rock lyrics with more cultural concerns, all conducted to an understated, rootsy backing. Boom is still striving for the kind of mainstream succes his talents deserve, and 1994 saw him reunited with Fashion again.

Selected album: *The Living Boom* (Fine Style 1990).

Boothe, Ken

b. 1948, Kingston, Jamaica. Boothe began his recording career with Winston 'Stranger' Cole in the duo Stranger And Ken, releasing titles including 'World's Fair', 'Hush', 'Artibella' and 'All Your Friends' during 1963-65. When the rocksteady rhythm began to evolve during 1966 Boothe recorded 'Feel Good'. He released a series of titles for Clement Dodd's Studio One label which revealed him to be an impassioned, fiery vocalist in an occasionally mannered style ultimately derived from US soul. During this period he was often referred to as the Wilson Pickett of Jamaican music. He continued recording with Dodd until 1970, releasing some of his best and biggest local hits. He made records for other producers at the same time, including Sonia Pottinger's Gayfeet label, for which he recorded the local hit 'Say You' in 1968. By the following year he had switched again, this time to Leslie Kong's Beverley's label where he stayed until 1971, notching two more local hits with 'Freedom Street' and 'Why Baby Why', as well as several other singles and an album. He then freelanced during the early 70s for various producers, including Keith Hudson, Herman Chin-Loy, Randy's and George 'Phil' Pratt. During the same period he began an association with former Gaylad, B.B. Seaton which resulted in an album in 1971. At this point in time he was hugely popular with Jamaican audiences, particularly teenage girls, who loved his emotive voice and good looks. When he started working with the pianist/vocalist/producer Lloyd Charmers in 1971 it was not long before the hits started to flow again, firstly in Jamaica and then in the UK charts. 'Everything I Own', a David Gates composition, topped the UK chart in November 1974. The follow-up, 'Crying Over You' also charted, reaching the number 11 position in February 1975. Pop singer Boy George covered Charmers' and Boothe's version of 'Everything I Own' when he scored in the UK chart with the song in 1987. Boothe sadly failed to capitalise on this success, having continued to record for a variety of Jamaican producers throughout the late 70s and 80s. He has also produced his own material with occasional commercial success. He regularly appears on Jamaican oldies shows, usually singing his classic 60s and 70s material, and remains one of the great Jamaican soul voices.

Ken Boothe

Selected albums: *Mr. Rock Steady* (Studio One 1968), *More Of Ken Boothe* (Studio One 1968), *A Man And His Hits* (Studio One 1970), *Freedom Street* (Beverley's 1971), *The Great Ken Boothe Meets B.B. Seaton And The Gaylads* (1971), *Black Gold And Green* (Trojan 1973), *Everything I Own* (Trojan 1974), *Let's Get It On* (Trojan 1974), *Blood Brothers* (Trojan 1975), *Live Good* (Liberty 1978), *I'm Just A Man* (Bunny Lee 1979), *Who Gets Your Love* (Trojan 1978), *Showcase* (Justice 1979), *Reggae For Lovers* (Mountain 1980), *Imagine* (Park Heights 1986), *Don't You Know* (Tappa 1988), *Power Of Love* (1993). Compilations: *Ken Boothe Collection* (Trojan 1987).

Bovell, Dennis

b. 1953, St. Peter, Barbados. Guitarist who, as co-founder of Matumbi, one of the UK's first and best indigenous bands, has had a long apprenticeship in reggae music. Though born in the West Indies, Bovell grew up in south London. There he fell in love with Jamaican dub music and its ethos, setting up an early British sound system: Jah Sufferer, in north London. It brought him his first clash with the establishment: he was imprisoned for six months on remand after one event, only to be released on appeal. Like many reggae musicians operating in the UK in the late 70s, Bovell discovered common ground with the punk/new wave movement. He was friends at school with keyboard player Nick Straker and producer Tony Mansfield (New Musik, Captain Sensible etc.), and this pair and others would help spice up his solo releases. In turn Bovell became embroiled in the early recordings of bands like the Pop Group and the Slits. Bovell's own efforts, particularly his first two sets, offered an impressive collection of experimental dubs. Indeed, at one point in time his name was linked in one way or another to no fewer than 18 singles in the British Reggae Top 20. Albums: As Blackbeard: *Strictly Dub Wize* (Tempus 1978), *I Wah Dub* (More Cut/EMI 1980). As Dennis Bovell: *Brain Damage* (Fontana 1981, double album). As Dennis

Bovell And The Dub Band: *Audio Active* (Moving Target 1986).

Brigadier Jerry

b. Robert Russell, Kingston, Jamaica. Brigadier was undoubtedly one of the most influential DJs of the 80s but the impact he created was achieved almost entirely through sound tapes, ie live recordings of sound system dances. As a spontaneous lyricist - speaking solely of cultural or reality issues - he is unsurpassed, despite a scarcity of recordings throughout his career. He was born in the Papine area of eastern Kingston, his sister Nancy also becoming a DJ. An early interest in music took him to King Strugav Hi-Fi, owned by the legendary U Roy, whom he acknowledges as his principal influence and mentor. By 1978 he had joined the Twelve Tribes of Israel organisation, spreading their message far and wide on the affiliated Jah Love sound system, and occasionally recording with other members like Fred Locks. Encouraged by Freddie McGregor and Judah Eskender Tafari he voiced three sides for Studio One, before in 1982 Delroy Stansbury released 'Pain' and 'Gwan A School' on the Jwyanza label. Outside of Jah Love he had made regular appearances on a number of other sound systems, including Supreme Love, Wha Dat and Black Star, and whilst in the US Downbeat International; accumulating a growing band of younger DJ admirers who frequently recorded his lyrics whilst his own trips to the studio remained a rare event.

In 1985 Jah Love Musik released his debut album proper, *Jamaica Jamaica*, which remains one of his best-ever works, and contains a definitive cut of Bunny Wailer's 'Armagideon'. A follow-up single, 'Roots Girl', proved less successful, but by 1986 it seems as though he was finally ready to grasp the challenge of transferring his skills to vinyl on a consistent basis, voicing several inspired sides for the Supreme label, Techniques and George Phang. Apart from 'Hard Drugs' for Pioneer however, there was little until his second album, *On The Road* in early 1991.

Dennis Bovell

In 1992 he again enjoyed a spell of relative activity; reactivating Jah Love in Jamaica, and recording the *Hail Him* set for Tapper Zukie.

Selected albums: *Live At The Controls* (Vista Sounds 1983), *Jamaica Jamaica* (RAS 1985), *On The Road* (RAS 1989), *Hail Him* (Tappa 1993).

Brooks, Cedric 'Im'

b. 1943, Kingston, Jamaica. At the age of 11 Brooks became a pupil at the Alpha Catholic School for Boys, where he learned clarinet and music theory, and in his late teens studied tenor saxophone and flute. In the early 60s he was a member of several groups including the Vagabonds and Granville Williams Band. He teamed up with trumpeter David Madden during 1968 for an excellent series of instrumentals for Coxsone Dodd, released under the name Im And David. Some of the best of these singles such as 'Candid Eye', 'Black Is Black' and 'Soul Brother' were included on the various artists album *Money Maker*. Brooks also played on many sessions for Dodd, and had several solo singles released in the early 70s.

In 1970 Brooks commenced his association with Count Ossie, the first fruits of which were 'So Long Rastafari Calling' and 'Give Me Back Me Language And Me Culture', released under the name Im And Count Ossie. Shortly after this, the two formed the Mystic Revelation of Rastafari, which combined the forces of Count Ossie's hand-drummers with a brass section arranged by Brooks. Together they recorded the ground breaking *Grounation* album. In 1974 Brooks left Count Ossie to form the Light Of Saba, taking some members of the Mystic Revelation Of Rastafari with him. The Light Of Saba retained the brass and Rasta drums that had characterized the previous group, added guitars, and incorporated a more pronounced reggae element. Around 1974, after recording a single for Randys, 'Demauungwani', they recorded their first album for the Institute Of Jamaica, *From Mento To Reggae To Third World Music*, under the name Cedric Brooks And The Divine Light. It gives a potted history of the development of Jamaican music, and includes beautifully performed pieces in the mento, junkunoo, ska, rocksteady and reggae styles, plus one forward looking Pan-Caribbean piece. Their superb *The Light Of Saba* included reworkings of 'Peanut Vendor' and Horace Silver's 'Song To My Father', but consisted mostly of original Rastafarian songs and instrumentals. *The Light Of Saba In Reggae* was an even stronger collection of original material. Shortly after this, Brooks left, although the Light Of Saba continued for one further album, the mediocre *Sabebe*.

In 1977 Studio One issued a brilliant solo album by Brooks, *Im Flash Forward*. This material may have been recorded in the early 70s, as it uses rhythm tracks from that period, but it is more likely that it was recorded shortly before its release. Whatever, Brooks's tenor playing on the album is beautifully restrained, and has a meditative quality that evokes a sublime, spiritual atmosphere. It has become firmly established as one of the greatest Jamaican instrumental albums. In 1978 Brooks assembled a large ensemble featuring a host of percussionists and horn players for *United Africa*, an album which not only utilized Jamaican musical forms such as reggae and nyahbinghi, but also incorporated African and Caribbean forms. It was a highly successful enterprise, but sadly, has never been followed up. Since then, Brooks has recorded widely as a session musician, but his only solo recordings have been some singles for Studio One. His thorough understanding of Jamaica's musical heritage, and the innovative and organic way in which he has built on that foundation to extend its scope ensures the longevity of his music. It seems inconceivable that others will not continue with the work that he has started.

Albums: *Im Flash Forward* (Studio One 1977), *United Africa* (Water Lily 1978). As Cedric Brooks And The Divine Light: *From Mento To Reggae To Third World Music* (Institute Of Jamaica 1975). As Cedric

Dennis Brown

Brooks And The Divine Light Of Saba: *The Light Of Saba* (Total Sounds 1976), *The Light Of Saba In Reggae* (Total Sounds 1977).

Brown, Al

b. Kingston, Jamaica. Smooth reggae artist, and an ex-member of Skin, Flesh And Bones, whose first recording was for Coxsone Dodd. He subsequently teamed up with the Volcanoes, but scored a UK solo hit with his version of Al Green's 'Here I Am Baby' for Trojan. Later singles included 'Caribbean Queen' and 'No Soul Today', but he proved unable to repeat the success, despite working with the Seventh Extension band and others.

Selected album: *Dying Love* (Studio One 1970), *Here I Am Baby* (Trojan 1978).

Brown, Dennis

b. Dennis Emanuel Brown, 1957, Kingston, Jamaica. Now regularly billed as 'The Crown Prince Of Reggae', it is only Brown's self-effacing nature that has denied him advancement to the office of king. He is loved in reggae music like no other singer and has been regularly courted by the major record labels, and even enjoyed a couple of token chart hits in Britain. More to the point, he has produced more reggae classics than just about anyone else. He began his career at the age of 11 as one of the Studio One label's many child stars. His first hit, 'No Man Is An Island' (1969), found him singing in much the same style he now uses, only with a far less croaky voice. 'If I Follow My Heart', his other chief hit at Studio One, was every bit as good. He spent the early 70s freelancing between studios, recording for Lloyd Daley, Impact, Joe Gibbs and Aquarius, before recording his third collection, *Super Reggae And Soul Hits*, a mature, classic record, full of Derrick Harriott's soulful arrangements and Brown's rich tones. A move to Winston 'Niney' Holness' label was no less profitable, with the two albums he made there, *Just Dennis* and *Wolf & Leopards*, recorded with a three year gap between them, yet with a seamless rootsy artistry making them clearly part of one body of work. Many regard the latter album as his best. A long, fruitful liaison with Joe Gibbs and Errol Thompson resulted in a further series of classic albums, among them *Visions*, *Joseph's Coat Of Many Colours*, *Spellbound*, and *Yesterday, Today & Tomorrow*. While the rock critics were latching onto dub in the mid-70s, it was Dennis who was drawing a mass audience almost unnoticed outside reggae's heartlands. His combination of serious, 'message' songs and soul-wailing love melodies was irresistible. His stage shows too were genuine 'events', and always packed a punch. 'Money In My Pocket' (1979) was the first of three incursions into chart territory, with Dennis eventually signing with A&M Records in the early 80s. Simultaneously, he became co-owner of the DEB label, successfully producing Junior Delgado and female lovers rock trio 15-16-17. Brown gradually spent more time in London as a consequence, eventually settling there for much of the 80s. His Joe Gibbs connection was terminated in 1982, marking the *de facto* end of Gibbs's prominence as a producer. Brown's series of reggae hits, including 'To The Foundation' for Gussie Clarke, 'Revolution' for Taxi or cuts on his own Yvonne's Special label (named after his wife), saw him become one of the few established singers to ride the early dancehall boom unscathed. However, when digital music exploded onto reggae in 1985-86, Dennis faltered for the first time in his career, seemingly unsure of his next move. Eventually he settled into the new style, recording *The Exit* for King Jammys in the digital mode. A move to Gussie Clarke's Music Works Studio in 1989 gave him more kudos with the youth market, particularly on the duet with Gregory Isaacs, 'Big All Around'. Once again Dennis Brown was in-demand in Jamaica, back at the roots of the music, and rolling once again, recording everywhere and anywhere for a few months. It remains to be seen what his next move will be: clearly he has the ability and energy to do whatever he wants.

Albums: *No Man Is An Island* (Studio One 1970), *If I Follow My Heart* (Studio One 1971), *Super Reggae & Soul Hits* (Trojan 1972), *Just Dennis* (Trojan 1975), *West Bound Train* (Third World 1977), *Visions* (Joe Gibbs 1977), *Wolf & Leopards* (DEB-EMI 1978), *Words Of Wisdom* (Laser 1979), *So Long Rastafari* (Harry J 1979), *Joseph's Coat Of Many Colours* (Laser 1979), *20th Century Dubwise* (DEB 1979), *Yesterday, Today & Tomorrow* (JGM 1982), *Satisfaction Feeling* (Tads 1983), *The Prophet Rides Again* (A&M 1983), *Love's Gotta Hold On Me* (JGM 1984), *Dennis* (Vista Sounds 1984), *Time And Place* (Clock Tower 1984), *Live At Montreaux* (Blue Moon 1984), *Slow Down* (Greensleeves 1985), *Revolution* (Yvonne's Special 1985), *Spellbound* (Blue Moon 1985), *Wake Up* (Natty Congo 1985), *The Exit* aka *History* (Jammys/Trojan 1986), *Money In My Pocket* (Trojan 1986), *Hold Tight* (Live & Love 1986), *Brown Sugar* (Taxi 1986), *Smile Like An Angel* (Blue Moon 1986), *In Concert* (Ayeola 1987), *Love Has Found Its Way* (A&M 1988), *Inseparable* (J&W 1988), *More* (Black Scorpio 1988), *My Time* (Rohit 1989), *Unchallenged* (Greensleeves 1990), *Overproof* (Greensleeves 1990), *Good Tonight* (Greensleeves 1990), *Go Now* (Rohit 1991), *Victory Is Mine* (Blue Moon 1991), *Friends For Life* (1992), *Some Like It Hot* (1992), *Limited Edition* (1992), *Blazing* (Greensleeves 1992), *Beautiful Morning* (1992), *Cosmic Force* (1993), *Unforgettable* (Charm 1993). With Gregory Isaacs: *Two Bad Superstars* (Burning Sounds 1984), *Judge Not* (Greensleeves 1984), *No Contest* (Greensleeves 1989), *Big All Around* (Greensleeves 1989). With Horace Andy: *Reggae Superstars Meet* (Striker Lee 1986). With John Holt: *Wild Fire* (Natty Congo 1986). With Enos McLeod: *Baalgad* (Goodies 1986). With Janet Kay: *So Amazing* (1993). Compilations: *Best Of* (Joe Gibbs 1975), *Best Of Vol. 2* (Joe Gibbs 1982), *Super Hits* (Trojan 1983), *Collection* (Dennis Ting 1985), *20 Classic Reggae Tracks* (Meteor 1985), *Good Vibrations* (Charthits 1989), *Classic Hits* (Sonic Sounds 1992), *20 Magnificent Hits* (1993).

Videos: *Live At Montreaux* (1987), *The Living Legend* (1992).

Brown, Glen

b. Glenmore Lloyd Brown, Jamaica. Brown started in the music business in the mid-60s as a singer recording duets with Lloyd Robinson and Dave Barker (see Dave And Ansell Collins) for various producers, including Duke Reid and Coxsone Dodd. However, it was in the early 70s that he found his true vocation as a producer, his legendary Pantomine label home to dozens of unique and often eccentric records. He scored a big hit in 1972 with 'Merry Up', a melodica instrumental much in the vein of Augustus Pablo, who had popularised the instrument some months earlier with his hit, 'Java'. Brown was adept at recycling his rhythms in new and interesting ways. If one of his backing tracks proved particularly popular, he would go on to cut a number of versions of it using different singers, instrumentalists and DJs, thereby prolonging its life and recouping the maximum potential for his outlay. He worked with many of the best DJs of the time, including Big Youth ('Come Into My Parlour', 'Opportunity Rock'), Prince Jazzbo ('Meaning Of One', 'Mr Harry Skank', 'Mr Want All'), I Roy ('Brother Toby Is A Movie From London'), Berry 'Prince Hammer' Simpson ('Whole Lot of Sugar') and U Roy ('No 1 In The World').

As well as providing fine vocal renditions himself on sides such as 'Realize' (with Richie MacDonald), 'Tell It Like It Is', 'Boat To Progress' and 'Away With The Bad', he recorded the likes of Roman Stewart, Keith Poppin, Johnny Clarke, Lloyd Parks ('Slaving') and Gregory Isaacs; the latter's 'One One Cocoa' being among that singer's finest vinyl moments. But perhaps the real grist to Brown's mill were the many instrumental sides his various labels carried, cuts like 'Dirty Harry' by Tommy McCook and Richard Hall, 'More Music' by McCook and trombonist Ron Wilson, and the melodica sides by the man himself;

'Pantomine Rock', 'Crisp As A Ball' and '2 Wedden Skank'. Brown's highly individual approach, coupled with the God Sons' tough bass and drum rhythms, has ensured these records a special place in the hearts of many reggae fans. In the latter half of the 70s the hits were fewer, but records like his own 'Father For The Living' and 'Lambs Bread Collie Man', Wayne Jarrett's 'Youthman' and a run of Sylford Walker gems like 'Lambs Bread', 'Eternal Day' and 'Chant Down Babylon', maintained his profile and reputation. During the 80s Brown became less visible on the reggae scene as he divided his time between Jamaica, New York and the UK. He recorded a melodica instrumental album for London's Fashion Records in 1990 that captured much of his charm, and reportedly has a Joseph Cotton album in the can.

Albums: *Horny Dub* (Grounation 1989), *Number One Sound* (Pantomine 1989), *Glen Brown Plays Music From The East* (Fashion 1990), *The Rhythm Master* (Pantomine 1991). With Mike Brooks: *In A Sound Clash* (Rhythm Foundation 1990). Productions: Sylford Walker: *Chant Down Babylon* (1989), *Dubble Attack* (Greensleeves 1989), *Boat To Progress* (Greensleeves 1989), *Dub From The South East* (Pantomine 1991). Various: *Check The Winner* (Greensleeves 1990).

Burning Spear

b. Winston Rodney, 1948, St Ann's Bay, Jamaica. Burning Spear, who appropriated the name from former Mau Mau leader Jomo Kenyatta, then president of Kenya, entered the music business in 1969 after fellow St. Ann's artist Bob Marley organised an audition for him with his erstwhile producer Coxsone Dodd. The three songs Spear sang for Dodd that Sunday afternoon included his eventual debut, 'Door Peep', a sombre, spiritual chant quite unlike anything that had so far emerged in the music, although perhaps a reference point may be found in the Ethiopians and Joe Higgs. 'Door Peep' and other early Spear sides like 'We Are Free' and 'Zion Higher' emerged in

the UK on the Bamboo and Banana labels. Spear continued to make records for Dodd until 1974, including 'Ethiopians Live It Out', 'This Population' and 'New Civilisation', nearly all in a serious, cultural style, mostly without any commercial success, although 'Joe Frazier' (aka 'He Prayed') did make the Jamaican Top 5 in 1972. Most of these songs can be found on the two albums Spear completed for Dodd. In 1975 Ocho Rios sound system owner Jack Ruby (real name Laurence Lindo) approached the singer who had been cooling his heels since leaving Dodd, and the two, along with pick-up backing vocalists Rupert Wellington and Delroy Hines, began working on the material that would eventually emerge as *Marcus Garvey* (1975), in honour of the great St Ann's born pan-Africanist. 'Marcus Garvey' and 'Slavery Days' emerged as singles perfectly capturing the mood of the times and becoming huge local hits. The public were at last ready for Burning Spear and when the album finally emerged it was hailed as an instant classic. Spear became recognised as the most likely candidate for the kind of international sucess Bob Marley And The Wailers were beginning to enjoy, and soon *Marcus Garvey* had been snapped up by Island Records which released it in the UK with an added track and in remixed form. This tampering with the mix, including the speeding up of several tracks, presumably in order to make the album more palatable to white ears, raised the hackles of many critics and fans. The album was very popular though, and soon Island had released a dubwise companion set entitled *Garvey's Ghost* (1976).

Rodney began to release music on his own Spear label at the end of 1975, the first issue being another classic, 'Travelling' (actually a revision of the earlier Studio One album track 'Journey'), followed by 'Spear Burning' (1976), 'The Youth' (1976), 'Throw Down Your Arms' (1977), the 12-inch 'Institution' (1977), 'Dry And Heavy' (1977), 'Free' (1977) and 'Nyah Keith' (1979). He also

Burning Spear

produced 'On That Day' by youth singer Burning Junior, and 'Love Everyone' by Phillip Fullwood, both in 1976. That same year Jack Ruby released 'Man In The Hills', followed by the album of the same name, again on Island, which marked the end of their collaboration. Spear also dropped Willington and Hines at this juncture. 1977 saw the release of *Dry & Heavy*, recorded at Harry J's Studio, which satisfyingly reworked many of his Studio One classics, including 'Swell Headed', 'Creation Rebel', 'This Race' and 'Free Again'. In October that year he made an electrifying appearance at London's Rainbow Theatre, backed by veteran trumpeter Bobby Ellis and the UK reggae band Aswad. Island released an album of the performance that inexplicably failed to capture the excitement generated.

In 1978 Spear parted with Island and issued *Marcus Children*, arguably his best album since *Marcus Garvey*, released in the UK on the Independent One Stop label as *Social Living*, again using members of Aswad alongside the usual crack Kingston session men. 1980 saw him strike a deal with EMI who issued his next album, the stunning *Hail H.I.M.*, produced by Spear and Family Man Barrett at Bob Marley's Tuff Gong studio, on his own Burning Spear subsidiary. Two excellent dubs of *Social Living* and *Hail H.I.M.* also appeared as *Living Dub Vols. 1 & 2*, mixed by ace engineer Sylvan Morris. Throughout the following years to the present, Spear has continued to release albums regularly, as well as touring the USA and elsewhere. *Resistance*, nominated for a Grammy in 1984, was a particularly strong set highlighting Spear's impressive, soulful patois against a muscular rhythmic backdrop. *People Of The World* similarly saw his backing group, the Burning Band, which now encompassed an all-female horn section, shine. His 1988 set, *Mistress Music* added rock musicians, including former members of Jefferson Airplane, though artistically it was his least successful album. *Mek We Dweet*, recorded at Tuff Gong studios, was a return to his unique, intense style. His lyrical concerns – black culture and history, Garveyism and Rasta beliefs, and universal love – have been consistently and powerfully expressed during his entire recording career. Selected albums: *Studio One Presents Burning Spear* (Studio One 1973), *Rocking Time* (Studio One 1974), *Marcus Garvey* (Mango/Island 1975), *Man In The Hills* (Fox-Wolf/Island 1976), *Garvey's Ghost* (Mango/Island 1976), *Dry & Heavy* (Mango/Island 1977), *Burning Spear Live* (Island 1977), *Marcus Children* aka *Social Living* (Burning Spear/One Stop 1978), *Living Dub* (Burning Spear/Heartbeat 1979), *Hail H.I.M.* (Burning Spear/EMI 1980), *Living Dub Vol. 2* (Burning Spear 1981), *Farover* (Burning Spear/Heartbeat 1982), *Fittest Of The Fittest* (Burning Spear/Heartbeat 1983), *Resistance* (Heartbeat 1985), *People Of The World* (Slash/Greensleeves 1986), *Mistress Music* (Slash/Greensleeves 1988), *Live In Paris: Zenith '88* (Slash/Greensleeves 1989, double album), *Mek We Dweet* (Mango/Island 1990), *Jah Kingdom* (Mango/Island 1992), *The World Should Know* (Mango/Island 1993). Compilations: *Reggae Greats* (Island 1985), *Selection* (EMI 1987), *100th Anniversary* (Mango/Island 1990, comprises *Marcus Garvey* and *Garvey's Ghost*).

Burrell, Phillip 'Fatis'

(see Exterminator)

Byles, Keith 'Chubby' Junior

b. 1948, Jubilee Hospital, Kingston, Jamaica. Growing up in the Jonestown district of Kingston, Junior Byles started work as a fireman in his late teens. By 1967 he had formed the Versatiles with Louis Davis and a youth named Dudley. The trio recorded a series of titles for producer Joe Gibbs during 1968-69, including 'Just Can't Win', 'Trust The Book' and 'Push It In'. By 1970 Junior was recording solo for producer Lee Perry as King Chubby. In 1972 Junior had two massive local hits, the dread anthem 'Beat Down Babylon', which was also the title of his first album released the following year, and the Jamaican Song Festival competition winner, 'Da Da'. He continued working with Perry, recording both militant roots material and intense love songs, nearly scraping into the UK charts with 'Curly Locks' (1975). That same year he had a hit in Jamaica with 'Fade Away' for Joseph 'Joe Joe' Hookim at Channel One, one of the best early rockers' tunes. He also recorded for the Ja-Man label, and producers Winston 'Niney' Holness and Pete Weston. In 1976, he entered Bellevue Hospital, retiring from music until 1978, when he wrote two songs for Joe Gibbs. He became less active as the 80s began, recording sessions for Maurice 'Blacka' Wellington (of the Morwells) in 1982 which were finally released in 1986 as *Rasta No Pickpocket*. He has recorded some of the most powerful reggae of the 70s, militant and deeply moving by turns, yet reamains relatively unknown.

Albums: *Beat Down Babylon* (Trojan 1973), *Jordan* (1976, reissued Heartbeat 1989), *Rasta No Pickpocket* (Night Hawk 1986), *Beat Down Babylon: The Upsetter Years* (Trojan 1987), *When Will Better Come* (Trojan 1988).

C

Cables

Although never achieving the legendary status of the Heptones or Maytals, the Cables perhaps deserved more than their fate of just one classic album and a handful of sundry tracks for various producers. At least if the standard of their best-known work, 'Baby Why', a huge Jamaican hit in 1969, is any indicator. Fronted by the fragile yet assertive voice of Keble (sometimes Keeble) Drummond, the Cables arrived at Studio One in the late 60s. It was a terrifically fertile time for the label, which, perhaps, did not bode well for the group: producer Coxsone Dodd already had his hands full with the Heptones, Delroy Wilson, Termites and a heap of other acts. However Drummond, whose christian name provided the group with its moniker, supported by harmony singers Elbert Stewart (baritone) and Vince Stoddart (tenor), cut a string of excellent singles for the label, including 'Be A Man', 'Love Is A Pleasure', the aforementioned 'Baby Why' and 'What Kind Of World'. Dodd later collected them on the frustratingly short, but still excellent *What Kind Of World* album. The rhythm tracks were classics, later re-used by Dodd for a slew of 'versions' with other artists. However, the original cuts remain much-prized by reggae enthusiasts today. By 1970 The Cables and Dodd had parted, and despite a few singles for other producers (JJ Johnson, Harry J), they failed to find their hit-making touch again. Drummond went solo in 1972, but his career petered out within a few years.
Album: *What Kind Of World* (Studio One 1970).

Campbell, Al

b. 31 August 1954, Kingston, Jamaica. Campbell first recorded as one of the Thrillers for Studio One in the late 60s. Though he provided backing vocals on many sessions for Coxsone Dodd, he is not the Al Campbell who sang the near legendary 'Take A Ride' for Coxsone. Throughout the 70s, 80s and 90s, Campbell has recorded successfully in just about all of the myriad styles that reggae music has gone through, the excellent 'roots' records that he made for Joe Gibbs and Phil Pratt being but one example of his talents. However, his greatest popularity was achieved when he covered lovers rock material for Phil Pratt again - with 'Gee Baby' in particular, which was a huge hit in 1975, both in Jamaica and the UK. From then on he flitted between the two countries and his recording of 'Late Night Blues', for London based JB Records, formed part of the soundtrack of 1980, and has been in constant demand ever since. He made many more records in a similar vein, several of which are collected on his *Mr Lovers Rock* set. He has retained his position as one of the music's foremost vocalists in the 90s, while his most recent recordings have been for King Jammys Kingston II label. He is still out there, despite the fickle nature of the traditional reggae audience, largely due to his smooth, relaxed, accomplished style, coupled with his ability to move with the times and give the public what they want.
Selected albums: *Rainy Days* (Hawkeye 1978), *Mr Lovers Rock* (Sonic Sounds 1980), *Other Side Of Love* (Greensleeves 1981), *Bad Boy* (CSA 1984), *Freedom Street* (Londisc 1984), *Forward Natty* (Move 1985), *Reggae '85* (Blue Mountain 1985), *Fence Too Tall* (Live & Love 1987), *Ain't That Loving You* (Vista 1989), *Shaggy Raggy* (Sampalau 1989).

Campbell, Cornell

b. c.1948, Jamaica. One of Jamaica's most distinctive falsetto voices, Cornell Campbell has been a reggae hitmaker for years, but has somehow never been bigger than his last record. He first recorded for Studio One in the ska era during the early 60s, either solo or as part of a duo with Alan Martin. After a

three-year gap he re-emerged in 1967 as a member of the Uniques, a popular but short-lived vocal group that also featured the exceptional falsetto of Slim Smith. By 1969 Cornell was leading his own group, the Eternals, and was back at Studio One recording hits with 'Queen Of The Minstrels' and 'Stars'. In 1971 he began a long association with producer Bunny Lee, re-cutting his Eternals hits solo and sounding better than ever. By 1974 Campbell was second only to Johnny Clarke in Lee's large stable, singing largely in the lovers rock style. His debut, *Cornell Campbell* (1973), was a shoddy affair despite the excellence of the music: the front cover featured an ice cream cone (no picture of the singer was available) and Campbell did not even hear of its existence until 1977. In 1975 he changed his approach, becoming a rasta singer as befitted his appearance, and immediately Campbell's stock increased: 'Natty Dread In A Greenwich Farm', the superb 'Natural Fact' and 'Dance In A Greenwich Farm' were all considerable Jamaican hits. The latter formed the title of his second album. A series of 'gorgon' records, with Campbell declaring himself 'the gorgon (ruler) of dis yah dance' set up another string of hits, as did 'Boxing', a brutal and much-covered record for Joe Gibbs. From time to time he would also return to Studio One for a one-off single. When his popularity began to wane in 1977, Campbell returned to love songs, with 'The Investigator', a consummate piece of lovers rock. By 1980, however, the joint creativity of Campbell and Bunny Lee had run its course and the duo parted company, reputedly acrimoniously. Campbell drifted from producer to producer until the mid-80s, when he became only an occasional visitor to Kingston's studios, occasionally turning up at Waterhouse to make a record with King Jammy or King Tubby. Since then only sporadic releases have increased the Campbell catalogue.
Albums: *Cornell Campbell* (Trojan 1973), *Dance In A Greenwich Farm* (Grounation 1975), *Gorgon* (Klik 1976), *Turn Back The Hands Of Time* (Third World 1977), *Stalowatt* (Third World 1978), *Sweet Baby* (Burning Sounds 1978), *Yes I Will* (Micron 1979), *The Inspector General* (Imperial 1979), *Reggae Sun* (AMO 1980), *Boxing* (Starlight 1982), *Fight Against Corruption* (Vista Sounds 1983), *Follow Instructions* (Mobiliser 1983). With the Gaylads: *Cornell Campbell Meets The Gaylads* (Culture Press 1985). Compilation: *The Cornell Campbell Collection* (Striker Lee 1985).

Capleton

b. Clifton Bailey, Jamaica. Capleton quickly captured the imagination of a dancehall audience hungry for 'slackness' and gun themes in 1990, the year he had his first big hit, 'Number One (On The Good Look Chart)', for Jah Life. Many of his recordings to appear over the next 12 months - for producers such as Philip 'Fatis' Burrell ('Bumbo Red'/'Bible Fi Dem'), King Jammys ('The Red'), Roof International ('Dem No Like Me'), Peterkins ('We No Lotion Man') and Black Scorpio ('Ghetto Youth'/'Somebody') were subsequently compiled on the *Capleton Gold* album, released in 1991. That year he voiced half an album for Gussie P ('Double Trouble'), combined with Johnny Osbourne on the highly successful 'Special Guest' for Outernational, and released several fine sides for African Star, as well as dueting with Bobby Zarro on 'Young, Fresh And Green'. In December he visited the UK with the late Pan Head, courting controversy over an unrelated gun incident at one London venue, and recording 'Dance Can't Done' for Brixton label Jungle Rock.
Back in Jamaica work began in earnest for Burrell's Exterminator label. 'Armshouse' was a stirring call for unification within the music, proving a massive hit in early 1992 and, like 'Prophesy' for Penthouse, revealed he could handle cultural and reality issues with the same formidable insight and raw power of delivery as his trademark slackness (of which 'Good Hole', in combination with Buju Banton for Stone Love, was an obvious

example). The singles 'F.C.T', 'Matey A Dead', 'Make Hay' and 'Unno Hear' previewed an eventual album for Fatis, whilst he continued a winning streak throughout 1992. The following year found him broadening his repertoire further still. 'Everybody Needs Somebody' and 'Mankind' for Colin Fat, 'Good Love' and Stampede' for Mad House, 'Cold Blooded Murderer' for Black Scorpio and the rabid 'Buggering' for African Star (also 'Good So'/'Bad So'), maintaining his growing reputation in avid fashion. As 1994 dawned he was proving popular on combinations with the likes of Brian and Tony Gold and Nadine Sutherland, working with Gussie Clarke, and looked poised to become one of the most radical cultural DJs of his era.
Selected albums: *We No Lotion Man* (Charm 1991), *Gold* (Charm 1991), *Armshouse* (Exterminator 1993). With General Levy: *Double Trouble* (Gussie P. 1991). With Cutty Ranks & Reggie Stepper: *Three The Hard Way* (Techniques 1991). With Tony Rebel & Ninjaman: *Real Rough* (1992).

Captain Sinbad

b. Carl Dwyer, Kingston, Jamaica. Now known as a producer, Dwyer began his career as DJ Captain Sinbad on the sound system Sound Of Silence alongside Sugar Minott in the mid-70s. Minott took him to Studio One where he recorded two songs, both unreleased. In 1978 Henry 'Junjo' Lawes produced the first of two albums and he teamed up with Little John for '61 Storm'. Sinbad's own debut as a producer was with Little John's 'A1 Sound'. He also guested on Minott's own 'Hard Time Pressure' and recorded unreleased albums for Black Roots and Linval Thompson. His next effort was for Dillinger's Oak Sound label in 1982, the year he moved to England. There he recorded 'Sister Myrtle' live on Saxon sound system for Rusty International (which later appeared on Studio One) and began recording UK artists on his own Rockfort imprint. John McLean's 'If I Give My Heart To You' was a notable success, although

issued on the Mad Professor's Ariwa label. By 1989 he was back in Jamaica, 'Wickedest Thing In Life' by Gospel Fish being the debut release on a new Sinbad label. Singles by Nerious Joseph, Capleton ('Two Minute Man'), Mike Ninja, Cobra ('Merciless Bad Boy'), O'Neil Shines, Daddy Woody and General T.K. followed with Frankie Paul's 'Heart Attack' a massive hit in 1991. Working closely between Fashion and Penthouse he began experimenting with hip hop remixes and released first *Sin Badda Than Them* and then *Gangster*, both 'version' albums of his popular rhythms. Meanwhile the roster of artists increased; established names like Anthony Red Rose, Glen Ricks and Prilly Hamilton sharing the credits alongside newcomers Sugar Black, Fragga Ranks and Poison Chang. In 1993 he started the *Romantic Ragga* series and introduced DJ Glamour Murphy. With his wide experience of working with both Jamaican and UK acts Sinbad is well placed for future success.
Selected albums: Cobra: *Merciless Bad Boy* (Sinbad 1991). Various: *Sin Badda Than Them* (Sinbad 1992), *Gangster* (Sinbad 1992), *Romantic Ragga Vols. 1* (Sinbad 1993), *Ambush* (Sinbad 1993), *Romantic Ragga Vols. 2* (Sinbad 1994).

Carlton And His Shoes

Carlton, Donald and Lynford Manning (and sometimes Alexander Henry of 'Please Be True' fame) made up the harmony group known as Carlton And His Shoes. Carlton Manning, probably the purest singer of love songs to ever come out of Jamaica, originally named the group Carlton And His Shades, but a printers' mis-spelling on their debut release for Sonia Pottinger stuck with them for their entire career. Their debut single vanished without trace but their subsequent work for Clement 'Coxsone' Dodd at Studio One established them as a seminal force in Jamaican music. 'Love Me Forever', for Dodd's Supreme label, was a massive rocksteady hit in the late 60s and has been re-released and interpreted countless times since its original recording. The b-side,

Chakademus

'Happy Land', formed the basis for 'Satta Amassa Ganna' - one of the most covered tunes in the history of reggae and its most enduring anthem, first performed by the Abyssinians: Donald and Lynford with the addition of Bernard Collins. Carlton, who had by now trademarked the double and treble tracking of his own sweet, aching lead vocals, continued to make fine records at Studio One. (He was also working at their Brentford Road Studios as a session guitarist). The last, 'Let Me Love You', was released on 12-inch in Jamaica in 1979 and showcased one of his finest-ever performances. He has also occasionally worked for other producers and released some excellent self-produced tracks since the halcyon days of the late 60s. Unfortunately, he has never been able to repeat his original success but remains a legendary figure in the development of Jamaican music.
Album: *Love Me Forever* (Studio One 1978), *This Heart Of Mine* (1980).

Chaka Demus & Pliers

The list of DJ/singer combinations in reggae is endless. None have been as successful - and deservedly so - as Chaka Demus & Pliers. Chaka Demus (b. John Taylor, 1965, West Kingston, Jamaica), the rapping half of the pairing, began his career chatting on a variety of sound systems, the most famous of these being Supreme and Jammy's, as Nicodemus Jr. In 1985 a name change provoked a shift of fortunes, and Chaka, whose gruff but avuncular tones made him a stand-out in any DJ company, cut his first single, 'Increase Your Knowledge' soon after. A sporadic string of 45s bearing his name arrived: 'One Scotch, One Bourbon, One Beer', an adaptation of the old Amos Milburn R&B chestnut, and '2 Foot Walk' among them. However, chiefly associated with Jammy's studio, Chaka's mild manner perhaps held him back in the company of what was then the biggest recording stable in Jamaica. A move to Penthouse Studio for 'Chaka On The Move' (1987) improved matters, and it was here that Chaka first became friendly with Pliers, a singer who, like Chaka, had not yet made the fullest indent on reggae's landscape.

Pliers (b. Everton Banner, 1965, Kingston, Jamaica) first found fame cutting sides with Black Scorpio (Maurice Johnson). Influenced by his brother, Spanner Banner, and fellow tool/tunesmith Pinchers, Pliers cut sides for a variety of labels, among them Pickout, Pioneer Musik ('Murder We Wrote', a song he would later return to), Jammys, Harry J and Studio One. Successful though he was, Pliers always seemed to trail in the wake of more celebrated, if faddish singers like Wayne Wonder and Sanchez. While playing shows together in Miami in 1991, Chaka and Pliers decided to team up. 'Gal Wine' for Ossie Hibbert was their first 45 together, which led to a slew of reggae chart successes: 'Rough This Year', 'Love Up The Gal', 'Without Love', 'Winning Machine' and 'Worl' A Girls' among them. A teaming with producers Sly Dunbar & Robbie Shakespeare created a new model of 'Murder She Wrote', which hit number 1 in the specialist charts world-wide. Evidently onto something, they secured a deal with Mango Records, Island's reggae division, and hit the charts with 'Tease Me', a fine, bright ragga-pop record. 'She Don't Let Nobody', the follow-up, also went Top 10, and a version of 'Twist & Shout', with extra vocal support from Jack Radics, became a UK number 1. All these titles were included on the *Tease Me* album. For a long time it seemed that Chaka & Pliers wouldn't make it as big as their peers. Now those same rivals can only gape in amazement and envy.
Selected albums: Chaka Demus solo: *Everybody Loves The Chaka* (Black Scorpio 1988), *The Original Chaka* (Witty 1989). With Shabba Ranks: *Rough & Rugged* (VP 1987). Chaka Demus & Pliers: *Gal Wine* (Greensleeves 1992), *Ruff This Year* (RAS 1992), *Chaka Demus And Pliers* (Charm 1992), *Tease Me* (Mango/Island 1993).

Channel One Records

(see Hookim, Joseph 'Joe Joe')

Chin, Clive

Record producer based at Randy's Studio 17, situated above the famous record shop of the same name in North Parade, Kingston. His first successful production came with the instrumental 'Java' in 1971, featuring the melodica playing of his old school friend, Augustus Pablo. He went on to score several more local hits in 1972 with such as Dennis Brown's 'Cheater', its accompanying horns cut: 'Harvest In The East' by Tommy McCook, and Junior Byles' 'King of Babylon'. He also produced Pablo's classic debut, *This Is,* in 1974, and two dub albums, one based around the 'Java' track, which was mixed by resident Randy's engineer, Errol 'T' Thompson. In 1975 he produced Carl Malcolm's 'Miss Wire Waist', a sizeable hit on the local market, in the wake of Malcolm's popular 'No Jestering' for fellow producer, Leonard 'Santic' Chin (no relation). Clive followed this with the ribald 'Fattie Bum Bum', whose inane catchy refrain appealed to the pop sensibilities of the British entrepreneur Jonathan King. He leased it to his UK label and hyped it into the British charts where it rose to number 8 in October of that year. Despite appearances to the contrary, this proved to be a less than satisfactory financial venture, and Chin concentrated once more on the grass roots audience with records like the stalking 'Guns In The Ghetto' and Jah Woosh's 'Shine Eye Gal'. Eventually he migrated to America, settling in the Bronx district of New York - to run the J & C Kitchen, serving Jamaican food to the local expatriate population. His family had established the VP record distribution company in the same locale. Over the last few years he has made tentative steps towards the music business again, but so far no new productions have been forthcoming.
Albums: *Java Java Dub* (White label 1973), *Randys Dub* (Randys 1974).

Chin-Loy, Herman

Of Chinese-Jamaican extraction, Herman Chin-Loy's earliest involvement in the music business came when he worked for his famous record producing cousin, Leslie Kong, in his Beverley's record shop in the 60s. In 1969 he opened up his own Aquarius Record Store in Half Way Tree and moved into record production via instrumentals like 'African Zulu' and 'Shang I'. To this end he utilised the talents of Lloyd Charmers and the Hippy Boys, featuring soon-to-be Wailers (see Marley, Bob) rhythm section Carlton & Family Man Barrett. On his later productions he is credited with being the first to use the highly influential Now Generation Band. He was also responsible for the debut recordings of Augustus Pablo: it was Chin-Loy, in fact, who gave Pablo his name. Chin-Loy had been releasing instrumentals, mainly organ-led affairs by Upsetter acolyte Glen Adams, and crediting them to an invented name, Augustus Pablo. When the young Horace Swaby (Pablo's real name) came on the scene, Herman saw no reason to change the credit, and so Horace Swaby became Augustus Pablo. In return Pablo made a number of records for the producer between 1971 and 1973, including 'Higgi Higgi', 'East Of The River Nile', 'Song Of The East' and 'The Red Sea'. Chin-Loy worked with a number of other artists in the early 70s, including Dennis Brown ('Song My Mother Used To Sing', 'It's Too Late') and Alton Ellis ('Alton's Official Daughter'). In May 1971 his production of Bruce Ruffin's 'Rain' became a crossover hit and secured the number 19 position in the UK pop charts.
According to his own testimony, *Aquarius Dub*, one of the first ever dub albums, emerged from a half hour mix-and-go session at Dynamics studio with Herman himself at the controls. He built his own 24 track studio, the first in Jamaica, in the mid-70s, which was used primarily for the recording of non-reggae music. In fact Chin-Loy's own productions were largely absent from the reggae scene until 1979. It was then that he began to score local hits once more with a number of 12" mixes on the cusp of the burgeoning dancehall style,

including material by Little Roy ('Long Time Rock Steady', 'Skanking On The Banking') and Ernest Wilson ('Truth & Rights'). Largely absent from the scene throughout the 80s, there were hints of activity in the 90s but nothing concrete has emerged as yet.
Albums: *Aquarius Dub* (Aquarius 1973), *Aquarius Dub Part 2* (Aquarius 1974).

Cimarons

The Cimarons' main claim to fame is the honour of being the UK's first indigenous reggae band. Like many later British outfits, the Cimarons, who formed in 1967 at a north London Methodist youth club, eked out a living in their early days supporting visiting Jamaican musicians on club dates, and they proved so adept that they were later invited to tour Africa. On their return they cut their debut 45, 'Mammy Blue', released on Downtown Records. By this time they had built themselves sufficient standing to make touring in their own right viable. These engagements paved the way for two album releases, the first of which, *In Time*, predominantly comprised soul standards given the reggae treatment. The second, *On The Rock*, was recorded in Jamaica. Riding on the crest of the reggae boom, they were picked up by Polydor in the late 70s. By recording *Reggaebility*, which included takes on several Beatles' songs, they certainly helped bring the genre mainstream attention. They have also backed a record by Australian songwriter Gary Shearston. Members of the band have included Sonny Binns (keyboards), Franklyn Dunn (bass), Locksley Gichie (guitars) and Winston Reid (vocals). In the 80s they were joined by former Matumbi drummer, Jah 'Bunny' Donaldson.
Selected albums: *In Time* (Trojan 1977), *On The Rock* (Vulcan 1977), *Maka* (Polydor 1978), *Live* (Polydor 1979), *Reggaebility* (Hallmark 1982).

Clarendonians

While Jamaican music is packed with child prodigies, to find three in one group is unusual even by reggae standards. The Clarendonians, originally Fitzroy 'Ernest' Wilson and Peter Austin, formed during 1965 in their home parish of Clarendon in rural Jamaica and after several talent competition victories came to the attention of producer Coxsone Dodd, owner of the Studio One label, while they were in their early teens. Dodd liked their feisty approach and soon put the pair in the studio, where they helped define the 'rude boy' era of ska alongside Dodd's other youthful protégés, Bob Marley And The Wailers. If anything, the Clarendonians were more successful than Marley's group at the time, scoring heavily with brash, loud singles like 'You Can't Be Happy', 'You Can't Keep A Good Man Down', 'Sho Be Do Be', 'Rudie Gone A Jail', 'Be Bop Boy', and their anthem, 'Rudie Bam Bam'. As young as their audience and the music they worked with, the Clarendonians were briefly the perfect ska vocal group. Somewhere along the line Dodd added another member, Freddie McGregor, who at the age of seven, had to stand on a box to reach the microphone; and Dodd permutated the members as Freddie And Fitzie, Freddie And Peter, or simply recorded them solo. Ernest Wilson was the first member to really strike out as a solo act with a cover of Billy Vera's 'Storybook Children' and Tim Hardin's 'If I Were A Carpenter', as well as recording under the unlikely monicker King Shark. He's still something of a star in Jamaica today, if only sporadically successful. Freddie McGregor was not so immediately successful, but after a series of excellent records with Studio One lasting right into the early 70s, he finally hit with 'Bobby Babylon'. Peter Austin's attempt at a solo career sadly faltered.
Compilation: *The Best Of The Clarendonians* (Studio One 1968).

Clarke, Gussie

b. Augustus Clarke, c.1953, Kingston, Jamaica. Clarke started in the reggae business by cutting dub plates. He grew up alongside reggae DJ Big Youth, and Gussie was an

early pioneer of the new DJ style. His first production was U Roy's 'The Higher The Mountain' in 1972, which became an instant classic. His initial album productions, Big Youth's *Screaming Target* and I Roy's *Presenting,* are among the best DJ albums of all time. Gussie was not one to push his own name at the expense of his acts however, and rather than the bizarre flash of contemporaries he preferred a low-key, crafted approach, reflected in the name of his 'house band', Simplicity People. During the 70s he recorded many of the greatest names in reggae including Augustus Pablo, Dennis Brown, Gregory Isaacs and Leroy Smart, and his Gussie and Puppy labels became synonymous with quality reggae. Clarke kept production almost as a sideline to his main business of dub cutting and record export. Unlike other producers in the grab-and-flee reggae business, he paid royalties and kept a publishing company. By the early 80s Gussie's activities as a producer were restricted to the occasional outing with reggae superstars such as Dennis Brown (*To The Foundation,* 1982), Gregory Isaacs (*Private Beach Party,* 1984) and vocal groups Cultural Roots (*Whole Heap A Daughters,* 1983) and the Mighty Diamonds (*The Roots Is There,* 1986, and *The Real Enemy,* 1988). The announcement that Gussie had recorded some of the Diamonds' *Real Enemy* at his own studio was met with indifference, but the first single to emerge from his Music Works Studio, Gregory Isaacs' 'Rumours', could not be ignored. Clarke had abandoned his solid, rather traditional sound and had 'gone digital', using computers and synthesizers to create an entirely new, dub-centred sound. The record was a massive hit, and another version of it, 'Telephone Love' from female singer JC Lodge, was the biggest reggae hit of 1988 in the USA. Suddenly Gussie appeared way ahead of the pack, and he spent 1989 and the start of 1990 with everyone queueing to record at his hi-tech studio, among them Aswad, Maxi Priest and jazz musician Courtney Pine. His 'Pirates Anthem' single with Home T, Cocoa Tea and Shabba Ranks was a huge underground hit in London, but then Clarke started to think about another project - a bigger, more 'international' studio. Once again his production work took a back seat as he block-booked Music Works to other producers and concentrated on his new baby. Towards the end of 1991 he put out a few singles, but it remains to be seen whether Clarke can once again deliver a shock to reggae, this time from brand-new premises.
Albums: Various: *Black Foundation* (Burning Sounds 1976), *Gussie Presents The Right Tracks* (1977), *Music Works Showcase* (Music Works 1984), *Music Works Showcase '88* (Greensleeves 1988), *Music Works Showcase '89* (Greensleeves 1989), *Ram Dancehall* (Mango/Island 1988), *Hardcore Ragga* (Greensleeves 1990). Big Youth: *Screaming Target* (Trojan 1973). I Roy: *Presenting* (Trojan 1973).

Clarke, Johnny

b. January 1955, Jamaica. After winning a talent contest at Bull Bay on the south-western coast of Jamaica, Johnny Clarke made his first record, 'God Made The Sea And Sun', which flopped. His next two releases for producer Rupie Edwards, 'Everyday Wandering' and 'Julie', both enjoyed considerable sales in Jamaica and with expatriate communities in the UK, USA and Canada. By 1974 Clarke was working with Bunny Lee in the studios of Treasure Isle, Randy's and Harry J, whilst voicing the finished instrumental tracks at King Tubby's studio in Kingston's Waterhouse district. Under Lee's tutelage during 1975-76 Clarke became the hottest new singer in Jamaica. His repertoire, an astute mix of militant 'dread' tunes and love songs given an up-to-the-minute gloss or 'style' by the Aggrovators studio band, found immediate favour with the discerning dancehall patrons of Jamaica and elsewhere. His hits in those two years included 'None Shall Escape The Judgement', 'Move Out Of Babylon', 'Rock With Me Baby', 'Enter Into His Gates With Praise', and 'Joshua's

Word', all new songs, while Lee encouraged him to cover classic Jamaican standards by artists such as John Holt. Holt's canon supplied further local hits for Clarke, including 'Fancy Make-Up', 'Stranger In Love', 'Left With A Broken Heart' and 'So Much Pain', all backed by the then current 'flying cymbal sound' of Lee's Aggrovators. Following this period, Clarke continued to record for Lee and other producers as diverse as Errol Thompson and Prince Jammy. He has continued to produce quality reggae material to the present day, after a period of inactivity in the mid-80s. Most recently he has recorded for Fashion Records and Jah Shaka in the UK, and the 90s' hitmaking production duo of Steely and Clevie.

Albums: *None Shall Escape* (1974), *Enter Into His Gates With Praise* (Attack 1974), *Put It On* (Vulcan 1975), *Authorised Version* (Virgin 1976), *Rocker's Time Now* (Virgin 1976), *Girl I Love You* (Justice 1977), *I Man Come Again* (Black Music 1982), *Yard Style* (Ariwa 1983), *Reggae Party* (Vista Sounds 1984), *Give Thanks* (Ariwa 1985), *Don't Trouble Trouble* (Attack/Trojan 1989). With Cornell Campbell: *Johnny Clarke Meets Cornell Campbell In New Style* (Vista Sounds 1983), With Sly & Robbie: *Sly & Robbie Present The Best Of Johnnie Clarke* (Vista Sounds 1985). Compilation: *20 Massive Hits* (1985), *Reggae Archives* (Gong Sounds 1991).

Cliff, Jimmy

b. James Chambers, 1948, St. Catherine, Jamaica. One of the great popularisers of reggae music, Jimmy Cliff blazed a trail into rock that Bob Marley later followed, but without ever capitalising on his great advantages as a singer-songwriter, nascent film star and interpreter of other peoples' material. Raised by his father, Cliff first moved to Kingston in 1962 after the dream of a musical career seduced him from his studies. An early brace of 45s, 'Daisy Got Me Crazy', with Count Boysie, and 'I'm Sorry', for sound system operator Sir Cavalier, did little to bring him to the public's attention. His career began in earnest when a song he

had written himself, 'Hurricane Hattie', describing the recent arrival in South America of the self-same meteorological disaster, became a local hit. He was still only 14 years old.

Cliff subsequently emerged as a ska singer for producer Leslie Kong in 1963, singing 'King Of Kings' and 'Dearest Beverly' in a hoarse, raucous voice to considerable local acclaim. He can be seen in this fledgling role on the video *This Is Ska*, shot in 1964. The same year Cliff joined a tour, promoted by politician Eward Seaga and headlined by Byron Lee And The Dragonaires, with the intention of exporting reggae music to the wider world. Though it would later collapse in acrimony, the jaunt at least brought Cliff to the attention of Island Records' boss Chris Blackwell, and in the mid-60s the young singer moved to London. By 1968 Cliff was being groomed as a solo star to the underground rock market. Musicians teamed with him included Mott The Hoople's Ian Hunter and vocalists including Madeline Bell and P.P. Arnold. The shift away from the conventional reggae audience was confirmed by a cover of Procul Harum's 'Whiter Shade of Pale' and appearances alongside the Incredible String Band and Jethro Tull on Island samplers.

1968 saw Cliff chancing his arm in Brazil, representing Jamaica in the International Song Festival. His entry, 'Waterfall' (a flop in England) earned him a considerable following in South America. More importantly the sojourn gave him the chance to take stock and write new material. He finally broke through in 1969 with 'Wonderful World, Beautiful People', a somewhat over-produced single typical of the era, which he had written in Brazil. 'Vietnam' was a small hit the following year, and was described by Bob Dylan as not only the best record about the war, but the best protest song he had heard. Paul Simon went one step further in his praises; after hearing the song he travelled to Kingston and booked the same rhythm section, studio and engineer to record 'Mother And Child

54

Jimmy Cliff

Reunion' - arguably the first US reggae song. In local terms however, its success was outstripped by 'Wild World', a cover of the Cat Stevens song, the link between the two singers perhaps strengthened by a shared Muslim faith.

While the albums *Jimmy Cliff* (1969), *Hard Road To Travel* (1970) and particularly *Another Cycle* (1971) were short on roots credibility, his next move, as the gun-toting, reggae-singing star of *The Harder They Come* (1972), was short on nothing. Cliff, with his ever-present five-point star t-shirt, was suddenly Jamaica's most marketable property. *The Harder They Come* was the island's best home-grown film, and its soundtrack one of the biggest selling reggae records of all time. Cliff seemed set for superstardom. Somehow it never happened: his relationship with Island soured and deals with EMI, Reprise and CBS failed to deliver him to his rightful place. In fact, his star began to wane directly as Bob Marley signed to Island. The company executed the same marketing process for both artists - rebellion, great songwriting, hipness - but it was Marley who embodied the new spirit of reggae and reaped the rewards. Cliff's artistic fortunes were revived, ironically enough, by the recruitment of Wailers' producer Joe Higgs as his bandleader. Despite their merits, Cliff's excellent records for his own Sunpower label did not really connect either. To many outside the reggae world he remains best known for writing the beautiful 'Many Rivers To Cross', a massive hit for UB40. However, his popularity on the African continent is enormous, arguably greater than that of any other reggae artist, Marley included. He is similarly venerated in South America, whose samba rhythms have helped to inform and enrich his latter day material. His 90s albums *Images* and *Breakout*, which highlight, as ever, his plaintive, gospel-tinged delivery, offer ample evidence to dislodge the widely-held belief (particularly in the West) that he is a perennial under-achiever.
Albums: *Jimmy Cliff* (Trojan 1969), *Wonderful World, Beautiful People* (A&M 1970, US), *Hard Road To Travel* (Trojan/A&M 1970), *Another Cycle* (Island 1971), *The Harder They Come* (Mango/Island 1972, film soundtrack), *Unlimited* (EMI 1973, Trojan 1990), *Struggling Man* (Island 1974), *Brave Warrior* (EMI 1975), *Follow My Mind* (Reprise 1976), *The Best Of Jimmy Cliff In Concert* (Reprise 1977), *Give Thanx* (Warner Bros. 1978), *Oh Jamaica* (EMI 1979), *I Am The Living* (WEA 1980), *Give The People What They Want* (Oneness/WEA 1981), *House Of Exile* (1981), *Special* (CBS 1982), *The Power And The Glory* (CBS 1983), *Can't Get Enough Of It* (Veep 1984), *Cliff Hanger* (Dynamic/CBS 1985), *Sense Of Direction* (Sire 1985), *Hang Fire* (Dynamic/CBS 1987), *Images* (Cliff Sounds 1989), *Save Our Planet Earth* (Musidisc 1990), *Breakout* (Cliff Sounds 1993). Compilations: *The Best Of Jimmy Cliff* (Island 1974), *The Collection* (EMI 1983), *Jimmy Cliff* (Trojan 1983), *Reggae Greats* (Island 1985), *Fundamental Reggae* (See For Miles 1987), *The Best Of Jimmy Cliff* (Mango/Island 1988).
Video: *Bongo Man* (1991).

Clint Eastwood & General Saint

Jamaican born Eastwood (Trinity's younger brother) came to prominence with British reggae fans in the late 70s with a series of big-selling singles recorded in his home country, and albums such as *African Youth*, *Death In The Arena* and *Sex Education*. In the early 80s he teamed up with General Saint, who had already established a serious following working in London's Front Line International sound system, and the pair formed a talented pop reggae duo. Their first release, a tribute to the late General Echo, topped the reggae charts and the follow-up, 'Another One Bites The Dust', repeated the feat in 1981, reaching as far as the lower rungs of the national chart. Their subsequent records and live appearances enhanced their reputation further and they were instrumental in the Jamaican DJ style crossing over to the early 80s pop audience.
Albums: Clint Eastwood: *African Youth* (Third World 1978), *Death In The Arena*

Cobra

(Cha Cha 1978), *Love & Happiness* (Burning Sounds 1979), *Sex Education* (Greensleeves 1980), *Jah Lights Shining* (Vista Sounds 1984). Compilation: *Best Of Clint Eastwood* (Culture Press 1984). Clint Eastwood & General Saint: *Two Bad DJ* (Greensleeves 1981), *Stop That Train* (Greensleeves 1983).

Clue J And His Blues Blasters

Double-bassist Cluett Johnson's most lasting contribution to the history of music happened by accident. From 1959, Jamaican-born Johnson led the first band to make records in Jamaica; the Blues Blasters' line-up included Ernest Ranglin (guitar), Emmanuel 'Rico' Rodriguez (trombone), Roland Alphonso (tenor saxophone), Theophilius Beckford (piano) and Arkland 'Drumbago' Parks (drums). Their early recordings, such as 'Shuffling Jug' (1959), were in a calypso or R&B vein and were promoted on producer Coxsone Dodd's Downbeat sound system, which played in and around Kingston. Having thus created a demand, Dodd would release their records on his Worldisc label. Rehearsing in the studio, Johnson reportedly instructed Ranglin to 'Play it like ska, ska', thus unwittingly coining the name of his island's predominant music of the 1962-66 period. By that time the Blues Blasters had evolved into the Skatalites and Johnson had slipped from view.
Album: Various: *All Star Top Hits* (Studio One 1961). With the Cecil Lloyd Trio: *Live At The Penthouse*.

Cobra

b. Ewart Everton Brown, 1968, Kingston, Jamaica. Brown grew up in St. Mary's and was nicknamed Cobra after a character in the G.I. Joe comic books. Early experience on the Mighty Ruler, Climax, Stereo One and Inner City sound systems led to his first record, 'Respect Woman', in 1989. The producer was his uncle, Delroy 'Spiderman' Thompson, then engineer at Tuff Gong. His first local hit was 'Nah Go Work', a duet with Tricia McKay, produced by Carl

Mitchell in 1990. Carl 'Banton' Nelson and Captain Sinbad were quick to follow their example in early 1991, encouraging him to voice titles like 'Ze Taurus' and 'Merciless Bad Boy' as a wave of gun lyrics - influenced by the Gulf War and championed by the DJ Ninjaman - began to gain popularity in the Jamaican dancehalls.
Next stop was Donovan Germain's Penthouse studio, where he immediately struck up a successful partnership with resident engineer Dave Kelly. Singles like 'Yush', 'Bad Boy Talk' and 'Gundelero' sealed his burgeoning reputation as an uncompromising lyricist, and were crowned by the best-selling *Bad Boy Talk* album. 1991 was his most prolific and rewarding year, with a glut of releases from King Jammys, Bobby Digital ('Tek Him' almost attained crossover status), Sly & Robbie, John John and Penthouse controlling the reggae charts, especially in the UK where he scored no less than five number 1 hits. UK producers played their part in helping widen his appeal, so too Montego Bay label Top Rank who'd followed the *Spotlight* album with Cobra's haunting 'Love Forever'. It was evidence of his shift towards romantic lyrics and softer, more R&B orientated rhythms as exemplified by 'Flex', which he'd voiced for Shang. It was this song which persuaded Columbia to sign him and by the end of 1992 he was number 1 on the US Billboard Chart. In 1993, after an impressive major label album debut with *Easy To Wet Hard To Dry* - complete with guest US rappers - he unexpectedly returned to the dancehall market, working with several of his former producers, including King Jammy.
Albums: *Bad Boy Talk* (Penthouse 1991), *Spotlight* (Top Rank 1992), Merciless Bad Boy (Sinbad 1992), *Easy To Wet Hard To Dry* (Columbia 1993).

Cocoa Tea

b. Calvin Scott, c.1960, Kingston, Jamaica. Cocoa Tea began his career while still a child in Kingston in 1974, singing on a couple of obscure records for an equally obscure

Cocoa Tea

producer Willie Francis, 'Searching In The Hills' being issued under the name of Calvin Scott.

He vanished again until 1983, when, sporting dreadlocks and his new nickname, he began to carve a niche in dancehall reggae with producer Henry 'Junjo' Lawes, hitting with 'Rockin' Dolly', and 'I Lost My Sonia'. Unlike other dancehall singers he did not find it necessary to attempt to dominate a song with energy, instead preferring a subtler, more melodic approach. His 1985 album debut, *Wha Them A Go Do, Can't Stop Cocoa Tea,* suggested that he would be around for a long time. This proved to be correct as *The Marshall, Sweet Sweet Cocoa Tea* (both 1986) and *Come Again* and *Cocoa Tea* (both 1987) established him further. A liaison with producer Gussie Clarke led to the formation of a group alongside the trio Home T and DJ Shabba Ranks. Their *Holding On* and the single 'Pirate's Anthem' were huge Jamaican hits in 1989. As a solo artist, *Riker's Island* established that he had more to say than most. The 'No Blood For Oil' single was one of the few lucid reggae comments on the Gulf war, also to be found on *One More For The Road* (1991), recorded with Home T after Cutty Ranks had replaced Shabba in the group. The only thing holding Cocoa Tea back from being a major star is his apparent reluctance to travel. Whether he will fulfil his potential remains to be seen.

Selected albums: *Wha Them A Go Do, Can't Stop Cocoa Tea* (Volcano 1985), *Sweet Sweet Cocoa Tea* (Blue Mountain 1985), *Cocoa Tea* (Firehouse 1986), *The Marshall* (Jammys 1986), *Come Again* (Super Power 1987), *Rikers Island* (Greensleeves 1991), *Authorized* (Greensleeves 1992), *I Am The Toughest* (King Jammys 1992), *Kingston Hot* (Greensleeves 1992), *One Up* (Exterminator/Greensleeves 1993). With Shabba Ranks and Home T: *Holding On* (Hawkeye 1988). With Tenor Saw: *Clash* (Greensleeves 1989). With Cutty Ranks and Home T: *One More For The Road* (1991).

Cole, Stranger

b. c.1945, Kingston, Jamaica. In 1962 Cole made his recording debut with Duke Reid, topping the local hit parade with 'Rough And Tough' and 'When You Call My Name', the latter a duet with Patsy Todd. His understated, laconic delivery could be heard on further hits for Reid including 'Stranger At The Door' (1963), 'We Are Rolling' (1964), and 'Run Joe' (1965). During this period, he also worked with other producers including a duet with Ken Boothe, 'Worlds Fair', for Coxsone Dodd, and sang harmony for Eric Morris' huge hit 'Penny Reel', a Prince Buster production. By the late 60s his voice had developed into a much more powerful, soulful instrument. He recorded for several producers including another duet with Patsy Todd, 'Down By The Tramline' (1967) for Sonia Pottinger, a duet with Gladstone Anderson, 'Just Like A River' (1968) for Joe Gibbs, 'Crying Every Night' (1970) for Byron Smith, and 'Lift Your Head Up High' (1970), a self production. In 1971 he emigrated to England where he toured extensively, before relocating to Canada in 1973, settling in Toronto. He released his first album, *Forward In The Land Of Sunshine*, in 1976. In the late 70s he produced two songs, 'Capture Land' and 'The Time Is Now', for the New York based Wackies label. Three albums were also issued on his own label, *The First Ten Years Of Stranger Cole* (1978), *Capture Land* (1980) and *The Patriot* (1982). He was less fortunate when working for other producers, as albums he recorded for Coxsone Dodd and Chinna Smith in the early 80s were not issued. His most recent album was *No More Fussing And Fighting*, his first to be released in the USA. Sadly, Stranger's rich back-catalogue has never been reissued.

Albums: *Forward In The Land Of Sunshine* (1976), *The First Ten Years Of Stranger Cole* (c.70s), *Capture Land* (c.80s), *The Patriot* (1982), *No More Fussing And Fighting* (1986).

Congos

Jamaican vocal group comprising Cedric

Myton (b. 1947, St. Catherine, Jamaica; falsetto), Roy Johnson (b. 1947, Hanover, Jamaica; tenor) plus Watty Burnett (baritone). Little is known about the formation of the Congos (sometimes spelt Congoes) and less about their demise. However, for a brief period they recorded some of the most alluring and exciting roots reggae of all time. Myton And Johnson, both serious rasta artists from Jamaica, first emerged as the Congos on a single, 'At The Feast', for producer Lee Perry (1976). Before teaming with Roy Johnson, Cedric Myton had been a member of the Tartans alongside Lloyd Robinson and had also sung with Ras Michael and recorded with Prince Lincoln And the Royal Rasses. Perry had been auditioning vocal groups at his Black Ark Studio in Kingston for a project he had in mind: a roots vocal album featuring a classic falsetto-tenor-baritone line-up. However, the Congos proved to be more than he had expected, even if they did not feature the baritone. Early singles 'Ark Of The Covenant' and 'Congo Man' confirmed that something special was going on, even by Perry's own high standards. Perry added Black Ark regular Watty Burnett to the group to handle deeper chores, and an album was completed. Unfortunately Perry was in dispute with Island, the label handling his international releases, at the time (1977), and hence did not offer the Congos', *Heart Of The Congos* to the company, preferring instead to press it on his own Black Art imprint. This caused a row with the group, who felt they were being sold short and the album only reached the specialist shops in small quantities. The group split with Perry and arranged another limited pressing of the album themselves and eventually signed to CBS in France. In 1980 UK label Go-Feet picked up *Heart Of The Congos* and gave it the release it deserved. However, it made their current efforts seem lack-lustre by comparison and subsequent records flopped, with Watty Burnett quitting the group. Roy Johnson was the next to go solo with *Congo Ashanti Roy* (1982). Present whereabouts of

members are unknown. The group's story is one typical of reggae; they had talent galore, but the business dealings were less than satisfactory. Whether they could have equalled *Heart Of The Congos* in different circumstances remains a moot point.

Selected albums: *Heart Of The Congos* (Black Art 1978), *Image Of Africa* (Epic 1979), *Congo Ashanti* (CBS 1980). Roy Johnson as Congo Ashanti Roy: *Sign Of The Star* (1981). Compilation: *Best Of The Congos*.

Count Ossie

b. Oswald Williams, c.1928, Jamaica, d. 18 October 1976. As a boy, Count Ossie became involved in the Rastafarian community where he learnt hand-drumming and the vocal chanting technique that reverberates back to pre-slavery days in Africa. By the late 50s, he had become a master-drummer and had formed a group of other percussionists around him, the Count Ossie Group. By the turn of the 60s Count Ossie was more of a cultural icon than pop star, and it was only the ingenuity of Prince Buster that made him a part of reggae. Buster, ever-eager to get one over on his rivals, was looking for a sound that no one else in Jamaica had managed to put on a ska record. Buster knew about Count Ossie, but everyone told him that Ossie would never agree to work on a commercial record, particularly since Buster was a Muslim and Ossie a Rastafarian. However, Buster went up into the hills and returned the next day with Ossie and several drummers in tow. The first and most famous record they made was 'Oh Carolina' and 'I Met A Man', featuring Ossie and ensemble thundering away on funde and kette drums and the vocals of the Folks Brothers out front. The record was a unique combination of ska, R&B and 'grounation' fundamentalist music that scored heavily both in Jamaica and on the London mod scene. Subsequent sessions for Coxsone Dodd followed accompanying the Mellocats' 'Another Moses', Bunny And Skitter's 'Lumumbo' and Lascelles Perkins' 'Destiny'. They also made some records

under their own name including 'Cassavubu' (for Prince Buster) and 'Babylon Gone' (for Harry Mudie). The group then refrained from recording until 1970, when they issued 'Whispering Drums' (for Harry Mudie), 'Back To Africa Version One' (for Lloyd Daley), and 'Holy Mount Zion' and 'Meditation' (for Coxsone Dodd). Around this time, Count Ossie's drummers were augmented by a bass player and a horn section led by Cedric Brooks, and the group took the name the Mystic Revelation Of Rastafari. In 1974 they recorded a triple album set, *Grounation*, which is a landmark recording in Jamaican music. The set included treatments of Charles Lloyd's 'Passin' Thru', the Jazz Crusaders' 'Way Back Home', Ethiopian melodies, improvisations, hymns and poetry. In 1975 the group recorded a follow-up album, the similarly excellent *Tales Of Mozambique*. Shortly after this, in 1976, Ossie died and left behind a unique legacy, to be carried on by Ras Michael And The Sons Of Negus and several less noteworthy outfits. During the 80s, the Mystic Revelation Of Rastafari reformed with several original members. Only two songs by the group have so far been released, 'Little Drummer Boy' and 'Hero Is He', the latter made for *A Tribute To Marcus Garvey*.
Albums: *Grounation* (Ashanti 1973), *Tales Of Mozambique* (Dynamic 1975).

Cousins, Roy
(see Royals)

Coxsone, Lloyd
An influential figure in the growth of the UK reggae scene, not to be confused with Coxsone Dodd, Lloyd Coxsone (b. Lloyd Blackwood) left his home in Morant Bay, Jamaica, and arrived in the UK in 1962, settling in south west London and setting up his first sound system, Lloyd The Matador. This venture floundered due to inexperience and Lloyd joined the UK-based Duke Reid sound (it was the habit for UK-based sounds to name themselves in honour of their big

Jamaican counterparts), but he eventually left in 1969, taking some of that operations' personnel with him, to form his own sound system, adopting the name of the biggest sound in Jamaica at the time, and also, pointedly, the main rival to Jamaica's Duke Reid, Sir Coxsone. This time he got it right and Coxsone sound soon gained a strong following that eventually led to his residency at the famous London nightclub, the Roaring Twenties in Carnaby Street. Throughout the 70s Sir Coxsone Sound led the UK sound system pack, staying on top by maintaining the sound to rigorous standards, playing the most exclusive dub plates direct from Jamaica, and keeping abreast of trends within the music. Rather than specialising in one particular style, Coxsone Sound, with the legendary selector Festus at the controls, offered music for all tastes.

Coxsone, like other sound men, also expanded into the record business licensing music from Jamaica at first, then trying his hand at his own productions using local UK artists. In 1975 he enjoyed huge success, and kickstarted the UK lovers rock phenomenon in the process, with his production of 'Caught You In A Lie' - originally a US soul hit by Robert Parker - featuring the vocal talents of 14 year old south London schoolgirl Louisa Marks. That same year he issued one of the best dub albums of the era, *King Of The Dub Rock*, which featured dubwise versions of his own productions and those of Gussie Clarke, mixed in part at King Tubby's. Other notable records appeared on his Tribesman and Lloyd Coxsone Outernational imprints and elsewhere during the late 70s/early 80s, including Faybiene Miranda's Jack Ruby-produced 'Prophecy', 'Love And Only Love' and 'Voice Of The Poor' by Fred Locks. Others included 'Stormy Night' and 'Homeward Bound' by the Creation Steppers, a version of the Commodores' 'Easy' by Jimmy Lindsay (many of which are available on *12 The Hard Way*) and many more. During the mid-80s Coxsone handed control of his sound over to the younger elements in his team, notably Blacker Dread, and a new breed of DJs. Blacker released his own productions by the likes of Fred Locks, Frankie Paul, Mikey General, Sugar Minott, Michael Palmer, Don Carlos, Earl Sixteen and Coxsone DJ, Jah Screechy. Recently, as interest in the roots music of the 70s has increased, Coxsone has emerged from his semi-retirement to once again stand at the controls of his sound.

Selected albums: *King Of The Dub Rock* (Safari 1975), *King Of The Dub Rock Part 2* (1982), *12 The Hard Way* (Tribesman 1989).

Culture

The runaway success of 1977 with their single 'Two Sevens Clash' for Joe Gibbs', and an album of the same name, Culture dominated reggae with their stark prophecy and apocalyptic warnings. They even found a sympathetic ear in the emergent punk audience of the period. The group was led by songwriter Joseph Hill, who had started his career at Studio One as a member of the Soul Defenders, releasing one solo single, 'Behold The Land'. With Albert 'Ralph' Walker and Kenneth Paley (aka Kenneth Dayes) providing the harmonies, the trio came from the same school of style and lyrical content as Burning Spear. Largely through the groundwork of artists such as Bob Marley And The Wailers, the aforementioned Burning Spear and the Abyssinians cultural or socio-political themes abounded in Jamaican music, and many new listeners were attracted to a genre they had previously dismissed. Culture were ready-made champions for this new-found reggae audience, and their popularity was further enhanced by electrifying live appearances with Hill, in particular, proving himself to be an effusive showman.

This level of interest attracted Virgin Records' Front Line label, who stepped in with the type of deal rarely offered to reggae

acts. Culture had by then finished working with Joe Gibbs and their all-important follow-up album was produced by Sonia Pottinger. *Harder Than The Rest* confounded the critics, and the hugely popular single 'Stop The Fighting' was further proof of their standing. A strange release from America at the same time, titled *Africa Stand Alone*, featured a number of tracks from the Virgin album, although the versions were substantially different. If anything this second album stimulated interest in the 'official' release and both boosted the sales of the other for months while consolidating Culture's reputation for militant lyrics set against raw roots rhythms. Culture have always remained rooted in the same lyrical preoccupations and, even if the rhythms have changed over the years - they have not. Joseph Hill split with his two backing singers in 1982, but continues to use the name Culture and his records always sell well despite being far removed from any current reggae trends. The indications that the 90s seem to be ushering in a second 'cultural' era might well prove fruitful for seasoned campaigners such as Hill.

Albums: *Two Sevens Clash* (Joe Gibbs/Lightning 1977), *Baldhead Bridge* (Joe Gibbs 1978), *Africa Stand Alone* (April Records 1978), *Harder Than The Rest* (Front Line 1978), *Cumbolo* (Front Line 1979), *International Herb* (Front Line 1979), *Lion Rock* (Sonic Sounds/Heartbeat 1981), *Culture In Culture* (Blue Track 1986), *Culture At Work* (Shanachie 1986), *Nuff Crisis!* (Blue Mountain 1988), *Good Things* (RAS 1989), *Wings Of A Dove* (Shanachie 1993), *Trod On* (Heartbeat 1993). Compilations: *Vital Selection* (Virgin 1981), *Too Long In Slavery* (Front Line 1989).

D

Daddy Freddie

b. Jamaica. Though the holder of the Guinness Book Of Records' 'World's Fastest Rapper' title, Daddy Freddie has emerged as more than a simple novelty act. Having enjoyed several hits in Jamaica, he emigrated to London in the mid-80s. Teaming up with Asher D he recorded 'Raggamuffin Hip Hop' for Music Of Life, which brought him to the wider public's attention for the first time, particularly in New York. While his patter blurs the distinction between ragga DJ and American-styled rap artist, Daddy Freddie's irreverent, quickfire mode has enhanced the possibilities of both genres.
Selected albums: *Cater Fi She* (Exterminator 1989), *Stress* (Music Of Life 1991).

Daley, Lloyd 'Matador'

b. Kingston, Jamaica, 1942. A reggae producer whose work, unusually, can be dignified by the motto of quality over quantity. Lloyd Daley's interest in music grew out of his work as an electrician, running his own shop, Lloyd's Radio & Television Service, in Waltham Park, Kingston. During the late 50s he started a sound system, Lloyd The Matador, and from there it was an almost inevitable step to production work. His early productions for his Matador (later Mystic) label were ska-based, but it was not until 1968 that he began to make an impact, his first big success being the Scorchers' 'Uglyman'. Hits with Little Roy ('Bongo Nyah', 'Scrooge'), the Heptones ('Righteous Man'), the Viceroys, and the Ethiopians were remarkable for their spare, unfussy quality, and his works with Little Roy were among the first explicitly Rasta-themed reggae releases. He also cut one of Dennis Brown's best early singles ('Baby Don't Do It'), a couple of Alton Ellis' most powerful 45s ('Back To Africa',

'Deliver Us'), one Abyssinians' classic ('Yim Mas Gan'), and was a pioneer in the DJ field, issuing records from U Roy and Big Joe. Perhaps because he wasn't dependent on music for an income, he faded from the scene in the early 70s, returning only to reissue his classic singles on two essential albums in 1992.
Selected albums: *Scandal* (Matador 1992), *Way Back When* (Matador 1992). Compilation: *Lloyd Daley's Matador Productions 1968-72* (Heartbeat 1992).

Dancehall

Dancehall, a particularly spare, uncluttered form of reggae, first emerged at the start of the 80s and was so-named because it literally began in the dances that have always been the lifeblood of Jamaican music. Essentially, a sound system would play a song, usually specially recorded on a dub plate, and a singer or DJ would extemporise over the top of it live. Drawing its lead from the empty, slow rhythms of Roots Radics, and, to a lesser extent, Sly & Robbie, dancehall was the least-fanciful genre of reggae to date, offering the rhythm, a voice, the dancers' energy and little else. By 1982 various acts had emerged who had recorded predominantly dancehall music, among them Yellowman, an albino MC with a witty, if rude, way about a lyric, Barrington Levy, a ferocious singer who never knew how to give less than 100 percent, and General Echo, another rudely talented chatter. Sound systems such as Jammy's, Volcano and Black Scorpio kept the public thirsting for more material, which they then began to supply on their own labels, with the sound bosses Prince Jammy, Henry 'Junjo' Lawes and Scorpio creating new stars like Junior Reid, Michael Palmer and Josey Wales. A similar process went on in the UK, with the sounds of Saxon Studio, Wassifa Hi-Fi and Unity all offering something different to their Jamaican counterparts. Dancehall never 'finished' as such. Instead, Jammy released a record in 1985 featuring singer Wayne Smith, 'Under Me Sleng Teng', which

single-handedly created the 'digital' style of dancehall, and subsequently, raggamuffin.
Selected albums: Various: *Best Of Reggae Dance Hall Vol. 1* (Rohit 1984), *Best Of Reggae Dance Hall Vol. 2* (Rohit 1985), *Dance Hall Session* (RAS 1986). Yellowman: *Nobody Move, Nobody Get Hurt.* (Greensleeves 1984). Barrington Levy: *Here I Come* (Time 1985). Josey Wales: *The Outlaw Josey Wales* (Greensleeves 1983).

Dave And Ansell Collins

A Jamaican duo who topped the UK charts in 1971 with 'Double Barrel', which was written and produced by Winston Riley. The duo comprised Dave Barker, a session vocalist and sometime pioneering DJ, and keyboard player Ansell Collins. Both had worked for Lee Perry in the late 60s before joining forces. 'Double Barrel' was one of the first reggae hits in the US too. The follow-up, 'Monkey Spanner', was also a UK Top 10 hit. However, they split shortly after the release of their sole long player. Ansell, who had previously worked solo in the late 60s, continued to record for small reggae labels throughout the 80s, principally as a session musician. Barker became a UK resident and fronted several short-lived soul bands. The duo briefly reunited as Dave and Ansell Collins in 1981, but the comeback passed by largely unheralded.
Selected albums: *Double Barrel* (Techniques/Trojan 1972), *In The Ghetto* (Trojan 1975). Compilation: *Classic Tracks* (Classic Tracks 1988).

Dekker, Desmond

b. Desmond Dacres, 16 July 1942, Kingston, Jamaica. Dacres spent much of his orphaned childhood near Seaforth in St. Thomas before returning to Kingston, where he worked as a welder. His workmates encouraged him to seek a recording audition and, after receiving rejections from leading producers Clement Dodd and Duke Reid, he found a mentor in the influential Leslie Kong. In 1963, the newly named Dekker released his first single, 'Honour Your Father And Mother', which was also issued in the UK courtesy of Chris Blackwell's Island label. During the same period, Dekker teamed up with his backing group, the Aces. Together they enjoyed enormous success in Jamaica during the mid-late 60s with a formidable run of 20 number 1 hits to their credit. The emergence of rocksteady in the latter half of 1966 propelled his *James Bond* inspired '007 (Shanty Town)' into the UK charts the following year. A catchy, rhythmically infectious articulation of the 'rude boy' street gang shenanigans, the single presaged Dekker's emergence as an internationally famous artist. In 1967, Dekker came second in the Jamaican Song Festival with 'Unity' and continued his chart-topping run in his home country with such titles as 'Hey Grandma', 'Music Like Dirt', 'Rudie Got Soul', 'Rude Boy Train' and 'Sabotage'.
1969 proved the year of Dekker's greatest international success. 'Get up in the morning, slaving for bread, sir, so that every mouth can be fed', was a patois-sung opening line which entranced and confused pop listeners on both sides of the Atlantic. The intriguing 'Israelites' was a club hit the previous year and by the spring of 1969 had become the first reggae song to top the UK charts, a considerable achievement for the period. Even more astonishing was its Top 10 success in the USA, a country that had previously proved commercially out-of-bounds to Jamaican performers. Back in Britain, Dekker's follow up was the Top 10 hit 'It Mek'. It was originally recorded the previous year under the title 'A It Mek', which roughly translated as 'That's Why It Happened'. 'It Mek' was inspired by Desmond's sister Elaine, who fell off a wall at her home and cried 'like ice water'. Dekker enjoyed translating everyday observations in sharp, incisive lines. 'Israelites' similarly articulated the plight of the downtrodden working man, while 'Problems' was a rousing protest number with the refrain '*everyday* is problems'. Dekker's success in the UK, buoyed by

Desmond Dekker

consistent touring, spearheaded the arrival of a number of Jamaican chart singles by such artists as the Harry J's All Stars, the Upsetters and the Pioneers. Until the arrival of Bob Marley, Dekker remained the most famous reggae artist on the international scene.

By 1969, Dekker had taken up residence in the UK where he was a regular club performer and continued to lay down his vocals over rhythm tracks recorded in Jamaica. A further minor success with 'Pickney Gal' was followed by a massive number 2 hit with the Jimmy Cliff composition 'You Can Get It If You Really Want', from the film *The Harder They Come*. When Dekker's long term manager/producer Kong died from heart failure in 1971, the artist joined the Cactus label. A reissue of 'Israelites' restored him to the UK Top 10 in 1975 and was followed by the pop/reggae 'Sing A Little Song', which reached number 16. During the 2-Tone ska/mod revival in 1980, Dekker recorded *Black And Dekker* with Graham Parker's Rumour, but the experiment was not commercially successful. A follow-up, also on Stiff Records, *Compass Point*, was his last major attempt at chart action, though he remained a perennial performer of old hit material and has frequently been featured on compilation albums. In 1984 he was found bankrupt by a British court, and publicly complained that he had failed to receive funds from his former manager. It was a sad moment for one of reggae's best-known personalities. In 1993, during another 2-Tone revival, Dekker released *King Of Kings* with four original members of the Specials. His unmistakable falsetto vocal remains one of reggae's most memorable, while his pioneering importance as the first major such artist to achieve international success deserves wider acknowledgement.

Albums: *007 (Shanty Town)* (Beverley's 1967), *Action* (Beverley's 1968), *The Israelites* (Beverley's 1969), *This Is Desmond Dekker* (Trojan 1969), *You Can Get It If You Really Want* (Trojan 1970), *Black And Dekker* (Stiff 1980), *Compass Point* (Stiff 1981), *Officially Live And Rare* (Trojan 1987, double album), *Music Like Dirt* (Trojan 1992). With the Specials: *King Of Kings* (Trojan 1993). Compilations: *Double Dekker* (Trojan 1974), *Sweet 16 Hits* (Trojan 1978), *Original Reggae Hitsound* (Trojan 1985), *20 Golden Pieces* (Bulldog 1987), *Best Of And The Rest Of* (Action Replay/Trojan 1989), *King Of Ska* (Trojan 1991), *20 Greatest Hits* (Point 2 1992), *Crucial Cuts - The Best Of Desmond Dekker* (1993).

Delgado, Junior

b. Oscar Hibbert, c.1958, Kingston, Jamaica. Junior 'Jux' Delgado started singing as a schoolboy, winning prizes at school concerts and local talent contests. His first recordings 'Reaction' and 'The Twenty Third Psalm' were produced by Lee Perry in 1973 with the band Time Unlimited, alongside Orville Smith and Glasford Manning, later of the Jewels. In 1974 Delgado recorded two solo sides for Rupie Edwards; 'Rasta Dreadlocks', on the producer's popular 'Skanga' rhythm, issued under the name the Heaven Singers and, under his own name, 'Run Baldhead'. Sessions with Total Sounds and Tommy Cowan and Warwick Lyn's Talent Corp, however, failed to emerge and Delgado left Time Unlimited for a solo career. During 1975 he recorded sides for producers Larry Lawrence and Winston 'Niney' Holness; a version of Ken Boothe/Garnett Mimm's 'Thinking' betraying the debt Delgado owed to that great singer - and 'Every Natty', before linking up with his friend Dennis Brown who released 'Tition', produced by Soul Syndicate/Aggrovators guitarist Earl 'Chinna' Smith, on his DEB label. 'Tition' (1975), short for politician, was a big reggae hit both in Jamaica and the UK, the raw bass, drum and piano rhythm, topped with Delgado's heartfelt, gritty moan and the hard hitting social commentary of the lyrics, set the tone for much of his subsequent output, and marked the beginning of a long musical collaboration between the two singers which lasted throughout the decade.

From 1976-79, Delgado recorded numerous

Junior Delgado

sides for DEB including 'Devils Throne', a version of the Heptones 'Love Won't Come Easy', the ever popular 'Trickster', 'She Gonna Marry Me', 'Warrior', and 'Famine' as well as completing an excellent album, *Taste Of The Young Heart*. Other tunes for different producers during this period include the storming Sons Of Slaves' for Lee Perry, 'Armed Robbery' and 'United Dreadlocks' for Joe Gibbs, 'Away With Your Fussing And Fighting' and 'Blackmans Heart Cries Out' for Augustus Pablo, and two self productions, 'Fisherman Row' and 'Jah Stay', utilising the 'Tition' rhythm, the latter appearing on his own Incredible Jux label in Jamaica. All of which served to create a reputation for himself as one of the most exciting roots singers on the 70s reggae scene.

In the early 80s he spent much of his time commuting between Jamaica and the UK, maintaining his reputation with further searing cuts including 'Fort Augustus' for Sly And Robbie. However, in 1983, disaster struck in the form of an 18 month prison sentence. On his release, his astonishing 'Broadwater Farm' 12-inch (1985), for London production outfit Maccabees, prophecised the riots in that troubled area of north London, and got banned immediately they occurred. Nevertheless it proved his enforced lay-off had diminished his potency not one jot, and he soon immersed himself in a flurry of recordings for Skengdon ('Nine Fence' 1985), Mikey Carrol's Creative Sounds ('Poverty' 1986), Prince Jammy ('Illegal Gun' 1987), and his own 'Bus I Skull' (1988), released on London's Fashion Records and recorded at their A Class Studio. His biggest hit in this period though was the epochal 'Ragamuffin Year' (1986) which saw him paired back with Augustus Pablo. More singles followed; 'Forward Revolution', the superb comment on events in South Africa; 'Hanging Tree', 'Riot Inna Juvenile Prison', and 'Dub School', all for Pablo, and 'We A Blood' for Fashion. He appeared with Pablo in concert at London's Astoria Theatre in 1986 and thrilled the crowd with a superb show-stopping performance, and somehow found the time to nurture the talents of two upcoming youngsters, Yammie Bolo and White Mice. Though he has been a little quiet in the early 90s, it is surely only a matter of time before reggae fans are once more treated to the generous talents of the Incredible Jux.

Albums: *Taste Of the Young Heart* (DEB-EMI 1978), *Effort* (DEB-EMI 1979), *Dance A Dub* (Jux 1980), *More She Love It* (Yvonne's Special 1981), *Disco Style Showcase* (Yvonne's Special 1981), *Bushmaster Connection* (Jux 1982), *Classics* (Maccabees 1985), *Sisters And Brothers* (Blue Moon 1985), *In Griechenland* (Arcade 1986), *Raggamuffin Year* (Mango/Island 1986), *Stranger* (Skengdon 1987), *Moving Down The Road* (Live & Love 1987), *Roadblock* (Blue Trac 1987), *It Takes Two To Tango* (Fashion 1987), *One Step More* (Mango/Island 1988), *Taste Of The Young Heart* (Incredible 1989), *Dub School* (Buffalo 1990). With Augustus Pablo: *Raggamuffin Dub* (Rockers International 1990), *Showcase* (Rockers International 1993).

Digital

A term used to describe reggae music from the mid-80s onwards when computer generated music took over. The first example of this type of music (although notably Lee Perry, Augustus Pablo and Sly And Robbie amongst others had all previously experimented with drum machines) was released by Prince (later King) Jammy by Wayne Smith, utilising a Casio 'music box'. The resulting 'Under Me Sleng Teng' spawned over 200 different versions during the next couple of months and the computer became ubiquitous. Jammys was at the forefront of this musical revolution and former employees producer Bobby Digital and musicians Steely And Clevie went on to become top names in their own right. Jammy's former employer King Tubby also proved adept at this music and many more famous names from reggae's illustrious past soon allied themselves to the new beat. Once again the music was opened up to all sorts of newcomers and possibilities as expensive studio time and costly session musicians were no longer a prerequisite for making records. Like all new forms it has its detractors but nothing succeeds like success and digital reggae has proved to be one of the most popular styles of the music outside of its immediate audience since the late 60s/early 70s.

Albums: *See King Jammy, Bobby Digital, Steely And Clevie.*

Digital B
(see Digital, Bobby)

Digital, Bobby
b. Robert Dixon, Kingston, Jamaica. Dixon was christened Digital because his arrival at King Jammys coincided with the rise of Steely And Clevie's computerised rhythm tracks in 1985. He quickly began to learn dub-cutting, voicing and mixing under Jammy's tuition; fulfilling a line of descendency that goes back to the late dub pioneer, King Tubby. Soon he was to play a pivotal role in the running of the studio, enhancing the careers of artists such as Cocoa Tea, Shabba Ranks, Chaka Demus, Admiral Bailey, Sanchez, Pinchers and many more. When he left in 1988 to form Heatwave sound system and build his own studio, all those artists voiced for the new Digital B label. Hits for Shabba included 'Wicked Inna Bed' and 'Gal Yuh Good', which led to the *Just Reality* album in 1990. He, Ninjaman and Admiral Tibet joined forces for 'Serious Time', and by 1991 he had attracted new talent like Cobra ('Tek Him'), Tony Rebel, Penny Irie and Shaka Shamba ('Reggae Fight'), as well as established names such as Gregory Isaacs, Johnny Osbourne and Cornell Campbell. Whether cutting hardcore rhythms or recreating classics from the past, the quality of his productions reaped equal success throughout that year; including albums by Pinchers, Sanchez and Admiral Tibet, various 'version' sets and Half Pint's 'Substitute Lover'.

1992 found Garnett Silk in the studio, recording his debut album and several hit singles which led to a major deal with Atlantic. By this time Digital was producing tracks for the international market; Shabba, Buju Banton, Cobra and Tiger among them. By the end of 1993 he had released a staggering volume of music, most of it exceptional. There were albums from Glen Ricks and Leroy Smart, some fine performances by Gregory Isaacs ('Easy'), Cocoa Tea, Red Dragon, Sugar Minott, Josey Wales and Lt. Stitchie, all of whom refreshed their careers accordingly. Mafia & Fluxy, Sly And Robbie and Danny Browne also created new, exciting rhythms like 'Mad Dog' and 'Top Ten', which a plethora of younger artists like Terror Fabulous, Daddy Screw, Roundhead, Jigsy King and Saaba Tooth seized upon with rapid results. As 1994 opened he was cutting rhythms specifically to reintroduce Shabba to his dancehall audience. With his credentials as a fellow ghetto youth made good, an extensive array of gifted artists and a burgeoning reputation with a wider audience after his work with international acts, Bobby Digital is well situated to stay a leading producer well into the 90s.

Selected albums: Shabba Ranks: *Just Reality* (Blue Mountain 1990). Sanchez: *I Can't Wait* (Blue Mountain 1991). Dirtsman: *Acid* (Supreme 1988). Admiral Tibet: *Separate Class* (Blue Mountain 1991). Pinchers: *Hotter* (Blue Mountain 1992). Leroy Smart: *Talk About Friend* (Blue Mountain 1992). Garnett Silk: *It's Growing* (Blue Mountain 1992). Various: *Wicked In Bed* (Blue Mountain 1989), *Gal Yuh Good* (Blue Mountain 1990), *Full House* (Digital B 1991), *Ripe Cherry* (Digital B 1991), *Moving Away* (VP 1992), *Top Ten* (VP 1993), *Mad Dog* (VP 1993), *Strictly Dancehall* (VP 1993).

Dillinger
b. Lester Bullocks, 25 June 1953, Kingston, Jamaica. In 1971, he commenced his career as a DJ, working on the sound systems of Prince Jackie and El Brasso, where he initially imitated U Roy, Dennis Alcapone

and Big Youth, before forging his own style. In 1974, he recorded the excellent 'Freshly' for Yabby You, and the following year had a glut of material released, including 'Brace A Boy' for Augustus Pablo, 'CB 200' for Joe Joe Hookim and 'Killer Man Jaro' for Coxsone Dodd. It was Dodd who released his stunning first album, *Ready Natty Dreadie* (1975), where he effortlessly delivered 10 strong toasts over a selection of Studio One's classic rocksteady and reggae rhythms. It is only the first pressing of the album that contains the brilliant title track, as it was subsequently replaced by 'Natty Kung Fu'. Hookim released his second album, *CB 200* (1976), which features several singles including the title track, 'Plantation Heights (1975), 'Cocaine In My Brain' (1976) and 'Crank Face' (1976). In late 1976, he made an album in the UK with Trinity, *Clash*, for producer Clement Bushay, which suffered from hurried recording sessions. Joe Joe Hookim released a further album, *Bionic Dread* (1977), which is far less compelling than its predecessor. 'Cocaine In My Brain' had proven to be so popular in Europe and the USA that he recorded a follow-up, 'Marijuana In My Brain' (1979), which became a number 1 hit in Holland, and an album of the same name quickly followed. Unfortunately, most of his material from this time did not match his earlier work, although he was still brave enough to attempt one of the first reggae electro recordings with *Badder Than Them* (1980). He was inactive for most of the 80s, but in 1990, he returned to the recording scene.

Albums: *Ready Natty Dreadie* (Studio One 1975), *CB 200* (Island 1976), *Bionic Dread* (Black Swan 1976), *Talkin' Blues* (Magnum 1977), *Top Ranking* (Third World 1978), *Answer My Questions* (Third World 1979), *Marijuana In My Brain* (Jamaica Sound 1979), *Badder Than Them* (A&M 1980), *Corn Bread* (Vista Sounds 1983), *King Pharaoh* (Blue Moon 1984), *Best Of Live* (Vista Sounds 1984), *Cocaine* (New Cross 1984), *Tribal War* (New Cross 1986), *Say No To Drugs* (Lagoon 1993), *Funky Punk* (1993). With Trinity: *Clash* (Burning Sounds 1978). With Clint Eastwood: *Live At London* (Vista Sounds 1983).

Dirtsman

b. Patrick Thompson, 1966, Spanish Town, Jamaica, d. 21 December 1993. The brother of Papa San, Dirtsman was a similarly inclined dancehall DJ until his brutal killing. His father was the owner of the Black Universe sound system, but he subsequently moved on to the Creation Rock Tower Sound, based in Willowdene. His first chart appearance came with 'Thank You' in 1990, preceding 'Borrow Man' on Steely & Clevie's label. Later he teamed up with Phillip Smart in New York, which offered him further success with 'Hot This Year'. On the cusp of mainstream success he signed to BMG, but his career was cut short in 1993 when he was shot on his veranda by four gunmen, being pronounced dead on arrival at Spanish Town Hospital.
Album: *Acid* (VP 1988).

Dobson, Dobbie

'The Loving Pauper', as he has been affectionately nicknamed, has crafted an impressively individual technique, built around a voice of rich, modular tone. Dobson was originally in a group at Kingston College with Howard Barrett (later to form the Paragons). They recorded their first song for the Tip Top label: 'Cry A Little Cry', written by Dobson, and produced by Sonia Pottinger. Though it proved a radio hit, the group split and Dobson continued to record solo for Pottinger: 'I'll Be Around' and 'Blue Am I' being good examples of his early craft. Afterwards he went to Duke Reid and recorded 'Loving Pauper', as well as cutting 'Seems To Me I'm Losing You' for Coxsone Dodd at roughly the same time. But it was 'Pauper' which became his signature tune. He recorded it twice more after its initial release on Treasure Isle, and many other reggae stars (Freddie McGregor, Ruddy Thomas) would also cover it. Dobson subsequently worked with several short-term outfits such as the Virtues, the Sheiks and Charles & The Teddy Boys.

More fruitful rewards came via a new partnership with Rupie Edwards. 'That Wonderful Sound' became a huge hit in Jamaica. The follow-up, 'Endlessly', nearly broke into the UK charts too. Despite his prolific past, it was not until Rupie Edwards compiled an album directly following the success of 'Wonderful Sound' that Dobson added a long player to his canon. Unfortunately, it failed to sell in the quantities which both parties anticipated. It was followed at close range by *Sweet Dreams* for Federal Records. This comprised big 50s and 60s ballads belted out in Dobson's smoothest lovers' tones. His bad luck was compounded though, when a third album, for a Miami imprint, failed to produce any royalties. Although reggae artists have rarely been fully reimbursed for their music, the fact that the label was American and that Dobson's popularity was soaring there proved an added irritant. Disenchanted, Dobson migrated to New York in 1979 and remained quiet during the 80s. Instead he worked in real estate and junior management (he had previously been a marketing student at the University of West Indies). There are clearly several strings to Dobson's bow: he was also responsible for producing the first two Meditations albums. He has since returned to recording, enjoying renewed popularity in the US.

Albums: *Wonderful Sound* (Success 1977), *Sweet Dreams* (Federal 1978), *History For Lovers* (Count Shelley 1990), *Through The Years* (Studio One 1991).

Doctor Alimantado

The 'Ital Surgeon' Winston Thompson came to the record buying public's attention with his DJ work for Lee Perry in the early 70s, but it was only when he started producing records for himself that he found his niche. His 'The Best Dressed Chicken In Town' (a version to 'Ain't No Sunshine') released on Capo Records leaned heavily on the production techniques of Lee Perry, but was an unmatched assault on the senses – later to be described as two-and-a-half minutes of dub lyricism. His manic approach and choice of top rhythms assured his cult status in the UK where his records on the Ital Sounds and Vital Food labels were eagerly awaited and purchased by a cult following. He was nearly killed when a downtown Kingston bus knocked him over in 1977, and his subsequent comeback single for Channel One, 'Born For A Purpose', and the DJ version 'Life All Over', brought him to the fore at the same time that the punk market discovered reggae. He moved to England not long after to capitalise on his new found fame and has remained there, on and off, ever since, where he still releases records on his ISDA label, none of which have matched the quality of his early recordings. He is now resident in Holland.

Selected albums: *Best Dressed Chicken* (Greensleeves 1978), *Born For A Purpose/Songs Of Thunder* (Greensleeves 1981), *Love Is* (Keyman 1983), *In The Mix Vol. 1-5* (Keyman 1985-1990), *King's Bread* (Ital Sounds 1986), *King's Bread Dub* (Keyman 1989), *The Priveleged Few* (Keyman 1990). Compilation: *Reggae Revue Part 1* (Keyman 1988).

Dodd, Coxsone

It is indisputable that without the vision and work of Clement Seymour Dodd there would not be reggae music as we now understand it. Always interested in music, he was amongst the first in Jamaica to run his own sound system – Sir Coxsone The Down Beat – (the Coxsone was taken from a popular Yorkshire cricketer of the 50s), a forerunner to the mobile discos of the 60s. The power and amount of amplification equipment ensured that you 'felt' the music in your chest rather than simply listened to it. Competition was fierce to be first with the latest and most exclusive discs. The music favoured was hard R&B, with Shirley And Lee, Amos Milburn and Lyn Hope being particular favourites. The 'sounds' would often play in competition with each

Doctor Alimantado

other, drawing wild cheers and ecstatic reactions when certain tunes were played. Titles were scratched out on the records and songs were renamed to prevent rival sounds unearthing their identity. For instance, 'Later For Gator' by Willis Jackson was known as 'Coxsone Hop' to Down Beat followers. The story goes that Coxsone had been playing 'Later For Gator' for months and his closest rival, Duke Reid, had been unable to discover its true identity. Later Reid acquired the record himself, and played it against Dodd at one of their 'clashes'. Dodd is said to have nearly passed out with shock. Small fortunes were spent on record buying-sprees in America to keep on top.

In the mid-50s the supply of hard R&B records dried up as the smoother productions began to find favour with the black American audience. These were not popular in Jamaica however and, starved of American records, the sound system operators started to make their own music. Initially these were intended solely for live use and were played as dub plates only, but their popularity proved overwhelming and the sound system owners began to offer them for sale to the public. Among the earliest sides to appear at the end of the 50s on Coxsone's Worldisc label were records by local artists such as Jackie Estick, Lascelles Perkins ('Destiny'), Bunny & Skitter ('Lumumba'), Basil Gabbidon & The Mellow Larks ('Time To Pray'), Clue J And His Blues Blasters ('Shufflin' Jug'), Aubrey Adams and the Dewdroppers ('Marjie') and Theophilius Beckford ('Easy Snappin''). Other artists recorded later included organist Monty Alexander & the Cyclones ('Stack Is Back'), the Jiving Juniors, featuring a young Derrick Harriott, Derrick Morgan, Clancy Eccles ('River Jordan' and 'Freedom'), Alton (Ellis) & Eddie ('Muriel'), the Charmers (featuring Lloyd Tyrell aka Lloyd Charmers), (Joe) Higgs & Wilson ('How Can I Be Sure'), Cornell Campbell, and Owen Gray ('On The Beach'), as well as the first sides by such legendary hornsmen as Don Drummond ('Don Cosmic') and Roland Alphonso.

Some of these early recordings can be found on *All Star Top Hits*, and *Oldies But Goodies Vol. 1 & 2*. Although his empire was growing rapidly, Dodd shrugged off the attention with a typical: 'I didn't realize that this could be a business. I just did it for enjoyment!'.

Dodd's productions caught the mood of the times, and as Jamaican R&B evolved into ska, with the accent firmly on the off-beat, he was always at the forefront with his teams of session musicians and raw young vocalists. Throughout the ska era he ruled with records like 'Joe Liges' and 'Spit In The Sky' by Delroy Wilson, 'Six & Seven Books Of Moses' and 'Hallelujah' by the Maytals, 'Simmer Down', 'Hooligan', 'Rudie' and many more by the Wailers, 'Rude Boy Gone A Jail' and 'Shoo Be Do Be' by the Clarendonians, 'I've Got To Go Back Home' by Bob Andy, a brace of Lee Perry tunes including 'Rub & Squeeze' and 'Doctor Dick', as well as dozens of fiery instrumentals by the Skatalites (often released crediting only the lead instrumentalist), the crack ensemble who also provided the backing on all Coxsone recordings during this time. Dodd opened his own studio on Brentford Road in the early 60s, known as Studio One, which became the generic title for all Coxsone productions thereafter. The advantages were numerous: multiple 'takes' to ensure that the final one is right; experimentation without having to worry about the high costs of studio time; and the capacity to attempt 'uncommercial' ventures. Dodd placed many of the island's top musicians on his payroll and the results were impressive. With accomplished arrangers and musicians supervising - such as Lee Perry, Jackie Mittoo, Leroy Sibbles and Larry Marshall - just about every top name in reggae music worked for Studio One at some stage in their careers - usually at the beginning, because Dodd was always keen to develop new talent, holding regular Sunday auditions for aspiring artists. During the 1967-70 period the hits flowed out of Brentford Road in a veritable deluge of unparalleled creativity. By late 1966 ska's furious pace was beginning to give way to the slower rocksteady beat, the sparser instrumentation and the availability of multi-track recording equipment allowed for a greater emphasis on melody and subtlety, and although it is recognised that Duke Reid's Treasure Isle productions represent much of the finest rocksteady extant, Dodd's raw, almost organic productions from this period have since gone on to form what amounts to the foundation of reggae music in the following decades.

Much of this incredible output appeared on a number of labels in the UK, notably the Coxsone and Studio One imprints handled by Island's B&C group, and, later, on the Bamboo and Banana labels. Such artists as Ken Boothe (a cover of Kenny Lynch/Garnett Mimm's 'Moving Away', 'Thinking', 'Without Love', 'Just Another Girl'), Bob Andy ('I've Got To Go Back Home', 'Too Experienced', 'Going Home', 'Unchained', 'Feeling Soul'), Alton Ellis ('I'm Just A Guy', 'I'm Still In Love With You', 'Can I Change My Mind', 'Still Trying'), the Heptones ('Fattie Fattie', 'Love Won't Come Easy', 'Heptones Gonna Fight', 'I Hold The Handle", 'Pretty Looks', 'Give Me The Right', 'Sweet Talking'), Marcia Griffiths ('Truly', 'Feel Like Jumping'), John Holt ('Strange Things', 'Love I Can Feel', 'OK Fred'), Slim Smith ('Born To Love You', 'Never Let Go', 'Rougher Yet'), Delroy Wilson ('Never Conquer', 'I Don't Know Why'), Carlton And His Shoes ('Love Me Forever'), Jackie Mittoo ('Ram Jam', 'Hot Milk', 'One Step Beyond', 'Drum Song', 'Peanie Wallie', 'In Cold Blood'), Ernest Wilson ('Undying Love'), Larry (Marshall) & Alvin ('Nanny Goat', 'Throw Me Corn', 'Mean Girl'), Ken Parker ('My Whole World Is Falling Down'), Roland Alphonso ('Jah Shaky'), the Gaylads ('Africa', 'Love Me With All Your Heart'), the Eternals featuring Cornell Campbell ('Queen Of The Minstrels', 'Stars'), the Cables ('Baby Why', 'What Kind Of World', 'Be A Man') and dozens of

instrumental sides by the in-house session band the Soul Vendors/Sound Dimension ('Full Up', 'Swing Easy', 'Psychedelic Rock', 'Frozen Soul', 'Real Rock', 'Mojo Rocksteady') and countless others made some of their finest records at Brentford Road. Many of these songs, arrangements and rhythm tracks in particular, are endlessly recycled by younger artists and producers. Indeed one recent trend in the music is to sample snatches of Dodd's classic old rhythms and build new versions out of the sample.

Other, younger producers, some of whom - Lee Perry and Winston 'Niney' Holness in particular - had learnt their trade while with Coxsone, began to take over in the early 70s, leaving Coxsone to take a less prominent role in the music's development. Nonetheless, throughout the decade Coxsone still produced a great deal of fine music including some of the earliest material from Horace Andy ('Skylarking', 'Just Say Who', 'Fever', 'Every Tongue Shall Tell'), Dennis Brown ('No Man Is An Island', 'If I Follow My Heart', 'Easy Take It Easy'), the Wailing Souls ('Mr Fire Coal Man', 'Back Out With It'), Burning Spear ('Door Peep', 'Joe Frazier', 'Swell Headed'), Dennis Alcapone ('Power Version', *Forever Version*), Dillinger (*Ready Natty Dreadie*) and Freddie McKay (*Picture On The Wall*). He also re-released much of his back catalogue through the 1974-79 period, which ensured his music was heard by a new generation of reggae music lovers. As the dancehall style began to supersede the rockers and steppers forms, he was once more in full swing with artists like Freddie McGregor, Sugar Minott, Johnny Osbourne, Judah Eskender Tafari, Willie Williams and DJs Michigan And Smiley and the Lone Ranger all recording fine singles and albums. This proved to be the final golden period for Studio One however, and in the mid-80s Dodd closed his Brentford Road studio and relocated to New York.

In 1991 Dodd celebrated 35 years in the business with two huge shows in Jamaica, featuring many of the people he had worked with over the years. He is not that interested in the past, however, and is reluctant to talk about it, preferring to look to the future. Sadly, apart from the odd gem, his newer work is not up to his previous high standards - he is more often in New York these days and Brentford Road is usually shut. He still presses hundreds of his old records and there is always a selection of his music available at specialist reggae shops; and, in a business controlled by the latest and the newest, they continue to sell. There are the usual rumours of Dodd mistreating his artists and not paying proper royalties but he has yet to tell his side of the story, and, at any rate, many of his artists feel that their time was well spent at Coxsone's 'musical college'. His position as the guiding light of Jamaican music is beyond question and the true extent of his influence has yet to be fully realised.

Selected albums: Various: *All Star Top Hits* (Studio One c.1961), *Oldies But Goodies (Vols 1 & 2)* (Studio One c.1968), *Best Of Studio One (Vols. 1, 2, & 3)* (Heartbeat 1983-87). The Skatalites: *Ska Authentic*. Dub Specialist: *Hi-Fashion Dub Top Ten*. Roland Alphonso: *Best Of* (Studio One c.1973). Jackie Mittoo: *Macka Fat* (Studio One 1970). Cedric Brooks: *Im Flash Forward* (Studio One 1977). Dennis Brown: *If I Follow My Heart* (Studio One 1971). Bob Andy: *Song Book* (Studio One 1972). Burning Spear: *Studio One Presents* (Studio One 1973). Carlton And His Shoes*: Love Me Forever* (Studio One 1978). Alton Ellis: *Sunday Coming*. Heptones: *On Top* (Studio One 60s). Freddie McGregor: *Bobby Babylon*. Bob Marley & The Wailers: *Wailing Wailers* (Studio One c.1965). Johnny Osbourne: *Truths & Rights*. Maytals: *Never Grow Old*. Sugar Minott: *Live Loving*. Wailing Souls: *Studio One Presents*. Delroy Wilson: *Feel Good All Over*.

Donaldson, Eric

b. 11 June 1947, Jamaica. Eric Donaldson, one of Jamaica's most accomplished falsetto voices, will forever be associated with the Jamaican Festival Song Competition. In particular one of his five winning entries in that contest, 'Cherry Oh Baby', which succeeded in 1971, and launched his career in reggae music. Donaldson attending school in Spanish Town before taking up a job as a house painter, singing in his spare time. In 1964 he cut some unreleased sides for Studio One in Kingston, and in the mid-60s he formed vocal group the West Indians, alongside Leslie Burke and Hector Brooks. A heap of sides for producer JJ Johnson produced one hit, 'Right On Time', in 1968. They also recorded for Lee Perry ('Oh Lord') the following year, to scant reaction A name-change to the Killowatts and a succession of songs for JJ Johnson and Lloyd Daley's Matador label ('Slot Machine', 'Real Cool Operator') failed to ignite the fire of fame and the group split.

In 1970 Donaldson cut some sides for Alvin Ranglin's GG label, the best of which was 'Lonely Night', but a trip to Dynamic Sounds studio for 'Never Going To Give You Up' again led nowhere, although it did bode well for the future. In 1971, apparently as a last stand, he entered the Festival Song Competition with 'Cherry Oh Baby'. By the day of the festival, he had enrolled the astute Tommy Cowan as manager, and was ready to sell the amazing 50,000 copies that the disc eventually shifted on Dynamic. Eric Donaldson had arrived. While it has not been a smooth ride from there, Donaldson has been periodically successful, cutting albums sporadically and recording a clutch of songs that are fondly remembered by reggae aficionados, notably 'Miserable Woman' (1972), 'What A Festival' (1973) and 'Freedom Street' (1977). Donaldson apparently still loves the festival, winning in 1971, 1977, 1978, 1984 and 1993, and always seems ready to give his career a shot in the arm by appearing there. He now lives in Kent Village, Jamaica, where he runs the 'Cherry Oh Baby Go-Go Bar'. The song itself is perennially popular, and should have made him very rich: UB40 and the Rolling Stones both covered it, and the rhythm was incredibly popular in 1991, with over 30 new versions issued in Jamaica, including

Donaldson's own update.
Selected albums: *Eric Donaldson* (Trojan 1971), *Keep On Riding* (Dynamic 1976), *Kent Village* (Dynamic 1978), *Right On Time* (Dynamic 1985), *Trouble In Afrika* (Blue Mountain 1992), *Love Of The Common People* (1993).

Dread, Mikey

b. Michael Campbell, Port Antonio, Jamaica. Dread achieved prominence in Jamaica in the late 70s as a DJ on the JBC station with his four hour Saturday night *Dread At The Controls* show. Campbell's show played strictly reggae (bizarrely, until the rise of IRIE FM, most official Jamaican radio consisted of anything but). His selections - many of them hot off the cutting lathe, dub plate specials - were punctuated by wild sound effects and suitably manic utterances. This made him a hero to the grass roots audience, but put him at odds with fellow broadcasters, jealous of his success, and the conservative, reggae-loathing JBC directorship, leading to his resignation in 1979. He had already entered the recording business with DJ sides like 'Dread At The Controls' and 'Homeguard' for Lee Perry, and 'Rootsman Revival' for Sonia Pottinger's High Note label. After a brief spell as engineer for Treasure Isle studio, he formed a working relationship with producer Carlton Patterson, for whom he cut 'Barber Saloon', and helped produce Ray I's popular 'Weatherman Skank'. He inaugurated his own DATC label in 1979 and began releasing records by Earl Sixteen, Rod Taylor, Edi Fitzroy, Sugar Minott and others, as well as his own popular DJ titles like 'Love The Dread', 'African Map' and 'Proper Education'. These were sought-after as much for the entertaining 'version' sides, mixed by Campbell and King Tubby. Perhaps his most enduring contributions are the two dubwise albums, *Dread At The Controls* and *African Anthem*, replete with many of the effects and jingles featured on his radio show. In 1982 he narrated Channel 4's six part *Deep Roots* programme, and

presented *The Rockers Road Show* for the same company the following year. He has also worked with UB40 and the Clash, toasting on the latter's 'Bank Robber'. He now resides in America where he continues to record, make stage appearances and host a music programme for television.
Albums: *Dread At The Controls* (DATC/Trojan 1979), *African Anthem* (DATC. 1979), *At The Control Dubwise* (Hawkeye 1979), *World War III* (DATC 1981), *S.W.A.L.K.* (DATC. 1982), *Dub Merchant* (DATC 1982), *Pave The Way* (Heartbeat 1984), *Pave The Way Parts I & II* (DEP 1985, double album), *Beyond World War III* (DATC 1986), *Happy Family* (RAS 1989).

Drummond, Don

b. 1943, Kingston, Jamaica, d. 1969, Kingston, Jamaica. One of the saddest things about Jamaican music is that one of its principal innovators died before ever seeing the growth and success of the genre he helped to create. Don Drummond was educated at the infamous Alpha Catholic Boys Home and School, in the heart of the Kingston ghetto where he, like so many others, was allowed to develop and express his musical talents, first as a pupil and later as a teacher. By the early 50s he had established his reputation as one of the island's top jazz trombonists. His main inspiration at this stage were the American big bands, but as the decade wore on, the influence of R&B and sound systems began to be felt in Jamaica. When the sound system operators began to make their own records, they naturally turned to accomplished musicians such as Don Drummond, Roland Alphonso and Rico Rodriguez, who had consolidated their reputations throughout the decade with residencies at clubs such as the Glass Bucket and the Silver Slipper. Their musical knowledge and expertise was critical in determining the feel and direction of these early recordings, which were usually credited to the Skatalites. Don Drummond was also an early convert to the Rastafarian faith and

Mikey Dread

his beliefs were reflected in records like 'Addis Ababa', 'Far East' and countless uncredited recordings. His fragile mental condition was not helped by the lack of either financial rewards or recognition for his talents. Following the murder of Marguerita (his common law wife) in 1965, he was committed to Belle Vue, Kingston's lunatic asylum, where he ended his days in 1969. Drummond was an early tragedy in Jamaican music and he was the precursor of much that was to follow. Since his death, his work has been assessed for its true worth, while one particularly perceptive critic stated that his music 'contained the hurt of his people'. Always a quiet, reserved and shy man, he let his music do the talking.

Albums: *Best Of* (Studio One), *100 Years After* (Studio One), *Memorial* (Treasure Isle), *In Memory Of* (Studio One), *Scattered Lights* (Top Deck 1985).

Dub

Essentially reggae in the raw, this cultish, perennially popular form strips out the majority of the music's melody at the mixing desk, leaving behind the rhythm section ('drum & bass' music in reggae parlance) and the residue of other instruments, often with massive layers of echo. The roots of dub are twisted and clouded in the passing of time. Reggae records with crashing effects and decidedly eccentric arrangements go back to the ska era. By 1969-70 many producers, among them Lee Perry, Chin-Randy's, Joe Gibbs, Bunny Lee and Lynford 'Andy Capp' Anderson were making largely instrumental music that was heavily dependent on the rhythm section (The Upsetters' 'Clint Eastwood' in 1970, for example), and it would only take the addition of delay units such as the Copycat and Echoplex to create the dub boom. In 1972, encouraged by Bunny Lee, King Tubby, an electronics engineer and sound system owner, began to mix records in four-track, and by late 1973 his name graced many b-side 'versions' (the name is a corruption of instrumental version, or 'Version 2') of other people's records,

notably those of Bunny Lee and Lee Perry. At the same time, engineer Sylvan Morris at Harry J/Studio One, and Errol Thompson at Randy's, also experimented with the dub sound. Occasional, very limited-pressing dub albums began to hit the shops, which quickly became collectors' items. Among the best-known of these were Perry/Tubby collaborations, including the ingenious stereo LP *Blackboard Jungle Dub*, which had three different mixes, one for each speaker and one for both, and *King Tubby Meets The Upsetter At The Grass Roots Of Dub*, a record which was *the* underground reggae album of 1974 in the UK. Tubby's uniquely precise, often stunningly heavy mixes also graced any number of Bunny Lee productions on his Jackpot, Justice and Attack labels.

By the mid-70s virtually no reggae singles were released without dub versions on the flip, and artists such as Augustus Pablo and Glen Brown had created a career from instrumental music in dub form. New engineers such as Prince Jammy, Pat Kelly (also a singer) and Scientist gradually took over from the original dub mixers, but by 1982 the original boom was pretty much finished, save a few die-hards such as UK engineer-producers Mad Professor and Adrian Sherwood. However, by 1991 a new breed of dub-inspired musicians, such as Jah Shaka, Sound Iration and the Disciples had founded the 'new roots' movement, and placed the music back on the map, albeit with digital equipment and modern intentions.

Albums: Various: *King Tubby Meets The Upsetter At The Grass Roots Of Dub* (Fay 1974), *Pick A Dub* (Atra 1975), *Beware* (Grove 1978), *King Tubby Meets Rockers Uptown* (Yard 1976), *Black Board Jungle Dub* (Upsetter), *King Tubby's Prophecy Of Dub* (Prophets).

Dub Plate

A dub plate is simply an acetate cut onto a plastic-coated metal disc, featuring an unusual mix of a well-known record, or a recording unavailable elsewhere, and used by

Dub Poet Benjamin Zephaniah

a sound system to help promote the exclusivity of the music it plays. 'Dubs' are highly-prized by collectors, particularly those cut by King Tubby's or King Jammy, or those which feature famous artists offering amended renditions of classics.

Dub Poetry

A type of reggae where poets recite their works over heavy 'dubbed' rhythms influenced by 70s DJs such as U Roy, I Roy and Big Youth. One of the originators was Linton Kwesi Johnson who was born in Jamaica in 1952 and moved to England in 1963. His early poetry was in the traditional European style until he began listening to DJs and decided to set his work to music. From early on he had found the English language too restricting and austere, and he set to work in the heavy patois which the DJs specialised in. His first album, *Dread Beat & Blood* was released in the late 70s and proved hugely influential. Almost single-handed it gave birth to a whole sub-genre of reggae music where poets such as Michael Smith, Benjamin Zephaniah, Jean Binta Breeze, Oku Onuora & Mutabaruka perform to the accompaniment of roots reggae rhythms. Probably the most successful of all has been the Jamaican based Mutabaruka, whose debut album in 1982 for Earl 'Chinna' Smith's High Times label was something of a classic.

In reggae music the rhythm or backing track is never completely subservient to the vocal, instrumental or DJ's contribution, and sometimes the poets forgot this in order to get their own voices across. The results were disappointing. DJs never forgot the importance of the rhythm - even if much of their output was doggerel, it usually worked well in combination with a given backing track. It was always delivered so as to be heard rather than read. That said, though much of the DJ output is revered in Jamaica, its Kingston patois means little to the uninitiated, and this is where the dub poets' clearer diction wins out every time. Especially in the US and Europe, where many have large, committed followings, outside of the usual reggae audience. Most are well aware of the irony of their position and Muta put it very succinctly: 'Revolutionary poets, Have become entertainers, Babblin' out angry words'.

Albums: Linton Kwesi Johnson: *Dread Beat & Blood* (Front Line 1978, originally credited to Poet & The Roots), *Forces of Victory* (Island 1979), *Bass Culture* (Island 1980), *In Concert With The Dub Band* (LKJ 1988). Mutabaruka: *Check It* (High Times 1982), *The Mystery Unfolds* (Shanachie 1986), *Out Cry* (Shanchie 1987), *Any Which Way* (Greensleeves 1989). Jean Binta Breeze: *Tracks.* (1989). Benjamin Zephaniah: *Dub Ranting* (Upright 1983), *Rasta* (Upright 1987), *Us And Dem* (Mango/Island 1990). Michael Smith: *Mi Cyaan Believe It* (Island 1982). Various: *Dread Poets Society*.

Dube, Lucky

b. 1967, Ermelo, Eastern Transvaal, South Africa. The most successful African reggae artist of all time, Lucky Dube (pronounced Doobay) has taken his Peter Tosh-influenced music further than his hero himself managed. Guitarist-vocalist Lucky formed his first group, a mbqanga combo entitled The Sky Way Band, while still at school. An interest in Rastafarianism instigated a musical predilection for reggae, although, as a member of the Love Brothers, his first album betrayed none of this. His first hit single, the 'Zulu soul' of 'Baxoleleni', arrived in 1983, from his debut solo set *Lengane Ngeyetha*. Several LPs later, he starred in a South African movie, *Getting Lucky*, and performed reggae cuts for its soundtrack. His first reggae LP, *Rastas Never Die*, was banned in South Africa for its militancy, and Lucky diversified into rap for *Help My Krap*. In 1986 his new band, the Slaves, cut 'Think About The Children', and their second LP, *Slave*, sold 300,000 copies. In 1989 he toured France and the US with the group and appeared in the movie *Voice In The Dark*. Two albums in that year, *Together As One* and *Prisoner*, sold heavily, the latter going double platinum in

South Africa in five days.

In 1991 Dube became the first South African artist to play the Reggae Sunsplash festival in Jamaica, and again he issued two albums in one year, *Captured Live* (incidentally also the title of a Peter Tosh LP) and *House Of Exile*. Tours of Japan and Australia were also a success, and Dube additionally played WOMAD with Peter Gabriel. 1993's *Victims* has again broken his own records for world-wide sales, shifting in excess of a million copies on various licensee imprints. Although Dube's style is probably too dated ever to score heavily in Jamaica, he remains head and shoulders above his African reggae compatriots. Should he finally tie himself to a major label internationally, he may eventually become the mainstream star he evidently desires to be.

Selected albums: *Lengane Ngeyetha* (1983), *Rastas Never Die* (1985), *Help My Krap* (1986), *Slave* (Shanachie 1986), *Together As One* (1989), *Prisoner* (Shanachie 1989), *Captured Live* (Shanachie 1991), *House Of Exile* (1991), *Victims* (1993).

Dunbar, Sly

b. Lowell Dunbar, 10 May 1952, Kingston, Jamaica. In 1969 Dunbar commenced his recording career with Lee Perry, playing drums on 'Night Doctor' by the Upsetters, which appears on both *The Upsetter* and *Return of Django*. The following year, he played on Dave Barker and Ansell Collins' massive hit 'Double Barrel'. Around this time he also joined the Youth Professionals who had a residency at the Tit For Tat Club on Red Hills Road, Kingston. He paid frequent visits to another club further up the same road, Evil People, where he struck up a friendship with bass player Robbie Shakespeare (b. 27 September 1953, Kingston, Jamaica). Deciding to work together, their professional relationship as Sly And Robbie began. In 1972/3, Sly joined Skin Flesh And Bones, backing Al Brown on his best-selling cover of Al Green's 'Here I Am Baby'. The same year, Sly and Robbie became founder members of the Revolutionaries, Channel One studio's houseband. They recorded hit after hit, and the studio soon became the most in-demand on the island. Sly's technical proficiency and relentless inventiveness drove him to constantly develop original drum patterns, and while most of the island's other drummers were copying his latest innovations, he would move on and create something new. In this way, he had an enormous influence on the direction that reggae took from the mid-70s onwards. Sly's inventive and entertaining playing can be heard on dub and instrumental albums such as *Vital Dub*, *Satta Dub* and *Revolutionary Sounds*, as well as supporting the Mighty Diamonds on their classic *Right Time*. He also recorded extensively with the Professionals, Joe Gibbs' houseband, playing on classics such as *Visions* by Dennis Brown, *Two Sevens Clash* by Culture and *African Dub Chapter 3*. Derrick Harriott went one step further and put him on the cover of *Go Deh Wid Riddim* (1977), which was credited to Sly And The Revolutionaries. He was then signed to Virgin, who released two disappointing solo albums, *Simple Sly Man* (1978) and *Sly Wicked And Slick* (1979). Around this time, Sly was the first drummer to integrate successfully synthesized drums into his playing, and a little later became the first reggae drummer to use a Simmons electronic drum kit.

In 1979 Sly And Robbie moved into record production with their own Taxi label, scoring with Black Uhuru's best-selling *Showcase*. Further recordings included Gregory Isaacs' *Showcase* and the various artists compilation, *Presenting Taxi* (1981). They had their greatest commercial success with Black Uhuru, with whom they recorded four further albums. In 1984, they became official members of the group, but left later that year after the departure of Michael Rose. At the same time, they established Ini Kamoze as a major new reggae artist, released Dennis Brown's *Brown Sugar* and Sugar Minott's *Sugar And Spice*, plus three ground-breaking albums with

Grace Jones which were hugely successful and introduced their talents to the world outside of reggae. They have since recorded widely with artists such as Mick Jagger, Carly Simon, Gwen Guthrie, Bob Dylan, Robert Palmer, James Brown, Manu Dibango and Herbie Hancock. They also teamed up with Bill Laswell for a series of innovative soul/funk/crossover albums including *Language Barrier, Rhythm Killers, Silent Assasin* and Material's *The Third Power*. They have continued to develop their own reggae sound with recordings from their new discoveries 54-46 and Kotch, some of which are included on the compilations *Sound Of The 90s* and *Carib Soul*. They have already changed the musical world, and their restless creativity ensures that they will continue to do so.

Selected albums: *Go Deh Wid Riddim* (Crystal 1977), *Simple Sly Man* (Virgin 1978), *Sly Wicked And Slick* (Virgin 1979), *Sly-Go-Ville* (Mango/Island 1982). For Sly & Robbie recordings see under Sly And Robbie.

Dunkley, Errol

b. 1951, Kingston, Jamaica. Dunkley had already cut his first records, a duet with Roy Shirley entitled 'Gypsy' for Lindel Pottinger's Gaydisc label, 'My Queen' with Junior English for Prince Buster, and 'Love Me Forever', issued on the Rio label in 1965, at the ripe old age of 14. Between 1967 and 1968 he recorded 'Please Stop Your Lying', 'I'm Going Home', 'I'm Not Your Man' and 'You're Gonna Need Me' for Joe Gibbs, before switching to Coxsone Dodd in 1969 where he cut 'Satisfaction' and 'Get Up Now', among others. In 1971 he recorded a medley of his Joe Gibbs hits entitled 'Three In One', 'Deep Meditation' and 'Darling Ooh' for Rupie Edwards. In an attempt to achieve musical and financial autonomy he teamed up with fellow singer Gregory Isaacs to form the African Museum label, scoring a local success with a version of Delroy Wilson's 'I Don't Know Why', retitled 'Movie Star'. However, the partnership floundered and Dunkley went on to form his own Silver Ring label, though no hits were forthcoming. In 1972 producer Jimmy Radway recorded him on two of his best sides: 'Keep The Pressure On' and the big hit, 'Black Cinderella'. An album also emerged produced by Sonia Pottinger entitled *Presenting Errol Dunkley* (re-released in 1981 as *Darling Ooh*), an excellent selection of originals and covers, including the classic, self-penned, 'A Little Way Different'.

Throughout the first half of the 70s Dunkley recorded a number of fine singles appearing on a variety of labels including 'Little Angel', 'Oh Lord', 'Where Must I Go', 'Down Below' and 'Act True To Your Man'. The second half of the decade saw Dunkley scoring successes amongst the UK reggae fraternity with tunes like 'I'm Your Man' and 'Eunoch Power' for Winston 'Niney' Holness, 'Stop Your Gun Shooting' for Tapper Zukie, and a new version of 'A Little Way Different' for Dennis Bovell. His biggest success, however, came in 1979 with his rendition of John Holt's naggingly catchy 'OK Fred', which managed to appeal to the pop sensibilities of Britain's wider record buying public, rising to number 11 in the UK national charts in September of that year, leading to unforgettable performances on great British television institutions such as *Top Of The Pops* and *Basil Brush*. Further forays into pop chart success proved elusive and Dunkley, now resident in the UK, had to be satisfied with the continued grass roots popularity of records such as 'Happiness Forgets', 'Rush Me No Badness', 'If I Can't Have You', 'Come Natural' and a version of the Stylistics 'Betcha By Golly Wow'.

Albums: *Presenting Errol Dunkley* (1972), *Darling Ooh* (Trojan 1972), *OK Fred* (Third World 1979), *Profile* (Third World 1980), *Special Request* (1987), *Aquarius* (1989).

Dynamites

The Jamaican houseband for producer Clancy Eccles during the early reggae years of the late 60s and early 70s, the Dynamites backed numerous Clan Disc artists such as Eccles himself, Cynthia Richards and pioneer DJ King Stitt. Their line-up fluctuated, though its nucleus was Winston Wright (organ/piano), Hux Brown (guitar), Jackie Jackson (bass), Gladstone Anderson (piano) and Paul Douglas (drums). This combo, with added saxophones, recorded the memorable *Fire Corner* (1969), a unique set of moody reggae instrumentals that also included King Stitt on the title track and 'Vigorton 2'.

Albums: With King Stitt: *Fire Corner* (Trojan 1969). With Clancy Eccles: *Herbsman Reggae* (Trojan 1970).

E

1983), *Super Duper* (Time 1986), *Showcase* (Studio One 1985), *Babylon Walls* (1991), *Boss Man* (Carib Sounds 1992), *Not For Sale* (Next Step 1993), *Phoenix Of Peace* (1993).

Earl Sixteen

b. Earl Daley, 1958, Kingston, Jamaica. After winning local talent shows Daley joined the group Flaming Phonics as lead vocalist before voicing the self-penned 'Malcolm X' for Joe Gibbs in 1975, later to be covered by Dennis Brown. In 1977 he became a member of the Boris Gardiner Happening who introduced him to Lee Perry at the Black Ark. There he recorded four tracks in 1978/9 and met Earl Morgan of the Heptones, who produced his debut album, *Singing Star*. His next collection was for radio DJ and DATC producer Mikey Dread, although there were singles for Augustus Pablo ('Changing World'), Linval Thompson, Derrick Harriott and others, released throughout the early 80s, including an excellent set for former Stur-Gav duo Ranking Joe and Jah Screw. By 1982/3 he was at Studio One where his third version of 'Love Is A Feeling' was recorded. The previous two were for Aston 'Family Man' Barrett and Stafford Douglas; to date it is Earl Sixteen's most popular song. Those Brentford Road sessions resulted in Coxsone Dodd's *Showcase* album of 1985. Shortly afterwards he switched allegiance to former Royals founder Roy Cousins, then Skengdon and Blacka Dread ('Batman And Robin') and Bert Douglas ('Problems'). In 1988 after a two year break he resurfaced in England, covering Simply Red's 'Holding Back The Years' and making a short-lived attempt to produce himself. During 1991/2 he was to be found at Ariwa, recording *Babylon Walls* and several fine singles for the Mad Professor. Since then he has voiced for a growing number of UK producers with varying degrees of success.

Selected albums: *Shining Star* (Vista 1980), *Reggae Sounds* (DATC 1981), *Julie* (Roy Cousins 1982), *Special Request* (Roy Cousins

Earth Messengers

Back in the mid-70s Vincent 'Vinnie' Taylor (b. c.1960, St. Anns, Jamaica) was a Rasta youth seeking an outlet for his singing talents. That outlet arrived in 1976 when Taylor formed Vinnie Taylor And The Revealers, a roots vocal trio modelled along the lines of local heroes Burning Spear. The Revealers logically went to Spear's producer, Jack Ruby, who recorded them on a single 'Hard Times'. When it flopped, Taylor returned to grass roots, changing the group's name to Earth Messengers and acting as a channel for frustrated Ocho Rios youth talent. Among those who passed through Earth Messengers were Donovan Francis, later to sign to Island as a solo singer, and Errol Douglas, later to turn up in Foundation. In 1988 Jack Ruby picked up on Earth Messengers, now comprising Vinnie Taylor, his brother Milton, and Bedster Henry, and they recorded *Ivory Towers*, which was critically well-received but commercially unsuccessful. However, persistence did not entirely pay off for Taylor: further recordings were stymied when Ruby died of a heart attack in the spring of 1989, and Earth Messengers' current activities are unknown. They remain yet another unlucky reggae act.

Album: *Ivory Towers* (Mango/Island 1989).

Eccles, Clancy

b. c.1940, Jamaica. One of the most loved and respected personalities in the history of Jamaican music, Clancy Eccles started making records for Clement 'Coxsone' Dodd in 1959, recording 'Freedom', initially as an acetate which was featured on Dodd's sound system for nearly two years before its official release in 1961. For the same producer he also recorded local hits 'River Jordan' and 'Glory Hallelujah'. He then provided 'Judgement' for Leslie Kong's

Earl Sixteen

business mentor Charlie Moo in late 1962. By the mid-60s he had completed three other records, 'Miss Ida' and 'Roam Jerusalem'/'Sammy No Dead' for Sonia Pottinger and 'I'm The Greatest' for Mike Shadeen. By 1967 he had started his own label, his first release being Eric 'Monty' Morris' local hit, 'Say What You're Saying'. During the next few years Eccles was one of reggae's leading producers. He was instrumental in helping Lee Perry set up his own operation when that producer left Coxsone, arranging Perry's huge local hit, 'People Funny Boy' in 1968.

From 1969 Trojan Records released Eccles's productions on UK Clandisc. Records like 'Fire Corner' by DJ King Stitt and the bawdy 'Fatty Fatty' by Eccles were very popular, not only with audiences in Jamaica and the Afro-Caribbean communities in North America and the UK, but also appealing to the British skinheads who followed Jamaican music at that time. In this period, utilizing his studio band the Dynamites, Eccles produced records by such artists as Alton Ellis, Lord Creator, the Fabulous Flames, Lee Perry, Larry Marshall, Joe Higgs, the Beltones, Busty Brown, Carl Dawkins and Cynthia Richards. He issued many records featuring his own vocals, singing either heart-felt love songs or stinging social comment. A lifelong socialist, Eccles has continued to record material on this theme right up to 1985, when he issued 'Mash Up We Country', a song that takes its place alongside such classics as the pro-PNP (People's National Party) anthem 'Rod Of Correction' (1972) and 'Generation Belly' (1976). Eccles was also an adviser to Michael Manley's PNP Government from 1972 on matters relating to the music business. He continues to release compilations of oldies, as well as the occasional new production. Eccles is the quintessential Jamaican producer, particularly in the attention he pays to his craft and his proximity to his audience's tastes.

Albums: *Freedom* (Trojan 1969), *Herbsman Reggae* (Trojan 1970), *Top Of The Ladder* (Top Of The Ladder 1973), *Jamaica Reggae Vol. 1* (1986), *Reggae Vintage Vol.2* (1987), *Fatty Fatty 1967-1970* (1988). The Dynamites with King Stitt: *Fire Corner* (Trojan 1969).

Edwards, Jackie

b. Wilfred Edwards, 1938, Jamaica, d. 15 August 1992. The honeyed tones of Jackie Edwards have graced hundreds of ska, R&B, soul, rocksteady, reggae and ballad recordings since he composed and sang 'Your Eyes Are Dreaming', a sentimental ballad, and the gentle Latin-beat 'Tell Me Darling', for future Island Records owner Chris Blackwell in 1959. Probably the most accomplished romantic singer and songwriter that Jamaica has ever produced, he has always had enough soul in his voice to escape the descent into schmaltz. In 1962, when Blackwell set up Island Records in London, Edwards made the trip to Britain with him. At Island in the early years, his duties included not only singing and songwriting but also delivering boxes of ska records by bus to the capital's suburban shops. His persistence paid off when, in 1966, the Spencer Davis Group scored two consecutive UK number 1 pop hits with his now classic compositions, 'Keep On Running' and 'Somebody Help Me'. In more recent years he has continued to issue records whose standards of production have been variable but on which his crooning has substantiated his soubriquet of 'the original cool ruler'.

Albums: *The Most Of ...* (Island 1963), *Stand Up For Jesus* (Island 1964), *Come On Home* (Island 1966), *By Demand* (Island 1967), *Premature Golden Sands* (Island 1967), *I Do Love You* (Trojan 1973), *Sincerely* (Trojan 1978), *King Of The Ghetto* (Black Music 1983), *Original Cool Ruler* (Vista Sounds 1983). With Millie Small: *Pledging My Love* (1967), *The Best Of Jackie & Millie* (1968). Compilations: *The Best Of* (Island 1966).

Edwards, Rupie

b. 4 July 1945, Goshen, near Brownstown, St. Anns, Jamaica. Edwards got his first musical inspiration while attending the Anglican church school in Sergeantville as a seven-year-old. In early 1958 he moved to Kingston, where he attended Kingston Senior School and, like others of similar musical inclination, he formed a band with home-made instruments, bamboo saxophone and thumb piano; and performed at school concerts. In 1962 he had appeared on Vere John's 'Opportunity Hour' and the same year he made four records, for the Hi-Lite label based from the Hi-Lite Haberdashery and the Little Wonder Music Store in Kingston. One title, 'Guilty Convict', was released in the UK on the Blue Beat label. Edwards was paid £15 for that session, but that did not stop him from making two more records for the President Bell's sound system, and then two further titles with Junior Menz, 'Mother's Choice', and a cover of the Impressions' 'Amen'. By the mid-60s, Edwards was a member of the Virtues, again with Junior Menz and guitarist Eric Frater.

From 1968, Edwards began to release his own productions; the first was 'Burning Love', recorded at Studio One and engineered by Coxsone Dodd and Graham Goodall. This and other early productions enabled him to devote himself full-time to music; and give up his job at a local garage, where he repaired cars owned by Dodd and Duke Reid. By the early 70s Edwards had produced hits by himself and other artists like Bob Andy, Joe Higgs, the Ethiopians, and the Tellers, and had been instrumental in bringing the talents of Johnny Clarke and Gregory Isaacs before the public. He also recorded DJs such as the late U Roy Junior, Shorty the President and I Roy as well as scores of excellent instrumentals by Jamaica's finest session musicians.

In December 1974 Edwards's single 'Ire Feelings (Skanga)' entered the UK charts and stayed there for the next 10 weeks, eventually reaching number 9. The follow-up, 'Leggo Skanga' charted for six weeks from February 1975. During this period Edwards issued an entire album on which all the tracks used the same backing track. This concept subsequently became an important feature of Jamaican music. The album, 'Yamaha Skank', utilized a rhythm given to Edwards by producer Bunny Lee; Slim Smith's 'My Conversation'. Following his UK chart success, Edwards took up residence in London, continuing his operations from there up to the present day. Edwards released a series of his own oldies in both 12-inch and album form and also leased some material to Creole during the 70s, though there were no further hits. He continued to record material for the religious and sentimental love song markets, enjoying steady sales, and operating his own retail outlet.

Albums: *Yamaha Skank* (Success 1974), *Rupie Edwards Dub Basket* (Cactus 1976), *Dub Basket Chapter 2* (Cactus 1976), *Jamaica Serenade* (Cactus 1976). Various: *Rupie's Gems Volumes 1 & 2* (Cactus 1976), *Dub Classic* (Success 1977), *Hit Picks Volume 1* (Cactus 1977), *Ire Feelings: Chapter & Version* (Trojan 1990), *Let There Be Version* (Trojan 1990).

Eek A Mouse

b. Ripton Joseph Hilton, 1957, Kingston, Jamaica. One of the most individual talents to emerge from Jamaica, Eek A Mouse's unique phrasing and singing style were to become as instantly recognisable as his 6' 6" frame (Eek A Mouse was the name of a racehorse Hilton frequently lost money on at the races; the one time he refused to back it, the horse duly won). His first two releases, 'My Father's Land' and 'Creation', he made under his real name in the mid-70s. After spells with the Papa Roots, Black Ark, Gemini, Jah Life, Black Scorpio and Virgo sound systems he began recording with Joe Gibbs in 1980. 'Once A Virgin', 'Modelling Queen' and 'Virgin Girl' became sizeable hits the following year, by which time he'd joined forces with producer and Volcano sound owner, Henry 'Junjo' Lawes. Utilising the Roots Radics at Channel One with Scientist invariably mixing the final results. Junjo and Linval Thompson coaxed a series of best-selling albums and numerous hit singles from the idiosyncratic DJ throughout the years 1980 to 1984.

In 1981 following his debut album *Wa Do Dem*, he became the unscheduled star of that year's Reggae Sunsplash. In 1982 singles like 'Ganja Smuggling', 'For Hire And Removal' and 'Do You Remember' maintained his rocketing profile, as did the album *Skidip*. 'Terrorists In The City', 'Anarexol' and 'Operation Eradication' - voiced in response to the death of his friend Errol Scorcher - all sold well, and *The Mouse And The Man* and *Assassinator* albums (not to mention several appearances on live dancehall albums) quickly followed in 1983, but already there were signs that his distinctive trademark 'biddy biddy bengs' were becoming all too familiar. After *Mouseketeer* - last of his albums with Junjo - his popularity began to wane despite the occasional good record and a steady reputation as a performing artist. *U-Neek* heralded a comeback in 1991 with tracks produced by Gussie Clarke, Daddy O and Matt Robinson. That year he enjoyed a walk-on part in the movie *New Jack City*, and recorded for both Wild Apache and former Channel One engineer, Soljie.

Albums: *Wa Do Dem* (Greensleeves 1981), *Skidip* (Greensleeves 1982), *The Mouse And The Man* (Greensleeves 1983), *Assassinator* (RAS 1984), *Mousekateer* (Greensleeves 1984), *King And I* (RAS 1987), *U-Neek* (Mango/Island 1991). Compilations: *The Very Best Of Eek A Mouse* (Greensleeves 1987).

Ellis, Alton

b. 1944, Kingston, Jamaica. Ellis, Jamaica's most soulful singer, celebrated 25 years in the business many years ago now and he is still making important records. In many ways he epitomizes the story of reggae vocalists: a start in the business at a very early age, massive popularity for a limited period, and a gradual slide from prominence while continuing to make excellent records purchased by discerning listeners. Apart from his songwriting abilities and voice Alton's

particular gift was his ability to take R&B or soul songs and place them in a specifically Jamaican context and so make them 'reggae songs' rather than mere cover versions. Alton was born into a musical family, and he first recorded in the late 50s as one of a duo with singer Eddy Perkins for Randys and Studio One as Alton And Eddy. They enjoyed some success in the R&B style and 'Muriel' was a massive hit for them. Perkins departed soon afterwards for a solo career and Alton continued with Studio One at Brentford Road as well as working with Coxsone Dodd's arch rival in the business Duke Reid at his Treasure Isle Studio in Bond Street, initially as Alton Ellis And The Flames. He came to undisputed prominence with the rise of rocksteady in 1965-66 when the ska beat slowed down and instrumental records became less important. This 'cool' music gave far greater freedom to singers' to express themselves - they no longer had to battle against the frantic ska pace and 'noisiness', and Alton Ellis reigned supreme - his 'Get Ready - Rock Steady' was one of the first records to actually use the term. Both Coxsone and Reid made many classic records with Alton as he moved between Brentford Road and Bond Street, but he recorded the definitive rock steady album for Treasure Isle - *Mr Soul Of Jamaica,* while his Studio One output is collected on three albums all of which have their high points.

In the late 60s and early 70s he went on to record for some of Jamaica's finest producers and he scored two huge hit records for Lloyd 'The Matador' Daley - 'Deliver Us' and 'Back To Africa', while a cover version of 'Too Late To Turn Back Now' that he made for Randys in the early 70s has remained a firm favourite with the reggae audience ever since. He toured the UK in the 60s as a vocalist for Studio One's Soul Vendors band and he returned to England in 1972 where he has based himself (on and off) ever since, making records that are never less than excellent. However, he is now sadly disillusioned with the reggae business. He accepts its machinations with a dignified

Alton Ellis

resignation just as in the early days when his songs were covered and no royalties were forthcoming: 'I was just proud that, whoever, would do an Alton Ellis song'. He was involved at the start of Janet Kay's career and a cover version of one of his greatest songs, 'I'm Still In Love With You', formed the basis for Althea And Donna's 'Uptown Top Ranking' - a UK number 1 in 1978 - but his records and live shows are now sadly few and far between.

Selected albums: *Sunday Coming* (Studio One), *Best Of Alton Ellis* (Studio One), *Sings Rock & Soul* (Studio One 1966), *Love To Share* (Third World 1979), *Showcase* (Studio One 1980), *25th Silver Jubilee* (Skynote 1984), *Still In Love* (Horse 1985), *Continuation* (All Tone 1985), *Jubilee Vol. 2* (Sky Note 1985), *Here I Am* (Angella Records 1988), *My Time Is Right* (Trojan 1990), *Alton And Hortense Ellis* (Heartbeat 1990), *Cry Tough* (Heartbeat 1993).

Ethiopians

The Ethiopians were originally a trio comprising Leonard 'Sparrow' Dillon (b 1945, Portland, Jamaica), Stephen Taylor (b. 1944, St. Mary, Jamaica), and Aston Morris. Prior to their formation in 1966, Dillon had recorded a series of ska/mento titles for the seminal Jamaican producer Coxsone Dodd under the name of Jack Sparrow, including 'Ice Water' (1965) and 'Suffering On The Land' (1965). In late 1966 Morris left, and the duo of Dillon and Taylor began recording for Dodd as the Ethiopians, mostly in a style that bridged ska and rocksteady. Titles recorded during late 1966 and early 1967 included 'Free Man', 'Live Good', 'Owe Me No Pay Me', 'I'm Gonna Take Over Now' and 'Dun Dead Already'. After leaving Dodd they recorded at Dynamic Studios for the WIRL label, enjoying massive local hits with the rocksteady 'Train To Skaville' (1967), and the title track of their first album, *Engine 54*. In late 1967 they recorded for Sonia Pottinger's Gayfeet label including 'Stay Loose Mama', 'The Whip' and 'Train To Glory'. They also worked

with Lee Perry and his fledgeling company, releasing 'Cut Down' and 'Not Me'. By 1968 they had begun an association with producer J.J. Johnson which turned out to be their most consistent, comprising a series of quintessential Jamaican vocal records that remain emblematic of the then new beat of reggae's first phase.

As well as being great dance tunes, their lyrics had begun to reflect and criticise ghetto life. Rasta themes also received an airing. Their first big hit for J.J., 'Everything Crash', was an incisive look at the post-colonial legacy and a classic rhythm. Many further titles were recorded for J.J. during 1968-71, including 'What A Fire', 'Gun Man', 'Hong Kong Flu', 'Woman Capture Man', 'The Selah', and many others. From 1969 they began to work with other producers; in that same year they scored with 'Fire A Mus' Mus' Tail' and 'Reggae Hit The Town' for H. Robinson. In 1970 they made 'Satan Girl' for Lloyd 'Matador' Daley, titles for Derrick Harriott - 'Lot's Wife', 'No Baptism', and 'Good Ambition', and sessions at Duke Reid's Treasure Isle Studios produced 'Mother's Tender Care', 'Condition Bad A Yard' and 'Pirate' (1971). They continued recording with many other label owners including Randy's (1971), Winston Riley (1972), Alvin 'GG' Ranglin (1972), Joe Gibbs (1971, 1975), Rupie Edwards (1972-73), Harry J (1972), and Lee Perry again (1973).

In 1975 Stephen Taylor died in a car crash, and Dillon carried on alone, occasionally using session singers, including members of the Cordells. In 1977 Winston 'Niney' Holness issued a solid Rasta-based album entitled *Slave Call*. 1978 saw the release of 'Open The Gate Of Zion', recorded at Channel One with Sly Dunbar, Robbie Shakespeare and the Revolutionaries. By 1980 Dillon was back with Dodd, releasing the album *Everything Crash*. This was a mature, rootsy set with new versions of the title song and 'No Baptism', and excellent new songs based on vintage Studio One rhythms. The late 70s saw the release of more 45s for Dodd, followed by a break until a lively self-produced reissue of 'Pirate' surfaced in 1986. Since then Dillon has worked with new members, Harold Bishop and former Burning Spear drummer, Neville Duncan.

Selected albums: *Engine 54* (1968), *Reggae Power* (Trojan 1969), *Woman Capture Man* (Trojan 1970), *Slave Call* (Third World 1977), *Open The Gate Of Zion* (GGs 1978), *Everything Crash* (Studio One 1979), *Dread Prophecy* (Night Hawk 1986), *Let's Ska And Rock Steady* (1992, reissue of *Engine 54*), *The World Goes Ska* (1993). Compilation: *Original Reggae Hit Sound* (Trojan 1986).

Exterminator

Record label/sound system run by Philip 'Fatis' Burrell (b. Kingston, Jamaica). It took Burrell a decade to become one of Jamaica's leading producers of the 90s. He was born in Trenchtown but spent part of his childhood in England before returning to Jamaica in his teens. George Phang and Robbie Shakespeare encouraged him to take up production, his first release being Sugar Minott's 'More Dogs To The Bone' in 1984, the year his shortlived Kings & Lions label made its appearance. *The Summit* was an early dub album featuring the rhythms of Sly And Robbie, although it was King Tubby's Firehouse Crew who played on most subsequent recordings at either Dynamics or Music Works. By 1987 he had founded the Vena label, and discovered Sanchez, Pinchers and Thriller U, all of whom featured on the label with some of their earliest works. Frankie Paul and Red Dragon both voiced hit tracks, and sampler albums from 1988 reveal established names like Gregory Isaacs, Charlie Chaplin and General Trees rubbing shoulders with Fatis protegés such as Quench Aid, Lukie D, Conrad Crystal and Daddy Freddy, whose 1989 *Cater Fi She* album for Burrell was his debut. That same year saw the introduction of 'live' dancehall sets, and some seriously militant marketing of the Exterminator label, which mirrored the hard, driving rhythm tracks and often uncompromising material found on it.

Throughout 1990-91 artists of the calibre of Ninjaman, Ini Kamoze ('Hot Stepper'), Cocoa Tea, Admiral Tibet, Tony Rebel ('Real Rough'), Frankie Paul, Gregory Isaacs, Beres Hammond ('Emptiness Inside'), Johnny Osbourne, Tiger - whose *Ready Fi Dem* was released the following year - appeared as part of Burrell's roster. He let loose a similarly prolific number of exceptional releases in the following two years also, beginning with Capleton's 'Armshouse' (which spawned two version albums) and culminating in long players by Cocoa Tea, Sugar Minott, Pinchers, Sanchez, Luciano and Beres Hammond, whose *Full Attention* crowned a richly creative body of work for Fatis. Dennis Brown, Yami Bolo, Nadine Sutherland, Cocoa Tea, Buju Banton, General Degree, Chaka Demus And Pliers, Singing Sweet, Marcia Griffiths and Brian and Tony Gold all voiced excellent tracks for Exterminator between 1993 and 1994, arguing that the long term potential of the Exterminator empire remains huge. Whether creating classic rhythms from the past or breaking new ground with adventurous hardcore beats, Burrell's standards remain impeccable.

Selected albums: (All on Exterminator label) Various: *Exterminator Vols. 1 & 2* (1988), *Turn On The Heat* (1989), *Exterminator Live Vols. 1 & 2* (1989), *Exterminator Presents* (1990). Sly And Robbie: *The Summit* (1988). Daddy Freddy: *Cater Fi She* (1989). Pinchers: *Lift It Up Again* (1987), *Mass Out* (1987), *Dirt Low* (1993). Sanchez: *Boom Boom Bye Bye* (1993). Frankie Paul: *Warning* (1987), *Easy Mover* (1988). Tiger: *Ready Fi Dem* (1991). Beres Hammond: *Full Attention* (1993). Cocoa Tea: *One Up* (1993). Sugar Minott: *Run Things* (1993). Luciano: *Moving Up* (1993).

F

Fashion Records

Founded in Summer 1980, Fashion Records has been a rare success amongst UK-based reggae labels, and alongside rival Ariwa, remains the only studio-owning, domestic-producing company to have survived since the early 80s. The label is the brainchild of John MacGillivray and Chris Lane, two reggae devotees, and is essentially a spin-off from MacGillivray's Dub Vendor record store. The first Fashion release hit number 1 in the UK reggae charts in the Summer of 1980 – Dee Sharp's 'Let's Dub It Up', with south London lovers rock band the Investigators supplying the rhythms (Lane had previously produced a couple of singles for the band as the Private I's). 'Let's Dub It Up' provided a benchmark in British reggae and set a standard that Fashion, incredibly, nearly always lived up to: fine, classy harmonies, punchy rhythms, bright arrangements and above all else, strong songs. In the next few years a veritable who's who of British reggae, and those passing through from Jamaica, turned up on the label: Keith Douglas, Carlton Manning (of Carlton And His Shoes), Alton Ellis and Carlton Lewis among many others. In 1982 Fashion opened a four-track studio, A-Class, in the basement of the new Dub Vendor shop at Clapham Junction. By this time the UK MC explosion had begun, and Fashion were at the centre of it with chatters Papa Face, Laurel & Hardy, Pato Banton, Bionic Rhona, Macka B and Asher Senator. A dub-cutting service saw Paul Robinson of One Blood and Maxi Priest's 'Caution' band (Lane was also a member, as was Priest himself) as regulars at the tiny subterranean studio. Robinson soon enjoyed hits with the label as 'Barry Boom', and the company was rarely out of the specialist charts.

Chirpy, fast-talking MC Smiley Culture had one of the biggest reggae hits of 1984 on the label with 'Cockney Translation', but bettered it when 'Police Officer' went top 12 in the national charts, as several Fashion band regulars frightened Britain on *Top Of The Pops*. Their connection with the UK MC boom made the step into ragga in the mid-80s a comparatively natural one. Meanwhile Fashion was also cutting lovers rock hits through Michael Gordon and the under-rated Nerious Joseph, often coming out on another imprint, Fine Style. Two female acts were also recruited, Winsome and Shako Lee (Janet Lee Davis). Winsome's 'Am I The Same Girl', 'Born Free' and 'Super Woman' (with Tippa Irie) proved themselves classics of their type. Fashion also began to work with a variety of Jamaican acts, including Junior Delgado, Joseph Cotton ('No Touch The Style'), Leroy Gibbon, Frankie Paul, Glen Brown and Augustus Pablo.

In 1988 the label opened the new A-Class Studio, a sixteen-track set up in Forest Hill, and began to use tracks laid at Penthouse Studios in Jamaica, voicing and mixing them in London. 1989/90 saw a string of reggae chart hits, with Shako Lee's 'Two Timing Lover' and Cutty Ranks' 'The Stopper' both hitting number 1. Fashion also became involved in distribution of other labels, such as Mafia & Fluxy's M&F, Paul Robinson's Merger, Captain Sinbad's Sinbad and Gussie Prento's Gussie P. The label now stands virtually alone in British reggae as an entity capable of working with almost all of the modern strands of the music. A second pop chart success at long last, Louchie Lou and Michie One's inspired ragga cover of the Isley's 'Shout', licensed to ffrr, and the rise of General Levy, also leased to ffrr and perhaps the most accomplished UK ragga rapper yet, should ensure that the label's future remains secure into the next century.

Selected albums: Various: *Great British MCs* (Fashion 1985), *JA To UK MC Clash Vol 2 - Papa San Meets Tippa Irie* (Fashion 1988), *Fashion Revives Classic Lovers* (Fashion 1989), *Fashion Revives Classic Lovers Vol 2* (Fashion

Dean Fraser

1988), *Jamaica's Finest Vol. 1* (Fashion 1990), *Funky Punany* (Fashion 1990). Glen Brown: *Plays Music From The East* (Fashion 1990). Cutty Ranks: *The Stopper* (Fashion 1990). General Levy: *The Wickeder General* (Fashion 1993).

Folks Brothers

To be labelled a one-hit wonder is generally something of an insult, but to be a one-record wonder is an accolade. The Jamaican artists who have made one perfect recording and then vanished, leaving a reputation forever untarnished by later lapses, could be counted on the fingers of one hand. The Folks Brothers are among that number: in 1961 or early 1962 they recorded 'Oh Carolina', a unique and perfect single, and never appeared again. The record has Count Ossie's Rastafarian drummers thundering out complex African cross-rhythms, Owen Gray contrastingly American-styled on piano, and the Brothers, a soulful lead singer and two lighter-voiced male accompanists, delivering the song. In 1993 an updated version of 'Oh Carolina' breached the number 1 position in the UK charts for Shaggy.

Foundation

A roots reggae vocal trio, styled after classic acts like Culture and Burning Spear, Foundation formed in 1977 around lead singer Errol 'Keith' Douglas in the St Anns area of Jamaica's north coast. Douglas's chief claim to fame prior to Foundation was as the writer of Dennis Brown's 'Jah Can Do It' - Douglas had recorded it himself for producer Joe Gibbs on a fame-hunting excursion to Kingston, but Gibbs had, instead, got Brown to re-voice the track. Douglas returned to the north coast for a rethink, and founded Foundation with Emilio 'Father' Smiley, ex-of the Revealers, and Euston 'Ipal' Thomas. The trio wrote and practised for months, but by the time they had arrived at the yard of producer Jack Ruby, who had overseen Burning Spear's classic *Marcus Garvey*, he was winding down his recording activities. He did however, promise that 'when the time

was right' he would take them into the studio, and Ruby kept that promise almost a decade later when he signed them to Island Records for their debut set, *Flames*, co-produced and somewhat overwhelmed by the guitar of Steven 'Cat' Coore of Third World. Live dates on Sly And Robbie's 1988 Rhythm Killers tour were more subtle, and their second set, *Heart Feel It* (1989) was far better. However, just after its completion producer Jack Ruby died of a heart attack, and Foundation's name has not surfaced since.

Albums: *Flames* (Island 1988), *Heart Feel It* (Mango/Island 1989).

Fraser, Dean

b. c.1955, Kingston, Jamaica. The premier modern Jamaican reggae saxophonist, Dean Fraser has long been known amongst the reggae cognoscenti for his fulsome, warmhearted tenor tone, a sound that matched both his size and demeanour. Fraser first emerged in the Jamaican music business in the mid-70s when horns were starting to diminish in importance within reggae bands. His own first musical experiments were as a clarinetist, at a youth club in Jonestown, as part of the National Volunteer programme. There he met fellow musicians Ronald 'Nambo' Robinson and Junior 'Chico' Chinn, who played trombone and trumpet respectively. Together with Fraser on sax they were to become the foremost horn section in Jamaica throughout the 80s. Initially they played at old people's homes, covering jazz and R&B standards, until Dean left to join Sonny Bradshaw's band, a large ensemble playing mainly jazz arrangements and offering much scope for young musicians seriously wishing to learn all aspects of the music business. In 1975 he played on his first recording session with Lloyd 'Gitsy' Willis and two years later joined the We The People Band, led by singer, producer and bassist Lloyd Parks. Nambo and Chico were enrolled shortly afterwards as the band achieved prominence backing Dennis Brown, then in the midst of recording a string of successful records for producer Joe Gibbs.

It was Gibbs who produced Dean Fraser's first album, *Black Horn Man*, in 1978, followed by *Revolutionary Dream* for Donovan Germain some two years later. Fraser's early singles included several vocal records rendered in a pure, gentle tone somewhat akin to that of Slim Smith. In the early 80s, known as 'Youth Sax', he would fire up the sessions of Sly & Robbie, and became a regular on both their world tours and in support of other acts like Gregory Isaacs. An emotional instrumental version of Bob Marley's 'Redemption Song' at the 1981 Reggae Sunsplash, the first held since the late Marley's death, put Fraser uncharacteristically in the spotlight, and prompted Mango to commission the *Pumping Air* set.

Ironically, as reggae was swept by 'computerized' music in the mid-80s, Fraser was suddenly in-demand as the best-known human instrumentalist, and his saxophone tones sweetened literally dozens of pre-recorded 'digital' rhythms. He would enjoy a surprise hit with 'Girlfriend' for Dennis Star in 1987, encouraging him to rediscover his singing voice for the excellent *Sings And Blows* and *Dancehall Sax* for the same producer, which delivered several Jamaican vocal hits. From 1988 onwards he worked increasingly with Gussie Clarke at Music Works, first as a session musician and guest instrumentalist on Gussie's one-rhythm albums, then as an invaluable part of the production team, arranging and playing on a variety of albums by artists such as Cocoa Tea, Gregory Isaacs, Dennis Brown and Freddie McGregor. It is a function he also provides for the producers Carlton Hines and Phillip 'Fatis' Burrell. Fraser remains as popular today as ever and forms part of a saxophone tradition that goes back to the likes of Tommy McCook and Roland Alphonso in reggae, and his records, like those of R&B player Ace Cannon, will remain endlessly popular with the older Jamaican community. In recognition of his musical services he was awarded the Musgrave Medal from the Jamaican government in 1993.

Selected albums: *Black Horn Man* (1978), *Revolutionary Dream* (1980), *A Touch Of Sax, Revolutionary Sounds* (1982), *Pure Horn* (1983), *Pumping Air* (Island 1984), *Big Bad Sax* (Super Power 1988), *Sings And Blows* (Greensleeves 1988), *Dancehall Sax* (Witty/Greensleeves 1988), *Raw Sax* (Greensleeves 1989), *Call On Dean* (1991), *Moonlight* (Greensleeves 1991), *Taking Chances* (1993). With Willie Lindo: *Double Dynamite* (1983).

G

Gardiner, Boris

b. 1954, Kingston, Jamaica. Boris Gardiner, bass player, vocalist and musical director, has never been one of reggae's most celebrated names, but he has remained a permanent fixture in the music, and has three huge UK chart hits to his credit. His bass playing skills first emerged in the late 60s, and the bands he graced included Byron Lee's Dragonaires, the Aggrovators, Crystalites and many more. His first brush with chart success was 'Elizabethan Reggae', cut for Byron Lee, which hit number 14 in January 1970. Gardiner toured the UK in support of his hit, which, at first, was incorrectly credited to its producer. His debut album, again produced by Byron Lee, was released the same year. In its wake Gardiner immersed himself in session work, regularly playing as part of the Now Generation band, and was later to be found as one of Lee Perry's Upsetters, following the Barrett brothers' defection to the Wailers. His solid, to-the-point basslines were seldom noticed, yet always effective. In the 80s, as reggae was on the cusp of the digital era, an age likely to put paid to the careers of bass players, Gardiner's mellow, soulful voice came to the fore on a MOR reggae ballad, 'I Want To Wake Up With You', which hit number 1 in the UK charts. Gardiner, who had been dogged by illness on and off throughout the 80s, was finally getting paid. His follow-up, 'You're Everything To Me', went to number 11, and a seasonal 'The Meaning Of Christmas' also scraped the charts.

Selected albums: *Reggae Happening* (Duke 1970), *I Want To Wake Up With You* (Revue 1986), *Everything To Me* (Revue 1986), *Its Nice To Be With You* (K&K 1986), *Soulful Experience* (Dynamic 1988), *Let's Take A Holiday* (WKS 1989). Compilations: *Classic Tracks* (Counterpoint 1988).

Gayfeet Records

(see Pottinger, Sonia)

Gaylads

A vocal trio consisting of Winston Delano Stewart (b. 5 January 1947, Kingston, Jamaica), Harris 'BB' Seaton (b. 3 September 1944, Kingston, Jamaica), and Maurice Roberts (b. 2 July 1945, Kingston, Jamaica). Together they began recording during the ska period but came to prominence during the rocksteady era in the mid to late 60s. Perhaps at any other time and in any other place their names would be highly revered and spoken of in hushed, awestruck tones, but such was the strength of the competition for three-part harmony vocal groups in Jamaica during the 60s that their names are seldom remembered outside of reggae's cognoscenti. Most of their finest ska and rocksteady material was recorded for Coxsone Dodd's Studio One organisation (where they also recorded in the calypso style) and the best of it is collected on two classic albums, *Soul Beat* and *The Best Of The Gaylads*, with Seaton writing most of their material. As with most other Dodd singers their talents were used extensively for harmony work for other Studio One artists such as Slim Smith and Peter Tosh. They also recorded some beautiful rocksteady sides for WIRL - 'Joy In The Morning' is one of their most enduring and much versioned songs - and 'ABC Rocksteady' and 'It's Hard To Confess' for Sonia Pottinger's Gayfeet label, two all-time classics of the genre. Stewart and Seaton pursued solo careers in the 70s with varying degrees of success Their legacy is a proud one, the Gaylords' name bedecking some of the most graceful three part harmonies ever recorded.

Albums: *Sunshine Is Golden* (Studio One c.60s), *Soul Beat* (Studio One late 60s). Compilations: *The Best Of* (Studio One 1992), *After Studio One* (Metronome 1992).

General Echo

Another DJ whose legend has gone before him. Echo (aka Ranking Slackness) was one

General Levy

of the first to challenge the predominantly 'cultural' approach of the majority of mid to late 70s DJs, and his influence on the upcoming DJs who made it big in the 80s (in particular the UK MC school) was profound. He was one of the first DJs to be heard and fully appreciated on yard tapes as he tore up Jamaica on his own Echo Tone Hi Fi set and his preference for 'slack' or risque lyrics, in particular his timing and tone of voice, were very popular and widely imitated. Echo felt no compunction about stopping the music altogether if the vibes were right in order to tell a joke or two - a facet which endeared him even more to his followers. His version of Winston Riley's 'Stalag' rhythm - 'Arleen' - was a number 1 hit for weeks in Jamaica and the future was looking very bright for Echo until he was shot dead by the police in Kingston in 1980, along with Flux and Big John (both from his sound system), in an incident that has never been fully explained.
Albums: *12-inches Of Pleasure* (Greensleeves 1980). As Ranking Slackness: *The Slackest LP.* (Techniques 1979).

General Levy

b. 1971, Park Royal, London, England. As ragga music finally made it into the mainstream in 1993 with Chaka Demus & Pliers, Shaggy, Shabba Ranks *et al* storming the UK national charts, it was left to just one home-grown DJ to fly the flag for British ragga music. A north London youth, Paul Levy began his career DJing as General Levy, working his way through Vigilante, Java and Robbo Ranx's Tipatone sound systems. His first release was for Robbo's Muzik Street label in 1988, and 'New Cockatoo' proved to be something quite different, as Levy's freshness, youth and enthusiasm hiccuped out of every groove.

His next move was to south London where Fashion Record's resident engineer, Gussie P, released his debut album, on which he shared the honours with Jamaican superstar DJ Capleton. Entitled *Double Trouble* the format (already tried and trusted) highlighted both Levy and Capleton's different styles and

approaches, spanning Jamaican and UK traditions. His popularity was boosted by numerous 'specials' for sound systems and he finally came to the public's attention in a big way with 'Original Length & Strength' on Fashion Records. His next trio of releases for Fashion, 'Heat', 'Breeze' and 'The Wig' established him as *the* British DJ. His lyrics ranged from serious culture to risqué 'slackness', with hardly a pause for breath while his live shows had to be experienced to be believed, as he exploded all over the stage, arms and legs flailing to the accompaniment of non-stop, infectious, raucous rhyming. His branching out with Justice Records for some hip hop based recordings further broadened his appeal, and the late 1992 long-playing release for Fashion of *The Wickeder General* was an immediate runaway success. His burgeoning talent was soon spotted by the majors (especially with all the frantic interest in ragga in the Spring of 1993), and ffrr/London clinched the big deal. They re-titled, re-packaged and re-promoted *The Wickeder General* as *Wickedness Increase* and the strength of the added tracks ensured healthy sales - even to the reggae market where his fans had already purchased the original pressing. Levy now stands on the brink of crossover success, his talent and personality have already made him the UK's number one reggae DJ, and many critics expect him to break big in the 90s.
Albums: *The Wickeder General* (Fashion 1993), *Wickedness Increase* (ffrr/London 1993). With Capleton: *Double Trouble* (Gussie P. 1988).

Germain, Donovan

b. 7 March 1952. A producer whose involvement in 80s and 90s reggae music has helped define and popularise the format. Germain started in the business with a record shop in New York, and he began producing his own work in 1972. From the outset his style was characterised by its dignified, musical approach and Germain soon proved that he could make lovers rock as adeptly as

'roots' records – his 'Mr Boss Man' with Cultural Roots was a huge underground hit in 1980. He made the UK national charts in the mid-80s with Audrey Hall's 'One Dance Won't Do' - strangely enough an answer version to Beres Hammond's 'What One Dance Can Do', which was not a hit outside of the reggae sphere. He had many more hits throughout the 80s. However, everything came together towards the end of the decade when he opened his own Penthouse Studio on Slipe Road in Kingston in 1987. The quality and feel of the studio ensured that it was in constant demand for outside sessions and many, many classic recordings have been made there under the auspices of Germain and Dave 'Rude Boy' Kelly. It continues to hold its position as one of the top Kingston studios - no mean feat in the hectic competition that abounds in this particular field and Penthouse's clean, sophisticated sound and production work have ensured the popularity of the music with a much wider audience. Germain is a modest man who would always rather let his music do the talking - a keen student of reggae, his involvement has always been imbued with a sense of, and sympathy for, the music's history and traditions. Now recognised as one of the very top reggae producers, he has proved himself many times over and there are few who would begrudge him the accolade. The discography lists just a small selection of the man's prolific output, any of which will demonstrate both the clean, crisp sound that has become a byword for Penthouse productions, and Germain's ability to get the best out of both vocalists and DJs.
Albums: Audrey Hall: *Just You Just Me* (Germain 1987). Marcia Griffiths: *Marcia* (Germain 1988), *Indomitable* (Penthouse 1993). Buju Banton: *Mr Mention* (Penthouse 1991). Beres Hammond: *A Love Affair* (Penthouse 1992). Various: *What One Rhythm Can Do* (Germain 1987), *Ninja Turtle (Volumes 1, 2 & 3)* (Penthouse 1989), *Good Fellas* (Penthouse 1989), *Reggae Ambassadors (Volumes 1 & 2)* (Penthouse 1990), *Rhythm Exclusive* (Penthouse 1992), *Best Of Penthouse* (Penthouse 1993), *Dance Hall Hits (Volumes 1, 2 & 3)* (Penthouse 1993), *Lovers Rock* (Penthouse 1993), *Penthouse Sampler* (Penthouse 1993).

Gibbs, Joe

b. Joel Gibson, 1945, Montego Bay, Jamaica. Gibbs started in the music business selling records in his television repair shop situated in Beeston Street, Kingston. In 1966 he moved into record production, releasing his material on the Jogib, Amalgamated, and Pressure Beat labels in Jamaica. He found instant success with Roy Shirley's 'Hold Them', one of the earliest records to introduce the new rocksteady beat, issued on the Doctor Bird label in the UK. By 1968 his productions were being released in the UK on Amalgamated, a subsidiary of Trojan Records set up exclusively for that purpose. The early issues were in the rocksteady format including 'Just Like A River' and 'Seeing Is Knowing' by Stranger (Cole) And Gladdy (Gladstone Anderson), and 'El Casino Royale' by guitarist Lynn Tait. Later came reggae sides by the Versatiles, who included Junior Byles in their number, Errol Dunkley, the Royals, the Reggae Boys, Ken Parker, the Immortals, the Slickers, Jimmy London, Ernest Wilson, Keith Blake (aka Prince Alla, also a member of the Leaders with Milton Henry), the Soulmates, and Nicky Thomas, whose 'Love Of The Common People' reached number 9 in the UK charts during July 1970. Other local hits came via the Pioneers who recorded extensively for Gibbs before defecting to the Leslie Kong camp. Their hits included 'Give Me A Little Loving', 'Long Shot', 'Jackpot', 'Catch The Beat', and 'Mama Look Deh'. Many of which were written and produced by Lee Perry who cut his own records 'The Upsetter' and 'Kimble' for Gibbs before leaving to set up his own label. The parting was not exactly sweet, Perry's first self-production, 'People Funny Boy', being a vitriolic attack on Gibbs, who responded on record with the identical sounding 'People

Grudgeful'. Once Perry had departed, Gibbs enlisted Winston 'Niney' Holness to perform similar duties. With Niney at the helm, working the board alongside Errol 'ET' Thompson at Randy's, Gibbs label entered into the nascent dub/version boom with instrumental sides like 'Nevada Joe' and its version, 'Straight To The Head', and 'Franco Nero' by Joe Gibbs And The Destroyers. Other popular instrumentals like 'Hi-Jacked' and 'Movements' were credited to the Joe Gibbs All Stars. In 1969 he installed a two-track studio at the back of his newly established Joe Gibbs Record Mart in West Parade, later moving to North Parade, and began producing successful records like 'Jack Of My Trade' by veteran DJ Sir Lord Comic, 'Them A Fi Get A Beatin'', 'Maga Dog' and 'Arise Black Man' by Peter Tosh, the first cut of 'Money In My Pocket' by Dennis Brown, and its DJ version 'A So We Stay' by Big Youth, 'Warricka Hill' by the Versatiles, and 'Pretty Girl' by Delroy Wilson. These appeared on a variety of labels in Jamaica and, primarily, on the Pressure Beat imprint through Trojan in the UK. Gibbs also released several albums including *Best Of Dennis Brown*, *Heptones & Friends Vols. 1 & 2* and two of the earliest dub albums; the elusive *Dub Serial* and the first chapter of his classic *African Dub* series, both mixed by ET.

By 1975 Gibbs had opened his own 16-track studio and pressing plant at 24 Retirement Crescent, Kingston 5. With Errol T installed at the controls, the hits soon poured forth from artists such as Leo Graham, Sylford Walker ('Burn Babylon'), Junior Byles ('Heart And Soul'), Dillinger ('Production Plan'), George Washington ('Rockers No Crackers'), Dhaima ('Inna Jah Children'), Earl Sixteen ('Malcolm X'), Ruddy Thomas ('Every Day Is A Holiday'), Gregory Isaacs ('Babylon Too Rough'), Jah Berry aka Prince Hammer ('Dreadlocks Thing'), Naggo 'Dolphin' Morris ('Su Su Pon Rasta'), Trinity's *Three Piece Suit* (1977), Prince Far I's *Under Heavy Manners* (1977), and a brace of Revolutionaries-style instrumentals by Joe Gibbs And The Professionals. This was his studio band, incorporating the talents of Lloyd Parks, Sly And Robbie, Bingy Bunny and Bopeep on keyboards, Sticky and Ruddy Thomas on percussion, and a horn section comprising Bobby Ellis, Tommy McCook, Herman Marquis and Vin Gordon. Two further instalments of the *African Dub* series also emerged, with the notorious *Chapter 3*, benefiting (or suffering, depending on your point of view) from a particularly over-the-top mix from ET and Gibbs, achieving great popularity amongst the UK's punk adherents in 1977. These records appeared on a variety of Gibbs affiliated labels including Joe Gibbs, Town & Country, Errol T, Reflections and Heavy Duty. The late 70s/early 80s were a fruitful time for Gibbs, with two of his acts, Culture and Dennis Brown, breaking internationally. Gibbs scored two more UK chart entries, with teenage female DJ duo Althea And Donna's novelty 'Up Town Top Ranking' in 1977 and Dennis Brown's re-cut of 'Money In My Pocket' in 1979. Gibbs' also produced popular sides by Eek A Mouse ('Virgin Girl'), Nigger Kojak And Liza ('Sky Juice'), and Junior Murvin ('Cool Out Son'). This activity continued on into the 80s, when after moving to Miami, he temporarily ceased his operations following a lawsuit over copyright. He sold his old studio to Bunny Lee, but continues to lease and reissue his old material.

Albums: Various: *Explosive Rock Steady* (1968), *Jackpot Of Hits* (1968), *African Dub Volumes 1, 2 & 3* (Joe Gibbs 1975, 1976, Lightnight 1978), *Top Ranking DJ Session Vol. 1* (1980), *Top Ranking DJ Session Vol. 2* (1982). Pioneers: *Greetings From The Pioneers* (1968), Heptones: *Heptones & Friends Volumes 1 & 2* (1972/3). The Professionals: *State Of Emergency* (1976). Culture: *Two Sevens Clash* (Lightning 1977), *Baldhead Bridge* (Joe Gibbs 1978). Prince Far I: *Under Heavy Manners* (1977). Dennis Brown: *Best Of* (1975). Joe Gibbs & Friends: *The Reggae Train 1968-1971* (1988). With Errol Thompson: *The Mighty Two* (Heartbeat 1990).

Gospel Fish

Gladiators

Formed in Jamaica c.1965, the group originally comprised Albert Griffiths (vocals/guitar), Clinton Fearon (vocals/guitar) and David Webber (vocals). Griffiths adopted the groups' name after a workmate suggested it to him. Their earliest recordings include 'The Train Is Coming Back' (1968) for Leeward Robinson, 'You Were To Be' (c.1969) for Duke Reid and 'Hello Carol' (1969) for Coxsone Dodd. During 1970, Webber was replaced by Dallimore Sutherland (bass/vocals). The group's focus became more roots orientated, and good examples of this approach include two fine songs they recorded for Lloyd Daley in 1971, 'Rock A Man Soul' and 'Freedom Train'. Throughout the early 70s they recorded a stunning body of work for Dodd including 'A Prayer To Thee', 'Bongo Red', 'Jah Jah Go Before Us', 'Roots Natty' and 'Serious Thing'. In 1976, they signed to Virgin Records. Their first album, *Trenchtown Mix-up*, was a strong collection of new songs and remakes, and this was followed by *Proverbial Reggae* (1978) and *Naturality* (1979). Between 1977 and 1978, further singles appeared from Studio One, including 'Mr Baldwin' and 'Peace'. In 1979, Dodd finally released a collection of their singles as *Presenting The Gladiators*. Meanwhile, their Virgin contract concluded with *Sweet So Till* (1979) and *The Gladiators* (1980), the latter being a misjudged crossover attempt. Further albums have all been consistent while not hitting the heights of their earlier recordings.

Albums: *Trenchtown Mix-up* (Virgin 1976), *Proverbial Reggae* (Front Line 1978), *Naturality* (Front Line 1979), *Presenting The Gladiators* (Studio One 1979), *Sweet So Till* (Front Line 1980), *The Gladiators* (Virgin 1980), *Symbol Of Reality* (1982), *Serious Thing* (Night Hawk 1984), *Country Living* (Heartbeat 1985), *In Store For You* (1988), *On The Right Track* (1989), *Dreadlocks The Time Is Now* (Front Line 1990), *Valley Of Decision* (1991), *A True Rastaman* (1993). Compilation: *Vital Selection* (Virgin 1987).

Glasgow, Deborahe

b. 1965, d. January 25, 1994. Glasgow's career began at the tender age of 12 when she first worked with the Mad Professor. Under the name Debbie G. she released 'Falling In Love' for his Ariwa label, which anticipated her powerful lovers rock style. She subsequently apprenticed herself to the London sound system circuit, mixing with the likes of Tippa Irie and Papa Levi, gaining a reputation for knowing her own mind and music. After meeting London producer Patrick Donegan she signed to UK Bubblers, a Greensleeves subsidiary, marking her debut for the label with 'You're My Sugar'. It gained her a first entry in the reggae charts. Other hits followed, including 'Knight In Shining Armour', 'Don't Stay Away' and 'When Somebody Loves You Back', a lovers rock standard. Later she travelled to Jamaica to work with Gussie Clarke, and these sessions would produce the best work of her tragically short life. A self-titled album emerged, which was strengthened by the presence of Shabba Ranks and the inclusion of singles 'Champion Lover' and 'Don't Test Me'. Later, Shabba's version of 'Champion Lover', re-titled 'Mr Lover Man', would become a huge international hit. After this career peak Deborahe kept her distance from the music business, concentrating instead on bringing up her family in Wandsworth, London. However, she did collaborate with General Lee for 'Weak' and 'Knocking The Boots'. Shortly after she was diagnosed as having cancer of the lymph gland, and died of a brain haemorrhage on the 25th of January, 1994.

Album: *Deborahe Glasgow* (Greensleeves 1989).

Gospel Fish

b. Everald Thomas, Spanish Town, Jamaica. Gospel's quirkily inventive lyrics are invariably marked by a maturity and intelligence that sets him apart from many of his contemporaries. He was raised in Thompson Pen, learning hand drums from his Rasta father before fellow DJ Jimmy

Crazy dubbed him Gospel Fish after watching him sing hymns in the local church choir. The pair dueted on their first ever release, 'Neighbourhood Cousin', in 1987, which Gospel - then working as a security guard - produced himself. 'Walk An' Wine', 'Ruff An' Tuff' and 'Cash Ready' followed, but his first two hits, 'Golden Rule' and 'Bandy Leg' did not arrive until a year later. His producer was now Dennis Star, who brought him to the UK in 1988 for his first shows outside Jamaica. Until then he had been a regular feature on the Happy Tone, Nite Flight, Lightning and Leo Taurus sound systems, inspired by DJs such as Lt. Stitchie, Tony Rebel and Professor Nuts.

In 1990 he began voicing for Captain Sinbad, Fashion and Gussie P, all of whom have been instrumental in helping him reach a wider audience. 'Wickedest Thing In Life', 'You Must Be Fool' and 'Too Much Gun Talk' revealed a shift from mildly 'slack' themes to something altogether more cultural; much as 'Ten' had done when released by Penthouse in 1991. Throughout 1991-92 he also recorded for Soljie, Top Rank, Bee Cat and Taxi before Sinbad coaxed him into writing a combative 'burial' tune called 'Brush Dem', which brought his biggest hit to date. During 1993 a stay in the UK found him guesting on the Aswad/Yazz collaboration 'Hold On', and enjoying further exposure with both Fashion and Sinbad, occasionally in combination, as with John McLean on *Romantic Ragga*.

Selected album: Various: *Romantic Ragga* (Sinbad 1993).

Grant, Eddy

b. Edmond Montague Grant, 5 March 1948, Plaisance, Guyana. Grant was 24 years old, with several hits to his credit, when he left the Equals to form his own production company. After producing other acts, he made his own debut in 1977 with *Message Man*. It was certainly a solo effort. Not only did he sing and play every note, but it was recorded in his own studio, the Coach House, and released on his own label, Ice

Records. Grant had developed his own sound - part reggae, part funk, strong musical motifs, strong melodies - pop with credibility. More than 10 years after the Equals' first hit, 'Living On The Front Line' (1979) was a UK number 11 hit, and the now dreadlocked Grant had found himself a whole new audience. 'Do You Feel My Love' and 'Can't Get Enough Of You' kept him in the UK Top 20. In 1982 he moved his home and studio to Barbados, signed Ice Records to RCA, and achieved a memorable UK number 1 hit with 'I Don't Wanna Dance'. The following year 'Electric Avenue' reached number 2 on both sides of the Atlantic, and the parent album *Killer On The Rampage* proved his biggest seller. The huge hits eluded him for four years until he stormed back in January 1988 with 'Gimme Hope Jo'anna', as if he had never been away. The dressing of the anti-Apartheid message in the apparent simplicity of a pop song was typically inspired.

Albums: *Message Man* (Ice 1977), *Walking On Sunshine* (Ice 1979), *Love In Exile* (Ice 1980), *Can't Get Enough* (Ice 1981), *Live At Notting Hill* (Ice 1981), *Paintings Of The Soul* (Ice 1982), *Killer On The Rampage* (Ice/RCA 1982), *Can't Get Enough* (Ice/RCA 1983), *Going For Broke* (Ice/RCA 1984), *Born Tuff* (Ice 1987), *File Under Rock* (Parlophone 1988). Compilations: *All the Hits: The Killer At His Best* (K-Tel 1984), *Hits* (Starr 1988), *Walking On Sunshine (The Best Of Eddy Grant)* (Parlophone 1989).

Video: *Live In London* (1986), *Walking On Sunshine* (1989).

Gray, Owen

b. 5 July 1939, Jamaica. Owen's singing won him a local talent contest at the age of nine, and three years later he began to appear in public, playing drums, guitar and keyboards. In 1960 he became one of the first artists produced by Chris Blackwell, later the owner of Island Records. His first single, 'Please Let Me Go' (though the lyrics suggested that 'Don't Let Me Go' should have been its title), with its easy shuffle rhythm and hard Ernest Ranglin guitar solo adding to the singer's appeal, was a number 1 hit in Jamaica. Gray's voice, light but with a cutting edge, won him favour throughout the decade; he turned his hand to R&B ('Let Me Go Free', based on Professor Longhair's 'Tipitina'), ska ('Millie Girl') and ballads ('Far Love') before emigrating to Britain. He maintained a prodigious output, following the trends of ska, rocksteady and reggae, scoring a big seller with 'Cupid' (1968) and recording one of the steamiest soul dances ever issued in England in 'Help Me' (1966). By the late 70s he was no longer in the forefront of British black music, and a 1982 attempt at 'Sexual Healing' was less than successful. He now lives in Miami where he still finds an audience for his extensive oldies repertoire.

Albums: *Cupid* (1969), *Fire And Bullets* (Trojan 1977), *Dreams Of Owen Gray* (Trojan 1978), *Forward On The Scene* (Third World 1978), *Little Girl* (Vista Sounds 1984), *Owen Gray Sings Bob Marley* (Sarge 1984), *Room At The Top* (World Enterprise 1986), *Watch This Sound* (Sky Note 1986), *Stand By Me* (Hitbound 1986), *Instant Rapport* (Bushranger 1989), *Ready Willing And Able* (Park Heights 1989). With Pluggy Satchmo: *Battle Of The Giants Round 1* (Vista Sounds 1983). With Delroy Wilson: *Oldies But Goldies* (Vista Sounds 1983). With Max Romeo: *Owen Gray Meets Max Romeo* (Culture Press 1984). Compilations: *Hit After Hit Vols. 1, 2 & 3* (Carib Gems 1980, Vista Sounds 1983).

Greensleeves

Despite its humble origins as a record shop in West Ealing, London, in 1975, Greensleeves continues to thrive in the keenly contested environs of the reggae marketplace. The label's first releases were Reggae Regular's 'Where Is Jah' and Doctor Alimantado's 'Born For A Purpose'. The latter artist also offered them their first long player, the *Best Dressed Chicken In Town* compilation. Tony McDermott's distinctive artwork soon established Greensleeves' visual

image and identity. The label further consolidated its name with the emergence of dancehall, licensing much of Henry 'Junjo' Lawes catalogue for domestic release. Others included Scientist, Channel One's technical guru, and Prince Jammy's productions, notably his early works with Black Uhuru. The UK side were equally productive with their UK Bubblers label, peaking commercially with Tippa Irie's UK Top 30 hit, 'Hello Darling', in 1986. Other notable successes on the domestic front included Clint Eastwood And General Saint.

The mid-80s saw impressive re-packagings of Jamaican standards (Hugh Mundell, Burning Spear, Yabby You) as well as major new works from Eek A Mouse, Josey Wales, Junior Reid and Yellowman. Their profile was enhanced further via the UK release of two groundbreaking singles: Wayne Smith's 'Under Me Sleng Ten', which kickstarted the digital revolution, and Gregory Isaacs' 'Rumours', the best-selling reggae record of 1988, and an important staging post in the development of ragga. A new wave of artists had their records released in the UK by Greensleeves: Shabba Ranks, Cocoa Tea and Papa San among them. The English lovers rock scene was represented by Deborahe Glasgow while the company scored their biggest seller to date when picking up Shaggy's 'Oh Carolina'. They also market several other independent labels, notably Jah Shaka's idiosyncratic roster.

Selected albums: *Greensleeves Sampler Vols. 1 - 8* (Greensleeves 1983 to 1993).

Griffiths, Marcia

b. 1954, Kingston, Jamaica. Griffiths is arguably the most consistently successful female vocalist ever in reggae music, having recorded in every one of the myriad of styles in Jamaican music from ska through to an 80s rap crossover record. Her precocious talent were recognised very early on by producers Coxsone Dodd and Byron Lee who were competing for her father's signature on a recording contract before Marcia's 10th birthday. Coxsone was the winner because she 'like his vibes' and Coxsone's Studio One set up was like a 'musical college'. It was there that Griffiths scored her first Jamaican number 1 in 1968 with the rocksteady hit 'Feel Like Jumping', a record that can still fill dance floors. She had worked very closely with Bob Andy during this period and he had written many of her biggest hits for her. In 1969, they recorded, as Bob And Marcia, an interpretation of Nina Simone's 'Young, Gifted And Black' for producer Harry 'J' Johnson and their bright, lilting reading of the song touched a nerve with UK buyers, particularly among the reggae-obsessed skinhead audience. The popularity of the record ensured crossover success and it rode high in the UK charts in 1970 and became a hit all over Europe. Their follow-up, 'Pied Piper', in 1971 was equally pop-oriented and another big hit in the UK. The duo toured extensively but both felt that there was very little financial reward during this period and they returned to Jamaica to reassess their respective careers. Marcia made some beautiful records for Sonia Pottinger's High Note label and in 1975, she became one of Bob Marley's I-Threes backing vocalists, along with Rita Marley and Judy Mowatt - recruited to fill the musical gap left by the departure of Bunny Wailer and Peter Tosh from the Wailers. For the remainder of the decade and on into the 80s she recorded and toured with Marley, still continuing with her solo career, but after Marley's death in 1981, she again recorded extensively as a solo artist. Her 'Electric Boogie' with Bunny Wailer was a hit in the USA in 1989 - seven years after it was recorded - and even inspired its own dance - 'The Electric Slide'. She continues to record and, furthermore, make records that matter.

Albums: *The Original - At Studio One* (Studio One c.70s), *Sweet Bitter Love* (Trojan 1974), *Naturally* (Sky Note 1978), *Steppin'* (Sky Note 1979), *Rock My Soul* (Pioneer International 1984), *I Love Music* (Mountain Sounds 1986), *Marcia* (Germain 1988),

Marcia Griffiths

Carousel (Mango/Island 1990), *Put A Little Love In Your Heart* (Penthouse 1993), *Indomitable* (Penthouse 1993).

Half Pint

H

Half Pint

b. c.1962, Western Kingston, Jamaica. One of the first and finest dancehall reggae singers, Half Pint has never entirely maintained his career at the highest level, but nonetheless has had an impressive, if sporadic string of huge Jamaican hits. An enthusiastic and exciting singer, Half Pint, one of seven children, left school in 1976 and spent the next six years trying to break into the music business before cutting a debut single, 'Sally'. 'Money Man Skank' was a major hit and kicked off a five-track debut album for Jammy's. Early hits 'One In A Million' and 'Pouchie Lou' for producer Prince Jammy established his style, and Half Pint's diminutive figure traversed the world on Sly And Robbie's 1985 Taxi Tour, paying the duo back with singles 'World Inflation', 'Hold On', and 'Night Life Lady'. A visit to producer George Phang brought about his biggest hit, 'Greetings' (1985), an unavoidable refrain in the world's reggae cities, and then the Rolling Stones covered his 'Winsome' to the outright astonishment of the singer. *Victory* followed the blueprint of *Greetings* to the letter and sold well in America. Since then, Half Pint has been less successful, but he carries a considerable following eagerly waiting for another *Greetings*, and in the spring of 1992 the big reggae hit 'Substitute Lover' was a sign of his reviving fortunes.

Albums: *Money Man Skank* (Jammys 1984), *Can't You Wait Till I Get You Home* (Power House 1984), *One In A Million* (Greensleeves 1984), *In Fine Style* (Sunset/Sonic Sounds 1984), *Greetings* (Power House 1986), *Victory* (RAS 1988), *One Big Family* (Powerhouse 1989), *Pick Your Choice* (1993). With Michael Palmer: *Joint Favourites* (1985). Compilation: *20 Super Hits* (Sonic Sounds 1993)

Hammond, Beres

b. Beresford Hammond, 1955, Kingston, Jamaica. Winning a string of awards for Best Male Vocalist throughout the early 90s meant that success had come late to Beres Hammond. He was still in his teens when he joined Zap Pow in 1975, after singing on local amateur shows. He'd met guitarist and producer Willie Lindo even before that, and by the time Hammond had left the group in 1980 Lindo had produced his debut album, *Soul Reggae*, and was already working on *Just A Man* which followed in 1981. It was to prove a harmonious partnership; although *Let's Make A Song* had been self-produced, Lindo was back in the chair for *Coming At You* in 1983. With his smoky, soulful vocals, Beres was accruing a reputation as a master stylist, and his choice of material reflected this, often bearing a distinctly R&B flavour. All that changed with his fifth album, *Beres Hammond*. 'Groovy Little Thing', 'One Dance Will Do' (which sparked off a saga of answer versions) and 'She Loves Me Now' all became best-selling singles which established his name on the dancehall market.

It wasn't until he was coerced into recording for Donovan Germain's Penthouse label in 1990 that he experienced similar success again. A major label deal with Cooltempo had failed in presenting his talents to a wider audience and despite a high profile duet with Maxi Priest for 'How Can We Ease The Pain' in 1988, he had seemingly lost direction. Germain voiced him over popular dancehall rhythms and 'Tempted To Touch' proved to be a runaway hit, resulting in the release of *A Love Affair* in 1992. By then Beres was in demand, and a wealth of material ensued from producers such as Willie Lindo, Richard Bell from Star Trail, Steely & Clevie and 'Fatis' Burrell, who was based at Music Works, adjoining the Penthouse studio. The hits flowed thick and fast, often in the shape of collaborations with artists like Marcia Griffiths, Buju Banton, Cobra, Cutty Ranks, Reggie Stepper and Tony Rebel. In 1992 Sly Dunbar remixed

Beres Hammond

earlier tracks Hammond had voiced for Tapper Zukie and 'Putting Up Resistance' won a JAMI award for the year's Best Song. The following year 'Fatis' built on the existence of a growing number of great tracks for his Exterminator label and issued the *Full Attention* album, which showcased Beres in unstoppable form over a selection of weighty rhythms. The result highlighted his abilities not only as a magnificent singer of ballads, reality and dancehall material, but also revealed him to be a writer of genuine merit. After recording further hits for New York producers Sting and Robert Livingston he signed for Elektra in the autumn of 1993. Selected albums: *Soul Reggae* (Water Lily 1979), *Just A Man* (Joe Gibbs 1981), *Let's Make A Song* (1982), *Coming At You* (WKS 1983), *Beres Hammond* (Charm 1986), *Have A Nice Weekend* (WKS 1987), *Live & Learn Present* (Live & Learn 1988), *Putting Up Resistance* (Tuff Gong 1989), *Just A Vibes* (Star Trail 1990), *A Love Affair* (Penthouse 1992), *Full Attention* (Exterminator 1993), *Sweetness* (VP 1993).

Harriott, Derrick

b. c.1942, Kingston, Jamaica. While a pupil at Excelsior High School, Harriott formed a duo with Claude Sang Junior, and in 1958 formed the Jiving Juniors with Eugene Dwyer, Herman Sang, and Maurice Winter. In 1960-61 they had hits with 'Over The River' for Coxsone Dodd and 'Lollipop Girl' for Duke Reid. In 1962, Harriott left the group and formed his own label, Crystal. His first solo recording, 'I Care', was a hit, as were 'What Can I Do' (1964), 'The Jerk' (1965) and 'I'm Only Human' (1965). All of these were included on his debut, *The Best Of Derrick Harriott*. In 1967 he had hits with his own 'The Loser' and 'Solomon', the Ethiopians' 'No Baptism' and Keith And Tex's 'Tonight' and 'Stop That Train'. Harriott's sophisticated, soul-styled sound had caught the imagination of the Jamaican public - his recordings in the rocksteady style were superlative and still sound fresh and vibrant today. In 1970 he issued the Crystalites' *The Undertaker*, an excellent instrumental album in a similar vein to that of the early Upsetters which had been huge hits with the skinhead audience in the UK. Other albums included DJ Scotty's *Schooldays* (1971), Dennis Brown's *Super Reggae And Soul Hits* (1972) and his own *14 Chartbuster Hits*. Under the Crystalites banner he issued one of the earliest dub albums, *Scrub A Dub*, becoming one of the first producers to use the talents of King Tubby at his Waterhouse Studio. He followed it with the sublime *More Scrubbing The Dub*, a collection of dub and instrumental versions of his best rhythms. In the late 70s he utilised the Revolutionaries for Winston McAnuff's *Pick Hits To Click* (1978), DJ Ray I's *Rasta Revival* (1978) and his own *Enter The Chariot* and *Disco 6*, a fine compilation featuring Dennis Brown, Cornell Campbell and Horace Andy. In the 80s he continued to have hits with soul covers such as 'Skin To Skin' and 'Checking Out', and in 1988 scored with 'Starting All Over Again', a duet with Yellowman, concerning the affects of Hurricane Gilbert. Albums: *The Best Of Derrick Harriott* (Island 1965), *The Best Of Derick Harriott Volume Two* (Trojan 1968), *14 Chartbuster Hits* (Crystal 1973), *Greatest Reggae Hits* (Trojan 1975), *Songs For Midnight Lovers* (Trojan 1976), *Disco 6* (1977), *Reggae Disco Rockers* (Charmers 1977), *Chartbusters 70s Style* (1978), *Enter The Chariot* (1978), *Songs For Midnight Lovers* (Trojan 1985), *Skin To Skin* (Sarge 1989), *Musical Chariot* (Charly 1990). As Derrick Harriott & Friends: *Step Softly* (Trojan 1988, covers 1965-72). Productions: Various: *Rock Steady Party* (1967), *Disco 6* (1977), *Those Reggae Oldies* (1978, covers c.1967-72), *Riding The Musical Chariot* (1990, covers 1967-71). Dennis Brown: *Super Reggae And Soul Hits* (1972). Crystalites: *The Undertaker* (1970), *Scrub A Dub* (Crystal 1974), *More Scrubbing The Dub* (Crystal 1975), *Sensimilla Dub* (1980). Winston McAnuff: *Pick Hits To Click* (1978). Ray I: *Rasta Revival* (1978). Scotty: *Schooldays* (1971). Sly And The Revolutionaries: *Go*

Derrick Harriott

Deh Wid Ridim (Crystal 1977). Keith And Tex: *Stop That Train* (Crystal 1992). Compilations: *Greatest Reggae Hits* (Trojan 1985).

Hartley, Trevor

b. Morant Bay, St Thomas, Jamaica. Dreaming of becoming a singer in his youth, Hartley managed to voice two sides on rhythms recycled from the Morwells at Joe Gibbs studio, which eventually saw release on the Pele label. He moved to London in the late 70s, recording with Dennis Bovell on the 1978 double a-side, 'Selassie I'/'Skip Away', followed by sessions with Phill Pratt for his debut album. Unfortunately, shortly after its release the record label went under, neutering its impact. Following a liaison with Sugar Minott's Black Roots label on 'Africa', Hartley worked with Arawak on two 45s before a placement with Top Ranking. Neither yielded the breakthrough Hartley's obvious talents craved. A revision of the Frankie Beverley/Maze nugget, 'Call On Me,' at least pushed him back into the reggae charts, and his profile was boosted by his participation in the British Reggae Artists Famine Appeal (BRAPA) as a featured vocalist, alongside Aswad and many others.
He topped the UK reggae charts again in 1988 with 'Hooked On You', which brought him a deal with London Records. However, like so many before him, the liaison between raw reggae talent and a major label proved a mis-match. Their relationship was not a happy one, though it did yield one minor hit, 'Nine Til Five'. The 90s saw him recording with a variety of production teams, notably Mad Professor, and Mafia & Fluxy, work which bodes well for his future, with a new album scheduled for release in 1994.
Selected album: *Innocent Lover* (Burning Sounds 1979).

Heptones

Leroy Sibbles (b. 1949, Jamaica), Barry Llewellyn (b. 1947, Jamaica) and Earl Morgan (b. 1945, Jamaica) were beyond doubt the foremost rocksteady and reggae vocal trio and their work together, especially for Studio One, set the standards for all other Jamaican harmony groups to measure their works by. They started with Ken Lack's Caltone label, but failed to record any hits even though they produced a memorable and bizarre version of the 'William Tell Overture' entitled 'Gun Men Coming To Town'. Their next move to Coxsone Dodd's Studio One set-up in 1966 coincided with the rise of rocksteady, and the Heptones proved to be masters of the genre. Not only did Sibbles possess a pure and delicate lead voice and a masterly songwriting talent, but he was also responsible for many of the music's most popular (and versioned) bass lines, which were sufficiently versatile and melodic enough to be able to record any number of different instrumental and vocal takes. The Heptones became the most imitated and influential vocal group in Jamaica and their collected works for Studio One have stood the test of time and countless cover versions. After their first big hit in Jamaica and the UK, the lewd and suggestive 'Fattie Fattie', which was a big seller despite being banned from the radio, there was no stopping them. Sibbles wrote love songs and social/protest/reality songs almost to order, but he really excelled with the sly misogyny of 'Tripe Girl': 'You tried to hurt me but you can't' and 'I Hold The Handle': 'I hold the handle, you've got the blade . . . When I wake up in the morning fix me some orange juice . . . When I wake up in the morning just put yourself to use'. His voice swooped and soared and all the time Morgan and Llewellyn filled in beautifully behind him taking occasional lead and even contributing songs such as Llewellyn's 'Pretty Looks' which proved every bit as popular and enduring as Sibbles' own compositions.
The Heptones left Studio One in 1971, a bitter parting for Sibbles in particular who had been employed at Brentford Road as a bassist, musical arranger and talent scout and, while Coxsone Dodd is reluctant to talk

Trevor Hartley

about the past, Sibbles has voiced many accusations. It was a sad end to an association that gave the world so much good music. This was by no means the end for the Heptones, however, and they went on to work for Joe Gibbs, Harry J, Augustus Pablo, Harry Mudie, Geoffrey Chung, Phill Pratt, Rupie Edwards and many more - a veritable litany of Who's Who in the Jamaican music world of the early 70s - and they made hit after hit. In 1973 they relocated briefly to Canada but returned to Jamaica and recorded what was their most commercially successful album ever, *Party Time* for the Upsetter - Lee Perry, which consisted mainly of re-cuts of their Studio One hits - songs this strong can take any amount of versioning. It looked, for a while, that the Heptones would follow Bob Marley And The Wailers into the realms of international stardom, but for whatever reasons - and it was certainly nothing to do with the power and strength of their music - it just did not happen. Leroy Sibbles left for a solo career, returning again to Canada where he has based himself, on and off, ever since, and he continues to tour and release records (which are always of interest) every once in a while. Barry Llewellyn and Earl Morgan recruited Naggo Morris and continued as the Heptones - solid and workmanlike but unfortunately failing to match the power and beauty of their earlier recordings.

Selected albums: *The Heptones* (Studio One c.60s), *On Top* (Studio One c.60s) *Black Is Black* (Studio One c.60s), *Ting A Ling* (Studio One c.60s), *Freedom Line* (Studio One c.70s), *Heptones & Friends* (Trojan 1973), *Party Time* (Island 1976), *Night Food* (Island 1976), *Better Days* (Third World 1979), *Good Life* (Greensleeves 1979), *Back On Top* (Vista Sounds 1983), *In A Dance Hall Style* (Vista Sound 1983), *Swing Low* (Burning Sounds 1985), *Changing Time* (Thunderbolt 1987), *On The Run* (Shanachie 1987), *Sing Good Vibes* (Clarendon 1988). Compilations: *Legends From Studio One* (Trenchtown 1985), *22 Golden Hits* (TTP 1986), *Big And Free* (Trenchtown 1989), *Original Heptones* (Trenchtown 1989), *Nightfood In A Party Time* (Trenchtown 1989), *On The Road Again* (Trenchtown 1990), *20 Golden Hits* (Sonic Sounds 1992).

Higgs, Joe

b. 3 June 1940, Kingston, Jamaica. In the late 50s Higgs joined Roy Wilson to form the duo Higgs And Wilson. In 1959 they recorded their first single, 'Mammy Oh', for politico Edward Seaga, and it became a massive hit. In the early 60s they worked for Coxsone Dodd, and had several further hits including 'How Can I Be Sure' and 'There's A Reward'. Higgs was sharing his time coaching a young group called the Wailers, and he subsequently introduced them to Dodd, who launched their career. In the mid-60s Higgs decided to pursue a solo career, and made further recordings for Dodd including 'Change Of Plans' and 'Neighbour Neighbour'. In the early 70s Higgs recorded for a variety of producers, and outstanding songs from this period include 'The Wave Of War' and 'The World Is Spinning Round' (1972) for Harry 'J' Johnson, 'Burning Fire' (1974) for Rupie Edwards, 'More Slavery' (1975) for Jack Ruby, and 'Creation' (1975), a self-production. In 1975, Higgs finally had an album released, the excellent *Life Of Contradiction*. The imaginatively arranged songs were given faultless jazz-tinged performances by a group that included jazz guitarist Eric Gale. Further albums followed with *Unity Is Power* (1979) and *Triumph* (1985), both of which are strong collections. Higgs' thoughtful lyrics and expressive voice have made him one of the most singular artists to come from Jamaica.

Albums: *Life Of Contradiction* (Grounation 1975), *Unity Is Power* (One Stop/Island 1979), *Triumph* (Alligator 1985), *Family* (Blue Mountain 1988), *Blackman Know Thyself* (Shanachie 1990).

High Note

(see Pottinger, Sonia)

Joe Higgs

Hinds, Justin

b. 7 May 1942, Steertown, St. Anns, Jamaica. Justin Hinds, together with backing vocalists the Dominoes (Dennis Sinclair and Junior Dixon) first recorded in late 1963 for producer Duke Reid. That first session brought forth an instant hit, 'Carry Go Bring Come', recorded in one take, and set a pattern from which Hinds rarely deviated; Hinds' expressive country/gospel tenor lead vocals with empathetic support from the two Dominoes, backed by the Treasure Isle studio band led by Tommy McCook and Herman Marquis. Hinds was Reid's most successful artist in the period 1964-66, reputedly recording 70 singles. He stayed with Reid until 1972; the relationship produced some of the finest Jamaican music, through ska, rocksteady and reggae. In the former style, 'King Samuel', 'Botheration', 'Jump Out Of The Frying Pan' (all 1964), 'The Ark', 'Peace And Love' and the bawdy 'Rub Up Push Up' (all 1965), are exemplary. The transition to the rocksteady format during 1966-67 brought forth hits like 'The Higher The Monkey Climbs', 'No Good Rudy', a new, rocksteady version of 'Carry Go Bring Come', 'On A Saturday Night', 'Once A Man', an anguished cover of the Rip Chords 'Here I Stand' and the sublime 'Save A Bread', both in 1968. Lyrically, Hinds is a master, utilising the rich Jamaican tradition of proverb and parable to reflect the wide range of issues thrown up by a society in transition from country to city. After Reid's death in 1975, Hinds made two albums with sound system owner and producer Jack Ruby. In 1978 he also recorded a handful of discs for producer Sonia Pottinger. Titles like 'What A Weeping', 'Rig-Ma'Roe Game' and 'Wipe Your Weeping Eyes' showed Hind's beautiful voice still expressively righteous. Since 1984, when he recorded the excellent album *Travel With Love* for Nighthawk Records of St. Louis, he has apparently preferred the rural lifestyle to the 'rat race' of Kingston.
Selected albums: *Best Of Justin Hinds & The Dominoes* (1968), *Jezebel* (Island 1976), *From Jamaica With Reggae* (High Note 1984), *Travel With Love* (Night Hawk 1985), *Justin Hinds* (Jwyanza 1990), *Early Recordings* (Esoldun/Treasure Isle 1992).

Holness, Winston 'Niney'

b. 1951, Montego Bay, Jamaica. Winston 'Niney' Holness, aka The Observer, is one of the great characters of reggae music. Called Niney when he lost a thumb in a workshop accident, he has been a singer, producer, engineer, DJ, fixer, arranger, manager and virtually everything else in reggae. Although Niney had organised bands to play at school dances in the 50s, it was not until he came under the tutelage of producer Bunny Lee in the late 60s that he achieved his entry into the professional music business. In 1967-68 he worked with Lee Perry for Joe Gibbs, taking over when Perry left in mid-1968 to start his own label. By 1970 he had set up his own operation, with his first production entitled 'Mr Brown'/'Everybody Bawling' by DJs Dennis Alcapone and Lizzy. It sold modestly, but his next record, 'Blood & Fire', released in December 1980, was an immediate smash, eventually selling 30,000 in Jamaica alone. The tune propelled Niney into the front rank of the new 'rebel' vanguard, establishing him as a producer fully capable of building original rhythms. The record bore a slight resemblance to Bob Marley's 'Duppy Conqueror' but far outsold it, and the pair clashed when Marley heard the record. Niney productions of the early 70s are characterised by their sparse simplicity and heaviness, often cultural/political in sentiment, and frequently espousing Rasta themes.
During 1973 he began an association with Dennis Brown, the results released initially by Joe Gibbs, but later that year records began appearing on Niney's 'Observer' label. Again Niney had changed the beat and Dennis Brown became the hottest singer of 1974. The local hits of the period included 'Westbound Train' (1973), 'Cassandra', 'I Am The Conqueror', and 'No More Will I

Justin Hinds

Roam' (all 1974). Brown's sessions with Niney constitute a high point in the development of reggae during the 70s. Niney also issued records by Gregory Isaacs, Michael Rose, Junior Delgado, Sang Hugh, Horace Andy, Delroy Wilson, Leroy Smart, Junior Byles and Cornell Campbell. He issued a dub album - *Dubbing With The Observer* - mixed by King Tubby's, and DJ music by such as U Roy, Big Youth, I Roy, Dillinger and Trinity. At the end of the 70s Niney vanished from view, only to turn up in Paris in 1982. During the mid-80s he worked at Kingston's Channel One studio in an unspecified capacity, and issued a few singles and an album. He was next spotted in New York, apparently retired, although no doubt his irrepressible good humour will enliven Jamaican music once again when he feels the urge, and he recently released his first new work in years, with recordings by Frankie Paul and Andrew Tosh (Peter Tosh's son).

Albums: *Dubbing With The Observer* (Attack 1975), *Live At The Turntable Club* (1975), *Sledgehammer Dub* (1976), *Blood & Fire 1971-1972* (Trojan 1988), *Bring The Couchie 1974-1976* (Trojan 1989), *Niney The Observer* (Charly 1990), *Turbo Charge* (Rounder 1991). Productions: Dennis Brown: *Just Dennis* (Trojan 1975). The Ethiopians: *Slave Call* (1977). Freddie McGregor: *Freddie* (1980).

Holt, John

b. 1947, Kingston, Jamaica. At the age of 12 Holt's voice was a regular feature of the talent contests run by Vere Johns at various Jamaican theatres, and by 1963 Holt had cut his first single, 'I Cried A Tear'/'Forever I'll Stay' for Leslie Kong's Beverley's label. Holt also recorded duets with Alton Ellis for Randy's, including 'Rum Bumper' (1964). Between 1965-70 he was lead singer with the Paragons, arguably the smoothest, most accomplished vocal trio in reggae, and heavily dependent on Holt's precise, creamy tenor. The group's work with producer Duke Reid was impeccable, and they enjoyed a string of hits: 'Ali Baba', 'Tonight' and 'I See Your Face' among them. Holt, sometimes with the Paragons, also worked with Studio One on sides such as 'Fancy Make-Up', 'A Love I Can Feel', 'Let's Build Our Dreams' and 'OK Fred' (later a chart smash for Errol Dunkley), as well as Prince Buster ('Oh Girl', 'My Heart Is Gone').

By the early 70s John Holt was one of reggae's biggest stars and ready to cross over into the pop market. His 'Stick By Me', one of dozens of songs he cut with producer Bunny Lee, was the biggest-selling Jamaican record of 1972. A year later his *Time Is The Master* set for producer Harry Mudie proved a masterpiece, and pointed the way ahead: fine songs (among them covers of Ivory Joe Hunter's 'It May Sound Silly' and Brook Benton's 'Looking Back'), heavy rhythms, and a sweetening of lush, orchestral arrangements laid in London. Trojan issued a series of Bunny Lee-produced best-selling John Holt LPs, including the *1000/5000/10,000 Volts* series, and brought him to London to work with Tony Ashfield, who again used string arrangements. December 1974 saw him score a huge pop hit across Europe with 'Help Me Make It Through The Night', but Holt was more than a balladeer, and by 1976 he was enjoying further Jamaican success with 'Up Park Camp', a massive roots hit for producer Joe Joe Hookim. A brief experiment with disco (*Holt Goes Disco*) was about the only blot on his copybook during the 70s, and he has continued to work in a contemporary style to the present day, occasionally scoring enormous roots reggae hits ('Police In Helicopter' in 1987) while still being willing to work in other styles, as demonstrated by the *Reggae, Hip House, R&B Flavor* album title he employed in 1993. He remains a unique talent, perhaps under-rated amongst more snobbish fans because of his flirtation with the pop world.

Albums: *A Love I Can Feel* (Studio One 1971), *Greatest Hits* (Studio One 1972), *Presenting The Fabulous John Holt* (Trojan 1973), *Holt* (Trojan 1973), *Still In Chains*

(Trojan 1973), *1000 Volts Of Holt* (Trojan 1973), *Time Is The Master* (Creole 1974), *Dusty Roads* (Trojan 1974), *Sings For I* (Trojan 1974), *Pledging My Love* (Trojan 1975), *Before The Next Teardrop Falls* (Klik 1976), *Up Park Camp* (Channel One 1977), *Holt Goes Disco* (Trojan 1977), *2,000 Volts Of Holt* (Trojan 1979), *Just The Two Of Us* (CSA 1982), *Sweetie Come Brush Me* (Volcano 1982), *Police In Helicopter* (Greensleeves 1983), *Further You Look* (Trojan 1983), *Let It Go On* (Trojan 1983), *For Lovers And Dancers* (Trojan 1984), *Live In London* (Very Good 1984), *3,000 Volts Of Holt* (Trojan 1986), *Reggae Christmas Album* (Trojan 1986), *OK Fred* (Spartan 1987), *Time Is The Master* (Creole 1988), *Rock With Me Baby* (Trojan 1988), *If I Were A Carpenter* (1989), *Why I Care* (Greensleeves 1989), *Reggae, Hip House, R&B Flavor* (1993), *Peacemaker* (1993). With Horace Andy: *From One Extreme To Another* (Beta 1986). Compilations: *Roots Of Holt* (Trojan 1983), *Greatest Hits* (Prince Buster 1984), *Pure Gold* (Vista Sounds 1985), *16 Songs For Soulful Lovers* (Platinum 1986), *Living Legend* (Classic 1986), *20 Golden Love Songs* (Trojan 1986), *Best Of* (Action Replay 1990), *Let Your Love Flow* (CSA 1988), *Love Songs Vol. 2* (Parish 1992).

Hookim, Joseph 'Joe Joe'

b. Jamaica. One of four brothers involved with music from an early age (the other brothers were Kenneth, Ernest and Paulie) Joe Joe and his brother, Ernest, started on the bottom rung of the entertainment industry ladder controlling juke boxes and one-armed bandits, but in 1970 the Jamaican government outlawed gaming machines. This gave the brothers a push up the ladder because they then decided to branch out and build their own recording studio - Channel One - in the heart of the Kingston ghetto on Maxfield Avenue. At first Joe Joe hired veteran Sid Bucknor as engineer because none of his family was particularly adept at the technical side of the business, but before long Ernest took over at the mixing desk

literally picking it up as he went along. By this time the Hookims also had their own pressing plant and label printing workshop - a truly independent family business. Channel One slowly established a name for itself with releases on a variety of different labels from established singers such as Leroy Smart, Junior Byles and Horace Andy, but it was when the Mighty Diamonds started work for them that everything came together and after the release of 'Right Time' in 1976 nothing ever seemed to go wrong for them. The Diamonds obviously had a lot to offer but what was exciting and different about their records was the 'rockers' rhythm dominated by 'militant' double drumming courtesy of Sly Dunbar of their in-house Revolutionaries band. The sound was to influence the entire Jamaican music business for the next two years with every producer on the island coming up with their own variaton of the beat.

The bestsellers never stopped coming from the Channel with the Diamonds along with DJs Dillinger and Trinity plus countless instrumental records from the Revolutionaries controlling the charts. Joe Joe said that he felt embarrassed sometimes to see up to nine out of the Top 10 records on his own Well Charge label! A lot of the rhythms were 'do-overs' of Studio One classics, which caused friction, and Joe Joe came in for criticism. He has, however, always been open about the fact that he has copied Coxsone Dodd's rhythms. Throughout the 70s and on into the mid-80s the Maxfield Avenue Studio was in constant demand by artists and producers all hoping to capture a bit of the magic and in 1979 the set up was updated to sixteen tracks to accommodate the demand. The Hookim brothers were the first to introduce 12-inch 45 rpm records to Jamaica with 'Truly' by the Jayes (a version of an old Marcia Griffiths Studio One hit) which was released with a DJ version by Ranking Trevor. The dynamic range of these 12-inch releases was a vast improvement on the 7-inch with far more bass and treble and the 12-inch 'Disco-

John Holt

Mix' went on to become an integral part of reggae music with vocal, DJ and instrumental cuts of the same rhythm all together on one release. Less successful were the 'Channel One Economic Packages' - 7-inch releases that played at $33^{1/3}$ rpm with vocal and DJ pieces of the same rhythm but, sadly, the sound quality left much to be desired and these were soon discontinued. Joe Joe founded a New York branch of Channel One and in the early 80s their future looked assured as he released a highly successful and much imitated series of 'Clash' albums from the USA - one different artist on each side. Even with hindsight it is difficult to see just what went wrong at Channel One, but the Kingston and New York operations were summarily shut down in the late 80s and the Hookim brothers are no longer active in the music business. Their insight and innovations are greatly missed.

Selected albums: Various: *Vital Dub* (Virgin 1976), *Jonkanoo Dub* (Cha Cha 1978), *General For All General - Dance Hall Style* (Hitbound 1984), *Hit Bound! Revolutionary Sound Of Channel One* (Heartbeat 1990). Mighty Diamonds: *Right Time* (Well Charge/Virgin 1976), *Stand Up To Your Judgement* (JJ/Hitbound 1978). Dillinger: *CB200* (Mango/Island 1976). The Wailing Souls: *The Best Of* (Empire). Revolutionaries: *Vital Dub, Strictly Rockers* (Well Charge/Virgin).

Hudson, Keith

b. 1946, Kingston, Jamaica, d. 14 November 1984, New York, USA. Hudson was only 14 years old when he produced his first recording, an instrumental featuring members of the Skatalites which eventually saw release with a blank label in 1968, and two years later was re-used for Dennis Alcapone's 'Shades Of Hudson'. After leaving school, he served an apprenticeship in dentistry, and subsidised his early recordings with money earned from these skills. In late 1967 he started his Inbidimts label with Ken Boothe's 'Old Fashioned Way', which subsequently became a number 1 in Jamaica. Over the next two years he released hits by Delroy Wilson ('Run Run') and John Holt ('Never Will I Hurt My Baby'), featuring himself as vocalist by 1970. Over the next two years, he had hits with U Roy's 'Dynamic Fashion Way', Alton Ellis' 'Big Bad Boy', Dennis Alcapone's 'The Sky's The Limits', Big Youth's 'S.90 Skank' and Soul Syndicate's 'Riot', and released a host of other singles on his Imbidimts, Mafia, Rebind and other labels. His willingness to experiment was evident on U Roy's 'Dynamic Fashion Way', and 'S.90 Skank', where he arranged for a motorcycle to be surreptitiously brought into Byron Lee's recording studio so that he could record it being revved-up. In 1974 he released *Flesh Of My Skin, Blood Of My Blood*, which still stands as a masterpiece. Sandwiched between two atmospheric instrumentals were a series of uplifting laments set to bare, understated rhythms, which sounded like nothing that had preceded them, and like nothing that has followed them, and forcefully convey not only a feeling of pain and oppression, but also an iron resolve to endure and defeat those obstacles. 1975 saw two further stunning releases: *Torch of Freedom* and *Pick A Dub*. In 1976 he moved to New York and signed a four year contract with Virgin Records, who had followed Islands' lead in signing reggae acts in response to increased interest in the music, primarily from a new, predominantly white audience. There he would put the Joint label into operation. In 1977 a dub album, *Brand* (aka *The Joint*) was issued, followed the next year by its companion vocal set, *Rasta Communication*. In early 1984 rumours circulated that Keith was recording with the Wailers in New York, but nothing was ever released. In August he was diagnosed as having lung cancer. He received radiation therapy, and appeared to be responding well to the treatment, but on the morning of 14th November he complained of stomach pains, collapsed and died.

Albums: *Furnace* (Imbidimts 1972), *Entering The Dragon* (1973), *Flesh Of My Skin, Blood*

Keith Hudson

Of My Blood (Mamba 1974), *Torch Of Freedom* (Atra 1975), *Too Expensive* (Virgin 1976), *Rasta Communication* (Joint 1978), *From One Extreme To Another* (1979), *Playing It Cool* (1981), *Steaming Jungle* (1982). Dub Albums: *Pick A Dub* (1975), *Brand/The Joint* (Joint 1977), *Nuh Skin Up Dub* (1979). Productions: Militant Barry: *Green Valley* (1979). Compilations: *The Big J Of Reggae* (1978, covers 1970-75), *Studio Kinda Cloudy* (Trojan 1988, covers 1967-72).

I

I Roy

b. Roy Reid, c.1949, Spanish Town, Jamaica. With a voice like your favourite uncle telling you a slightly risque story, I Roy, aka Roy Reid, aka the Godfather, aka Roy Senior, is one of the great originals of Jamaican music. Always the most intellectual of his peers, he arrived right at the start of the 70s as an accomplished DJ with a neat line in storytelling and the ability to ride a rhythm as if it was first recorded for him and not simply 'borrowed' by him from a singer or group. He drew his name from U Roy, the first truly popular reggae toaster, and his first records were slightly derivative of the elder man's style, and also owed a little to another DJ pioneer, Dennis Alcapone. However, I Roy soon hit his stride and cut a mighty series of singles for producer Gussie Clarke, including 'Black Man Time', 'Tripe Girl' and 'Magnificent Seven'. 'Brother Toby Is A Movie From London' emerged for Glen Brown; 'Dr Who' for Lee Perry and innumerable sides for Bunny Lee. His debut album *Presenting* was magnificent, collating most of his hits for Gussie Clarke. It remains a classic of its genre today. Further albums *Hell And Sorrow* and *Many Moods Of* were nearly as strong. In 1975 he became involved in an on-record slanging match with fellow DJ Prince Jazzbo, a bizarre name-calling affair that nonetheless presented the public with a new twist to such rivalries and helped maintain sales. In 1976 a liaison with producer Prince Tony Robinson brought I Roy a deal with Virgin Records and Roy's albums graced the label five times: *General, Musical Shark Attack, World On Fire, Crisis Time* and the excellent 1977 set *Heart Of A Lion*. By the early 80s I Roy had burnt out his lyrical store and was overtaken by younger, madder DJs. However, he is still to be found on the periphery of reggae today,

sometimes, ironically, on Ujama, the label owned by his old rival, Prince Jazzbo.
Albums: *Presenting* (Gussie/Trojan 1973), *Hell & Sorrow* (Trojan 1974), *Many Moods Of* (Trojan 1974), *Truths & Rights* (Grounation 1975), *Can't Conquer Rasta* (Justice 1976), *Crisis Time* (Caroline/Virgin 1976), *Dread Baldhead* (Klik 1976), *Ten Commandments* (Micron 1977), *Heart Of A Lion* (Front Line 1977), *Musical Shark Attack* (Front Line 1977), *The Best Of* (GG's 1977), *The Godfather* (Third World 1977), *World On Fire* (Front Line 1978), *The General* (Front Line 1977), *African Herbsman* (Joe Gibbs 1979), *Hotter Yatta* (Harry J 1980), *I Roy's Doctor Fish* (Imperial 1981), *Outer Limits* (Intense/Hawkeye 1983), *The Lyrics Man* (Witty 1990), *Straight To The Heart* (1990). With Prince Jazzbo: *Step Forward Youth* (Live & Love 1975). With Jah Woosh: *We Chat You Rock* (Trojan 1987). With Prince Jazzbo: *Head To Head Clash* (1990). Compilations: *Crucial Cuts* (Virgin 1983), *Classic I Roy* (Mr. Tipsy 1986).

I Threes

The I Threes were formed, at the instigation of Bob Marley, on the departure of Peter Tosh and Bunny Wailer. Having lost his two main backing vocalists he recruited Marcia Griffiths, Judy Mowatt and Rita Marley to fill out the Wailers' sound. The trio's harmonies added substantially to many of Marley's most successful records, and they also added visual depth to live concerts, with dance steps choreographed by Mowatt. All three had recorded solo previously, and returned to those careers following the death of their band leader. They have not recorded as a trio outside of the Wailers' legacy, aside from the 'Music For The World' 12-inch, credited to Marley, Mowatt and Griffith, in 1983, although there have been several reunion concerts.

Icho Candy

b. Winston Evans, Jamaica. Perhaps the first the world heard of roots enigma Icho Candy was his anonymous appearance on Channel

Gregory Isaacs

4's Deep Roots programme in 1982, where he was seen twisting his tortured Horace Andy-styled tonsils around 'Where Do The Children Play' in company with DJ Bobby Culture, singing live on the late Jack Ruby's sound system. His earliest vinyl outing 'Little Children No Cry' was for Ruby, followed by 'Bandulu' for Joe Gibbs, finally achieving some prominence with titles such as 'Captain Selassie I', on the Jwyanza label and 'Mr User' and 'Bloodsuckers' for Prince Jazzbo's Ujama label, thus creating a small cult following for himself in the UK. Never the most prolific of singers, he embarked on, what was for him, a burst of recording activity during the latter part of the decade with singles like 'In Texas Town' (1987) a bizarre cowboy variation on the cajun standard 'Jambalaya', and the apocalyptic roots anthem 'Babylon' (1987) for Augustus Pablo's Rockers label, 'Cool Down Sufferer' (1989) for Tesfa McDonald, and 'Jah Calling All Over The World' (1990) for Cashima Steel's Creation label, for whom he also recorded a (so far) unreleased album. He also provided an albums worth of material for Finnish producer Tero Kaski, of which only one track, 'Resign Babylon' (1994), has so far emerged. Another period of obscurity was broken in 1993 by the release of *Glory To The King*, issued on Jah Shaka's King Of The Zulu Tribe imprint.

Album: *Glory To The King* (King Of The Zulu Tribe 1993).

Inner Circle

Inner Circle first emerged in the early 70s, comprising brothers Ian and Roger Lewis (guitars) and three future members of Third World, Stephen 'Cat' Coore, Ritchie Daley and Michael 'Ibo' Cooper. As Third World reassembled, the Lewis brothers recruited drummer Calvin McKenzie, keyboard players Charles Farquharson and Bernard 'Touter' Harvey. Together they won the prestigious 'Best Band Contest' on the 'Johnny Golding Show'. Though they would enjoy moderately successful album sales and a hit 45, 'I See You', it wasn't until the brothers brought in singer Jacob 'Killer' Miller that they became a viable commercial proposition. Miller, a child prodigy, who had created a series of classic roots records ('Tenement Yard', 'Forward Jah Jah Children') before joining Inner Circle, was somewhat rotund, and the Lewis brothers were hardly skinny either: the trio made a formidable, imposing combination. Early albums showed the band fusing dancefloor rhythms and reggae to reasonable success. However, in 1976 they signed to Capitol Records releasing two albums for the label, *Reggae Thing* and *Ready For The World*, rising rapidly up the reggae hierarchy in the process. At one point Miller was more popular in Jamaica than Bob Marley, the band playing the now-legendary Peace Concert in 1978 above him on the bill.

Everything Is Great, their first album for Island gave the band an overdue international hit with its title song, and its disco rhythms made it a huge seller in Europe. 'Stop Breaking My Heart' was also a hit 45, and *New Age Music* consolidated their position. However, disaster struck in 1980 when Jacob Miller was killed in a car crash. The remainder of Inner Circle quit, with the Lewis brothers and Harvey eventually opening a studio in Miami. In 1987 the band got itchy feet, and cut an album for RAS, *One Way*, with new singer Carlton Coffey. US dates were critically acclaimed, and the band, with the addition of Lance Hall (drums) and Lester Adderley (guitar), signed to WEA/Metronome. *Identified*, their first LP for the label, brought the band to wider recognition with 'Bad Boys', which was employed as the theme to US television series *Cops*. 1993 saw their long-overdue return to pop success with 'Sweat (A La La La La Long)', a catchy, upbeat single from the *Bad To the Bone* album. Bright, unsentimental, and thoroughly professional, Inner Circle deserve their long overdue success.

Selected albums: *Dread Reggae Hits* (Top Ranking 1973), *Heavy Reggae* (Top Ranking 1974), *Blame It On The Sun* (Trojan 1975),

Rock The Boat (Trojan 1975), *Reggae Thing* (Capitol 1976), *Ready For The World* (Capitol 1977), *Everything Is Great* (Island 1978), *New Age Music* (Island 1979), *One Way* (RAS 1987), *Identified* (WEA 1989), *Bad To The Bone* (RAS 1993). Compilation: *Reggae Greats* (Island 1985).

Isaacs, Gregory

b. 1951, Kingston, Jamaica. Reggae superstar Gregory Isaacs has seldom looked back during a three decade career which has gone from strength to strength, and while many rock stars like to play with an 'outlaw' image, Gregory is the real thing - the ultimate rude boy reggae star - who shows no signs of letting up in the 90s. Like so many other others before him he began by doing the rounds of Kingston's producers and entering various talent competitions, before scoring with Rupie Edwards' Success Records in the early 70s. He set up his own African Museum shop and label in 1973 with Errol Dunkley in order to gain artistic and financial control of his own destiny. He continued to record for many other producers during the rest of the decade to finance his own label, notably Winston 'Niney' Holness, Gussie Clarke, Lloyd F. Campbell, Glen Brown, Alvin Ranglin and Phil Pratt.

His early recordings were romantic ballads crooned in the inimitable Isaacs style, cool, leisurely, and always sounding vulnerable or pained by his adventures in love. But these translated effortlessly into social protest or 'reality' songs as the decade progressed and the pre-occupations of reggae music shifted towards songs with a more cultural emphasis. By 1980 Gregory was the number one star in the reggae world, touring the UK and the USA extensively, and his live appearances resulted in frenzied crowd scenes, with audiences eating out of the palm of his hand. He had by now signed with Virgin Records' Front Line label and was gaining a considerable name for himself outside of the confines of the traditional reggae music audience and, even though he had recorded

many classic sides for outside producers, he still managed to put out his best 45s on African Museum (and subsequently Front Line). His pre-eminence during this period was confirmed in the mantle of 'Cool Ruler', chosen for him by critics and fans after the title of the album.

A new contract with Charisma's Pre label set up the UK release of two further classic albums, though he was never less that prodigious even by Jamaican standards. He was, however, beset by personal and legal problems in the mid-80s and was even jailed in Kingston's notorious General Penitentiary. His release was celebrated with *Out Deh*. His spell inside left him short of ready money and he proceeded to record for anyone and everyone who was prepared to pay him the necessary cash to get back on his feet. Because of his name he was inundated with offers of work and the market was soon flooded with Gregory Isaacs' releases on any amount of different labels. Incredibly his standards did not drop, and he generally stuck to original material which was still head and shoulders above the competition. Most weeks in the latter half of the decade would see the release of yet more Gregory material, voiced with current hot producers such as Jammys, Red Man, Bobby Digital and Steely And Clevie among others; by so doing he took on the youth of Jamaica at their own game and won.

Rumours abound about Gregory's 'rude boy' lifestyle - but he would claim he has to be tough to maintain his position within Kingston's notorious musical industry. Certainly the reasons for his lofty seat in the reggae hierarchy are purely musical; a combination of his boundless talent and his uncompromising attitude. Alone - out of all reggae's star performers - Gregory has actually improved over the years and to look forward to more quality releases from him is not mere wishful thinking, but a justifiable expectancy cultivated by his high standards. It is very difficult to see how anyone will now be able to take away his crown - his legendary status and reputation in the reggae

Israel Vibration

business are truly second to none.

Selected albums: *In Person* (Trojan 1975), *All I Have Is Love* (Trojan 1976), *Extra Classic* (Conflict 1977, Shanachie 1981), *Mr Isaacs* (Earthquake 1977), *Slum Dub* (Burning Sounds 1978), *Best Of Vol. 1 & 2* (GG's 1976, 1981: not compilations), *Cool Ruler* (Front Line 1978), *Soon Forward* (Front Line 1979), *Showcase* (Taxi 1980), *The Lonely Lover* (Pre 1980), *For Everyone* (Success 1980), *More Gregory* (Pre 1981), *Night Nurse* (Mango/Island 1982), *The Sensational Gregory Isaacs* (Vista 1982), *Mr. Isaacs* (Shanachie 1982), *Out Deh!* (Mango/Island 1983), *Reggae Greats (Live)* (Mango/Island 1984), *Live At The Academy Brixton* (Rough Trade 1984), *Private Beach Party* (RAS 1985), *Easy* (Tad's 1985), *All I Have Is Love, Love Love* (Tad's 1986), *Victim* (C&E 1987), *Watchman Of The City* (Rohit 1988), *Sly And Robbie Presents Gregory Isaacs* (RAS 1988), *Talk Don't Bother Me* (Skengdon 1988), *Come Along* (Live & Love 1988), *Encore* (Kingdom 1988), *Red Rose For Gregory* (Greensleeves 1988), *I.O.U.* (RAS 1989), *Call Me Collect* (RAS 1990), *Dancing Floor* (Heartbeat 1990), *Come Again Dub* (ROIR 1991), *Can't Stay Away* (1992), *Pardon Me* (1992), *No Luck* (1993), *Absent* (Greensleeves 1993). With Ronnie Davis: *Gregory Isaacs Meets Ronnie Davis* (Plant 1970). With Dennis Brown: *Two Bad Superstars Meet* (Burning Sounds 1984), *Judge Not* (Greensleeves 1984), *No Contest* (Music Works 1989). With Jah Mel: *Double Explosive* (Andys 1984). With Sugar Minott: *Double Dose* (Blue Mountain 1987). Compilations: *The Early Years* (Trojan 1981), *Lover's Rock* (Pre 1982, double album comprising *The Lonely Lover* and *More Gregory*), *Crucial Cuts* (Virgin 1983), *My Number One* (Heartbeat 1990), *Love Is Overdue* (Network 1991).

Israel Vibration

Comprising Cecil 'Skeleton' Spence, Albert 'Apple' Craig and Lascelles 'Wiss' Bulgrin, this vocal group was formed while the members, all crippled in infancy during the polio epidemic that swept the island in the 50s, were inmates at Kingston's Mona Rehabilitation Centre. Resident since childhood, they were expelled after they began to grow dreadlocks in accordance with their Rastafarian beliefs. For six years they lived rough, literally singing for their supper. Their attempts to survive on handouts from the institution they had lived in for most of their lives were met with indifference, hostility, and sometimes brutality. Their first release, 'Why Worry' (1976), financed by the Twelve Tribes organisation to whom they had become affiliated, and recorded at Treasure Isle Studio, was a big success, as were their live shows supporting Dennis Brown and Bob Marley among others. In 1978 they teamed up with the Inner Circle's Lewis Brothers; Ian and Roger aka the Fatman Riddim Section, to record their debut, *The Same Song,* for Tommy Cowan's Top Ranking label. It swiftly became hailed as an instant roots classic, as did its dub companion *Israel Tafari. Same Song* and its follow-up *Unconquered People* (1980) appeared through a licensing deal with Harvest Records in the UK, as did the 12-inch 'Crisis' which featured a melodica version by Augustus Pablo. The group's unique brand of gentle rural sounding harmonies and sincere Rasta lyrics have sustained them for a number of albums - mostly released through RAS Records in the US - over the years, especially in the international market, where they continue to flourish.

Albums: *The Same Song* (Top Ranking 1978), *Same Song Dub* (Top Ranking 1978), *Israel Tafari* (Top Ranking 1978), *Unconquered People* (Israel Vibes/Greensleeves 1980), *Strength Of My Life* (RAS 1988), *Praises* (RAS 1990), *Forever* (RAS 1991), *Israel Dub* (Greensleeves 1992), *Why You So Craven* (RAS 1992). Compilation: *Best Of* (Sonic Sounds 1988).

J

Jah Shaka

An enigmatic and highly individual personality on the UK sound system scene, Jah Shaka (his real name remains a mystery) came to the UK from Jamaica with his parents at the age of eight, settling in south east London. Succumbing to a passion for music, he began his career a few years later in the late 60s, playing in a band and travelling around in an obscure local sound system named Freddie Cloudburst. Inspired spiritually by his interest in Rastafari, and consciously by the American Civil Rights movement (particularly such exponents of black awareness as Angela Davis and George Jackson), he began to assemble equipment for his own sound, to be named after the great 18th Century Zulu King Shaka, the 'Black Napoleon'. From quite modest beginnings in the early 70s, Shaka's sound became, by the end of the decade, one of the top three in the country, alongside such luminaries as Lloyd Coxsone and the Mighty Fatman, specialising in heavyweight, dubwise steppers material, and exclusive cuts on dub plate. But whereas these and other sounds usually supported a team of selectors and DJs, Shaka performed all these functions alone, assistance in setting up the sound coming from a team of devoted youths for whom Shaka's music was almost a way of life.

His dances became famous for their spiritually charged atmosphere and the acrobatic, stylised dancing of the participants. Shaka would operate his sound like a single instrument, the music played at ear-splitting distortion levels, the air rent by his trademark sirens and syndrums, the man himself caught up in the spirit, alternatively chanting, singing and dancing as furiously as many of those in the crowd. In 1980 Shaka inaugurated his Jah Shaka King Of The Zulu

Tribe label with the release of 'Jah Children Cry' by African Princess, which sold well in the reggae market. This was followed by the first instalment in his long-running *Commandments Of Dub* series. Over the years the label has carried well over 50 releases by UK based artists like Junior Brown, Sgt Pepper, Vivian Jones, Sis Nya and the Twinkle Brothers, as well as dozens of releases by Shaka himself, and Jamaican artists such as Horace Andy, Icho Candy and Max Romeo. With the decline of interest in Rastafarianism in the 80s, Shaka's dances became more and more isolated affairs, the crowd thinning to a hardcore of older followers. However, Shaka's adherence to Rasta, and the particular type of heavy, spiritual reggae with which his name has become synonymous, remained unswerving. By the latter part of the decade a new, young, multi-racial crowd of disaffected roots fans had begun to appear. Out of this crowd emerged a number of artists and sound systems who largely shunned contemporary reggae in favour of the revived sounds of the 70s and early 80s that Shaka still specialised in. Though seen by some observers as anachronistic and irrelevant, this 'new dub school', inspired almost to a man by Shaka, has nevertheless gained much support over the last few years, nurturing and sustaining its own network of musicians, record labels, studios, sound systems, clubs and radio shows.

Selected albums: *Commandments Of Dub Chapters 1-10* (Jah Shaka 1980-1991), *Revelation Songs* (Jah Shaka 1983), *Kings Music* (Jah Shaka 1984), *Message From Africa* (Jah Shaka 1985), *The Music Message* (Jah Shaka 1988), *My Prayer* (Jah Shaka 1990).

Jet Star

(see Pama Records)

Johnson, Harry 'J'

Harry Johnson started his career in the music business playing in a band whilst still at school. Success failed to materialise however, and he made a living as an insurance

Jah Shaka

salesman until the music bug bit him again in 1968. This time he went into record production, and it paid off. One of his earliest productions, 'No More Heartaches', by the Beltones, was a huge local smash. Other hits from this period included Lloyd Robinson's 'Cuss Cuss', whose rhythm remains one of the most versioned ever, then, in 1969, he released 'Liquidator' by the Harry J All Stars, which became a crossover and international hit, reaching number 9 in the UK charts in November 1969. Further international success came his way with Bob & Marcia's 'Young Gifted & Black', one of the first reggae records to use strings, dubbed on in the UK, where the record reached number 5 in March 1970.

In 1972 Harry sold his record shop and invested the money, and what he had earned from his UK hits, into his sixteen-track studio at 10 Roosevelt Avenue. Later he installed former Studio One engineer Sylvan Morris at the controls in place of Sid Bucknor, who moved to England, to ensure that Harry J's became one of the most popular studios for recording live on the island, utilised by such as Burning Spear, Augustus Pablo, and, prior to the advent of Tuff Gong, Bob Marley. Harry's own productions continued to do well, including 'Pied Piper' by Marcia Griffiths which reached number 11 in the UK pop charts in July 1971, 'Breakfast In Bed' by Lorna Bennett, and its DJ version, 'Skank In Bed', by Scotty. Island released an album with the Heptones entitled *Night Food* (1976), from which a number of popular singles such as 'Book Of Rules' and 'Mama Say' were plucked. In the late 70s Harry moved down a gear and produced mainly DJ records for the local market. His studio remained popular though, and in 1981 he was tempted back into the production seat to score another international hit with Sheila Hylton's 'The Bed's Too Big Without You', which reached number 35 in February of that year.

Selected albums: Heptones: *Night Food* (Island 1976). Harry J All Stars: *Liquidator*.

Johnson, Linton Kwesi

b. 1952, Chapelton, Jamaica. Johnson's family emigrated to London in 1963, and he quickly developed a keen awareness of both literature and politics, culminating in a degree in sociology at Goldsmith's College, London, in 1973. An interest in poetry manifested itself in two books, *Voices Of The Living And The Dead* (1974) and *Dread Beat And Blood* (1975), both written in a style that put on paper the patois spoken in black Britain, often with a rhythm reminiscent of Jamaican DJs. Johnson also wrote about reggae for *New Musical Express*, *Melody Maker* and *Black Music*, as well as being writer-in-residence for the London Borough of Lambeth and heavily involved in the *Race Today* co-operative newspaper. Experiments with reggae bands at his poetry readings culminated in 1977's *Dread Beat An' Blood* recorded as Poet And The Roots, an album that virtually defined the 'dub poetry' genre. An intoxicating mixture of Johnson's lucid, plain-spoken commonsense and rhetoric, and Dennis Bovell's intriguing dub rhythms, it sold well. In 1978 Johnson changed labels from Virgin to Island and issued the strong *Forces Of Victory*, this time under his own name. Johnson became a media face, introducing radio histories of reggae and cropping up on television arts shows, but to his credit he did not exploit his position, preferring instead to remain politically active at grass roots level in Brixton, London. *Bass Culture* was a more ambitious project that met a mixed reception, with tracks including the love-chat 'Lorraine' and the title song offering a far broader sweep of subjects than his previous work. *LKJ In Dub* contained Dennis Bovell dub mixes of tracks from his two Island albums. In the same year *Inglan Is A Bitch*, his third book, was published and he also opened a record label, LKJ, which introduced Jamaican poet Michael Smith to a UK audience. In the early 80s Johnson seemed to tire of the 'dub poet' tag and became far less active in the music business. In 1986 he issued *In Concert With The Dub Band*, a double live set which consisted

Judge Dread

chiefly of older material. He finally returned to the studio in 1990 to record *Tings An' Times* for his own label, a more reflective, slightly-less brash set. While Johnson has undoubtedly added a notch to reggae's canon in providing a solid focus for the dub poetry movement, offering an alternative stance to that of straightforward reggae DJs, he appears to view his musical involvement as secondary to his political and social activities, and is not therefore the 'name' in the media he might have been. However, no other artist would have tackled subjects like 'Black Petty Booshwah' (petit-bourgeois) or 'Inglan' (England) Is A Bitch', and for that, his place in reggae history is assured.

Albums: *Dread Beat An' Blood* (Front Line 1978, as Poet & The Roots), *Forces Of Victory* (Island 1979), *Bass Culture* (Island 1980), *LKJ In Dub* (Island 1980), *Making History* (Island 1984), *Linton Kwesi Johnson Live* (Rough Trade 1985), *In Concert With The Dub Band* (LKJ 1988), *Tings And Times* (LKJ 1990), *LKJ In Dub Vol. 2* (1992). Compilation: *Reggae Greats* (Island 1985).

Judge Dread

Real name Alex Hughes, Kent-born Judge Dread was a bouncer in London clubs at the end of the 60s and became familiar with reggae through his work, where he had run into (not literally) the likes of Derrick Morgan and Prince Buster. In 1969 Buster had a huge underground hit with the obscene 'Big 5', a version of Brook Benton's 'Rainy Night In Georgia'. It was clear there was a yawning gap waiting to be filled when Buster failed to effectively follow his hit, so Alex Hughes, aka Judge Dread (a name borrowed from a Prince Buster character) plunged in. His first single, 'Big Six' went to number 11 in 1972, and spent more than half the year in the charts. No-one heard it on air: it was a filthy nursery rhyme. 'Big Seven' did better than 'Big Six', and from this point on Dread scored hits with 'Big Eight', a ridiculous version of 'Je T'Aime', and a string of other novelty reggae records, often co-penned by his friend, Fred Lemon.

Incidentally, 'Big Six' was also a hit in Jamaica. Five years and eleven hits later (including such musical delicacies as 'Y Viva Suspenders' and 'Up With The Cock'), the good-natured Hughes, one of just two acts to successfully combine music hall with reggae (the other was Count Prince Miller, whose 'Mule Train' rivalled Dread for sheer chutzpah) had finally ground to a halt in chart terms. He can still be found occasionally working the clubs, and has also sought employment as a local newspaper columnist in Snodland, Kent.

Selected albums: *Bedtime Stories* (Creole 1975), *Last Of The Skinheads* (Cactus 1976), *Rub-A-Dub* (Creole 1981), *Dreadmania* (Trojan 1981), *Working Class 'Ero* (Trojan 1981), *40 Big Ones* (Creole 1983), *Not Guilty* (Creole 1984). Compilations: *The Best Worst Of Judge Dread* (Creole 1978), *The Very Worst Of Judge Dread* (Creole 1991).

K

Kay, Janet

b. Janet Kay Bogle, January 17, 1958, London, England. Kay attended Brondesbury High School, Wembley, and later took up secretarial studies, skills which she has returned to at various junctures in her recording career. Her first recordings came under the aegis of Alton Ellis in 1977. This had been brought about by a chance meeting with members of Aswad that summer, who recommended her to the reggae stalwart. The first results of the collaboration, 'Loving You', topped the reggae charts. In many ways she was the prototype lovers rock singer, with her spirited vocals floating over some of the genre's most inspired bass lines. 'That's What Friends Are For' and 'I Do Love You' followed. However, her breakthrough arrived with 'Silly Games', produced by Dennis Bovell for the Arawak imprint. It became a huge crossover hit, going all the way to number 2 in 1979. Kay has returned to recording intermittently, predominantly in the lovers rock style, and has also acted extensively as part of the Black Theatre Co-operative, appearing several times in straight acting roles on television. Her work has never lost its popularity with the reggae audience, despite her low profile for much of the 80s and 90s, and she has the talent and personality to make it big on her own terms - it can only be a matter of time before the kind of success she so obviously deserves is finally hers.

Selected albums: *Capricorn Woman* (Solid Groove 1979), *Silly Games* (Arawak 1980), *Loving You* (Burning Sounds 1988), *Sweet Surrender* (Body Music 1989). With Dennis Brown: *So Amazing* (Body Work 1987). With Dennis Bovell: *Dub Dem Silly* (Arawak 1994).

Keith And Tex

Texas Dixon and Keith Rowe first auditioned for Derrick Harriott in the late 60s, and the producer was so enamoured with their voices that he immediately took them under his wing and into his studio. Backed by musicians of the calibre of Lynn Tait and Hux Brown, they recorded two of reggae's most enduring and versioned staples, 'Tonight' and 'Stop That Train'. However, they faded into obscurity soon after these releases, though 'Hypnotizing Eyes' and a cover of the Temptations' 'Don't Look Back' prolonged their career. Rowe went on to release 'Groovy Situation' for Lee Perry, but afterwards emigrated to the US and joined the army, while Dixon relocated to Canada. The duo might well have languished in obscurity had it not been for rapper Vanilla Ice's version of 'Stop That Train'. In its wake Crystal Records put together an admirable retrospective package of early recordings, which, rather than bursting the bubble, confirmed their legendary status.

Selected compilation: *Stop That Train* (Crystal 1992).

Kelly, Pat

b. 1949, Kingston, Jamaica. Kelly spent a year in Springfield, Massachusetts, USA, during 1966 studying electronics, before returning to Jamaica. In 1967 he replaced Keith 'Slim' Smith as lead singer of the Techniques, who along with Alton Ellis, the Paragons and the Melodians were spearheading Duke Reid's campaign to dominate Jamaican music via his epochal rocksteady productions. With Kelly's wholly distinctive and utterly beautiful falsetto soaring over the impeccable harmonies of Winston Riley and Bruce Ruffin, the trio easily maintained the flow of hits they had begun when Smith had been lead singer. Their first record, an adaptation of a Curtis Mayfield tune, 'You'll Want Me Back', but re-titled, 'You Don't Care' in Jamaica, held the number 1 position in the local chart for six weeks. Their next, another Mayfield

Janet Kay

cover, this time adapted from the Impressions 'Minstrel And Queen' and retitled 'Queen Majesty', enjoyed similar hit status, as did the subsequent 'My Girl' and 'Love Is Not A Gamble'. All are *bona fide* classics of Jamaican vocal harmony, rocksteady style. In 1968 Kelly went solo, joining the roster of artists under the wing of the leading producer Bunny Lee. His first effort for Lee was another Curtis Mayfield cover version, 'Little Boy Blue'. Subsequently he provided Lee with the biggest-selling Jamaican hit of 1969, 'How Long Will It Take', a landmark recording in that it was the first Jamaican record to feature a string arrangement, overdubbed when the song was released in the UK by the Palmer brothers on their Unity label. Other hits and an album for Lee soon followed, and Kelly's superb, Sam Cooke-derived falsetto even came to the attention of the Beatles' Apple label, who reputedly offered Kelly a £25,000 contract. Unable to act on this offer because of prior contractual commitments, he returned to Jamaica disillusioned, where he recorded sporadically, enjoying a huge local hit for producer Phill Pratt in 1972, 'Talk About Love', as well as recording songs at Treasure Isle studios in the same period with former Gaylad, B.B. Seaton. He then returned to engineering, principally for the Channel One studios owned by the Hookim brothers. Throughout the late 70s and early 80s he continued recording, for Winston Riley, Phill Pratt, Bunny Lee and the London-based sound system owner Fatman. He still records occasionally, his latest album being issued in 1989, and his contribution as one of the great Jamaican soul voices cannot be underestimated.

Albums: *Pat Kelly Sings* (Pama 1969), *Talk About Love* (Terminal 1975), *Lonely Man* (Burning Sounds 1978), *One Man Stand* (Third World 1979), *From Both Sides* (Ital 1980), *I Wish It Would Rain* (Joe Gibbs 1980), *Pat Kelly And Friends* (Chanan-Jah 1984), *One In A Million* (Sky Note 1984), *Ordinary Man* (Body Music 1987), *Cry For You No More* (Blue Moon 1988).

Compilation: *The Best Of Pat Kelly* (Vista Sounds 1983).

King Jammys

b. Lloyd James, Kingston, Jamaica. Jammy, the undisputed king of computerized, digital reggae music for the 80s, was interested in little else but the sound system business from a very early age. He began by building amplifiers and repairing electrical equipment from his mother's house in the Waterhouse area of downtown Kingston and was soon playing out with his own sound system. His prowess earned him a deserved local reputation and as Prince Jammy he built equipment for many Waterhouse sounds - he was even acknowledged by the legendary King Tubby, another Waterhouse resident, with whom Jammy often worked. In the early 70s Jammy left Jamaica to work in Canada where his reputation had gone before him and he was soon working in live stage shows, employed in various studio activities and sound system work. He stayed for a few years but returned to Kingston and set up his first studio (with extremely limited facilities) at his in-laws' home in Waterhouse. At the same time Tubby's number one engineer, Phillip Smart, left for New York and Jammy joined Tubby's team. It was during his time with Tubby that Jammy got to know the people in the business who really mattered and how the reggae business actually worked - he acknowledges Bunny Lee and Vivian 'Yabby You' Jackson as particular influences. Jammy was continually expanding his own studio and sound system and in the late 70s he began to release his own productions including the debut Black Uhuru album, coming into contact with many rising dancehall artists such as Half Pint, Junior Reid and Echo Minott. His constant involvement with the grass roots side of the business meant that Jammy always knew what was happening and, more importantly, possessed a sense of what was *going* to happen. In 1985 he recorded a youth singer called Wayne Smith with a tune called

'Under Me Sleng Teng' which was to irrevocably alter the nature and totally revolutionize the sound of reggae music. The basis for 'Sleng Teng' was a Casio 'Music Box' and one of the 'rock' rhythms from the box was adapted and slowed down to become a 'reggae' rhythm. The shock waves were scarcely believable and before long there were over two hundred different versions of the rhythm available as every producer and artist jumped aboard the bandwagon. More than anything else it opened the music right up for young independent producers and artists because expensive studio time and 'real' musicians were no longer a prerequisite for recording. Digital reggae ruled. Jammy, the originator, rode the crest of the wave and his records and sound system dominated and controlled reggae music for the remainder of the decade and on into the 90s.

Bobby 'Digital' Dixon, now an established producer in his own right, was brought into Jammy's camp and he soon became right hand man in the set-up with Steely & Clevie providing the rhythms. Both were established musicians with a real feeling for the new sound and a bewildering array of 7-inch and 12-inch singles and albums were released every month. Most were massive Jamaican hits and with the help of long-time associate, Count Shelly, the records were released simultaneously in New York and London while Jammy took care of business in Jamaica. Countless artists made their debut on the Jammys label, but veteran singers and vocal groups were all keen to play their part in the new sound. There was no one to touch him and in 1987 Jammys won the coveted Rockers Award for best producer. Jammy's 90s output is not so prolific (by his standards) but he still continues to lead while others follow. It is impossible to overstate his contribution to Jamaican music because as the top producer throughout the digital era he has altered the sound of reggae music without ever losing touch with its foundation – the sound system.

Selected albums: Various: *Superstar Hit Parade Vols 1 - 7* (Greensleeves 1984-1992), *Ten To One* (Jammys 1985), *Superstar Hit Parade Vol. 2* (Jammys 1986), *Sleng Ten Extravaganza Vols 1 & 2* (Jammys 1986), *Superstar Hit Parade Vol. 3* (Jammys 1987), *A Man And His Music Vols 1, 2 & 3* (RAS 1991). Lieutenant Stitchie: *Great Ambition* (Jammys 1987). Frankie Paul: *Sara* (Jammys 1987). Leroy Gibbon: *Four Season Lover* (Jammys 1987). Further reading: *King Jammy's*, Beth Lesser (Muzik Tree/Black Star 1989).

King Kong

b. Dennis Anthony Thomas, Kingston, Jamaica. First named Junior Kong after his father, he started out as a DJ at Tuff Gong, releasing his debut tune, 'Pink Eye', in 1982. After stints with GT and his own Love Bunch sound system, he went on to record for King Tubby's Firehouse label, using a powerful, gospel-tinged wail not dissimilar to that of Tenor Saw. The gravity and realism of early songs like 'Aids' and 'Babylon' when matched to Tubby's prototype digital 'riddims' in 1985 quickly established his reputation alongside Anthony Red Rose, with whom Tubby teamed him for their debut album, *Two Big Bull Inna One Pen*. By the following year he was voicing for King Jammys, with 'Trouble Again', 'Mix Up' and 'Legal We Legal' becoming notable hits and leading to his first solo album release in the UK via Greensleeves. Jammys was one of many producers in both the UK and Jamaica to record him throughout 1986/7. Others included Black Scorpio, Harry J ('Musical Terrorist'), Errol Scorcher, Ossie Hibbert, Prince Jazzbo, Java ('Toots Boops') and Jah Life. Albums for Bunny Lee, Black Solidarity and King Jammys ensuing before he took up residency first in New York then Canada as the 80s drew to a close, recording only intermittently on his own short-lived Conscious Music label. 'He Was A Friend' was prompted by the death of Tenor Saw in 1989. The following year he relocated to England and attempted a comeback with strong work for Mafia & Fluxy and Gussie P.

in 1991/2, since when he has been inactive. Selected albums: *Legal We Legal* (King Jammys 1986, retitled *Trouble Again* in UK, Greensleeves 1986), *Dancehall Session* (Striker Lee 1986), *Big Heavy Load* (Striker Lee 1987), *Identify Me* (Black Solidarity 1987). With Anthony Red Rose: *Two Big Bull Inna One Pen* (Firehouse 1986). With Nitty Gritty: *Confrontation* (King Jammys 1987).

King Stitt

The 'Ugly One', apparently born Winston Spark, never let his seriously disfigured facial features inhibit his progress in the highly competitive Kingston music world. By 1969 he was the regular DJ for Coxsone Dodd's Number One Set. His success paved the way for U Roy, I Roy and Big Youth but, unfortunately, their new style and approach soon superseded Stitt. His style was firmly rooted in the older tradition of Jamaican DJing influenced by American radio DJs - shouted introductions and interjections as opposed to 'riding the rhythm' and filling out the entire length of the record. Stitt's contributions were fragmentary and explosive as hit followed hit for Clancy Eccles in the early 70s - 'Herbman', 'Fire Corner', 'The Ugly One' and, possibly the most interesting of all, 'Dance Beat' where Clancy and Stitt reminisce about the old ska days, the dances and the dancehalls. Sadly, there is no album of strictly King Stitt material, although *Fire Corner* credited to the Dynamites (Clancy's Studio band) has a fairly representative cross-section of his work. His few recordings at Studio One failed to match the quality of his Clancy's output, but he has continued to work there in a non-recording capacity.
Albums: With The Dynamites: *Fire Corner* (Clandisc 1969). Various: *Dance Hall '63* (Studio One 1994).

King Tubby

b. Osbourne Ruddock, 28 January 1941, Kingston, Jamaica, d. 6 February 1989. King Tubby grew up around High Holborn Street in Central Kingston before moving to Waterhouse in 1955. He started repairing radios and by the late 50s had begun to experiment with sound system amplifiers. By 1968 he was operating his own Tubby's Home Town Hi-Fi, where he later incorporated a custom reverb and echo facility into his system. At the same time he was working as disc-cutter for Duke Reid and it was here that he discovered that he could make special versions of well-known and loved rocksteady tunes. By cutting out most of the vocal track, fading it in at suitable points, reducing the mix down to the bass only, and dropping other instrumental tracks in or out, Tubby had invented dub. Initially the technique was used for 'specials' or dub plates - custom acetates made exclusively for sound system use. The spaces left in the mix allowed sound system DJs to stretch out lyrically, predating the emergence of US rappers by some years. Record producers soon began to see the potential of the version thus created. Joe Gibbs' engineer, Errol Thompson, working at Randy's Studio 17, started rhythm versions as b-sides by 1971. To keep ahead of the competition Tubby acquired the old four-track mixing console from Dynamic Studios. He then introduced further refinements - delay echo, slide faders, and phasing. By late 1971 he was working with producers like Bunny Lee, Lee Perry, Glen Brown, Augustus Pablo and 'Prince' Tony Robinson. The latter issued records that credited Tubby as mixer, including 'Tubby's In Full Swing', b-side to a DJ track by Winston Scotland.
Throughout the 70s Tubby mixed dubs for all the previously-mentioned producers, in addition to Roy Cousins, Vivian 'Yabby You' Jackson, Winston Riley, Carlton Patterson and Bertram Brown's Freedom Sounds. His most important work, for sheer quantity, was with Bunny Lee. Lee used Tubby for dub and voicing, on rhythms he had built elsewhere with the Aggrovators session band. All the singers who worked with Lee at this time - Johnny Clarke, Cornell Campbell, Linval Thompson, Jackie

Edwards, Derrick Morgan, Delroy Wilson, Horace Andy, John Holt and Owen Grey - made records with Aggrovators rhythms, voiced and mixed at King Tubby's. Lee began to issue dub albums featuring Tubby's mixes, and other producers soon followed that lead. Tubby's name as mixer soon appeared on well over 100 albums.

A generation of engineers trained under Tubby's supervision, including King Jammys and 'Prince' Phillip Smart, both subsequently finding success on their own terms. Throughout this period Tubby had laid plans to build his own studio, and by 1988 he had begun to issue computer-generated digital music featuring many of the new-wave ragga singers and DJs, including Pad Anthony, Courtney Melody, Anthony Redrose, Pliers, Ninjaman, as well as established talents like Cornell Campbell. Just as it seemed Tubby was poised to challenge top producers like Jammys and Gussie Clarke, tragedy struck. On 6 February 1989, a lone gunman murdered King Tubby outside his home, the motive apparently robbery. The loss shocked Jamaican music. Many innovations, not only in Jamaican music but in other 'dance' forms as well; the 'dub mix', the practice of DJing extended lyrics over rhythm tracks, the prominence of bass and drums in the mix - all were developed by King Tubby, both on his sound system and in the studio during the period 1969-74. His place as a seminal figure in the music's development through three decades is assured.

Selected albums: *Black Board Jungle* (Upsetter 1974), *Dub From The Roots* (Total Sounds 1974), *The Roots Of Dub* (Grounation 1975), *Shalom Dub* (Klik 1975), *King Tubby Meets the Aggrovators At Dub Station* (Live & Love 1975), *King Tubby Meets The Upsetter At The Grass Roots Of Dub* (Fay Music 1975), *Harry Mudie Meets King Tubby In Dub Conference Volumes 1, 2 & 3* (Moodisc 1975/76/77), *Dubbing With The Observer* (Trojan 1975), *King Tubby Meets Rockers Uptown* (Clocktower 1976), *King Tubby's Prophesy Of Dub* (Prophets 1976), *Ital Dub* (Trojan 1976), *Beware* (Grove Music 1978), *Rockers Meets* *King Tubby In A Firehouse* (Yard Music 1980), *Dangerous Dub: King Tubby Meets Roots Radics* (Copasetic 1981), *King Tubby's Presents Soundclash Dubplate Style* (Taurus 1989), *King Tubby's Special 1973-1976* (Trojan 1989).

Kong, Leslie

b. 1933, Kingston, Jamaica, d. 1971. In partnership with his three brothers Chinese Jamaican Kong ran a combination ice-cream parlour and record shop called Beverley's on Orange Street in Kingston. He became a record producer in 1961 after hearing Jimmy Cliff sing 'Dearest Beverley' outside his establishment, which he subsequently recorded and released on the Beverley's label. The following year he recorded Bob Marley's first records, 'Judge Not' and 'One Cup Of Coffee', and had huge hits with Jimmy Cliff's 'Miss Jamaica' and Derrick and Patsy's 'Housewives Choice'. For the rest of the decade he worked with nearly all of the top names in Jamaican music such as John Holt, Joe Higgs, Derrick Morgan, Stranger Cole, Desmond Dekker, the Maytals, the Melodians and the Pioneers, and many of these recordings were licensed for release in the UK on Chris Blackwell's Island label.

In 1967 Kong scored a big international hit with Desmond Dekker's '007', and a massive world-wide smash with the same artist in 1969 with 'Israelites'. In late 1969 Kong again recorded Bob Marley, this time with the Wailers, and he released these sessions as *The Best Of The Wailers*. He crossed over again into the UK national charts with the Pioneers' 'Long Shot Kick The Bucket', the Melodians' 'Rivers Of Babylon' (the blueprint for Boney M's hit version a decade later) and 'Sweet Sensation', and the Maytals' 'Monkey Man' - only one of a long series of hits that he enjoyed with the group. Kong's work has for too long been viewed as 'unfashionable' by reggae's self-appointed experts. Much of this is due to professional jealousy - few producers ever came near to matching Beverley's in terms of hit records, and many of Beverley's releases were also huge international successes – Kong was one of the first producers to popularise Jamaican music outside of its immediate target audience. His productions were always clean and sharp and he used the best available musicians. His reputation has sadly never matched these achievements – a highly unusual situation in the reggae field – but time will, hopefully, redress the balance, and allow his work to be appreciated on its true merits.

Albums: Various: *Reggae Party* (MFP 1970), *The Best Of Beverley's* (Trojan 1981), *The King Kong Compilation* (Island 1981).

Kotch

Kotch have been in existence since 1981, although only drummer Steven Lee and his guitarist uncle Pablo Stewart have remained constant. First called Psalms, the band offered straightforward roots reggae at a time when dancehall was starting to rise. Their first single, 'In The Hills', produced by themselves and Third World's Willie Stewart, flopped, but it was followed by the better-received 'Ska-ba', produced by Ibo Cooper, also from Third World. By that time, 1982, their lead singer, Parry Hinds, had been replaced by the distinctive, soulful baritone of Rueben 'Norman' Espuet and the line-up settled to Espuet, Lee, Pablo Stewart, Ian Heard (saxophone), Al Wilson (trombone), Earl Thorpe (bass) and Herbie Harris (keyboards). Four singles arrived in 1983, the last two; 'Head Over Heels' and 'Jean' charting in Jamaica. Their first album, *Sticks And Stones* was also issued that year. Steven Lee's other job at his father's Sonic Sounds record distribution company in Kingston gave Kotch an important connection. Upstairs at Sonic Sounds was a tiny computerized studio, Megabyte, that Sly Dunbar rented. Kotch's keyboard player, Herbie Harris, became resident programmer and, with reggae changing in 1986 to a fully-digital sound, Sly was looking for his Taxi label to follow suit. In 1988 it arrived: a rocking, woodblock snare, a sub-sonic, growling bass, and a simple keyboard and guitar arrangement that owed something to rocksteady. When Sly needed a voice, he called on the band downstairs. Kotch's first new hit, 'Cruising', caused confusion. Many believed that it was the work of a girl group. Norman Espuet's baritone had been side-lined for a falsetto worthy of the Stylistics. An appearance at the Reggae Sunsplash festival in 1988 confirmed that it was Espuet with the high-rise larynx. 'Cruising' hit number 1 in Jamaica, and it was quickly followed by 'Tears', (a Top 10 hit) and a cover of Smokey Robinson's 'Ooh Baby Baby', which Mango issued in England to considerable reggae chart success. 'Heartbreak', a cover of Eric Clapton's 'Wonderful Tonight', and 'Tracks Of My Tears' have all since sold well. The album *Kotch* was released internationally and to support it they toured Africa, South America and Europe and played extensively, backing singers and DJs in Jamaica – a facet of their work which success forced them to abandon. 'Don't Take Away' with U Roy, and 'Clock' maintained their profile in 1990.

Albums: *Sticks And Stones* (Sonic Sounds 1983), *Kotch* (Mango/Island 1989).

L

Lady Patra

b. c.1973, Kingston, Jamaica. A DJ, singer and hopeful actor widely touted/hyped as the female equivalent of Shabba Ranks, Patra signed to the same management, under the aegis of Clifton 'Specialist' Dillon, in 1989. She also shares the same record company, Epic. Accordingly, with the new, commercial expectations placed on her shoulders, her material has moved from strict dancehall to include smooth love songs. Patra was brought up singing in churches in Westmoreland, where she moved from Kingston at an early age. Her ambition as a child was always evident, and she soon entered neighbourhood singing/DJing competitions in high school. Early supporters, who included Major Mackerel, encouraged her to return to Kingston and try her luck in the studios. Gussie Clarke was the first to 'voice' her after she had been declined by several others. Such rejections were only a short-term problem, however. Following the sessions with Clarke she found herself in demand by Shocking Vibes, Exterminator and several others. Sides like 'Holler Fe The Wok', Visa Hole', 'Man Me Love' and 'Worky Worky' showcased her considerable talents. On the back of this moderate success she played her first major show at the Sting '88 celebrations. By the time the deal with Epic was struck, Patra's singing voice had taken precedence over her DJ skills, as highlighted by the single 'Sweet Memories', the first product of new sessions (though it was actually released by Tachyon's Sonny Ochai). Curiously, it rose to number 1 in the Japanese reggae charts, but Epic will surely demand much more concrete domestic success in return for their investment.
Album: *Queen Of The Pack* (Epic 1993).

Lawes, Henry 'Junjo'

b. Henry Lawes, Kingston, Jamaica. One of the most prolific and influential producers of the 80s, Lawes was born and raised in Olympic Way, West Kingston. In 1978 he made his musical debut singing in the trio Grooving Locks. The following year he took Barrington Levy to Channel One. Subsequently 'Collie Weed', 'Looking My Love' and 'Shine Eye Gal' all reached number 1 on the Jamaican charts, and the resulting *Bounty Hunter* album is generally considered to be the first of the new dancehall era. With the Roots Radics and Scientist working on the majority of his releases, Lawes began voicing a dazzling array of talent. Michael Prophet ('Gun Man'), Papa Tullo, General Echo, Ranking Toyan ('How The West Was Won'), Billy Boyo, Little Harry, Little John ('Dancehall Style'), Barry Brown ('Give Another Israel A Try'), Anthony Johnson and Eek-A-Mouse ('Wa Do Dem') were among those who recorded for his Arrival and Volcano labels throughout 1980-82.
Apart from pioneering the concept of two artist 'clash' albums and presenting dubmixer Scientist as an artist in his own right, his next step was to instigate albums of live dancehall sessions, often featuring Yellowman, whose rapid rise owed much to the many hit singles and albums recorded for Lawes. Early B, Josey Wales ('Outlaw Josey Wales'), Nicodemus, Buru Banton, Michigan And Smiley ('Diseases'), Peter Metro, Charlie Chaplin, Audie Murphy and Lord Sassafras all recorded over his rhythm tracks, which began to dominate the dancehall market. Quick to spot new talent, he also reawakened the careers of several established acts who had slipped into decline. Under his direction John Holt enjoyed a revival, voicing hits such as 'Sweetie Come Brush Me' and then 'Police In Helicopter'; Alton Ellis, Ken Boothe, Johnny Osbourne ('Fally Lover'/'Ice Cream Love'), Al Campbell, the Wailing Souls and Earl 16 similarly benefiting from his winning touch. In 1983 he formed his own Volcano sound system.

Bunny Lee

With access to unlimited dub plates and using state-of-the-art equipment, Volcano soon became the number one sound in Jamaica. By the following year Yellowman ('Zungguzungguguzungguzeng'), Barrington Levy ('Prison Oval Rock') and Eek-A-Mouse ('Anaxerol') were vying for the top slot, and he had already added new talents like Cocoa Tea ('Rocking Dolly'/'Lost My Sonia') and Frankie Paul ('Pass The Tushenpeng') to his roster, co-writing an ever-increasing number of hit songs himself. In 1985 he took Volcano to New York, where he remained for six years. He had missed out on the digital revolution that had swept through Jamaican music during those years, but worked with several of his former artists on his return, including John Holt, Linval Thompson, Cocoa Tea ('Kingston Hot') and Yellowman, to varying degrees of success. By 1994 he had recorded albums with Ninjaman, General TK and Shaka Shamba, voiced an increasing number of younger artists and had plans for his own studio in Kingston. With his uncanny eye for new talent, his lyrical ability and shrewd marketing sense, few would bet against him making further significant contributions to reggae music in the future.

Selected albums: Barrington Levy: *Bounty Hunter* (1979), *Englishman* (1989), *Robin Hood* (1981). Scientist: *Heavyweight Dub Champion* (Greensleeves 1980), *Wins The World Cup* (Greensleeves 1983). Michael Prophet: *Gun Man* (1981). Ranking Toyan: *How The West Was Won* (1982). Eek-A-Mouse: *Wa Do Dem* (1981), *The Mouse And The Man* (Greensleeves 1983), *Mouseketeer* (Greensleeves 1984). Yellowman: *Mr Yellowman* (Greensleeves 1982), *Zungguzungguguzungguzeng* (Greensleeves 1984). Yellowman with Josey Wales: *Two Giants Clash* (1983). Josey Wales: *The Outlaw Josey Wales* (1983). John Holt: *Police In Helicopter* (1983). Johnny Osbourne: *Fally Lover* (1981). Don Carlos: *Day To Day Living* (1983). Wailing Souls: *Inchpinchers* (1983). Frankie Paul: *Pass The Tushenpeng* (1984). Cocoa Tea: *Wha Dem A Go* (1984), *Kingston Hot* (1992). Ninjaman: *Booyakka! Booyakka!* (1994). Various: *Live At Aces International* (1983), *Total Recall* (VP 1991), *Total Recall Vol. 2* (VP 1992).

Further reading: *Reggae Inna Dancehall Style*, Tero Kaski & Pekka Vuorinen (Black Star 1984).

Lee, Bunny

b. Edward O'Sullivan Lee, 23 August 1941, Jamaica. Bunny Lee, aka Bunny and Striker, was introduced to the music business by vocalist Derrick Morgan in 1962. Morgan, at that time one of Jamaica's most prolific and successful performers, took Lee to producer/sound system operator Duke Reid, who gave him a job as record plugger for his Treasure Isle label. Following his stay with Reid, Lee began working with Ken Lack, erstwhile road manager for the Skatalites band. By 1966, Lack had started releasing records by Ken Boothe, the Clarendonians, Max Romeo, the Tartans, the Heptones and others. Lee's first production, 'Listen To The Beat' by Lloyd Jackson And The Groovers, was released on Lack's Caltone label in 1967. His first hit was 'Music Field' by Roy Shirley (1967), on the WIRL label. He then began releasing his productions on his own imprint, Lee's. He enjoyed local hits during 1967-68 with Derrick Morgan's 'Hold You Jack', Slim Smith And The Uniques' 'My Conversation', Lester Sterling and Stranger Cole's 'Bangarang', Pat Kelly's 'Little Boy Blue' and the Sensation's 'Long Time Me No See You Girl'. Lee's talent for producing music that was commercially and artistically satisfying ensured his position as the leading hitmaker in Jamaica by 1969. During the following four years Lee scored hits with Slim Smith's 'Everybody Needs Love' (1969), Pat Kelly's 'How Long?' (1970), Delroy Wilson's 'Better Must Come' (1971) and the Jamaica Song Festival winner, Eric Donaldson's 'Cherry Oh Baby' (1971), later a UK hit for UB40, and John Holt's 'Stick By Me' (1972). By 1974 he was producing Johnny Clarke on a string of local hits, beginning with 'None Shall Escape The

Byron Lee

Judgement' and 'Move Out Of Babylon'. Owen Grey had showcased 'Bongo Natty' that same year, whilst 1975 saw Cornell Campbell release a series of strong-selling tunes beginning with 'The Gorgon'.

Lee, along with producer Lee Perry and engineer King Tubby, had changed the face of Jamaican music, breaking the dominance of the big producers like Clement Dodd and Duke Reid. Bunny Lee's contribution had been to grasp the commercial opportunities created by technological innovations such as the multi-track studio. A rhythm track could be made which could then be used as the backing for many songs or 'versions', often remixed or 'dubbed'. In addition to King Tubby, engineers like Prince Jammy and Philip Smart developed their talents on Bunny Lee productions. During the period 1969-77 Lee produced literally thousands of tracks - vocals, DJ records and dubs - with a wide range of artists. As well as those already mentioned he produced music for singers, including Jackie Edwards, Leroy Smart, Linval Thompson, David Isaacs, Alton Ellis, Dave Barker, Ken Boothe and Frankie Jones; DJs like Dennis Alcapone, U Roy, I Roy, Prince Jazzbo, U Brown, Big Joe, Trinity, Dr. Alimantado, Jah Stitch, Tapper Zukie, most with additional corresponding dub versions. The early 80s saw a reduction in output; Lee was hampered because he did not control his own studio, although he continued to release music through his connection with Count Shelley in London and New York. He bought Joe Gibbs' old studio in North Parade, Kingston, and released material in the late 80s using computer-generated rhythms, but seems content to hire his studio to newer producers.

Selected album: *Leaping With Mr. Lee* (1968). Compilation: *Jumping With Mr Lee 1967-1968* (Trojan 1989).

Lee, Byron, And The Dragonaires

b. 27 June 1935, Jamaica. Lee and his manager, Ronnie Nasralla, first put together the Dragonaires in 1956 and worked as a support act for touring singers including Harry Belafonte, and their debut single 'Dumplins' in 1960 was the first release on the UK's Blue Beat label (although it originally came out on his own Dragons Breath label in Jamaica). The 14-piece Dragonaires featured an ever fluctuating line-up and are often cited as one of Jamaica's first ska bands, although they were firmly an 'establishment' band and their success was largely due to Lee's business and political connections. They toured extensively in the West Indies, North America and Canada and did much to popularise the ska sound. In 1969 Lee bought out the old WIRL set-up and established Dynamic Sounds as the best equipped and most popular studio in the Caribbean. As well as supporting home grown talent, visiting stars such as the Rolling Stones, Eric Clapton and Paul Simon all recorded at Dynamic hoping for a piece of the reggae action. Lee still records occasionally but concentrates on the soca style these days.

Selected albums: *Reggae Fever* (1968), *Sparrow Meets The Dragon* (1970), *The Midas Touch* (Dragon 1975), *Mighty Sparrow* (Dynamic 1976), *Reggae International* (Dynamic 1976), *Six Million Dollar Man* (Dynamic 1976), *This Is Carnival* (Dynamic 1976), *Art Of Mas* (Dynamic 1977), *Jamaica's Golden Hits* (Stylus 1977), *More Carnival* (Dynamic 1978), *Carnival Experience* (Dynamic 1979), *Jamaican Ska* (Rhino 1980), *Soft Lee Vol. 3* (Vista 1983), *Soul-Ska* (Vista 1983), *Best Of Carnival* (Dynamic 1984), *Jamaica's Golden Hits Vol. 2* (Dynamic 1984), *Wine Miss Tiny* (Creole 1985), *Soca Girl* (Dynamic 1986), *Soca Thunder* (Dynamic 1987), *De Music Hot Mama* (Dynamic 1988), *Reggae Blast Off* (Trojan 1988), *Reggae Round The World* (Trojan 1988), *Soca Bachannal* (Dynamic 1989), *Play Dynamite Ska* (Dr Buster Dynamite 1992), *Wine Down* (Dynamic 1992).

Levi, Ijahman

b. Trevor Sutherland, 1946, Manchester, Jamaica. Levi received his earliest musical

Ijahman Levi

tutoring as a youth living in Trenchtown from Joe Higgs, eventually becoming proficient enough to appear on Vere John's 'Opportunity Hour', the launching pad for many a reggae career. He made his first recording, 'Red Eyed People', under the name Youth for producer Duke Reid in 1961. Levi emigrated to England in 1963 settling in Harlesden, London, and formed a short-lived group called the Vibrations. Once the Vibrations folded, he and another singer, Carl Simmons, formed a stage act called Youth & Rudie And The Shell Shock Show, performing a Tamla Motown and Stax-style soul revue at the famous London niterie the Q Club, as well as touring Europe. He recorded a number of obscure singles at this time for various labels including Polydor, Pama, and Deram, for whom he cut a reggae version of P.P. Arnold's 'Angel Of The Morning', as well as a reggae version of 'White Christmas' for Trojan, under the unlikely handle of Nyah And The Snowflakes. None of these recordings made any impact, and Levi put his career on hold while he settled down to pursue a normal family life.

His career was resuscitated in 1972 when he was reborn as Ijahman Levi, after turning to the Bible. In 1976 he recorded three excellent singles for Dennis 'Dip' Harris; 'Chariot Of Love', 'I'm A Levi' and 'Jah Heavy Load'. At this time he also contributed some vocal harmonies to Rico Rodriguez's 'Man From Warieka'. This brought him to the attention of Island Records boss Chris Blackwell, who set about producing his debut, *Haile I Hymn* (1978). Hampered by Blackwell's stated intention of creating a reggae *Astral Weeks*, the album contained only four extended tracks, including new versions of 'Jah Heavy Load' and 'I'm A Levi', and garnered mixed reviews. And yet, despite accusations of self-indulgence and pretension, *Haile I Hymn* remains Levi's most important and popular album. After the follow-up, *Are We A Warrior*, Levi parted company with Island. He set up his own labels Tree Roots and

Jahmani, releasing several Jamaican pressed singles in the early 80s including 'Thank You', another version of 'Jah Heavy Load' and 'Tradesman', as well as a new, more conventional album, *Tell It To The Children*. During the 80s Levi's style of roots Rasta reggae fared less well, in common with many of his contemporaries. Nevertheless in 1985 he was to score perhaps his biggest reggae hit with the sentimental 'I Do', a duet with his wife Madge, a radical departure from his usual militant spiritual style.

Albums: *Haile I Hymn (Chapter 1)* (Island 1978), *Are We A Warrior* (Mango/Island 1979), *Tell It To The Children* (Jahmani/Tree Roots 1982), *Africa* (Jahmani/Tree Roots 1984), *Lily Of My Valley* (Jahmani 1985), *Culture Country* (Tree Roots 1987), *Forward Rastaman* (Fat Shadow 1987), *Ijahman & Friends* (Tree Roots 1988), *Inside Out* (Tree Roots 1989), *Live Over Europe* (Jamaica Sound 1989), *Love Smiles* (Jahmani 1991), *On Track* (Jahmani 1991). With Maj: *I Do* (Jahmani 1986).

Levy, Barrington

b. 1964, Kingston, Jamaica. Barrington Levy was one of the first singers to challenge the dominance of DJs in 80s dancehall reggae, although his earliest recording, under the name of the Mighty Multitude ('My Black Girl' in 1977), predated that era. Another early single, 'A Long Long Time Since We Don't Have No Love' in 1978, followed the first into obscurity, but Barrington, undaunted, went into the dancehalls. By 1981 Levy's effortlessly buoyant voice had spread his fame to the point where Henry 'Junjo' Lawes, then the hottest producer in Jamaica, came hunting for him. His first Junjo single was 'Ah Yah We Deh', which sold moderately well, as did two further releases. His fourth single, 'Collie Weed', really took off. Barrington did not sound much like anyone else: maybe revealing some of Jacob Miller's style, and a little of Bob Andy's influence, but with the raw energy of the dancehalls in his phrasing. While other singers were struggling,

Barrington Levy

Barrington was slugging it out at the top. His first album, *Bounty Hunter*, sold well and a string of singles consolidated his position: 'Robber Man', 'Black Rose', 'Like A Soldier', the massive 'Money Move', the monster hit, 'Shine Eye Gal', and the stunning 'Prison Oval Rock', and a series of albums were released between 1982-85 to capitalise on his success. He was later to denounce many of these as 'joke business', being packaged with old singles, out-takes and one-off private sound system recordings. He did his first UK gigs in 1984, including a slot as a winner at the UK Reggae Awards. He then linked with young producer Jah Screw and scored a huge hit with the anthemic 'Under Me Sensi'. He followed it with 'Here I Come', which was a hit in the soul clubs and scraped the UK charts when licensed by London Records, who also issued an album of the same title. However, Screw and Levy made the fatal mistake of courting crossover success and he sounded lost on subsequent rocky singles.

Levy travelled between Jamaica, London and New York, and although he lost momentum at the end of the 80s he still had all the talent of his peak, as *Love The Life You Live* made clear. Two Bob Andy covers, 'Too Experienced' and 'My Time' brought him back to the forefront of reggae, and he signed to Island Records in 1991 for the fine *Divine* set. While it remains to be seen whether he can ever achieve the broader success that seemed to be his in the mid-80s, he remains one of reggae's most powerful and original voices.

Albums: *Bounty Hunter* (Jah Life 1979), *Shine Eye Gal* (Burning Sounds 1979), *Englishman* (Greensleeves 1980), *Robin Hood* (Greensleeves 1980), *21 Girls Salute* (Jah Life 1983), *Poor Man Style* (Trojan 1983), *Run Come Yah* (1983), *Lifestyle* (GG's 1983), *Teach Me Culture* (Live & Learn 1983), *Barrington Levy* (Clock Tower 1984), *Here I Come* (Time/London 1985), *Hunter Man* (Burning Sounds 1988), *Love The Life You Live* (Time/London 1988), *Open Book* (Tuff Gong 1988), *Prison Oval Rock* (Volcano 1989), *Divine* (Mango/Island 1991), *Turning Point* (Greensleeves 1992). With Frankie Paul: *Barrington Levy Meets Frankie Paul* (Ariwa 1984). Compilations: *The Collection* (Time/London 1991), *20 Vintage Hits* (Sonic Sounds 1992).

Lieutenant Stitchie

b. Cleveland Laing, Spanish Town, Jamaica. In 1979 the young Stitchie was a singer, eventually joining Django sound system as the DJ Ranking Noseworthy in 1983, whilst working as a biology teacher in a Spanish Town school. Within two years he'd graduated from City Lights Disco and Lightning Super Mix to Stereo One, adapting the name Citchie from a love of citrus fruit. His first tune was 'If I Don't Care' for Nonsul as Ranking Citrus. By his second ('Two Is Better Than Too Many') he was Stitchie thanks to a label mis-spelling. Hits for Stereo One ('Nice Girl', 'Story Time' and 'Natty Dread') followed before he visited King Jammys in 1986. Immediately his perfectly observed and humorous lyrics caught on: 'Wear Yuh Size' and 'Broad Hips' attaining instant success. In 1987 he was voted DJ Of The Year in Jamaica and celebrated with a debut album, *Great Ambition*. Atlantic signed him in 1988, releasing *The Governor* album but failing to retain his dancehall audience with the next (*Wild Jamaican Romances*). In 1993 he returned to the Kingston studios eager to recapture lost ground, recording a spate of local hits for Danny Browne, Penthouse, Digital B, King Jammys ('Hot Like The Sun'), Shocking Vibes ('Bun It Down'), Carib ('Bandy Leg'), John John and his own Drum And Bass label, on which he produced emergent talents such as the late Pan Head. His third Atlantic album, *Rude Boy*, was released that year and he made successful tours of both Europe and America. Always entertaining on stage or record, he is currently enjoying his most popular spell since his 1987 heyday.

Selected albums: *Great Ambition* (King Jammys 1987), *The Governor* (Atlantic 1989),

Lieutenant Stitchie

Wild Jamaican Romances (Atlantic 1991), *Rude Boy* (Atlantic 1993).

Little John

b. John McMorris, c.1970, Kingston, Jamaica. McMorris first recorded with Captain Sinbad for the Youth In Progress label at the tender age of nine, where his piping interjections contrasted neatly with Sinbad's gruff style, and throughout the 80s he was seldom out of the reggae charts. Claimed by many to be the first dancehall singer, his ability to fit lyrics over any rhythm or backing track became something of a legend in a business that has scant regard for second takes and 'dropping in'. Little John did it every time – and he rode on the crest of the 80s dancehall music explosion, becoming a superstar by the age of 17.

He began his career on Romantic Hi Fi, moving up through Killermanjaro, Gemini and Volcano Hi Power (the importance of sound systems such as these to the rise in popularity of Little John and dancehall music cannot be overstated) where he honed and perfected his craft with a constant string of live appearances. Simultaneously he was recording for just about every producer in Jamaica, notably Henry 'Junjo' Lawes, Joe Joe Hookim, George Phang, Jah Thomas and Jammys, and he has released countless records on a bewildering string of labels. He no longer records as extensively as he once did, and limits his live appearances these days too – a stance that is only fitting for a veteran of his status. He's certainly not living on past glories either, as recent hits for Exterminator proved, and his talent, warm personality and skill as a raconteur are bound to ensure his place at the top for a long time to come.
Selected albums: *True Confession* (Power House 1984), *Unite* (Vista Sounds 1984), *Clark's Booty* (Live & Love/Jammys 1985), *River To The Bank* (Power House 1985), *Warriors & Trouble* (World Enterprise 1986), *Youth Of Today* (Skengdon 1987), *Reggae Dance* (Midnight Rock 1989). Compilations: *Best Of Little John* (R&M 1985). Various: *Junjo Presents A Live Session With Aces*

International (Volcano/Greensleeves; includes Little John).

Little Roy

b. Earl Lowe, c.1950, Jamaica. Little Roy is perhaps the archetypal roots reggae artist, with a career that stretches back to the early 70s, and hardly a non-'cultural' lyric on any of his records. He first recorded for producer Lloyd 'Matador' Daley in 1969, both as a solo act and alongside Joy Lindsay as Roy And Joy. From the outset he wrote about Rasta themes – slavery, the wearing of dreadlocks, exile – his best record of the period was 'Righteous Man'. By 1972 he had formed the Tafari label with the help of Lloyd Barnes and Munchie Jackson, and his records soon received simultaneous release in New York through Barnes' Aries label. Often part of a trio alongside two mysterious characters, Ian and Rock, he recorded some alluring and atmospheric tracks: 'Tribal War', 'Blackbird' and 'Prophecy'. Barnes put them together to form an album, *Tribal War*, a record of a decidedly limited pressing. In 1978 he recorded *Columbus Ship*, a far less artistically successful set, and then dropped below reggae's horizon altogether, though there were occasional sightings of him confined to New York. His business associate Munchie Jackson was shot by his own son in a bizarre Brooklyn domestic killing in 1977. However, in one of those twists unique to reggae, ragga rulers Steely And Clevie decided to remake the 'Prophecy' rhythm in 1990, and it was an instant hit for Freddie McGregor. Not slow to spot an opportunity, Little Roy emerged from nowhere with a 10-track compilation of his now in-demand old material, *Prophecy*, and then cut the extremely good *Live On* the following year. He is rumoured to be assembling yet another comeback set.
Albums: *Tribal War* (Tafari 1975), *Free For All Dub* (1975), *Columbus Ship* (Copasetic 1978), *Prophecy* (1990), *Live On* (1991).

Livingstone, Dandy

b. 1944, Kingston, Jamaica. Livingstone was

at one time a member of the 60s duo, Sugar And Dandy with Sugar Simone and he was a very popular performer in the UK as a solo artist after he relocated there at the age of 15. His records appeared on a variety of different labels under different names and he was responsible for many of the UK's rocksteady and reggae hits throughout the 60s, 'Reggae In Your Jeggae' proving particularly popular in 1969. His first UK chart entry was 'Suzanne Beware of the Devil' in 1972, when reggae was briefly enjoying great popularity in the charts due to the skinhead connection. The follow up, 'Big City', was a smaller hit the following year. His name was revered by many ska/2-Tone fans who recalled his 60s heyday, and the Specials recorded a cover of his 'A Message To You Rudy'.

Selected albums: *Your Musical Doctor* (Downtown 1965), *Dandy Livingstone* (Trojan 1972), *South African Experience* (Night Owl 1978).

Locks, Fred

b. Stafford Elliot, c.1955, Kingston, Jamaica. Locks began his sporadic career as a member of the Lyrics, who recorded tracks like 'A Get It', 'Girls Like Dirt', and 'Hear What The Old Man Say' for Coxsone Dodd in the late 60s, 'Give Praises' for Randy's, and the self-financed 'Sing A Long', both in 1971. The Lyrics disbanded shortly afterwards, and Locks, discouraged by the lack of financial reward endemic to the Jamaican music business, immersed himself in the Rasta faith then gaining significant ground amongst Jamaica's ghetto youth, and retired to live a spartan existence out on the beach at Harbour View. Whilst enduring this bucolic lifestyle, Locks allowed his dreads to grow to formidable proportions - hence his nickname - and continued to write songs, one of which, a prophetic Garveyite vision of repatriation entitled 'Black Star Liners', he was persuaded to record by producer Hugh Boothe.

Released in 1975 on the Jahmikmusic label in Jamaica, and on Grounation in the UK, 'Black Star Liners' struck a resounding chord amongst the new generation of Rastafarian youth on both islands, propelling Locks to cult figure status in the process. Two years later Grounation off-shoot Vulcan finally officially released the long awaited *Black Star Liners/True Rastaman*, a classic example of 70s roots Rasta reggae, packed with fine songs including former singles 'Last Days' (retitled 'Time To Change') and 'Wolf Wolf', and raw, guileless vocals. Throughout this time Locks had also been a member of the vocal trio Creation Steppers with Eric Griffiths and Willy Stepper, who had been releasing singles on their Star Of The East imprint in Jamaica, achieving considerable local success with 'Stormy Night' - later covered at Channel One by the Rolands. A various artists album entitled *Love & Harmony* featured the title track (also a 12-inch in Jamaica) credited to Fred Locks, and 'Kill Nebuchadnezzar' by the Creation Steppers also emerged, in 1979. In 1980 Locks and the Creation Steppers went to the UK for several shows and linked up with the legendary sound system operator and record producer, Lloydie Coxsone, who released a number of discs by both the group and Locks including the classic 'steppers' 'Homeward Bound', 'Love And Only Love' and 'Voice Of The Poor'. These and other tracks were eventually released on *Love And Only Love*. Locks moved to the USA in 1982, effectively halting his and the Steppers career. Settling in Philadelphia, he immersed himself in the local Twelve Tribes organisation, after which he recorded only sporadically.

Albums: *Black Star Liners/True Rastaman* (Vulcan 1977), *Love And Only Love* (Tribesman 1981).

Lodge, J.C.

b. June Carol, hence the JC initials. JC's entrance into the reggae world came courtesy of an audition for Joe Gibbs, who was won over by her voice. Their first recording together was a version of Charley Pride's 'Someone Loves You, Honey', which

went straight to the top of the Jamaican charts. Ironically, the result for Gibbs was bankruptcy, after he failed to pay royalties to the songwriter. In 1988 she recorded 'Telephone Love' for Gussie Clarke, which subsequently became a big hit in Jamaica and America, where, after being housed on the Pow Wow imprint, it achieved crossover status. Its success brought her to the attention of the predominantly hip hop-focused Warners owned Tommy Boy subsidiary. In the process she became the first female reggae star to pick up a major label deal. Her debut for Tommy Boy played safe by revisiting 'Telephone Love', and branching out musically to encompass soul and rock. Also a talented painter, Lodge has exhibited in Kingston art galleries, and appeared as an actor in several theatrical productions.
Selected albums: *I Believe In You* (Greensleeves 1987), *Revealed* (RAS 1988), *Tropic Of Love* (Tommy Boy 1992).

Lone Ranger

b. Anthony Waldron, the Lone Ranger was one of the most lyrically inventive late 70s DJs, with a considerable influence on the British school of MCing. Waldron spent a large proportion of his formative years in the UK, which perhaps accounted for his radically different stance, and, like so many others, he began his own recording career at Studio One. Welton Irie partnered him at first, but he soon graduated to working solo, setting himself loose on several classic Studio One rhythms, after which he became virtually unstoppable. His version of Slim Smith's seminal 'Rougher Yet', re-titled 'Love Bump', was a major success. So too his reading of Slim Smith's 'Never Let Go', a version known as 'The Answer', which has become more famous than the original. As top DJ for Kingston's Virgo Sound, he kept up appearances in the dance halls and Virgo Hi Fi were voted the top sound of 1980.
His recordings for Alvin 'GG' Ranglin assured his legendary status. 'Barnabas Collins' (about a vampire show on

television) contained the immortal line: 'chew ya neck like a Wrigley's', and was a UK reggae chart number 1 in 1980. His additional work for Winston Riley and Channel One, which included the memorable 'M16', proved almost as popular. His tour of the UK that year reiterated that he could do it on stage as well as on record and for the sound systems. Any performer who could deliver priceless lyrics such as 'Lightning clap and thunder roll . . . Noah at the ark control', would always be guaranteed a receptive audience. His repertoire of strange voices, 'oinks' and 'ribbits', were widely imitated. Ranger recorded sparingly, sometimes branching out in keeping with other DJs into self-production, and his catalogue has always been assembled with style, class and a dash of great humour.
Selected albums: *Barnabas Collins* (GG's 1980), *On The Other Side Of Dub* (Studio One 1981), *M16* (Channel One 1982), *Hi-Yo Silver Away!* (Greensleeves 1982), *Badda Dan Dem* (Studio One 1982), *Dee Jay Daddy* (Techniques 1984), *Learn To Drive* (Bebo's Music 1985).

Lord Creator

b. Kentrick Patrick, c.1940, Trinidad. As his imperious name makes clear, Lord Creator began his career as a calypso singer. Some time in the mid-to-late 50s he arrived in Jamaica where the music scene was just starting its own recording business. Lord Creator's smooth, honeyed tones were not ideal for the raucous jump to R&B soon to emerge from ska, but as a big band crooner in Jamaica, he had no equal. 'Evening News' (1959) was his first massive hit, and it was a song he returned to at several points in his career. The storyline of a barefoot kid feeding his siblings by selling newspapers he could not even read, had greater resonance at a time when Jamaica was struggling for its independence. In 1962 his 'Independent Jamaica' was the first single on the Island label in the UK, although legend has it that Owen Gray's 'Twist Baby', scheduled as Island 002, made it to the shops first. 'Don't

Stay Out Late' (1963) was a major Jamaican hit, and Lord Creator was generally regarded as the island's biggest star of the time. 'Little Princess' (1964) helped maintain his status. He also released a calypso album for the Studio One label. He was overtaken by other smooth voices such as Ken Boothe and Bob Andy, both of which offered more contemporary songs.

In 1969 he teamed up with producer Clancy Eccles and recorded the single 'Kingston Town', perhaps the finest sentimental reggae record ever released. However, by this time Creator was hardly well-off and a week after recording the record, he borrowed $30 from Eccles. A couple of months later Eccles spotted Creator in a Kingston street and the singer ran off. Eventually Eccles caught him, and Creator immediately began to make excuses for not paying back the money he owed. Eccles explained that he owed Creator $1,000 in royalties for 'Kingston Town'. The record had sold thousands of copies in Britain without ever making the charts. During the 70s, Lord Creator's croon became rare in a reggae music obsessed with roots, Rasta and heavy dub. He did record one powerful single in 1977, however, 'Life', an updated version of a 1967 single, 'Such Is Life'.

During the 80s rumour had it that Lord Creator had succumbed to the life of the homeless rum drinker on the streets of Kingston, and eventually Clancy Eccles helped organise enough money for Creator to be returned to his family in Trinidad. That seemed to be the end of the story, but in 1989 UB40 covered 'Kingston Town', and Clancy Eccles and Creator were recruited to give their seal of approval in the accompanying video. While it seems sadly ironic that he never got the hit he deserved with his own version, at least UB40's success meant that a royalty cheque would go to the song's creator.

Selected albums: *Songs My Mother Never Taught Me* (Port O Jam 1964), *Big Bamboo* (Dynamic 1974).

Lovers Rock

Although love songs have been staple fare in reggae, and other musics, since time began, lovers rock as a genre emerged in the mid-70s, chiefly in London. Mixing Philly soul with sweet skanking rhythms, it was the antithesis of the roots reggae movement and provided non-Rasta reggae fans with something to identify with, and party to, in an era otherwise dominated by dub. Early exponents such as 15-16-17, Brown Sugar (who featured Caron Wheeler, later of Soul II Soul) and Carroll Thompson, all sold incredibly well. The critics reviled them for their sickly, barely-trained harmonies and schoolgirl voices, but meanwhile, this truly working class music was to be found in teenagers' bedrooms in every British city centre. There were few lovers chart hits, one exception being Janet Kay's 'Silly Games' (number 2 in 1979), but the music thrived away from the mainstream music business, and some records, such as Louisa Mark's 'Caught You In A Lie' and 'Six Sixth Street' were real artistic successes, albeit largely unheralded ones. Throughout the 80s and early 90s lovers has remained a largely underground music, while artists like Winsome, The Investigators, The Instigators, Deborahe Glasgow and Sandra Cross have built huge followings. One international success has been Maxi Priest, who combined lovers with ragga, roots and soul to produce that long-awaited breakthrough fusion.

Selected albums: Various: *Pure Lovers Volume 2* (Charm 1992), *Lovers For Lovers Volume 6* (Business 1992), *Fashion Revives Classic Lovers* (Fashion 1989). Deborahe Glasgow: *Deborahe Glasgow* (Greensleeves 1989). Sandra Cross: *Country Life* (Ariwa 1985).

Luciano

b. Jepther McClymont, Davey Town, Jamaica. Luciano was one of the most promising new singer/songwriters to emerge in 1993. He began singing in his local parish church before assuming the name of Stepper John and migrating to Kingston in April 1992. There he voiced his debut tune for

Herman Chin-Loy at Aquarius, then half an album with Pressley for Mau Mau producer Sky High. Homer Harris of Blue Mountain had by now changed McClymont's name to Luciano. His first Jamaican hit, 'Give My Love A Try', was for Castro Brown and a clutch of ballads and self-penned reality songs soon followed, initially for Brown's New Name label. Phillip 'Fatis' Burrell produced his first two UK hits, 'Chant Out' and 'Poor And Simple', in the summer of 1993 on Exterminator, and was later to release his debut solo album *Moving Up*. Singles for Exterminator, Blacka Dread ('Time Is The Master') and Sly And Robbie's Taxi label helped establish Luciano's fast-growing reputation before he joined Freddie McGregor's Big Ship organisation, 'Shake It Up Tonight' becoming his first UK reggae number 1 and leading to a well-received album of the same name.

Selected albums: *Moving Up* (RAS/Exterminator 1993), *Shake It Up Tonight* (Big Ship 1993). With Pressley: *Meets Pressley* (Sky High 1993).

Macka B

M

Macka B

Macka B is the most productive, distinctive and certainly among the most talented of MCs to emerge in Britain in the 1980s. Born Christopher MacFarlane, Wolverhampton, England, he first rose to local fame chatting for Birmingham-based Wassifa hi-fi, with a melodic but gruff voice which perhaps most closely resembled that of Prince Far-I, although Macka B was of the new breed and capable of a pace of delivery that made his predecessors look lazy by comparison. His large physique, stunning, topical lyrics and dreadlocked features made him an imposing presence on the mic, and after one local release his fame quickly spread to London, occasioning the release of a well-received 45, 'Bible Reader', for Fashion Records (1985). Perhaps recognising that Macka B's future did not lay in the dancehall MC trade the label were currently having hits with, Fashion suggested that Macka B try his luck at Ariwa Records, their South London rivals. With the help of fellow Wolverhamptonite Macka Dub, Ariwa producer Mad Professor unleashed a monster with Macka B's debut LP, *Sign Of The Times*, which remains a classic to this day. Mixing comic material with roots anthems like 'Invasion', drenched in tight horns and heavy dub mixing, the album was a huge hit in the reggae community. Macka B appeared on ITV's *Club Mix* and was something of a celebrity, but he shunned the limelight, preferring instead to work in the roots market, issuing a series of strong albums over the next five years, among them *We've Had Enough*, *Natural Suntan* and *Peace Cup*. He retains his credibility and goodwill, and has even made the occasional trip to Jamaica to record with producer Black Scorpio on a couple of sides, as well as cutting 'DJ Unity' at Penthouse Studio, Kingston, with Jamaican counterpart Tony Rebel.

Albums: *Sign Of the Times* (Ariwa 1986), *We've Had Enough* (Ariwa 1987), *Looks Are Deceiving* (Ariwa 1988), *Buppie Culture* (Ariwa 1989), *Natural Suntan* (Ariwa 1990), *Peace Cup* (Ariwa 1991), *Jamaica No Problem* (Ariwa 1992), *Here Comes Trouble* (Ariwa 1993).

Mad Professor

(See Ariwa Sounds)

Mafia And Fluxy

Initially inspired by Sly And Robbie, brothers Mafia (b. Leroy Heywood, 1962, London, England; bass) and Fluxy (b. David Heywood, 1963, London, England; drums) are the UK's foremost rhythm section, and are becoming increasingly well-known for their own productions. Early encouragement came via Uncle Wizard's sound system and then Fatman, who released their debut, 'Let's Make Love', after they had formed Tottenham, London, band the Instigators in 1977. By 1985 they had earned several hits and gained valuable experience backing touring Jamaican acts, quickly coming to terms with the new digital technology. In 1987 they visited Jamaica, building rhythm tracks for Bunny Lee, Blacker Dread, King Jammys and Exterminator. That year they started their own self-titled label, producing Cinderella, Billy Melody, Sugar Minott and later Private Collection ('Dreamer'). Their debut album *Dancehall Connection Vol. 1* featured such diverse talents as General Trees, King Kong and General Levy when released in 1990. That year Mafia And Fluxy returned to Jamaica, providing many notable hits for Penthouse, Black Scorpio, King Jammys, Gussie Clarke, Mikey Bennett, Mr Doo and Roy Francis. In the UK they backed Maxi Priest and Lloyd Brown while being voted Producers Of The Year, the Instigators winning the Best Reggae Band Award. On their own label tracks by Tiger ('Winery'), Gregory Isaacs, Johnny Osbourne, Sugar Black, Cornell Campbell, Sanchez ('Whip Appeal') and Sugar Minott

Mafia And Fluxy

were released at regular intervals. In 1992 Mafia issued his debut album, *Finders Keepers*, while hits by Cobra ('Off Guard'), Dirtsman, Poison Chang ('Do Me A Favour'), Sweetie Irie, Red Dragon, Cutty Ranks ('Armed And Dangerous'), Tenor Fly and Chaka Demus And Pliers ('Wining Machine') witnessed no shortage of success throughout 1992/3. Back in Jamaica Mafia And Fluxy laid further tracks for Bobby Digital, Penthouse and Stone Love, with whom they won a Jamaican award for 'Best Juggling (mixing) Record'. By 1994 they were remixing the likes of Boy George, Barrington Levy and the Rhythm Kings, Mega Banton's 'First Position' was a number 1 hit and they had become one of the most in-demand rhythm sections in reggae music, even occasionally pairing with Sly (Mafia) and Steely (Fluxy).
Selected albums: Various: *Danchall Collection Vol. 1* (Mafia & Fluxy 1990). Mafia solo: *Finders Keepers* (Mafia & Fluxy 1992). Mafia And Fluxy: *Revival Hits Vol. 1* (Mafia & Fluxy 1992).

Marley, Bob, And The Wailers

This legendary vocal group originally comprised six members: Robert Nesta Marley (b. 6 February 1945, St. Anns, Jamaica, d. 11 May 1981, Miami, Florida, USA), Bunny Wailer (b. Neville O'Riley Livingston, 10 April 1947, Kingston, Jamaica), Peter Tosh (b. Winston Hubert McIntosh, 19 October 1944, Westmoreland, Jamaica, d. 11 May 1987, Kingston, Jamaica), Junior Braithwaite, Beverley Kelso, and Cherry Smith. Bob Marley And The Wailers are the sole Jamaican group to have achieved global superstar status together with genuine penetration of world markets. The original vocal group was formed during 1963. After extensive tuition with the great vocalist Joe Higgs, they began their recording career later that year for Coxsone Dodd, although Marley had made two singles for producer Leslie Kong in 1962 - 'Judge Not' and 'One Cup Of Coffee'. Their first record, 'Simmer Down', released just before Christmas 1963 under the group name Bob Marley And The Wailers, went to number 1 on the JBC Radio chart in January 1964, holding that position for the ensuing two months and reputedly selling over 80,000 copies. This big local hit was followed by 'It Hurts To Be Alone', featuring Junior Braithwaite on lead vocal, and 'Lonesome Feeling', with lead vocal by Bunny Wailer. During the period 1963-66, the Wailers made over 70 tracks for Dodd, over 20 of which were local hits, covering a wide stylistic base; from covers of US soul and doo-wop with ska backing to the newer, less frantic 'rude-boy' sounds which presaged the development of rocksteady, and including many songs which Marley would re-record in the 70s. In late 1965, Braithwaite left to go to America, and Kelso and Smith also departed that year.

On 10 February 1966, Marley married Rita Anderson, at the time a member of the Soulettes, later to become one of the I-Threes and a solo vocalist in her own right. The next day he left to join his mother in Wilmington, Delaware, returning to Jamaica in October 1966; the Wailers were now a vocal trio. They cut the local hit 'Bend Down Low' at Studio One late in 1967 (though it was actually self-produced and released on their own label, Wail 'N' Soul 'M'). This and other self-produced output of the time is amongst the rarest, least re-issued Wailers music, and catches the group on the brink of a new maturity; for the first time there were overtly Rasta songs. By the end of that year, following Bunny Wailer's release from prison, they were making demos for Danny Sims, the manager of soft-soul singer Johnny Nash, who would hit the UK charts in April of 1972 with the 1968 Marley composition, 'Stir It Up'. This association proved incapable of supporting them, and they began recording for producer Leslie Kong, who had already enjoyed international success with Desmond Dekker, the Pioneers, and Jimmy Cliff. Kong released several singles and an album called *The Best Of The Wailers* in 1970. By the end of 1969, wider commercial success still eluded them. Marley, who had spent the summer of 1969

working at the Chrysler car factory in Wilmington, Delaware, returned to Jamaica, and the trio began a collaboration with Lee Perry that was to prove crucially important to their future development. Not only would Perry help focus the trio's rebel stance more effectively, but they would work with the bass and drum team of the Barrett brothers, Aston 'Family Man' (b. 22 November 1946, Kingston, Jamaica) and Carlton (b. 17 December 1950, Kingston, Jamaica, d. 1987, Kingston, Jamaica), who would become an integral part of the Wailers' sound.

The music Bob Marley And The Wailers made with Perry during 1969-71 represents possibly the height of their respective collective powers. Combining brilliant new songs like 'Duppy Conqueror', 'Small Axe' and 'Sun Is Shining' with definitive reworkings of old material, backed by the innovative rhythms of the Upsetters and the equally innovative influence of Perry, this body of work stands as a zenith in Jamaican music. It was also the blueprint for Bob Marley's international success. The group continued to record for their own Tuff Gong label after the Perry sessions and came to the attention of Chris Blackwell, then owner of Island Records. Island had released much of the Wailers' early music from the Studio One period, although the label had concentrated on the rock market since the late 60s. Their first album for the company, *Catch A Fire* (1973), was packaged like a rock album, and targeted at the album market in which Island had been very successful. The band arrived in the UK in April 1973 to tour and appear on television. In July 1973 they supported Bruce Springsteen at Max's Kansas City club in New York. Backed by an astute promotional campaign, *Catch A Fire* sold well enough to warrant issue of *Burnin'*, adding Earl 'Wire' Lindo to the group, which signalled a return to a militant, rootsy approach unencumbered by any rock production values whatsoever.

The rock/blues guitarist Eric Clapton covered 'I Shot The Sheriff' from this

Bob Marley

album, taking the tune to the number 9 position in the UK chart during the autumn of 1974, and reinforcing the impact of the Wailers in the process. Just as the band was poised on the brink of wider success internal differences caused Tosh and Livingston to depart, both embarking on substantial solo careers, and Lindo left to join Taj Mahal. The new Wailers band, formed mid-1974, included Marley, the Barrett brothers and Bernard 'Touter' Harvey on keyboards, with vocal harmonies by the I-Threes, comprising Marcia Griffiths, Rita Marley and Judy Mowatt. This line-up, with later additions, would come to define the so-called 'international' reggae sound that Bob Marley and the Wailers played until Marley's death in 1981. In establishing that form, not only on the series of albums recorded for Island but also by extensive touring, the band moved from the mainstream of Jamaican music into the global market. As the influence of Bob Marley spread, not only as a musician but also as a symbol of success from the so-called 'Third World', the music made locally pursued its own distinct course. 1975 was the year in which the group consolidated their position, with the release of the massively successful *Natty Dread* and rapturously-received concerts at London Lyceum. These concerts attracted both black and white patrons; the crossover had begun. At the end of the year Marley scored his first UK chart hit, the autobiographical 'No Woman No Cry'. His first live album, comprising material from the Lyceum concerts, was also released this year. He continued to release an album a year until his death, at which time a spokesman for Island Records estimated worldwide sales of $190 million. Marley survived an assassination attempt on 3rd December 1976, leaving Jamaica for 18 months early in 1977. In July he had an operation in Miami to remove cancer cells from his right toe.

His albums *Exodus* and *Kaya* enjoyed massive international sales. In April 1978, he played the One Love Peace Concert in Kingston, bringing the two leaders of the violently-warring Jamaican political parties together in a largely symbolic peacemaking gesture. The band then undertook a huge worldwide tour that took in the USA, Canada, Japan, Australia and New Zealand. His own label, Tuff Gong, was expanding its interests, developing new talent. The album *Survival* was released to the usual acclaim, being particularly successful in Africa. The song 'Zimbabwe' was subsequently covered many times by African artists. In 1980, Marley and the Wailers played a momentous concert in the newly-liberated Zimbabwe to an audience of 40,000. In the summer of 1980, his cancer began to spread; he collapsed at Madison Square Garden during a concert. Late in 1980 he began treatment with the controversial cancer specialist, Dr Josef Issels. By the 3rd of May, the doctor had given up. Marley flew to Miami, Florida, where he died on the 11th. His global success had been an inspiration to all Jamaican atists; his name became synonymous with Jamaican music, of which he had been the first authentic superstar. His contribution is thus immense: his career did much to focus attention on Jamaican music and establish credibility for it. In addition, he was a charismatic performer, a great singer and superb songwriter; a hard act to follow for other Jamaican artists. Marley was rightly celebrated in 1992 with the release of an outstanding CD box set chronicling his entire career, though his discography remains cluttered due to the legal ramifications of his estate.

Albums: *Wailing Wailers* (Studio One c.1965), *The Best Of The Wailers* (Beverley's 1970), *Soul Rebels* (Trojan/Upsetter 1970), *Catch A Fire* (Island 1973), *Burnin'* (Island 1973), *African Herbsman* (Trojan 1974), *Rasta Revolution* (Trojan 1974), *Natty Dread* (Island 1975), *Live* (Island 1975, later re-titled *Live At The Lyceum*), *Rastaman Vibration* (Island 1976), *Exodus* (Island 1977), *Kaya* (Island 1978), *Babylon By Bus* (Island 1978, live double album), *Survival* (Tuff Gong/Island 1979), *Uprising* (Tuff Gong/Island 1980), *Marley, Tosh Livingston & Associates* (Studio

One 1980). Compilations: *In The Beginning* (Psycho/Trojan 1979), *Chances Are* (WEA 1981), *Bob Marley - The Boxed Set* (Island 1982, 9-album box set), *Confrontation* (Tuff Gong/Island 1983), *Legend* (Island 1984), *Mellow Mood* (Topline 1984), *Reggae Greats* (Island 1985), *Soul Revolution I & II* (Trojan 1988, the first UK release of the 70s Jamaican double album), *Interviews* (Tuff Gong 1988), *Talkin' Blues* (Tuff Gong 1991), *All The Hits* (Rohit 1991), *Upsetter Record Shop Parts 1&2* (Esoldun 1992), *Songs Of Freedom* (Island 1992, 4-CD box set), *Never Ending Wailers* (RAS 1993).

Videos: *One Love Peace Concert* (1988), *Live At The Rainbow* (1988), *Caribbean Nights* (1988), *Legend* (1991), *Time Will Tell* (1992).

Further reading: *Bob Marley: The Roots Of Reggae*, Cathy McKnight & John Tobler (Star 1977), *Soul Rebel - Natural Mystic*, Adrian Boot & Vivien Goldman (Eel Pie 1981), *Bob Marley: The Biography*, Stephen Davis (Arthur Baker 1983), *Catch A Fire, The Life Of Bob Marley*, Timothy White (Elm Tree 1983), *Bob Marley: Reggae King Of The World*, Malika Lee Whitney (Plexus 1984), *Bob Marley: In His Own Words*, Ian McCann (Omnibus 1993), *The Music Of Bob Marley*, Ian McCann (Omnibus 1994).

Marley, Rita

Wife of Bob Marley, Rita (b. Rita Anderson, Jamaica) has enjoyed a successful solo career in her own right, both before and after her husband's death. She had originally worked with the Soulettes, a Studio One trio, where she first met Bob. She subsequently enjoyed several solo hits in Jamaica, among them 'Pied Piper'. Prophetically, she would back the Wailers on several early recordings before hooking up with Marcia Griffiths and Judy Mowatt to form the I-Threes. Perhaps her most poignant statement is the album, *Who Feels It Knows It*, recorded while Bob was dying of cancer. Rita's biggest hit came with 'One Draw', a pro-marijuana lyric recorded in 1981, shortly after Bob's death. However, she continued to score single successes with

'Many Are Called' and 'Play Play'. By the mid-80s she was largely retired, concentrating on untangling Bob's legal estate, and fostering the career of her children, Ziggy Marley And The Melody Makers.

Albums: *Who Feels It Knows It* (Shanachie 1980), *Harambe* (Teldec 1984).

Marley, Ziggy, (And The Melody Makers)

b. 1968, Kingston, Jamaica. Stephen Marley, one of Bob Marley's four children with his wife Rita Marley, started his career as one of the Melody Makers with siblings Sharon, Cedella and Stevie, whose appearance at their father's funeral in 1981 was their first introduction to the rest of the world. The following year 'What A Plot', released on Rita's label, was a big hit, and Ziggy's lead vocals sounded so uncannily like his late father's as to be almost frightening. The Melody Makers were allowed the time and space to mature and practise before committing themselves needlessly to vinyl - unlike so many of their Jamaican counterparts where recording activities were an economic necessity - and by the late 80s they were a headline act - especially in the USA. Their *Play The Game Right* debut, the only album to be credited simply to the Melody Makers, included one notable excerpt from their father's songbook, 'Children Playing In The Street', which he had originally written for them. Despite their tender years, the record stands up to repeated listening and suggests that Marley's maturity and wisdom may well be hereditary. The album to confirm this was *Conscious Party*. Produced by Chris Frantz and Tina Weymouth from Talking Heads, and featuring an inspired selection of backing musicians, the set boasted high-calibre material like 'Tomorrow People' and 'We Propose', which would not have disgraced any Wailers album. *One Bright Day* is a similarly delightful collection, comprising slick dance reggae with articulate rebuttals of the South African apartheid system.

Ziggy Marley And The Melody Makers

The Melody Makers have resisted the obvious temptation to re-record too many of their father's songs, and instead forged a career in their own right. Stephen Davis recounts in his excellent book – *Bob Marley - Conquering Lion Of Reggae* – just how popular they are in America by detailing a short exchange between two youngsters after seeing Bob Marley on video. One's question: 'Who's that?', being met by the cursory response: 'Ziggy Marley's father'. In his own lifetime Bob and the Wailers never really cracked the American market in the way that the Melody Makers have done. It must be pointed out that they are also very popular in Jamaica too – and not just because of Ziggy's lineage, though his ability to sing over his father's songs as 'specials' for some of Kingston's top sound systems, adapting the lyrics to espouse the prowess of a particular system, has made him widely popular. Irie FM have been known to play their favourite Ziggy songs such as 'Garden' three times in a row when the vibes are right. Ziggy & The Melody Makers have transcended the 'famous parent' tag to become stars in their own right, following on from their fathers' tradition without ever leaning too heavily on it. As Bob once remarked: 'All a my family are music'.

Albums: *Play The Game Right* (EMI 1985), *Hey World* (EMI 1986), *Conscious Party* (Virgin 1988), *One Bright Day* (Virgin 1989), *Jahmekya* (Virgin 1991), *Joy & Blues - Ghetto Youths United* (Virgin 1993). Compilation: *Time Has Come: The Best Of Ziggy Marley And The Melody Makers* (EMI/Manhattan 1988).

Marshall, Larry

b. c.1945, St. Anns, Jamaica. In 1963, Marshall had minor hits with 'Too Young To Love' for E Henry, and 'Please Stay' for Coxsone Dodd's Studio One label. Subsequently he enjoyed a big hit with 'Snake In The Grass', a Top Deck production, and, in 1967, recorded 'I've Got Another Girl' and 'Suspicion' for Prince Buster. However, he had his greatest successes at Studio One where, in addition to singing in a duo with Alvin Leslie, he also worked as an engineer. Larry And Alvin had a massive hit with 'Nanny Goat' (1968), and followed with 'Hush Up' (1968), 'Your Love' (1969) and 'Mean Girl' (1969). Another of their songs, 'Throw Me Corn', became hugely popular at dances through 1969-70 when played on acetate, and was eventually released in 1971. Marshall then recorded solo, and had a further hit with 'Thelma'. A compilation of his Studio One recordings, *Presenting Larry Marshall*, was issued around 1973. By this time, he was also doing production work at Studio One. He left around 1974, and had success with his self-produced 'I Admire You' (1975), with a strong album of the same name following. Since then, he has issued a steady stream of singles, and had moderate hits with remakes of 'Throw Me Corn' (1984) and 'I Admire You' (1985), both Gussie Clarke productions.

Albums: *Presenting Larry Marshall* (Studio One 1973, covers 1968-1971), *I Admire You* (Java 1975), *Dance With Me Across The Floor* (1988), *Come Let Us Reason* (1992).

Matumbi

Nowadays largely remembered for being home to Dennis Bovell's first musical adventures, Matumbi should nevertheless be considered in their own right as a leading voice in the UK's 70s reggae scene. Formed in south London in 1971 by Tex Dixon (vocals), he pulled together a nucleus which comprised Uton Jones (drums), Errol Pottinger (guitar), Bevin Fagan, Glaister Fagan and Nicholas Bailey (vocals), alongside the aforementioned Bovell (guitar). They took their name from the African word for 'rebirth', and in the customary manner of early UK reggae bands, first found employment backing visiting Jamaican musicians. After signing to Trojan early singles included 'Brother Louie' and 'Wipe Them Out', but it was the subsequent singles, 'After Tonight' and 'Man In Me', which brought them major commercial recognition. The latter was the biggest

selling UK reggae single of 1976. However, success almost immediately brought internal friction, exacerbated by Trojan's attitude. They were diquietened by the way individual members were partaking of several outside projects, rather than concentrating on establishing the band as a top name. An injunction was finally served, with the result that Bailey and Dixon quit, and Uton Jones was replaced on drums by Jah 'Bunny' Donaldson. Bailey would go on to solo 'pop' successes with Nick Straker. The remaining members moved on to a contract with EMI subsidiary Harvest, bolstering their profile by joining Ian Dury And The Blockheads on tour. *Seven Seals* was an effective long playing debut, but it was the follow-up, *Point Of View*, with garnered most plaudits. The title-track, a mix of reggae, soul and Glen Miller, reached the Top 40, and for a time it seemed Matumbi might occupy the commercial high ground which many UK reggae bands had aspired to. It was not to be, two albums followed but popular taste had bypassed Matumbi, and the members resumed their solo projects. Bunny joined the Cimarons, and Glaister Fagan and Blake came to be known as the Squad, seeing some chart success as such. Bovell pursued his own idiosyncratic vision working both inside and outside of the reggae medium.

Albums: *Seven Seals* (Harvest 1978), *Point Of View* (EMI 1979), *Dub Planet* (Extinguish 1980). Compilation: *Best Of* (Trojan 1978).

Maytals

Arguably the Maytals were only ever kept from becoming 'international' artists by the runaway success of Bob Marley And The Wailers in the 70s. Rumour has it that Island Records' Chris Blackwell only originally signed the Wailers because he was unable to obtain the Maytals' signatures at the time! Frederick 'Toots' Hibbert, Nathaniel 'Jerry' Matthias/McCarthy and Henry 'Raleigh' Gordon came together in 1962 at the start of Jamaica's ska craze and began recording for Coxsone Dodd's Studio One organisation. Ska vocalists needed to work very hard indeed to make themselves stand out against the heavy, frantic and often overpowering rhythms, and Toots sang himself hoarse in true Baptist preacher style, while Jerry and Raleigh filled in whatever gaps were left to make a solid, impenetrable wall of sound. Subtlety was not their strong point, but the sheer, vibrant joy of all that they were doing is evident in every note. It was not too long before the Maytals were the number one vocal group in Jamaica - a position they would maintain throughout the 60s and on into the 70s.

They left Coxsone after some massive hits and moved on to his ex-employee and arch-rival Prince Buster, celebrating with the vengeful 'Broadway Jungle'/'Dog War': 'We were caught in the jungle . . . In the hands of a man . . .' However, their stay with Buster was also short-lived and the Maytals moved on again to Byron Lee's BMN stable. In 1965 they made Jamaican musical history when both sides of 'Daddy'/'It's You' topped both Jamaican charts, and in 1966 they won the prestigious Jamaican Festival Song Competition with 'Bam Bam'. Many of their releases in these early days were credited to 'The Vikings' or 'The Flames', for as Toots says: 'Promoters in Jamaica called us all kinds of different names because they didn't want us to get our royalties'. The future was looking bright for the group, but Toots was imprisoned in late 1966 for possession of ganja (marijuana) and he was not released until 1968. The Maytals began work for Leslie Kong's Beverleys label, and their first release was a huge hit in Jamaica and the UK - '54-46 That's My Number' featured one of reggae's most enduring bass lines as Toots details his prison experiences in song (54-46 was his prison number). This was the beginning of a hugely successful period - both artistically and financially - for the group, and they recorded many classic records for Beverley's including 'Do The Reggay' one of the first songs ever to use 'reggae' in the title, 'Monkey Man', which actually made the UK charts, and 'Sweet and Dandy', which won the Festival Song

Competition again for them in 1969. They also appeared in a cameo role in the hugely popular film *The Harder They Come,* singing one of their all- time favourites, 'Pressure Drop'.

Kong's untimely death in 1971 from a heart attack robbed them of their mentor. Many believed that their best work was recorded while at Beverley's; evidence of its popularity was found in the 2-Tone craze in the late 70s when the new bands formed a large part of their repertoire from Toots Hibbert's Beverleys song book. They returned to Byron Lee - now the very successful owner of Dynamic Sounds, a state-of-the-art recording, mastering and record pressing complex. In 1972 the Maytals won the Festival Song Competition yet again with 'Pomps and Pride'. Through their work with Dynamic they attracted the attention of Chris Blackwell and became Toots And The Maytals. For the first time in 14 years they became widely known outside of reggae circles. Their UK and USA tours were sell outs, and Island Records released what was to be their biggest selling album ever, *Reggae Got Soul*, which took them into the UK album charts.

They made history again in 1980 when, on 29 September, they recorded a live show at London's Hammersmith Palais which was mastered, processed, pressed and in the shops 24 hours later. Few live excursions have been able to capture the feel and spontaneity of this album, which showcases the Maytals at their best : live without any embellishments. By now they had left their Jamaican audiences far behind but their nebulous 'pop' audience soon moved on to the next big sensation. While the Maytals continued to tour and make records on into the 90s, real lasting international success always seemed to elude them. Toots dispensed with the services of Jerry & Raleigh for his 1982 tour and has even experimented with non reggae line-ups. It will be interesting to see what direction he will now take to match the myriad achievements of his illustrious past.

Tommy McCook

Selected albums: *The Sensational* (Wirl c.1965), *Never Grow Old* (Studio One c.1966), *Original Golden Oldies (Volume Three)* (Fab Prince Buster c. 1967), *Sweet & Dandy* (Beverley's 1969), *From The Roots* (Trojan 1970), *Monkey Man* (Trojan 1970), *Funky Kingston* (Dragon 1973), *In The Dark* (Dragon/Dynamic 1974), *Slatyam Stoot* (Dynamic), *Reggae Got Soul* (Mango/Island 1976), *Toots Live* (Mango/Island), *Life Could Be A Dream* (Studio One 1992). Compilations: *Reggae Greats* (Mango/Island 1988), *Do The Reggae 1966-70*, (Trojan 1988).

McClean, Bitty

b. c.1972, Birmingham, England. Bitty was so named by his grandmother because he was underweight as a baby. As a teenager he went on to study Sound Recording and Media at Sandwell College in Birmingham. He impressed in his studies, and lecturer Alan Cave, previously engineer to UB40 on *Labour Of Love*, recommended him to his former employers as a tape operator. He went down to the band's Abattoir Studio and remained there for three years. Although nominally recording local bands, Bitty would more often find himself sneaking back into the studio late at night to record demos. By chance the band's Ali Campbell got to hear some of his material and was impressed enough to invite Bitty to provide backing vocals and harmonies on UB40's UK number 1, 'Can't Help Falling In Love'. He also co-produced and engineered their subsequent album, *Promises And Lies*. Having given notice of his talents, he was signed by the newly invoked Brilliant Record Company in June 1993. His debut single, 'It Keeps Rainin', surged to number 2 in the UK charts in September of that year, and was a good example of the fare on offer for his debut long playing set. As Bitty himself described it: 'Fresh, infectious, accessible reggae'. The follow-ups were versions of Bunny Wailer's 'Pass It On' and Justin Hinds' 'Here I Stand', both of which followed a similar pattern.

Album: *Just To Let You Know* (Brilliant 1994).

McCook, Tommy

b. c.1932, Jamaica. From the age of 10, McCook attended the Alpha Catholic School For Boys, where he learnt tenor saxophone, flute and music theory. He left Alpha at 14, and played with the dance bands of Eric Deans and Ray Coburn, subsequently developing into a fine jazz player. During the late 40s and early 50s he was a frequent visitor to Count Ossie's camp, where he would jam with Ossie's Rastafarian hand-drummers, developing a deep love for their music in the process. In 1954 McCook joined a dance band in the Bahamas, and further developed his jazz technique. On his return to Jamaica in 1962, he became involved in the development of ska, emerging as a founder member of the Skatalites in 1963. His understanding of jazz, R&B and Jamaican musical forms enabled him to make a huge contribution to the group, which changed the course of Jamaican music. The group backed all of the major ska vocalists, and recorded a huge body of instrumental music. Some of the best examples of his work with the Skatalites are compiled on *Ska Authentic*. After the Skatalites split up in 1965, McCook formed the Supersonics, who became Duke Reid's houseband at Treasure Isle studios. Their sublime, cool style made Treasure Isle the most popular studio of the rocksteady era with hits from the Techniques, Alton Ellis And The Flames, Justin Hinds And The Dominoes and many more. A compilation of Supersonics instrumentals from this period, simply entitled *Tommy McCook*, was later released in the UK. Since this time, he has played on many recordings for Coxsone Dodd, Bunny Lee, Channel One, Joe Gibbs, Randys and other producers. Solo albums released by Bunny Lee include *Cookin'*, *Brass Rockers* and *Hot Lava*. Glen Brown also issued an excellent blank-labelled album, usually called *Horny Dub* (1976), and with trumpeter Bobby Ellis he made an album for

Yabby You, *Blazing Horns* (1978). He is also a featured soloist on most Aggrovators, Revolutionaries and Professionals instrumentals from this period. He continues to tour and work as a session player.

Albums: *Tommy McCook* (Attack 1974, rec. 1965-6), *Cookin'* (c.1974), *Brass Rockers* (1975), *Horny Dub* (Grounation white label 1976), *Hot Lava* (Third World 1977) *Instrumental* (Justice 1978). With Bobby Ellis: *Blazing Horns* (1978).

McGregor, Freddie

b. c.1955, Clarendon, Jamaica. McGregor entered the Jamaican music business at the precocious age of seven, singing backing vocals with ska duo the Clarendonians at Coxsone Dodd's Studio One. He stayed with Dodd throughout the rest of the decade and into the early 70s, acting as a session drummer and backing singer as well as cutting sides such as 'Why Did You Do It', and 'Do Good' (c.1965) with Clarendonian Ernest 'Fitzroy' Wilson as Freddie And Fitzy, versions of Johnny Ace's 'Pledging My Love' and Junior Byles' 'Beat Down Babylon' (c.1972), and his own compositions, 'Go Away Pretty Woman', 'What Difference Does It Make' and 'Why Is Tomorrow Like Today'. In 1975, after adopting the Rasta faith through the Twelve Tribes organisation, he recorded two of his finest singles, 'I Man A Rasta' and 'Rastaman Camp', both heavyweight slices of roots Rasta reggae. In the early 70s he worked stage shows as lead singer with the Generation Gap and Soul Syndicate bands and maintained strong links with both sets of musicians throughout his career. The late 70s saw his star rise with excellent singles such as 'Jogging' for Tuff Gong, the herbsman anthem 'Natural Collie', based around the melody and arrangement of Norman Collins' soul opus, 'You Are My Starship', and 'Mark Of The Beast', 'Leave Yah', and a cover of George Benson's 'Love Ballad', all for Earl 'Chinna' Smith. Winston 'Niney' Holness produced his debut set *Mr McGregor* and there were further recordings for Studio One

including 'Homeward Bound', 'Come Now Sister', 'Africa Here I Come', and the classic *Boby Babylon*. In 1979 McGregor was also involved in the production of Judy Mowatt's excellent *Black Woman*.

McGregor's reputation as one of the most vocally gifted singers in reggae, able to turn his hand to lovers or roots material with equal potency, had been increasing steadily when he recorded *Big Ship* for Linval Thompson. Released in the UK on Greensleeves, the album was a great success. He followed this up with *Love At First Sight* (1982) for Joe Gibbs. Coxsone capitalized on McGregor's popularity, which by now was rivalling that of Dennis Brown and Gregory Isaacs', with *I Am Ready* (1982), like its predecessor comprised mainly of singles and previously unreleased tracks from the singers sojourn at Studio One in the early 70s. In 1984 McGregor inaugurated his own Big Ship label with *Across The Border*, and completed a licensing deal with RAS Records in the US for the release of *Come On Over*. In 1985 he recorded the duet 'Raggamuffin' with Dennis Brown for Gussie Clarke, and the dancehall hit 'Don't Hurt My Feelings' for George Phang's Powerhouse label. Throughout the 80s McGregor enjoyed a position as one of reggae's most popular performers touring the world with the Studio One Band, and scoring a huge hit in Colombia with a version of the Sandpipers' 'Guantanamera', sung in Spanish, for RAS. He signed a contact with Polydor which resulted in the UK chart-nudging 'Push Come To Shove' (1987) and 'That Girl', finally scoring a UK hit with a cover of Main Ingredient's 'Just Don't Wanna Be Lonely', which reached number 9 in August 1987. Now established as a senior reggae statesman McGregor completed a pair of albums, *Sings Jamaican Classics* (1991) and *Jamaican Classic Vol. 2* (1992), on which he offers his interpretations of reggae standards such as Little Roy's 'Prophecy' and Derrick Harriott's 'The Loser', re-titled 'The Winner'. McGregor again narrowly missed the UK charts with

Freddie McGregor

his interpretation of Justin Hinds And The Dominoes' 'Carry Go Bring Come' (1993), but has since had huge success in the reggae charts with his production of Luciano's 'Shake It Up Tonight', sung over the rhythm used for his own 'Seek And You Will Find', which also provides the vehicle for Big Youth's excellent 'Jah Judgement'. Already a veteran in the business at the age of 37, McGregor's future as a reggae superstar looks assured.

Selected albums: *Mr Macgregor* (Observer 1979), *Boby Babylon* (Studio One 1980), *Lovers Rock Showcase JA Style* (Third World 1981), *Love At First Sight* (Intense/Vista Sounds 1982), *Big Ship* (Greensleeves 1982), *I Am Ready* (Studio One 1982), *Come On Over* (RAS 1983), *Freddie* (Vista Sounds ·1983), *Across The Border* (RAS 1984), *All In The Same Boat* (RAS 1986), *Freddie MacGregor* (Dynamic/Polydor 1987), *Rhythm So Nice* (Dynamic 1988), *Don't Want To Be Lonely* (Studio One 1988), *Now* (Steelie & Clevie/VP 1991), *Sings Jamaican Classics* (Jetstar/VP 1991), *Hard To Get* (Greensleeves 1992), *Jamaican Classics Vol. 2* (Jetstar/VP 1992). Compilation: *Reggae Rockers* (Rohit 1989).

Video: *So I Wait* (1989).

McKay, Freddie

b. 1947, St Catherine, Jamaica. McKay recorded for producer Prince Buster in 1967 and scored his first hit, 'Love Is A Treasure', for Duke Reid in that same year. Later he moved from Treasure Isle to Coxsone Dodd's Studio One to record a number of popular titles in the early reggae idiom, including 'High School Dance', 'Sweet You Sour You', 'Drunken Sailor' and 'Picture On The Wall', which was also the title of a debut album which remains McKay's most consistent set. Never in the major league of Jamaican singers, Freddie nevertheless commanded a faithful following and continued to make excellent records right up to his untimely death in the mid-80s

Albums: *Picture On The Wall* (Studio One 1971), *Lonely Man* (Dragon 1974), *The Best Of Freddie McKay* (GG's 1977), *Creation* (Plant 1979), *Tribal In A Yard* (Move/Charly 1983).

Meditations

Jamaican vocal group comprising Ansel Cridland, Danny Clarke and Winston Watson. Clarke had previously been a member of The Righteous Flames, the group fronted by Winston Jarrett (who in turn had been formed from the ashes of Alton Ellis' Flames). He would go on to step out on his own in 1975, forming the Meditations alongside Cridland and Watson. The trio, a roots group closer to the Mighty Diamonds in style than anyone else, recorded a series of strong singles for producers Dobbie Dobson and Lee Perry: 'Running From Jamaica', 'No Peace', 'House Of Parliament' and 'Much Smarter', songs which cast them as righteous Rastafarians who had no truck with the system. Further hits for a variety of producers revealed their pedigree: 'Wake Up', 'Fly Your Natty Dread' and the massive 'Woman Is Like A Shadow' (1978). Their first LP, *Message From The Meditations*, was a minor classic. Resourceful beyond the limits of most bands, the Meditations rode out the dancehall era, cutting a series of strong, if hardly spectacularly successful albums for a variety of labels, including *Guidance* and *Wake Up*. Their 1986 set, *No More Friend*, was favourably received, and they remain revered ambassadors of rasta reggae, and retain much goodwill in America to this day.

Selected albums: *Message From the Meditations* (1977), *Wake Up* (Third World 1978), *No More Friend* (Greensleeves 1983), *For The Good Of Man* (Greensleeves 1988), *Return Of* (1993). Compilations: *Greatest Hits* (Greensleeves 1984).

Melodians

Vocal trio comprising Brent Dowe, Tony Brevett and Trevor McNaughton. Robert Cogle was also a member of the group throughout their career. He made a major contribution as songwriter on many of the trio's biggest hits, but apparently not as a vocalist. They started singing in Kingston's amateur talent contests from 1960, but did not record until April 1966, when they made four titles for Coxsone Dodd, only two of which were released. During 1967-68 the Melodians recorded a series of big local hits for the Treasure Isle label owned by producer Duke Reid that endure to this day as classics of the rocksteady school. The trio's cool, precise harmonies are showcased to near-perfection on 'You Don't Need Me', 'I Will Get Along', 'I Caught You', all released in 1967, and 'Come On Little Girl' in 1968. Later in 1968, the group made two more massive local hits for Sonia Pottinger; 'Little Nut Tree', freely adapted from the nursery rhyme, and the celebratory 'Swing And Dine'. The following year, while still continuing to record occasional titles for Pottinger's Tip-Top label ('No Nola'), they began an association with the producer Leslie Kong which was to bring them international success, firstly with *Sweet Sensation* and then with the Rasta-influenced, anthemic *Rivers Of Babylon*, the latter reputedly selling 75,000 copies in the UK alone.

They continued recording for Kong until his death in 1971, not only as a trio but as solo vocalists. Following this they recorded for Lee Perry, Harry J, Dynamics and Sonia Pottinger and Duke Reid again in 1972. Two years later the group split up. Brent Dowe recorded for Lee Perry in 1975 ('Down Here In Babylon'), and produced himself at Channel One the same year on the sublime 'Deh Pon The Wicked'. Tony Brevett enjoyed success again with 'Don't Get Weary', a self-production. In 1976, they re-formed, recording many of their old hits for producer Harry J, with backing by the Soul Syndicate band, but failed to maintain momentum. In the mid-80s the trio attempted a reunion, with little success; nonetheless, much of the music they made in the 60s remains emblematic of the best in rocksteady and reggae, and their recent stage shows at revival concerts have proved to be hugely popular.

Selected albums: *Rivers Of Babylon* (1970), *Sweet Sensation* (1976), *Sweet Sensation: The Original Reggae Hit Sound* (Island 1980), *Premeditation* (Skynote 1986), *Swing And Dine* (Heartbeat 1993).

Mighty Diamonds

One of the most famous Jamaican vocal groups of the 70s and 80s, the Diamonds consisted of Donald 'Tabby' Shaw (lead vocals), with Fitzroy 'Bunny' Simpson and Lloyd 'Judge' Ferguson providing the harmonies and occasional lead. They recorded unsuccessfully for Stranger Cole and Rupie Edwards, among others, before their breakthrough in 1975 with Joe Joe Hookim's Channel One studio. 'Hey Girl' and 'Country Living' were big reggae hits, but their next release, 'Right Time' on Hookim's Well Charge label, brought everything together. The Diamonds initial success was due to a number of reasons: the influence of Burning Spear's championing of Jamaican national hero, Marcus Garvey; the definitive three-part rocksteady harmonies of the Heptones, together with Sly Dunbar's militant rockers style of drumming on 'do-overs' of timeless Studio One rhythms; and, of course, their own superb songwriting, vocal abilities and the odd knack of somehow managing to sound urgent and relaxed at the same time.

Jamaica erupted into Diamonds-mania while the Channel One 'rockers' sound they had brought to prominence was to dominate reggae music for the next few years, with every drummer in the business developing his very own Sly Dunbar impersonation. Virgin Records was busy acquiring reggae artists in 1976, and the Diamonds and Hookim signed with them for the release of their debut, *Right Time*. It was a classic collection, showcasing perfectly the Diamonds uncanny ability to write catchy, meaningful songs - whether about 'love' or 'reality' - and set them to updated versions of some of the greatest Studio One rhythms. They sold throughout the reggae world and picked up many crossover sales. Virgin sent

Mighty Diamonds

the Diamonds to New Orleans to work with veteran producer Allen Toussaint, which resulted in *Ice On Fire*. It was not well-received, and sold poorly - mainly because its misguided approach baffled reggae fans, while the Diamonds name still meant very little to a wider audience.

They continued to work at Channel One, and many more hit singles came through during the 70s. In 1981, the dub plates of tunes they had recorded for Gussie Clarke were the most played on the Kingston and London sound system circuits. The most popular of these tunes was released on a 10-inch, dub plate style record in New York, a 7-inch in Jamaica and a 12-inch in England; 'Pass The Kouchie', an updating of a 60s Studio One instrumental 'Full Up', was a massive hit. This eventually became 'Pass The Dutchie' for the English group, Musical Youth, which was a worldwide pop hit. (A 'kouchie' is a pipe for smoking ganja, while a 'dutchie' is a type of cooking pot.) The rest of their work with Gussie was released on *Changes*, which consisted of the same combination of new songs and old rhythms, with some classic reggae songs, including 'Party Time' and 'Hurting Inside', performed in the inimitable Diamonds style.

For the rest of the decade and on into the 90s, the Diamonds have continued to consolidate their reputation as one of the best vocal harmony trios in the business with regular releases for a variety of different producers and some lovely self-produced records. Their harmonies are always tight, and their songs usually manage to avoid obvious and naive statements. In the constantly changing world of reggae, they are always a reliable and dependable source of top-quality music, and if their performances have not been quite up to the exalted standards of *Right Time* and *Changes*, it is perhaps too much to expect of them to change direction in a radical fashion at this stage in their careers.

Selected albums: *Right Time* (Well Charge/Virgin 1976, Shanachie 1984), *Ice On Fire* (Front Line 1977), *Stand Up To Your* *Judgement* (Channel One 1978), *Tell Me What's Wrong* (JJ 1979), *Planet Earth* (Virgin 1978), *Deeper Roots - Back To The Channel* (Front Line 1979), *Changes* (Music Works 1981), *Vital Selection* (Virgin 1981), *Leader Of Black Countrys* (Mobiliser 1983), *Kouchie Vibes* (Burning Sounds 1984), *Struggling* (Live & Love 1985), *If You're Looking For Trouble* (Live & Love 1986), *The Roots Is There* (Shanachie 1987), *Real Enemy* (Greensleeves 1987), *Reggae Street* (Shanachie 1987), *Dubwise* (Music Works 1988), *Get Ready* (Greensleeves 1988), *Never Get Weary* (Live & Love 1988), *Live In Europe* (Greensleeves 1989), *Go Seek Your Rights* (Frontline 1990), *The Moment Of Truth* (Mango/Island 1992), *Bust Out* (Greensleeves 1993).

Miller, Jacob

b. c.1955, Jamaica, d. 23 March, 1980. Miller recorded his first record for Coxsone Dodd, entitled 'Love Is A Message' (aka 'Let Me Love You') in 1968, aged just 13. The song did little business though, and Miller had to wait a few years before he returned to the studio. In 1974 he recorded a number of singles for Augustus Pablo, including 'Each One Teach One', 'Keep On Knocking', 'False Rasta', 'Who Say Jah No Dread' and 'Baby I Love You So', most of which were popular on the pre-release circuit in the UK. Unfortunately when Island released 'Baby I Love You So' they failed to credit Miller, and even relegated his vocal to the b-side in favour of its thrashing King Tubby's/Pablo dub, 'King Tubby's Meets Rockers Uptown'. Miller's biggest hits would come as a member of Inner Circle. In 1976 they scored a couple of roots hits with 'Tenement Yard' and 'Tired Fe Lick Weed In A Bush' (both credited to Miller). These and Miller's explosive stage act made them the top act in Jamaica in the latter part of the 70s. Miller, an exuberant, amply proportioned man, possessed of a fine tenor which often employed a trademark stutter, went on to make a number of excellent records with Inner Circle, including 'All Night Till Daylight' and 'Forward Jah Jah Children'.

He took part in the notorious 1978 One Love Peace Concert in Kingston, where Bob Marley joined hands with Edward Seaga and Michael Manley, flanked by representatives of Kingston's warring factions, and starred via an amusing cameo in the 1979 film, *Rockers*. He died in a road crash on March 23rd 1980.

Albums: *Killer Miller* (Top Ranking 1978, RAS 1988), *Natty Christmas* (Top Ranking 1978, RAS 1988), *Unfinished Symphony* (Circle 1984), *Who Say Jah No Dread* (Greensleeves 1992). Compilations: *Reggae Greats* (Island 1985), *Greatest Hits* (RAS 1988).

Millie

b. Millicent Small, 6 October 1942, Clarendon, Jamaica. After leaving home at the age of 13 to further her singing career in Kingston, Millie recorded several tracks with producer Coxsone Dodd, who teamed her up with Roy Panton. As Roy And Millie, they achieved local success with 'We'll Meet' and 'Oh, Shirley' and caught the attention of entrepreneur Chris Blackwell. On 22 June 1964, Millie accompanied Blackwell to the UK and recorded Harry Edwards' 'Don't You Know', before being presented with the catchy 'My Boy Lollipop', formerly a US R&B hit for Barbie Gaye, which became a transatlantic Top 5 hit, the first crossover ska record. Such chart fame proved evanescent. A carbon copy follow-up, 'Sweet William', was only a minor hit, and 'Bloodshot Eyes' failed to breach the Top 40. Thereafter she languished in relative obscurity. Even a brief tie-up with Jackie Edwards in Jackie And Millie, and a nude spread in a men's magazine failed to revitalise her career. Ultimately handicapped by her novelty hit, Millie's more serious work, such as the self-chosen *Millie Sings Fats Domino*, was sadly ignored.

Selected album: *The Best Of* (Trojan 1970).

Minott, Sugar

b. Lincoln Minott, 25 May 1956, Kingston, Jamaica. Minott was, perhaps, reggae music's brightest hope throughout the early 80s, but his refusal to compromise and turn his back on either his roots or his ghetto companions has marginalized his influence, and he is now a peripheral figure, as opposed to the major force he arguably deserves to be. Minott first recorded in the mid-70s as one of the African Brothers with Tony Tuff and Derrick Howard for a variety of Kingston producers; a couple of all-time classics evolved from this period, including 'Torturing' and 'Party Night'. The African Brothers eventually arrived at Studio One, where Sugar's precocious talent was immediately recognised and he was taken on as a studio apprentice where he sang whatever was required, often providing percussion and guitar where necessary. His sweet vocals were only one facet of his talent, and his ability to write new songs to fit over existing rhythms was remarkable. The results, in many cases, eclipsed the originals. He had a few steady sellers for Studio One, but it was his debut long player, *Live Loving,* that made his name and extended his popularity. He became a bigger star in the UK than in his homeland, and his first release in Britain, the self-produced 'Hard Time Pressure', was a major underground hit in 1979. He travelled to England later that year, and stayed for a lengthy period, adding immeasurably to the indigenous reggae scene. He became a focus for UK reggae, while releasing many records in the accepted local lovers rock style, which demonstrated his ability to work successfully in any flavour of reggae music. A national chart hit, for Hawkeye Records, followed in 1980, and crossover success seemed to be the next obvious step for Minott.

He had previously parted company with Studio One because of his desire for independence, and set up his own Youth Promotion/Black Roots collective organisation to foster and develop the abundant talent in the Kingston ghettos. Consequently, when he was offered deals for recording and concert work with established companies, Minott refused to sign unless the

Sugar Minott

rest of the Youth Promotion team were a part of the arrangement. This proved too altruistic for the large labels, and Minott continued to work in his own way, recording solo outings for many independent producers to finance his ideals. Sadly, his single-minded determination to help out the youths in the ghetto did not work in his favour, and many young singers and DJs who came to prominence on Sugar's Youth Promotion sound system (one of the top Kingston Sounds of the 80s) went on to greater success elsewhere, while his personal strength, too, seemed to be sapped by his constant caring for others less fortunate. His releases for the latter part of the decade were often lacklustre, relying too heavily on the stringing together of dancehall catchphrases and clichés. However, in the 90s he began to make some excellent records both for himself and other producers, including King Jammy, which at last recalled former glories. Selected albums: *Live Loving* (Studio One 1978), *Showcase* (Studio One 1979), *Black Roots* (Island 1979), *Bittersweet* (Ballistic 1979), *Ghetto-Ology* (Trojan 1979), *Roots Lovers* (Black Roots 1980), *Give The People* (Ballistic 1980), *African Girl* (Black Roots 1981), *Good Thing Going* (RCA 1981), *Dancehall Showcase* (Black Roots 1983), *With Lots Of Extra* (Hitbound 1983), *Herbman Hustling* (Black Roots 1984), *Slice Of The Cake* (Heartbeat 1984), *Wicked A Go Feel It* (Wackies 1984), *Leader Of The Pack* (Striker Lee 1985), *Rydim* (Greensleeves 1985), *Time Longer Than Rope* (Greensleeves 1985), *Inna Reggae Dancehall* (Heartbeat 1986), *Sugar And Spice* (Taxi 1986), *Them Ah Wolf* (C&F 1987), *Jamming In The Streets* (Wackies 1987), *African Soldier* (Heartbeat 1988), *Buy Off The Bar* (Sonic Sounds 1988), *Sugar Minott And Youth Promotion* (NEC 1988), *Lovers Rock Inna Dancehall* (Youth Promotion 1988), *Ghetto Youth Dem Rising* (Heartbeat 1988), *Sufferer's Choice* (Heartbeat 1988), *The Boss Is Back* (RAS 1989), *Smile* (L&M 1990), *A Touch Of Class* (Jammys 1991), *Run Things* (Exterminator 1993). With the African Brothers: *Collectors Item* (Uptempo 1987).

With Leroy Smart: *Rockers Award Winners* (Greensleeves 1985). Compilations: *Best Of Vol. 1* (Black Roots 1988), *The Artist* (L&M 1989, double album), *20 Super Hits* (Sonic Sounds 1990).
Video: *Official Sugar Minott Dance Hall Video* (1988).

Misty In Roots

One of Britain's foremost roots reggae groups, fronted by brothers Walford (lead vocals) and Delvin Tyson (rhythm guitar, vocals), with other regular members including Delbert McKay (guitar, vocals), Chesley Samson (lead guitar), Tony Henry (bass) and Dennis Augustine (rhythm guitar), who took over Delvin's role on the instrument when he elected to concentrate on vocal duties. Samson was replaced by Lorrance Crossfield in 1983, though this was just the most serious of numerous line-up revisions. Through eight John Peel Radio 1 sessions (he numbered them among his favourite groups for several years in the early 80s) they exhibited radically different line-ups for each, happily adding and subtracting musicians and vocalists as the occasion demanded.
The band's origins can be traced to Southall, Middlesex, where they first formed in 1974, backing Jamaican singer Nicky Thomas on his British tour a year later. From early on their commercial brand of reggae attracted supporters, but they relinquished the opportunity of singing to a major in order to set up their own People Unite label. On successive releases they honed a crafted, pleasing sound which would later see them become the first band in the reggae idiom invited to play Russia. They were also heavily involved in the Rock Against Racism movement playing alongside punk bands such as 999 and the Ruts. The fact that their staunch Rastafarian views were aired regularly on Radio 1 via Peel could only strengthen links between the two musical camps. Their Rasta beliefs were reinforced in the 80s by playing shows in their spiritual homeland of Africa, which

helped them to define: 'A feeling which has always been there'. Alongside Steel Pulse and Aswad, Misty In Roots rank as the most important UK reggae band of their generation.

Albums: *Live At The Counter-Eurovision* (People Unite 1979), *Wise And Foolish* (People Unite 1981), *Earth* (People Unite 1983), *Musi O Tunya* (People Unite 1985), *Forward* (Kaz 1989).

Mittoo, Jackie

b. 1948, Kingston, Jamaica, d. 1990. The self-effacing Jackie Mittoo was perhaps reggae's premier keyboard player, and had as much influence on the direction of reggae in the 60s and 70s as any single musician. Mittoo was taught to play the piano by his grandmother, first performing in public before he was 10 years old. After playing with local Kingston bands the Rivals and the Sheiks, Mittoo came to the attention of Coxsone Dodd at Studio One. At 15 Mittoo was playing piano and organ in the Skatalites, thereafter performing scouting and arranging duties for Dodd's labels. His own 'Got My Bugaloo' (1966) 45, a rare vocal outing, was one of the best records of the ska era and presaged the arrival of rocksteady, and his work with the Soul Brothers and, later, Soul Vendors bands, helped keep Studio One ahead of rival production houses. His playing behind the Heptones, Cables, Wailers and innumerable solo acts helped create the sound of reggae for years to come: later artists and studios, such as Augustus Pablo, Channel One and almost the entire dancehall movement of the early-80s based their rhythm arrangements on material that Mittoo had pioneered in the 60s. Dodd also issued solo albums by Mittoo from 1967 onwards, and they (*Now* and *Macka Fat* particularly) rank amongst the most artistically pleasing organ instrumental LPs outside of Booker T and jazz maestros like Jimmy Smith. For proof, try his radical arrangement of 'Eleanor Rigby' on *Now*, transforming a worn-out song with an astonishing roots sound.

In the mid-70s Mittoo left Dodd to work in Canada, where he set up the Stine-Jac label to moderate success, with music that was similar to that which he had left behind at Studio One, and cut several albums for producer Bunny Lee in both Jamaica and London. He also worked extensively on some fine sessions for Sugar Minott's Youth Promotion outlet, still displaying the same taste and rhythmic acumen that had always been his trademark. He was deeply respected as an elder statesman amongst Sugar's young reggae guns. He died in 1990, an event that brought about a long-overdue reassessment of his work among reggae cognoscenti. Undoubtedly, if he had been an American musician, his name would be spoken in the same breath as the greats of black music.

Selected albums: With the Soul Vendors: *On Tour* (Studio One 60s). Solo: *Evening Time* (1967), *In London* (Coxsone 1967), *Keep On Dancing* (1969), *Now* (1969), *Macka Fat* (Studio One 1970), *Hot Blood* (1977), *Cold Blood* (1978), *Keyboard King* (1978), *Showcase* (Studio One 1983). Compilation: *The Original Jackie Mittoo* (Third World 1979).

Monyaka

This six-piece Jamaican-born, Brooklyn, New York, USA based reggae act was led by guitarist/vocalist Errol Moore. At the time of their hit in 1983 other group members included Beres Barnet (guitar/vocals), Paul Henton (bass/vocals), Richard Bertram (drums/percussion), William Brown and John Allen (keyboards). Formed in 1974 as the Soul Supersonics they backed visiting reggae stars and released their first single, 'Rocking Time', in 1977. They followed this with *Classical Roots*, both records being released in the USA on their Hevyaka label. Under the new name Monyaka (Swahili for 'good luck') they recorded 'Stand Up Strong' in 1982. A year later, with just three original members left, they had a UK Top 20 hit with 'Go Deh Yaka'(patois for 'go to the top'), which cleverly fused reggae and contemporary R&B. The follow-up 'Reggae-matic Funk' failed to continue the interest and this unique band joined the ranks of reggae one-hit wonders.

Album: *Classical Roots* (Monyaka 1977).

Morgan, Derrick

b. March 1940, Stewarton, Jamaica. Morgan's recording career stretches back to the birth of the Jamaican record industry, c.1959-60. An imposing figure invariably topped with an almost brimless pork-pie hat, his cool, hip and rhythmic voice, enlivened by the occasional excited yelp, applied itself successfully to a variety of styles in those formative years, such as the Latin beat of 'Fat Man' (1960), the gospel fervour of 'I Pray For You' (1961) and the shuffling R&B of his Jamaican Independence anthem, 'Forward March' (1962). He duetted with female singer Patsy on a series of Shirley And Lee-styled numbers, that duo being currently popular in Jamaica, before settling into a ska style with 'Shake A Leg' (1962) and other recordings for Prince Buster.

His split from Buster to join the Chinese-owned Beverley's Records led to an entertaining, and successful, exchange of insults on singles like Morgan's 'Blazing Fire' and Buster's unequivocal 'Blackhead China Man' (Buster resented the idea of the Jamaican music industry being controlled by non-blacks). Morgan recorded prolifically throughout the 60s and into the 70s, recording rocksteady cuts such as 'Greedy Gal' (1967). He quickly became a very popular figure with reggae's UK skinhead followers.About this time his sight, always impaired, deteriorated to the extent where he could see only 'light and clouds', and he is now musically less active, though as recently as 1990 he travelled to London for a ska revival concert.

Selected albums: *Forward March* (Island 1963), *Seven Letters* (1969), *Forward March* (Beverley's 1964), *Moon Hop* (1970), *In The Mood* (Magnet 1974), *Development* (1975), *People Decision* (Third World 1977). Compilations: *Blazing Fire Vol. 1 & 2* (1988), *I Am The Ruler* (Trojan 1993).

Morwells

Formed in 1973, Kingston, Jamaica, this group featured Maurice 'Blacka' Wellington (vocals/percussion) and Eric 'Binghi Buny' Lamont (vocals/guitar). Prior to forming the group, Wellington had been a record salesman, and Lamont had recorded with Bongo Herman for Derrick Harriott. The group's name is a contraction of Maurice Wellington. In 1974 they released 'Mafia Boss' and 'You Got To Be Holy' on their own Morwell Esquire label, and followed these with their debut, *Presenting The Morwells* (1975). The album is a blend of strong original songs and covers of hits by the Melodians and Delroy Wilson. A dub version of the album, *Dub Me*, was also released, and proved even more popular than the vocal album. In 1976 Wellington became an engineer and producer for Joe Gibbs, and Lamont became the rhythm guitarist with the Revolutionaries, Channel One's houseband. This gave them fairly free access to the island's top musicians and studios, and in this period they reached peak form. Singles on Morwell Esquire included 'Proverb' (1976) and 'Crab In A Bag' (1977), and eight tracks from their first album plus four singles were released in the UK as *Crab Race*.

Bassist Errol 'Flabba' Holt now joined the group on a permanent basis, and further singles in 1977 included ''77 Festival' for Joe Gibbs, 'Mix-up' for Winston 'Niney' Holness and 'Africa We Want To Go' for Tony Robinson. Excellent albums followed with *Cool Runnings* (1978), *Kingston 12 Toughie* (1979) and *The Best Of The Morwells* (1981). The group then broke up, with Maurice Wellington continuing with the Morwell label, and Eric Lamont and Errol Holt forming the Roots Radics.

Albums: *Presenting* (Morwells 1975), *Dub Me* (1975), *Crab Race* (Burning Sounds 1978), *Cool Runnings* (Bushays 1979), *Kingston 12 Toughies* (Carib Gems 1980). Compilation: *The Best Of The Morwells* (Night Hawk 1981).

Blacka Morwell (the Morwells)

Moses, Pablo

b. Pablo Henry, c.1953, Jamaica. In 1975 Pablo made his debut recording 'I Man A Grasshopper'. It was immediately evident that an extraordinary talent was at work, an impression that was sustained by the release of 'We Should Be In Angola' (1976), produced by Clive Hunt. His first album, *Revolutionary Dream*, was released in 1977, and it still stands as a genuine mid-70s reggae classic. Pablo's detached delivery of his parable-like songs coalesced with Geoffrey Chung's brilliant production and arrangements to form a truly remarkable whole. Two further excellent albums under Chung's supervision followed: *A Song* (1980) and *Pave The Way* (1981). Pablo then decided to produce himself, but could not sustain the quality of his previous releases. Since the early 80s he has toured extensively, and gained a strong reputation internationally as a live performer.
Albums: *Revolutionary Dream* (Tropical Sound Track 1976), *A Song* (Island 1980), *Pave The Way* (Mango/Island 1981), *In The Future* (Alligator/Mercury 1983), *Tension* (Alligator/Mercury 1985), *Live To Love* (Rohit 1985), *We Refuse* (Profile 1990), *Charlie* (Profile 1990), *The Confessions Of A Rastaman* (Musidisc 1993).

Mowatt, Judy

b. c.1952, Kingston, Jamaica. In her teens Mowatt joined a dance troupe which toured the Caribbean. There she met up with Beryl Lawson and Merle Clemonson, with whom she formed the Gaylettes (aka the Gaytones). Together they backed many artists on releases for the Federal label in the mid-60s, until Mowatt's two accomplices left for America in 1970. Deciding to press ahead with a solo career, she recorded widely in both soul and reggae styles, under a variety of names due to contractual complications. The most notable of these releases was 'I Shall Sing', the first of a string of reggae chart successes. Subsequently Mowatt joined the Twelve Tribes Of Israel organisation, aligning herself with fellow Jamaican musicians such as Dennis Brown and Freddie McGregor. She formed her own label, Ashandan, and in the early 70s joined Marcia Griffiths on stage, alongside Rita Marley. Eventually the three way partnership was cemented as the I-Threes, Bob Marley having been suitably impressed by their performance as a trio. While working with Marley she continued her solo career, and also managed to find time to raise a family. She also had the honour of being the first to record at Bob Marley's Tuff Gong studio in Kingston, sessions which produced the *Black Woman* set. It was the first time that a female artist had produced her own album in Jamaica. Not only was it an outstanding work in its own right, but it offered an articulate voice for Jamaican women, who had previously been either under or mis-represented in the reggae idiom. Largely self-penned (with notable contributions from Bob Marley and Freddie McGregor) it proved a landmark work, her sweet, plaintive voice giving excellent service to her deeply held Rastafarian and feminist beliefs. She has continued to forge a solo career which rivals that of her old sparring partner Griffiths for the title of Jamaica's first woman of reggae. However, attempts to crossover have been less successful, notably *Love Is Overdue* which included takes on 'Try A Little Tenderness' and UB40's 'Sing Our Own Song'. The album did bring her a Grammy nomination though, the first occasion on which a female reggae artist had been so honoured.
Albums: *Mellow Mood* (Ashandan 1975), *Black Woman* (Tuff Gong/Shanachie 1979), *Only A Woman* (Shanachie 1982), *Mr D.J.* (Ashandan 1982), *Working Wonders* (Shanachie 1985), *Love Is Overdue* (Greensleeves 1986).

Mudie, Harry A.

b. c.1940, Spanish Town, Jamaica. One of the unsung pioneers of Jamaican recording, Mudie first developed his interest in music while a pupil at St. Jago High School during the mid-50s. His debut with the legendary

Pablo Moses

Judy Mowatt

Rasta drummer Count Ossie and saxophonist Wilton Gaynair, entitled 'Babylon Gone', aka 'Going Home', backed with 'So Long' by Winston And Roy, was released in the UK on the Blue Beat label in 1962. The same year he opened the Scaramouch Garden Amusement Center in Spanish Town. Little seems to have emerged, though, between 1962 and 1970, when Trojan Records began releasing his productions on the specially formed Moodisc label. A year later Rita and Benny King's R&B Discs Ltd created their own Moodisc label. Using a studio band led by pianist Gladstone Anderson, Mudie deftly combined sweet, tuneful melodies with heavy rhythms. The records issued on these and his Jamaican labels, including organist Winston Wright's 'Musically Red', Winston Shand's 'Time Is The Master', the Eternal's 'Push Me In The Corner', the Ebony Sisters' 'Let Me Tell You Boy', John Holt's 'It May Sound Silly', Dennis Walk's 'The Drifter' and 'Heart Don't Leap', Count Ossie's 'Whispering Drums', Lloyd Jones' 'Rome' and trumpeter Jo Jo Bennett's instrumental version 'Leaving Rome', established Mudie's name among the very best of the reggae producers of the day. He launched DJ I Roy on record with 'Musical Pleasure' and a version of 'The Drifter'. He was probably the first to use strings in the music, notably on John Holt's classic love song album, *Time Is The Master* (1973), and it is arguably this fact that seems to have prejudiced his standing among some of the more reactionary elements of the reggae audience.

In 1973 he scored a big reggae hit with Dennis Walks' calypso-flavoured 'Margaret', released on the Cactus label in the UK, following it with vibist Lennie Hibbert's version 'Margaret's Dream'. He also produced the Heptones on the classic 'Love Without Feeling', DJ tunes by Count Sticky, Big Joe ('Set Your Face At Ease' on the 'Rome' rhythm), and Jah Lloyd, and a plethora of 'Drifter' cuts by Bongo Herman and others. During the mid-70s Mudie issued three classic dub albums mixed by

King Tubby, instrumental sets by Gladstone Anderson and Ossie Scott, vocal albums by Dennis Walks and Bunny Maloney, for whom he produced the popular Jamaican lovers favourite 'Baby I've Been Missing You', and two excellent various artists collections. During the 80s and 90s he concentrated on his back catalogue with re-presses and some excellent new compilations such as *Reggae History Volume One* and *Reggae Bible*, the latter being a whole album based on the 'Drifter' rhythm. This prolific period produced over 100 singles and several 12-inch 'discomix' singles as the decade closed. Mudie recorded a variety of other artists, including Gregory Isaacs, Freddy Mckay, Joe White, Cornell Campbell, Jah Walton (now known as Joseph Cotton), and Prince Heron. During the 80s he kept a low profile, moving to Miami, Florida, issuing his back catalogue and an album by Bunny Maloney.
Selected albums: Rhythm Rulers: *Mudies Mood* (1970). Jo Jo Bennett: *Groovy Joe* (1970). Gladstone Anderson: *It May Sound Silly* (1972), *Gladdy Unlimited* (1977). John Holt: *Time Is The Master* (1973). Bunny Maloney: *Magic Woman* (1978). Ossie Scott: *Reggae Exposure With Sax* (1983). With King Tubby: *Harry Mudie Meets King Tubby In Dub Conference Vols. 1, 2 & 3* (Mudies 1975/6/7). Harry Mudie & Friends: *Let Me Tell You Boy 1970-71* (Trojan 1988). Various: *Quad Star Revolution Vol. 1* (1974), *Quad Star Revolution Vol. 2* (1976), *Reggae History Vol. 1* (Moods 1985).

Mundell, Hugh

b. 14 June 1962, Kingston, Jamaica. Hugh Mundell made his first recording for producer Joe Gibbs, the unreleased 'Where Is Natty Dread', while barely in his teens. After this false start his career really got under way when his precocious talent impressed session player/producer Augustus Pablo. Pablo enlisted his services as a DJ alongside Jah Bull on his Rockers sound system, and produced his first single release, 'Africa Must Be Free', in 1975. Several more singles were released over the next two years, including 'My Mind', 'Don't Stay Away Too Long', 'Let's All Unite' and 'Book Of Life', before the classic *Africa Must Be Free By 1983*, which was released in 1978, swiftly establishing Mundell's name as a bright new roots star in the ascendant.

Pablo further recorded Mundell on such sides as 'That Little Short Man', 'Feeling Alright', 'Jah Says The Time Has Come', 'One Jah One Aim And Destiny' and 'Great Tribulation'. Sundry other recordings were undertaken in his DJ mode as Jah Levi, surfacing mainly on 12". In 1979 Mundell tried his hand at self-production on 'Stop Them Jah' and 'Blackman's Foundation', as well as producing the teenage 'Little' Junior Reid on his debut, 'Speak The Truth', which emerged on Pablo's Rockers label in Jamaica. Another excellent song, 'Rastafari's Call' appeared on Mundell's own Muni Music label, while 'Can't Pop No Style' surfaced in 1981 on Greensleeves, coupled with Junior Reid's 'Know Myself'. The same year Mundell issued a co-produced album with Pablo entitled *Time And Place*, containing many of those tracks previously released as singles listed above, after which he broke with Pablo altogether, going on to record 'Jah Fire Will Be Burning' for Prince Jammy and *Mundell* for Henry 'Junjo' Lawes. Ironically it was in 1983, the year he prophesised for Africa's emancipation on his first record, that Hugh Mundell was tragically shot and killed whilst sitting in his car after an argument over a fridge.

Albums: *Africa Must Be Free By 1983* (Message 1978), *Time & Place* (Ja Mun Rock 1981), *Mundell* (Greensleeves 1982), *Black Man Foundation* (Shanachie 1985), *Arise* (Atra 1987).

Murvin, Junior

b. c.1949, Port Antonio, Jamaica. Murvin first recorded for producers Sonia Pottinger and Derrick Harriott in the early 70s as Junior Soul (not to be confused with the New York-based reggae singer of the same name). 'Solomon', a traditional Jamaican air, sold fairly well in 1972, but shortly after,

Murvin vanished from the public eye. In 1976 he turned up, guitar in hand, at Lee Perry's Black Ark studio in Kingston, with a song that he had been working on for some time. No-one was aware that this singer, now calling himself Junior Murvin, had ever recorded before, but Perry liked what he heard and within weeks 'Police And Thieves' was the biggest-selling Jamaican record of the year. Its popularity crossed the Atlantic to the UK and, released on Island, became the anthem for that year's violence-troubled Notting Hill Carnival. Perry recorded another couple of versions of the rhythm before issuing a strong album of the same title in 1977. The single was finally a UK chart hit in 1978. Junior's Curtis Mayfield-styled falsetto (he covered Mayfield's 'People Get Ready' and 'Closer Together') worked well with Perry's silky, complex arrangements, but the pair never put together another album; Perry was about to crack up and demolish his studio. Murvin moved on to work with Joe Gibbs, Mikey Dread, Henry 'Junjo' Lawes and Prince Jammy, but he has never quite captured the moment as 'Police And Thieves' did. Murvin's influence spilled over into rock, however, with 'Police And Thieves' right-on rude-boy image suiting the Clash's first album.

Albums: *Police And Thieves* (Island 1977), *Bad Man Posse* (Dread At The Controls 1982), *Muggers In The Street* (Greensleeves 1984), *Apartheid* (1986), *Signs And Wonders* (Live & Love 1989).

Musical Youth

Formed at Duddeston Manor School, Birmingham, England, this pop/reggae-influenced group featured two sets of brothers, Kelvin and Michael Grant and Junior and Patrick Waite (d. February 18 1993). The latter pair's father, Fred Waite, was a former member of Jamaican group the Techniques, and sang lead with Junior at the start of the group's career in the late 70s. Although schoolboys, the group managed to secure gigs at certain Birmingham pubs and

Musical Youth

released a single, 'Political'/'Generals' on local label 021 Records. An appearance on BBC DJ John Peel's evening show brought further attention to the group and they were signed to MCA Records. By that time, founding father Fred Waite had backed down to be replaced by Dennis Seaton as lead singer. During the winter of 1982, the group issued one of the fastest selling singles of the year in 'Pass The Dutchie'. Based on the Mighty Diamonds' 'Pass The Kouchie' (a song about marijuana), the title had been subtly altered to feature the patois 'Dutchie' (literally a 'cooking pot'). The infectious enthusiasm of the group's performance captured the public's imagination and propelled the record to number 1 in the UK charts. A US Top 10 hit also followed. The catchy follow-up 'Youth Of Today' also reached the UK Top 20 and early in 1983 'Never Gonna Give You Up' climbed to number 6. Minor successes with 'Heartbreaker' and 'Tell Me Why' were succeeded by a surprise collaboration with Donna Summer on the UK Top 20 hit 'Unconditional Love'. A revival of Desmond Dekker's '007' saw them back in the Top 30, but after one final hit with 'Sixteen', they fell from commercial grace and subsequently split up in 1985 when Seaton left the band. Plans to reform were scotched when Patrick Waite, who had gone on to a career of juvenile crime, died of natural causes while awaiting a court appearance on drug charges. The Grant brothers remain involved in music, while Seaton has released a solo set and formed his own band, XMY.
Albums: *The Youth Of Today* (MCA 1982), *Different Style* (MCA 1983). Dennis Seaton: *Imagine That* (Bellaphon, Germany 1989).

Mutabaruka

Jamaican dub poet who combines social commentary with scathing personal analysis and endearing humour. Having published several volumes of poetry (also writing for *Swing* magazine), Mutabaruka reserves his aural adventures for his most effective tirades against hypocrisy, injustice, or more particularly, stupidity. His favoured means of denouncing his enemies rests strongly with the latter, vilifying them and the contradictions of their positions by means of a languid, inviting slur. His debut album for Earl 'Chinna' Smith's High Times imprint was a genre classic. Muta tore through a set which railed against oppression on all fronts, aided and abetted by Chinna's imaginative rhythms and arrangements. 'Everytime A Ear De Soun', from the album, was also a big hit on 45. In the interim he has ensured his position as Jamaica's most popular, radical poet, with a series of inspiring albums. Despite such militancy, his metaphorical feet are kept on the ground by his day job: operating a health food store in Jamaica and broadcasting on Jamaica's Irie FM radio station.
Selected albums: *Check It* (High Times 1982), *The Mystery Unfolds* (Shanachie 1986), *Out Cry* (Shanachie 1987), *Any Which Way* (Greensleeves 1989), *Blakk Wi Black...Kkk* (Shanachie 1991).

N

Ninjaman

b. Desmond Ballantine, Kingston, Jamaica. Notorious from his long history of fearless controversy on record, stage show and sound system, Ninjaman's popularity in the Jamaican dancehalls has been unrivalled. He began DJing when he was 12, progressing to the Black Culture sound system and then Kilimanjaro, where from 1984 onwards he was apprentice to Supercat and Early B, known as Double Ugly. When another DJ appeared with the same name he became Uglyman, recording his debut for the Soul Carib label. That name too was short-lived; a second Uglyman arrived and, determined to forge an invincible identity of his own, 'Ugly' quickly became Ninja. His first hit, 'Protection', was self-produced, and voiced alongside Courtney Melody in 1987. The following year Lloyd Dennis teamed him with Tinga Stewart for a notable string of hits including 'Cover Me' and then 'Zig It Up', duetted with Flourgon. His early producers included King Jammys, Witty, Redman and Ini Kamoze, but it was with the advent of the Gulf War in 1990 that he became transformed into the archetypal outlaw; brandishing the title of 'Original Front Tooth, Gold Tooth, Gun Pon Tooth Don Gorgon', recording a bounty of apocalyptic 'burial' tunes interspersed with the most uncompromising 'reality' lyrics heard from any DJ of the ragga era. His sense of melodrama and stuttering verbal walkabouts are unique; he spread his fiery invective over many fine sides for Bobby Digital ('Permit To Bury', 'Fulfilment'), King Jammys ('Border Clash'/'Reality Yuh Want'), Mr. Doo ('Murder Weapon'), Gussie Clarke ('Above The Law'), Steely & Clevie ('Murder Dem') and Exterminator throughout 1991-1992. Among his many targets have been Shabba Ranks, who has

had to endure an incessant stream of taunts over the years. By the end of 1992, after surviving a bout of Christianity, arrest on gun charges and a flood of imitators, his talents had become over-exposed, though he remained one of the few genuinely original DJs to remain without a major record deal. Instead he made unremarkable albums for Henry 'Junjo' Lawes and then Junior Reid, still waiting for a much-deserved wider audience.

Selected Albums: *Super Star* (Witty 1989), *Kill Them & Done* (Tassa 1990), *Out Pon Bail* (Exterminator 1990), *Move From Here* (1990), *Run Come Test* (RAS 1990), *Reggae Sunsplash* (Pickout 1991), *Warning You Now* (Jammys 1991), *Nobody's Business But My Own* (Shanachie 1991), *My Weapon* (Mr Doo 1991), *Bounty Hunter* (Blue Mountain 1991), *Target Practice* (Jammys 1992), *Original Front Tooth, Gold Tooth, Gun Pon Tooth Don Gorgon* (Greensleeves 1992), *Sing-A-Ling-A-Ling School Pickney Sing Ting* (Greensleeves 1992), *Hardcore Killing* (Greensleeves 1993), *Booyakka! Booyakka!* (Greensleves 1994). With Courtney Melody: *Protection* (1989). With Capleton & Tony Rebel: *Real Rough* (1990). With Johnny P and Japanese: *Rough, Mean & Deadly - Ninja Man With Johnny P* (Pickout 1990).

Nitty Gritty

b. Glen Augustus Holness, 1957, August Town, Kingston, Jamaica, d. 24 June 1991, Brooklyn, New York, USA. Nitty Gritty rose to prominence as computerised rhythms took hold in Jamaica, alongside Tenor Saw, King Kong and Anthony Red Rose, all of whom shared a similar vocal style. Gritty's was a deep-throated, gospel-tinged wail distinguished by improvised catchphrases. He was born the second eldest of 11 children in a church-going family, and he trained as an electrician before founding a local group called the Soulites. In 1973 he sang 'Let The Power Fall On I' with Dennis Brown, George Nooks and the Mighty Diamonds for Joe Gibbs, but his first solo release, 'Every Man Is A Seller', did not arrive for

Niney The Observer (see Holness, Winston 'Niney')

another decade, being voiced for Sugar Minott's Youth Promotion label. After a spell on the Zodiac sound system with Danny Dread he cut several sides at Channel One, and two for Eric 'Bubbles' Howard of the African Brothers, before moving on to George Phang in 1984. By the following April he had joined forces with King Jammys and their first release together, 'Hog In A Minty', was an instant success with its haunting vocal refrain and shuffling 'tempo' rhythm track. It was promptly followed by 'Good Morning Teacher', 'Sweet Reggae Music', 'Run Down The World' and 'Gimme Some Of Your Something', all of them sizeable hits. His debut album, *Turbo Charged,* arrived in 1986 as did *Musical Confrontation,* on which credits were shared with King Kong.

Soon afterwards he moved to London and then to New York, his output becoming more varied but lacking the impact of his work with Jammys. Singles appeared for Uptempo, Black Solidarity and Skengdon. He returned to form with *General Penitentiary*, recorded with the Studio One Band in 1987. This was far more like the Nitty Gritty of old. By 1989 an album for Blacker Dread had arrived with material dating back to his first visit to England in 1986, after which he became relatively inactive. At the age of 34 he was shot dead outside Super Power record shop in Brooklyn, New York.

Selected albums: *Turbo Charged* (Greensleeves 1986), *General Penitentiary* (Black Victory 1987), *Nitty Gritty* (Witty 1988), *Jah In The Family* (Blacker Dread/SCOM 1989). With King Kong: *Musical Confrontation* (Jammys 1986). With Tenor Saw: *Powerhouse Presents* (Powerhouse 1989).

Now Generation

One of the great unsung bands (or session teams) in the history of Jamaican music. Led by Geoffrey Chung on keyboards, the band included Mikey Chung on lead guitar, Val Douglas on bass, Mikey 'Boo' Richards on drums, Robert Lynn on keyboards and Earl 'Wire' Lindo on organ. They worked on sessions for all the top producers in the early 70s, including Derrick Harriott, Herman Chin-Loy, Ken Khouri, Sonia Pottinger, Joe Gibbs and some of the late Duke Reid's reggae recordings. Their music was 'uptown' and soul influenced (they covered many soul classics), but they proved that they could provide raw roots records too - Glen Brown's better work, or Herman's 'Aquarius Dub' being notable examples. Their tightness and all round panache distinguished them from other session bands at the time, but they have never, sadly, been quite as celebrated as other less skilful outfits - perhaps due to a lack of show and stage work. They certainly deserve much wider recognition.

Selected album: *For The Good Times* (Trojan 1974).

O

Osbourne, Johnny

b. c.1948, Jamaica. During 1967 Osbourne became lead vocalist of the Wildcats, and recorded for producer Winston Riley, although nothing was issued. The Wildcats' manager then financed a session at Coxsone Dodd's Studio One, from which his debut single, 'All I Have Is Love', was released. In 1969 he recorded an album, *Come Back Darling*, for Riley. It was a strong collection on which Johnny was supported by the Sensations on harmony vocals. On the day that he completed the album, he emigrated to Toronto, Canada, to join his family. After singing with various soul and reggae groups, he became lead vocalist for Ishan People, and recorded two albums with them. The group broke up in 1979, and Johnny decided to return to Jamaica. Shortly after returning, he recorded 'Forgive Them' and 'Jealousy, Heartache And Pain' for the Studio One label. Through late 1979 and early 1980 he recorded extensively for Dodd, with these sessions culminating in a stunning album, *Truths And Rights*. This beautifully understated set of classic songs is Osbourne's major work. In 1979 he also had a hit for Prince Jammy with 'Folly Ranking', and an excellent album of the same name followed in 1980. The success of these recordings made him one of the most in-demand vocalists on the island, and a glut of material was released, including *Fally Lover*, *Warrior*, *Innah Disco Style* and *Never Stop Fighting*, between 1980-82. In 1983, he began the year with two big hits, 'Yo Yo' and 'Lend Me A Chopper', and later in the year enjoyed massive success with 'Water Pumping', an adaptation of Hopeton Lewis' 'Take It Easy', which had also served as the basis for Johnny Clarke's 1976 hit 'Rockers Time Now'. The hits continued with 'Get Cracking', 'Check For You', 'Rewind' (1984), 'Buddy Bye', 'No Sound Like We' and 'In The Area' (1985). In the late 80s he was particularly successful when recording for Bobby Digital, and had hits with 'Good Time Rock' (1988) and 'Rude Boy Skank' (1988), both of which are included on the album *Rougher Than Them* (1989). Throughout the 80s he continued to record for Coxsone Dodd, and excellent singles included 'Keep That Light', 'Unity' and 'A We Run Things', but a long-promised second album from Dodd has not materialised. Johnny's versatility and talent have enabled him to remain at the forefront of reggae, and no matter how thin the lyrics he has sung have been, often no more than encouragements to dance or endorsements of a particular sound system, he always manages to inject artistry and vitality into the proceedings. He is doubtless capable of another *Truths And Rights*.

Albums: *Come Back Darling* (Trojan 1969), *Truths And Rights* (Studio One 1980), *Folly Ranking* (Jammys 1980), *Fally Lover* (Greensleeves 1980), *Never Stop Fighting* (Greensleeves 1982), *Water Pumping* (Greensleeves 1984), *Reggae On Broadway* (Vista Sounds 1984), *Dancing Time* (Londisc 1984), *Johnny Osbourne* (Lix 1984), *In The Area* (Greensleeves 1984), *Rub A Dub Soldier* (Jammys 1985), *Bring The Sensi Come* (Midnight Rock 1985), *Reality* (Selection 1985), *Rock Me Rock Me* (Top Rank 1986), *Cool Down* (1989), *Johnny Osbourne* (Jetstar 1989), *Rougher Than Them* (1989), *Smiling Faces* (Blue Mountain 1989), *Nuh Dis (Come Ya Fe Drink Milk)* (Star 1990). With Michael Palmer: *Michael Palmer Meets Johnny Osbourne* (Vibes & Vibes 1984).

P

Pablo, Augustus

b. Horace Swaby, c.1954, St. Andrew, Jamaica. Pablo was responsible for putting the humble melodica on the musical map when one day in 1969 he walked into Herman Chin-Loy's Aquarius Records shop clutching the instrument and was taken down to Randy's studio the following day to cut his first record, 'Iggy Iggy'. His next release for the same producer was the prototype 'Far East' sound of 'East Of The River Nile'. Moving from Chin-Loy to Clive Chin as his new producer at Randy's, the next single, 'Java', proved to be Pablo's biggest, and one of his most influential. Chin later worked on the classic instrumental set, *This Is Augustus Pablo,* on which Pablo played a number of lead keyboard instruments. He worked with other producers at this time, cutting 'Lovers Mood' for Leonard Chin, 'Hot And Cold' with Lee Perry and others for Gussie Clarke, Keith Hudson and Bunny Lee. Dissatisfied with the financial and artistic arrangements with the producers, Pablo set up his own label named Rockers, after the sound system he and his brother Garth operated. His first releases were a mixture of new versions of old Studio One rhythms; 'Skanking Easy' (from 'Swing Easy') and 'Frozen Dub' (from 'Frozen Soul'), plus original compositions 'Cassava Piece', '555 Crown Street' and 'Pablo's Theme Song'. *King Tubby Meets Rockers Uptown* is regarded by many as one of the finest dub albums of all time. It contains dubwise versions of most of Pablo's productions mixed by the legendary independent studio engineer King Tubby. Other artists have benefitted from Pablo's skills as a producer, notably Jacob Miller, Hugh Mundell and Tetrack. Pablo was also in demand as a session musician and played on countless recordings throughout the 70s.

East Of The River Nile in 1978 remains his most compelling instrumental set after *This Is Augustus Pablo.* On this release, Pablo and his Rockers All Stars band, featuring guitarist Earl 'Chinna' Smith, created vast landscapes of rhythmic sound awash with Pablo's string synthesizer and melodica. The sound bore the unmistakable production stamp of Lee Perry's Black Ark studios.

The early 80s saw Pablo floundering somewhat in the early throes of the dancehall revolution, though he later rallied with his production of Junior Delgado's 'Raggamuffin Year' single and album in 1986. Since then he has released a number or recordings with varying degrees of artistic success, both of his own music and that of artists such as Yammie Bolo, Icho Candy, Delroy Williams, Norris Reid and Blacka T. Ironically, he has managed to adapt to the new computerised technology that many of his fans blame for what they see as the decline in musicianship in reggae music in the 80s and 90s. A withdrawn slip of a man, often in ill-health, Pablo's music has, at its best, always reflected a humility and inner peace. Although most critics agree his influential and commercially successful period was over by the end of the 70s, his most recent instrumental set, *Blowing With The Wind,* was his best since *East Of The River Nile,* and belies criticisms of artistic demise.

Albums: *This Is Augustus Pablo* (Tropical 1974), *Thriller* (Tropical/Nationwide 1975), *Ital Dub* (Trojan 1975), *King Tubby Meets Rockers Uptown* (Clocktower 1977), *East Of The River Nile* (Message 1978), *Africa Must Be Free By 1983 Dub* (Greensleeves 1979), *Earth Rightful Ruler* (Message 1982), *Rockers Meet King Tubby In A Fire House* (Shanachie 1982), *King David's Melody* (Alligator 1983), *Rising Sun* (Greensleeves 1986), *East Man Dub* (Greensleeves 1988), *Rockers Comes East* (Greensleeves 1988), *Blowing With The Wind* (Greensleeves 1990), *Heartical Chant* (Rockers International 1992), *Pablo And Friends* (1992). With Junior Delgado: *Raggamuffin Dub* (Rockers International

Augustus Pablo

1990). Compilations: *Original Rockers* (Greensleeves 1979), *Original Rockers 2* (Greensleeves 1989), *Authentic Golden Melodies* (Rockers International 1992).

Pama Records

Once the chief rival to Trojan, Pama has since evolved into Jet Star, the main reggae distributors in the UK. Originally the brainchild of occasional Jamaican record producers, the Palmer Brothers, Pama was founded in London in 1967, releasing an almost endless supply of Jamaican productions on a series of labels that were less high-profile than Trojan's in the white market, but which were every bit as musically strong as its rival's. Among Pama's subsidiary labels were Pama Supreme, Supreme, Crab, Bullet, Gas, New/Nu Beat, Success, Camel, Escort, Unity and Punch, the latter perhaps epitomising reggae's attitude, depicting a fist punching through a top 10 pop chart. Through these labels the brothers worked with nearly all of the top reggae producers, including Laurel Aitken (chiefly Nu Beat), Lee Perry (chiefly Punch), Rupie Edwards (Success), Bunny Lee (Unity, which scored a massive hit with Max Romeo's 'Wet Dream' in 1969) and virtually everyone who was anyone in reggae at the time. They also issued a series of *Straighten Up* albums in competition with Trojan's *Tighten Up* series, which remain highly collectable today, plus a scattering of non-reggae LPs, including *Butlins Red Coat Revue* and an album commemorating the investiture of the Prince Of Wales! By the mid-70s the business was chiefly in the hands of the youngest Palmer brother, Carl, who began to concentrate on setting-up a distribution network in the UK, which has gradually expanded to the point of ubiquity: if Jet Star don't distribute it, it's probably not reggae.
Selected albums: Various: *Crab's Biggest Hits* (Crab 1969), *Straighten Up Volume 1* (Pama 1970). The Upsetters: *Clint Eastwood* (Pama 1970). Max Romeo: *Let The Power Fall* (Pama 1972).

Papa Levi, Phillip

b. Phillip Williams. Papa Levi originally rose to fame on south London's Saxon sound system in the early 80s. His committed and uncompromising stance has, perhaps, denied him the kind of mainstream success that his talent deserves. As the premier UK MC of the period he was notable for a number of firsts: he was the first from the Saxon posse to make a record – 'Mi God Mi King' (for Paul Robinson aka Barry Boom), the first UK MC to have a number 1 record in Jamaica when the same record was released on the Taxi label – and the first to sign a major recording deal – with Island Records. But while others reaped the spin off benefits from these achievements Levi never moved from Saxon Sound System. Live on the mic. he dominated the proceedings and little was lost in the transfer to vinyl, as demonstrated on 'Mi God Mi King' when he dropped into the 'fast style' at the end of the record. The effect really was shattering. The rest of the decade saw him notching up some notable away performances in both Kingston and New York with Saxon on tour. Sadly he has never actually recorded that often, although when he does the results are always of interest. The 90s have neither seen nor heard too much from Levi but judging by his past performances the fireworks will start again once he returns to the studio.
Albums: *Trouble In Africa* (1987), *Code Of Practice* (Ariwa 1990). Various: *Coughing Up Fire - Saxon Studio Live* (Greensleeves 1985), *Great British MCs* (Fashion 1985, includes 'Mi God Mi King').

Papa San

b. Tyrone Thompson, 1966, Spanish Town, Jamaica. Probably the fastest DJ in the world and certainly one of the most inventive, Papa San began his career on the People's Choice, Small Axe and Creation sound systems, based around Spanish Town, where he spent most of his early years. In 1983 he joined Lee's Unlimited and by the following year could be heard on Metromedia. He first recorded in 1985. 'Animal Party' on Black

Solidarity being one of his earliest releases, so too 'Talking Parrot' for Rosie's Uprising, and both were distinguished by an ingenious lyrical slant and a quick-fire delivery, inspired in part by the fast-talking style instigated by UK MCs on the Saxon sound system. Over the next two years he recorded for Isiah Laing's Supreme label, Bunny Lee, Prince Jazzbo, Harmodio, King Jammys and the late King Tubby among others, voicing mainly cultural material and intricate tales of ghetto living complete with vivid descriptions of local characters. In 1988, after a successful spell in New York with the African Love and Papa Mike sets, he recorded 'DJ Business' for Fashion Records in London, an eight minute *tour de force* that listed in detail the entire history of reggae DJs. By all accounts it was voiced in one take and remains an essential illustration of his unique abilities. Fashion later teamed him with Tippa Irie for their *JA To UK MC Clash (Vol. 2)* album.

The next two years were spent recording in Jamaica with varying degrees of success. Gussie Clarke reunited him with his former Creation partner Lady G for 'Round Table Talk', but it was not until 1990 that he found another winning streak, sharpening his skills with Black Scorpio on both sound and record, voicing for Mikey Bennett, Captain Sinbad, Penthouse, Digital B and King Jammy's son, John John, before really getting into his stride around 1991-92. 'Strange' and the bizarre 'Maddy Maddy Cry' he produced himself. 'Hippity Hippity Hop' arrived on Robbie Shakespeare's Powermatic label, and fine tunes for Exterminator, Tan Yah, Shocking Vibes, Wild Apache and Lloyd Honeyghan tumbled after. He then began a rewarding stint with Sly And Robbie's Taxi label in 1993, though in December of that year his elder brother Dirtsman, also a DJ, was shot and killed in Jamaica..

Albums: *Animal Party* (Sonic Sounds 1986), *Lyric Shop* (Black Solidarity 1988), *Style And Fashion* (Black Scorpio 1989), *Fire Inna Dancehall* (Pipper 1991). With Tippa Irie: *JA To UK MC Clash Vol. 2* (Fashion 1988).

Paragons

One of the classic reggae vocal groups, the Paragons recorded extensively throughout the 60s, and, by the time of their disbandment in 1970, had left behind a string of classic sides that few of their rivals could compete with. Originally a quartet comprising Garth 'Tyrone' Evans, Bob Andy, Leroy Stamp and Junior Menz, the Paragons evolved from a group called the Binders. In 1964 Stamp left, and was replaced by John Holt, whose controlled lead vocals, supported by sumptuous, never-wavering harmonies, became the group's trademark. Junior Menz also left that year, to join the Techniques, his place taken by Howard Barrett. During 1964-65 the group cut a few singles for Coxsone Dodd at Studio One, including 'Good Luck And Goodbye'. In 1965 Bob Andy left to go solo, and in 1966 the trio began recording for Duke Reid, scoring a series of Jamaican number 1 hits in the new rocksteady style. Reid's productions were almost serene compared to those of his rivals, somehow utterly harmonious, and the Paragons came to epitomise the classy, warm sound of Reid's Treasure Isle Studio with a heap of wonderful releases: 'Happy Go Lucky Girl', 'On The Beach', 'Riding High On A Windy Day', 'Wear You To The Ball', 'The Tide Is High' and 'Only A Smile' among them. The trio also recorded a couple of marvellous singles that showed them to be just as adept at the more furious early reggae beat as they were at rocksteady: 'Left With A Broken Heart' and 'A Quiet Place'. In 1970 the trio split, with Holt rising to even dizzier heights as a solo act and Evans and Barrett relocating to New York, where Evans occasionally recorded for Lloyd Barnes' Bullwackies label. The pop world belatedly discovered the Paragons' genius in the following decade with the Slits murdering 'A Quiet Place' as 'The Man Next Door', and Blondie having a world-wide number 1 with an inferior remake of 'The Tide Is High'. Perhaps encouraged by this, the original trio reformed in 1983 to cut a few sides for

Island Records under Sly & Robbie's production aegis, but to little reward.

Albums: *On The Beach* (Treasure Isle 1968), *The Paragons With Roslyn Sweat* (1971), *The Paragons Return* (Island 1981), *Sly & Robbie Meet The Paragons* (Island 1981), *Now* (Starlite 1982). Compilations: *The Original Paragons* (Treasure Isle 1990), *My Best Girl Wears My Crown* (Trojan 1992), *Golden Hits* (1993).

Parks, Lloyd

b. 26 May 1948, Walton Gardens, Jamaica. A singer and bass player, Lloyd Parks began his career in the late 60s with the Invincibles band, whose personnel at that time also included Ansell Collins on organ, Sly Dunbar on drums and Ranchie Mclean on guitar, and was half of the Termites who recorded one album for Studio One. He then replaced Pat Kelly as lead vocalist in the Techniques vocal trio, joining Dave Barker and producer Winston Riley. He cut his debut solo single for Riley – 'Say You Love Me' (1969) – and played bass on Dave Barker and Ansell Collins' international hits 'Double Barrel' (1970) and 'Monkey Spanner' (1970). By 1970 he was recording solo again, for producers Sonia Pottinger ('We Will Make Love') and Harry 'J' Johnson ('A Little Better'). He then joined the Thoroughbreds house band playing Kingston's 'Tit-for-Tat' club. He continued making records in an expressive falsetto/tenor voice for a variety of producers including Glen Brown ('Slaving') and Prince Tony Robinson. When Parks launched his own label in 1973 it was initially distributed from Prince Tony's shop. Among his Jamaican hits were the huge smashes 'Officially' (1974), 'Mafia' (1974), 'Girl In The Morning' and 'Baby Hang Up The Phone' (1975). Parks continued session work on bass with Skin Flesh and Bones, and by 1976 was playing bass in both the Revolutionaries and Professionals studio bands. In 1978 he formed We The People Band, recording and touring, principally with Dennis Brown. He continued to combine session work and touring with the same band into the early 90s.

Albums: *Officially* (Trojan 1974), *Girl In The Morning* (Trojan 1975), *Loving You* (Trojan 1976).

Paul, Frankie

b. Jamaica. Blind from birth, Paul Blake had his sight partially restored as a child on a hospital ship. When Stevie Wonder visited Paul's special school he was encouraged by his school friends and teachers to sing for him. Legend has it that Stevie was so impressed by the youth's precocious talent that from then on Paul Blake decided to make singing his career. He first came to the record buying public's attention in a big way as Frankie Paul in the early 80s when he shared the honours with Sugar Minott (one side each) on a Channel One 'clash' album. Minott was the established superstar while Frankie was billed as the 'up and coming superstar' and it was not long before he became one of the most prolific singers in the history of reggae music. Every important (and not so important) producer in dancehall reggae from Jamaica, the USA and the UK queued up for Frankie Paul and his consistency was amazing. It seemed as if he only came alive in the studio and although, at first, the Dennis Brown and Stevie Wonder influences were apparent, it was not too long before Frankie became his own man. His voice had a power and dignity too often lacking in 80s reggae and his interpretations of other people's material were masterful.

Reggae singers and DJs are not usually contracted to any particular label or producer but they work for whoever is willing to record them if the price is right – usually little more than a session fee and the promise of royalties to come if the record sells. When this occurs, the market will be immediately flooded with every recording he has made up until that point on a variety of different formats and on a bewildering number of labels. Frankie was one of the very few with enough talent to overcome this overkill

Frankie Paul

syndrome and the amount of records he released was staggering, especially when one takes into account just how good most of them are. He was one of the only 'real' singer of note to come through in reggae music for the whole of the decade, and a major label deal has to be on the cards for Paul, after a mooted arrangement with Motown fell through. No evidence has come to light of any new deal as yet, but if someone can harness some of Frankie's vibrant energy to specific projects and stop him recording for anyone and everyone, the results promise to be very exciting.

Albums: *Strange Feeling* (Techniques 1983), *Be My Lady* (Joe Gibbs 1984), *Strictly Reggae Music* (Londisc 1984), *Pass The Tu-Sheng-Peng* (Greensleeves 1984), *Tidal Wave* (Greensleeves 1985), *Rich And Poor* (Classic 1986), *Alesha* (Powerhouse 1987), *Sara* (Jammys 1987), *Warning* (RAS 1987), *Give Me That Feeling* (Moodies 1987), *Rub A Dub Market* (Mango/Island 1987), *Casanova* (Live & Love 1988), *The Classic* (Tappa Zukie 1988), *Easy Mover* (Vena 1988), *True* (Black Scorpio 1988), *Ripe Mango* (Scom 1988), *Reaching Out* (Blue Mountain 1988), *Shut Up B'way* (Ujama 1988), *Sizzling* (Skengdon 1988), *Slow Down* (Redman 1988), *Love Affair* (Techniques 1989), *Love Line* (Glory Gold 1989), *Frankie Paul* (Blacka Dread 1989), *Can't Get You Out Of My Mind* (Rohit 1990), *Heartical Don* (Superpower 1990), *Close To You* (Jammys 1991), *Star Of A Romance* (Black Scorpio 1991), *At His Best* (Techniques 1991), *At Studio One* (Studio One 1992), *Fire Deh A Mus Mus Tail* (1992), *Should I?* (Hearbeat 1992). With Little John: *Showdown Volume 6* (Empire 1984). With Michael Palmer: *Double Trouble* (Greensleeves 1985). With Leroy Sibbles: *The Champions Clash* (Kingdom 1988). With Pinchers: *Dancehall Duo* (RAS 1988), *Turbo Charge* (Super Supreme 1988). Compilations: *The Best Of* (Abraham 1988), *20 Massive Hits* (Sonic Sounds 1990), *FP The Greatest* (Fashion 1992).
Video: *Musical Explosion* (Jettisoundz).

Penthouse Records
(see Germain, Donovan)

Perry, Lee
b. Rainford Hugh Perry, 28 March 1936, Hanover, Jamaica, aka Scratch and the Upsetter. Small in stature, but larger than life, 'Little' Lee Perry began his musical career working for seminal producer Coxsone Dodd during the late 50s and early 60s acting as a record scout, organising recording sessions, and later supervising auditions at Dodd's record shop in Orange Street, Kingston. By 1963, as well as handling production and songwriting for Delroy Wilson ('Joe Liges', 'Spit In The Sky') and the Maytals, Perry had released the first of his own vocal records through Dodd. Featuring a bluesy, declamatory vocal style over superb backing from the legendary Skatalites, these tracks set a pattern from which Perry, throughout his career, would rarely deviate. Social and personal justice, bawdy, sometimes lewd sexual commentary, and, like the material he wrote for Delroy Wilson, stinging attacks on musical rivals - mainly former Coxsone employee Prince Buster - are all prefigured on these early tracks like 'Prince In The Pack', 'Trial And Crosses', 'Help The Weak', 'Give Me Justice', 'Chicken Scratch' (from which he acquired his nickname), 'Doctor Dick' with Rita Marley and the Soulettes on backing vocals, and 'Madhead', recorded between 1963 and 1966. Incidentally, there were obviously no hard feelings involved between Buster and Perry, as the latter often appeared on Buster's records, including 'Ghost Dance' and 'Judge Dread'. Also during his sojourn with Dodd he began an association with the Wailers that had further repercussions later in the decade.

In 1966 Perry fell out with Coxsone and began working with other producers including J.J Johnson, Clancy Eccles and, in 1968, Joe Gibbs, for whom he wrote songs and produced artists like Errol Dunkley, and the Pioneers. With Gibbs, he also voiced a bitter snipe directed at Dodd entitled 'The

Upsetter' from which he gained his next apt epithet. On parting with Gibbs, Perry recorded several fine titles, including the big local hit, 'People Funny Boy' (1968), a vicious record, featuring a chugging rhythm in the new reggae style given to him by Clancy Eccles, wherein Perry took his former employer to task for allegedly ignoring his role in Gibbs' success, the slight made all the more pointed by employing the melody he had used for the Pioneers' hit 'Longshot'. 1968 also saw the setting up of his own Upsetter label in Jamaica, again with help from Clancy Eccles. Right away he began having hits with David Isaacs ('Place In The Sun') and the Untouchables ('Tighten Up', which lent its title to the classic series of early 70s reggae compilations on Trojan Records), and, in common with other early reggae producers, secured a deal with Trojan whereby his records were released under his imprint in the UK.

Perry experienced his first taste of UK chart success with tenor saxophonist Val Bennett's spaghetti western-inspired title, 'Return Of Django', which spent three weeks at number 5 in the UK charts during October 1969. At the same time he began producing the Wailers on a series of records including 'Small Axe', 'Duppy Conqueror', and 'Soul Rebel', mostly available on a number of recent compilations, which are now considered to be among that group's finest work. Just over 100 singles were released on Upsetter between 1969 and 1974 by artists such as Dave Barker (Dave And Ansell Collins) ('Shocks Of Mighty', 'Upsetting Station'), Dennis Alcapone ('Alpha & Omega'), the Stingers ('Give Me Power'), the Bleechers ('Come Into My Parlour', 'Check Him Out'), Neville Hinds ('Blackmans Time'), Leo Graham ('Newsflash'), Big Youth ('Mooving (sic) Version'), and the legendary Junior Byles ('Beat Down Babylon', 'Place Called Africa'). He also unleashed a welter of intense, energetic, and just plain barmy instrumentals: 'Night Doctor', 'Live Injection', 'Cold Sweat', 'Django Shoots First', 'The Vampire' and 'Drugs & Poison'. Other productions such as 'Selassie' by the Reggae Boys, the instrumentals 'Dry Acid', 'Return Of The Ugly', 'Clint Eastwood', and many more, appeared on other B&C and Pama labels.

From 1972-74 Perry slowed the rhythm down and consolidated his position as one of the leading innovators in Jamaican music. He released instrumentals like 'French Connection', 'Black Ipa', and DJ tracks by artists such as U Roy (who had cut two of his earliest records 'Earths Rightful Ruler' and the demented 'OK Corral' for Perry in the late 60s), Dillinger, Dr. Alimantado, I Roy and Charlie Ace (on the unique and bizarre cut-and-mix extravaganza, 'Cow Thief Skak'). Perry was also one of the first producers to utilise the talents of King Tubby, then just starting his own operations, and released important early dub albums like *Rhythm Shower* (1972) and the glorious *Blackboard Jungle Dub* (1973). Perry's productions from this period: the Gatherers' monolithic 'Words Of My Mouth', Milton Henry's 'This World' - whose rhythm also served Junior Byles' reading of Little Willie John's 'Fever' and Augustus Pablo's melodic workout 'Hot & Cold', Perry's own 'Jungle Lion', the Classics' 'Civilisation', and many others, are amongst the heaviest and most exciting reggae records of their day.

In 1974 Perry opened his own studio, dubbed the Black Ark, situated in his back yard at Washington Gardens, Kingston. Almost immediately he scored a big Jamaican hit with Junior Byles' hugely influential 'Curly Locks'. In 1975 his production of Susan Cadogan's seminal lovers rock tune 'Hurt So Good' reached number 4 in the UK charts. He also released the overlooked but innovative dub album *Revolution Dub* (1975), featuring some of his heaviest contemporary productions like Bunny And Rickey's 'Bushweed Corntrash', Junior Byles' 'The Long Way', and Jimmy Riley's 'Womans Gotta Have It', all garnished with Scratch's crazy sing-along rhymes and bursts of dialogue 'sampled' off the Perry TV.

From 1975 he began to employ studio technology, notably phase shifters and rudimentary drum machines, to produce a dense, multi-layered mixing style that is instantly recognizable, and eminently inimitable. It is all the more remarkable for the fact that all this was achieved in a four-track studio. By 1976 Island Records had begun to release the fruits of this latest phase, including music by the Heptones (*Party Time*), Max Romeo (*War Inna Babylon*), Bob Marley And The Wailers ('Jah Live', 'Punky Reggae Party'), George Faith (*To Be A Lover*), Junior Murvin (*Police & Thieves*, the single of the same title being very popular in Jamaica at the time, and becoming a belated chart hit in the UK in May 1980), Prince Jazzbo (*Natty Passing Through*, released on Black Wax), and the Upsetters (the classic *Super Ape*). However, Island rejected his own vocal album *Roast Fish, Collie Weed & Corn Bread* (1978), and missed out on the Congos classic, *Heart Of The Congos,* which finally gained a UK release some years later on the Beat's Go Feet label.

With commercial success now coming infrequently the frustrations and personal problems began to build. He was still making wonderful records; 'Mr Money Man' by Danny Hensworth, 'Open The Gate' by Watty Burnett, 'Garden Of Life' by Leroy Sibbles, and many others, but his style was now so far removed from the reggae mainstream that they met with little success in Jamaica or abroad. Perry's behaviour became increasingly strange and bewildering, and in 1980 he destroyed his studio and left for Britain, where he conducted a number of puzzling interviews that seemed to add credence to reports of his mental decline. Since then he has made a long series of eccentric, often self-indulgent solo albums with a variety of different collaborators including Adrian Sherwood, Lloyd Barnes, and Neil 'Mad Professor' Fraser (see Ariwa Sounds), totally outside the mainstream of Jamaican music. Simultaneously, his earlier work began to receive significant critical and cult attention as well as commanding high prices in the collectors market. After living in the Netherlands in the mid-80s he moved back to London, occasionally performing live. In 1990 he went to Switzerland, worked with a new management team, and reputedly married a Swiss millionairess. He also returned to Jamaica with the intention of rebuilding the trashed and burnt out Black Ark, though sadly this plan does not seem to have come to fruition so far. Whatever the future holds, Lee 'Scratch' Perry, the Upsetter, the man Bob Marley once described as a 'genius', has already made one of the most individual contributions to the development of Jamaican music, whether as producer/arranger/writer, or simply as a singularly powerful guiding force during several crucial phases.

Selected albums: As Lee Perry/Lee Perry And The Upsetters: *The Upsetter* (Trojan 1969), *Many Moods Of The Upsetter* (1970), *Scratch The Upsetter Again* (1970), *Africa's Blood* (1972), *Battle Axe* (1972), *Cloak & Dagger* (Rhino 1972), *Double Seven* (Trojan 1973), *Rhythm Shower* (Upsetter 1973), *Blackboard Jungle* (Upsetter 1974), *Kung Fu Meets The Dragon* (D.I.P. 1974), *D.I.P. Presents The Upsetter* (D.I.P. 1974), *Revolution Dub* (Cactus 1975), *The Super Ape* (Mango/Island 1976), *Return Of The Super Ape* (Lion Of Judah/Mango 1977), *Roast Fish, Collie Weed & Corn Bread* (Lion Of Judah 1978), *Scratch On The Wire* (Island 1979), *Scratch And Company: Chapter 1* (Clocktower 1980), *Return Of Pipecock Jackson* (Black Star 1981), *Mystic Miracle Star* (Heartbeat 1982), *History Mystery & Prophecy* (Mango/Island 1984), *Black Ark Vol. 1 & 2* (Black Ark 1984), *Black Ark In Dub* (Black Ark 1985), *Battle Of Armagideon: Millionaire Liquidator* (Trojan 1986), *Satan Kicked The Bucket* (Wackies 1988), *Scratch Attack* (RAS 1988, CD only), *Chicken Scratch* (Heartbeat 1989), *Turn And Fire* (Anachron 1989), *Build The Ark* (Trojan 1990, triple album), *From The Secret Laboratory* (Mango/Island 1990), *Message From Yard* (Rohit 1990), *Blood Vapour* (La/Unicorn 1990), *Spiritual Healing* (Black Cat 1991), *God Muzick*

(Network/Kook Kat 1991), *The Upsetter And The Beat* (Heartbeat 1992), *Soundz From The Hot Line* (Heartbeat 1993). With Dave Barker: *Prisoner Of Love: Dave Barker Meets The Upsetters* (Trojan 1970). With Dub Syndicate: *Time Boom X De Devil Dead* (On-U-Sound 1987), *Magnetic Mirror Master Mix* (Anachron 1990). With Prince Jazzbo: *Natty Passing Through* (Black Wax 1976) aka *Ital Corner* (Clocktower 1980). With Bullwackie: *Lee 'Scratch' Perry Meets Bullwackie - Satan's Dub* (ROIR 1990). With Mad Professor: *Lee Scratch Perry Meets The Mad Professor, Volumes 1 & 2* (Ariwa 1990), *Lee 'Scratch' Perry Meets The Mad Professor In Dub, Volumes 1 & 2* (Angella 1991). Compilations: *The Upsetter Collection* (Trojan 1981), *Reggae Greats* (Island 1984), *Best Of* (Pama 1984), *The Upsetter Box Set* (Trojan 1985), *Some Of The Best* (Heartbeat 1986), *The Upsetter Compact Set* (1988), *All The Hits* (Rohit 1989). As Jah Lion: *Colombia Colly* (Mango/Island 1976). As Lee Perry And Friends: Compilations: *Give Me Power* (Trojan 1988, early 70s recordings), *Open The Gate* (Trojan 1989, triple set, 70s recordings), *Shocks Of Mighty 1969-1974* (Attack 1989), *Public Jestering* (Attack 1990). As the Upsetters: *Version Like Rain* (Trojan 1990). Various: *Heart Of The Ark, Volume 1* (Seven Leaves 1982), *Heart Of The Ark, Volume 2* (Seven Leaves 1983), *Turn & Fire: Upsetter Disco Dub* (1989), *Megaton Dub* (Seven Leaves 1983), *Megaton Dub 2* (Seven Leaves 1983). Important productions: Bob Marley & The Wailers: *Soul Revolution 1 & 2* (Trojan 1988, double album).

Video: *The Ultimate Destruction* (1992).

Pinchers

When Pinchers first came to England in 1985, he had already recorded an album for Blue Trac, alongside Peter Chemist. It was the release of his 45, 'Abracadabra', that first won him significant attention. He followed-up with minor hits for a variety of producers, including 'Fatis' Burrell and Redman. The single to make the breakthrough for him, however, was 'Agony', recorded for King Jammy. It quickly made him a minor celebrity in Jamaica, to the point where he was offered (and accepted) advertising endorsements from a local wine vineyard. His other notable hits include 'Bandolero', the wild west imagery of which neatly seduced the dancehall audience, whose preoccupation with guns and violence it echoed. However, Pinchers' main source of fame continues to centre on sound system 'specials', live appearances at which he excels, and on which he has built a considerable reputation as one of reggae's emerging stars.

Albums: *Agony* (Live & Love 1987), *Mass Out* (Exterminator/RAS 1987), *Lift It Up Again* (Exterminator/Vena 1987), *Got To Be Me* (Live & Love 1987), *Return Of The Don* (Supreme 1989), *Hotter* (Blue Mountain 1992), *Dirt Low* (Exterminator 1993). With Frankie Paul: *Dancehall Duo* (RAS 1988), *Turbo Charge* (Super Supreme 1988). With Pliers: *Pinchers With Pliers* (Black Scorpio 1988). With Sanchez: *Pinchers Meets Sanchez* (Exterminator 1989). With Tweetie Bird: *Two Originals* (King Dragon 1990).

Pioneers

The original Pioneers, formed in 1962, consisted of the brothers Sydney and Derrick Crooks, and Glen Adams. The latter later enjoyed a career as vocalist and studio musician, playing organ as a member of Lee Perry's Upsetters. The Pioneers' debut, 'Sometime', was recorded for Leslie Kong's Beverleys label during 1965. By late 1967 they were recording for the Caltone label, owned by Ken Lack, former road manager of the Skatalites. In 1968, Sidney teamed up with Jackie Robinson to record a series of local hits for producer Joe Gibbs, hitting number 1 in the Jamaican chart with their first attempt, 'Gimme Little Loving'. They followed up with another number 1, 'Long Shot', a song celebrating the victories of a famous Jamaican racehorse. Further successes for Gibbs included 'Dem A Laugh', 'No Dope Me Pony', 'Me Nah Go A Bellevue', 'Catch The Beat', and 'Mama Look Deh',

Pinchers

which the Maytals used as the basis for their huge local hit of 1968, 'Monkey Man'. Sidney and Jackie then teamed up with Desmond Dekker's brother George, and returned to record for Leslie Kong, initially releasing another local hit, 'Nana', under the group name the Slickers. Subsequent records for Kong were recorded under the name of the Pioneers, including their famous continuation of the racehorse saga, 'Long Shot Kick De Bucket', which tells how Long Shot and a horse named Combat died in a race at Caymanas Park track in Kingston. Other local hits for Kong included the Jamaican chart-topper, 'Easy Come Easy Go' (a return volley against rival group the Royals), the frenetic 'Samfie Man', about a confidence trickster, and 'Mother Rittie'. After their sojourn at Beverleys, they took up residence in England, where 'Long Shot Kick De Bucket' had reached the UK chart, peaking at number 21 in early 1970. They toured Egypt and the Lebanon later that year, returning in 1971 to record in a much more lightweight 'pop' reggae style. Their greatest success came with the Jimmy Cliff-penned 'Let Your Yeah Be Yeah' which reached number 5 in the autumn of 1971. Smaller success came with the cover versions '100 lbs Of Clay' and 'A Little Bit Of Soap'. Since 1973, George has pursued a singing and composing career, Jackie has been a solo vocalist, while Sidney Crooks has concentrated on production, since the late 80s operating his own studio in Luton, Bedfordshire, England. Their best records remain those they recorded for Joe Gibbs and Leslie Kong during 1968-70.
Albums: *Greetings From The Pioneers* (1968), *Long Shot* (Trojan 1969), *Battle Of The Giants* (Trojan 1970), *Let Your Yeah Be Yeah* (1972), *I Believe In Love* (1973), *Freedom Feeling* (1973), *Roll On Muddy River* (1974), *I'm Gonna Knock On Your Door* (1974), *Pusher Man* (1974). Compilation: *Greatest Hits* (1975).

Pliers
(see Chakademus And Pliers)

Pottinger, Sonia
b. c.1943, Jamaica. In the mid-60s Pottinger opened her Tip Top Record Shop on Orange Street, Kingston, and in 1966, launched her career as a record producer with 'Every Night' by Joe White And Chuck with the Baba Brooks Band, recorded at Federal Recording Studios. This sentimental C&W ballad with an R&B beat became a massive hit which stayed high in the Jamaican charts for months. As the music changed to rocksteady, she recorded a string of sweet sounding hits such as 'The Whip' by the Ethiopians (1967), 'That's Life' by Delano Stewart (1968), and 'Swing And Dine' by the Melodians (1968), all released on her Gayfeet and High Note labels. In 1974, after Duke Reid's death, she took over his business and reissued and repackaged the Treasure Isle catalogue. In the late 70s, she issued several best-selling albums by Bob Andy, Marcia Griffiths and Culture. She retired from the recording business in 1985.
Albums: Various: *Put On Your Best Dress* (Trojan 1990, rec. 1967-68), *Musical Feast* (Heartbeat 1990, rec. 1967-70).

Priest, Maxi
b. Max Elliot, London, England. Former carpenter Maxi Priest is now a hugely successful solo reggae artist. He made his initial music industry breakthrough by employing his artisan's skills in building sound systems. He went on to tour with Saxon International, the UK's premier reggae assembly, where he rubbed shoulders with Peter King, Phillip Levi, Smiley Culture and Asher Senator. He made his name and reputation as a 'singing' DJ, vocalising off the cuff observations over prime 70s roots music, but he soon progressed to a more soulful style which was captured by producer Paul Robinson (aka Barry Boom) on his debut, *You're Safe*. After recording this album, he started a run of hits in 1986 with 'Strollin' On', 'In The Springtime' and 'Crazy Love'. In 1987 he scored a minor hit single with a cover of Robert Palmer's 'Some Guys Have All The

Pliers

Maxi Priest

Luck'. However, most successful was his 1988 cover of Cat Stevens' 'Wild World', though it owed more of a debt to the Jimmy Cliff reggae version. Further chart appearances followed with 'Close To You', 'Peace Throughout The World' and 'Human Work Of Art'. 1990's *Bona Fide* included contributions from, amongst others, Soul II Soul, a group undoubtedly influenced by Priest's mellow but evocative brand of lovers rock.

Albums: *You're Safe* (Virgin 1985), *Intentions* (Virgin 1986), *Maxi* (Ten 1987), *Bona Fide* (Ten 1990), *The Best Of Me* (Ten 1991), *Fe Real* (Ten 1992).

Prince Buster

b. Cecil Bustamante Campbell, 28 May 1938, Kingston, Jamaica. Buster was named after Alexandra Bustamante, the leader of the Jamaican Labour Party, and began his career as a boxer, but soon found his pugilistic talents being put to use as a bouncer/strong arm man and minder for Coxsone Dodd's Down Beat sound system. Competition was fierce in those early days, with fights often breaking out between the supporters of rival sounds with wires (and people) being cut regularly, and Buster still carries the scars (literally). He claims, like so many others, to have personally invented the ska sound, and he was certainly involved from the very early stages - at first with his work for Coxsone and after they had parted company with his own Voice Of The People sound system, record label and shop. His very first recording session produced one of the all-time classics of Jamaican music, 'Oh Carolina', with vocals by the Folks Brothers and musical accompaniment from Count Ossie. Inventive and innovative at the time, the record still sounds every bit as exciting now as it did then. Buster released countless records both by himself and other top acts on his Wild Bells, Voice Of The People and Buster's Record Shack labels, which were subsequently released in the UK on the Blue Beat imprint. They proved as popular there as they had been in Jamaica, firstly with the

Jamaican community and secondly with the mods, who took the Prince to their hearts with songs such as 'Al Capone' and 'Madness'. He toured the UK in the mid-60s to ecstatic crowds and appeared on the hugely popular *Ready, Steady, Go* television show.

He recorded in many different styles but his talking records were the most popular, including the hilarious 'Judge Dread' where he admonishes rude boys and sentences them to 400 years; the wildly misogynistic 'Ten Commandments'; the evocative 'Ghost Dance' - a look back at his early Kingston dancehall days; the confused and confusing 'Johnny Cool'; and the not so well known but equally wonderful 'Shepherd Beng Beng'. He also claims to have taught Georgie Fame to do the ska and he influenced other white pop acts - Madness named themselves after his song (debuting with a tribute, 'The Prince') and inspired doorman/bouncer Alex Hughes to adopt the name Judge Dread and have UK chart hits with variations on Prince Buster's lewd original 'Big Five'. Buster had tended towards 'slack' or rude records towards the end of the 60s which were only mildly risqué compared with what was to follow but caused a sensation at the time. He wisely invested his money in record shops and juke box operations throughout the Caribbean and, in the early 70s, took to recording many of the current top names including Big Youth, Dennis Alcapone, John Holt, Dennis Brown and Alton Ellis with varying degrees of success. He soon realised that his older recordings would outsell his newer efforts every time and he turned to re-pressing his extensive back catalogue on single and releasing his old albums both in Jamaica and the UK. He also put together some brilliant compilations where the superb sleevenotes, written by the Prince himself, attack in no uncertain terms the music of the day: 'They have used guns to spoil the fun and force tasteless and meaningless music upon the land.'

Throughout the rest of the 70s and on into the 80s he lived on his shops, his juke boxes

Prince Buster

and his past glories but he returned to live work in the latter half of the 80s. He has become a crowd puller again for, as he says: 'The people know my songs and loved them.' He even started, for the first time in years, to record new music again (1992). While it is impossible to forecast if this will prove successful or not one cannot ever take away the fact that Prince Buster's music has already inspired generations of performers. He is respected abroad – probably more than in his native Jamaica – but he will always have his place as one of the few Jamaican artists to reach directly to the international audience. Many more have played their part indirectly but his name was known both through his own recordings ('Al Capone' reached the lower regions of the UK national charts) and his work with other people. It is unlikely that any other Jamaican artist (apart from Bob Marley) still has his records so regularly played in clubs and dances throughout the world.

Selected albums: *Judge Dread Rock Steady* (Blue Beat 1967), *I Feel The Spirit* (1968), *Wreck A Pum Pum* (Blue Beat 1968), *She Was A Rough Rider* (Melodisc 1969), *Big Five* (Melodisc 1972), *On Tour* (1966, reissued 1988), *Judge Dread* (1968, reissued Blue Beat 1991), *Tutti Fruitti* (Melodisc). Various: *Pain In My Belly* (Islam/Blue Beat 1966). Compilations: *Prince Buster's Fabulous Greatest Hits* (Fab 1968), *Original Golden Oldies Vol. 1 & 2* (Prince Buster 1989).

Prince Far I

b. Michael Williams, c.1944, Spanish Town, Jamaica, d. 15 September 1983. Prince Far I, the voice of thunder, was originally a bouncer at the premises of Studio One, Jamaica's premier record label of the 60s and early 70s. A huge, muscular figure with impressive facial scars, he was known as a gentle giant with hidden depths. One day in 1970 King Stitt, the regular DJ at Studio One, had failed to turn up to voice a track, and Michael the bouncer persuaded the producer, Coxsone Dodd, to give him a try. Impressed, Dodd named the new artist King Cry-Cry and a legend was born. After a couple of records as Cry-Cry, he renamed himself Prince Far I. A gruff, deep, slow-burning rhymer, his talents at first appeared limited although Far I was built to last: while other DJs' careers fizzled like firecrackers, Far I retained his status throughout his life. When he really let rip, as on his 1977 album *Under Heavy Manners*, he was awesome. His *Psalms For I* (1976) remains a roots classic today, and his Trojan Records albums, *Free From Sin, Jamaican Heroes* and *Voice Of Thunder*, were all of a high standard. A brief liaison with Virgin Records brought him a wider, rockier audience, as did his *Cry Tuff Dub Encounter* (1976-79) series of dub albums, originally cut for his own Jamaican label Cry Tuff. Eventually Far I spent a fair portion of his time in England, where he recorded as part of Singers And Players for Adrian Sherwood's On-U Sound label. The pair worked together well, particularly on the 'Virgin' single, an undisguised swipe at Far I's previous label. UK gigs were frequent, with Far I, dressed in biblical robes, 'chanting down babylon' with the help of hundreds of white kids, whom he genially met and signed autographs for after the show. However, just as he was starting to build this new following, he was shot dead in Jamaica, yet another victim of Kingston's regular street violence, one year short of his 40th birthday.

Albums: *Psalms For I* (Carib Gems 1976), *Under Heavy Manners* (Joe Gibbs 1977), *Message From The King* (Front Line 1978), *Long Life* (Front Line 1978), *Cry Tuff Dub Encounter* (Cry Tuff/Hit Run 1978), *Free From Sin* (Trojan 1979), *Cry Tuff Dub Encounter, Part 2* (Cry Tuff/Front Line 1979), *Jamaican Heroes* (Trojan 1980), *Showcase In A Suitcase* (Pre 1980), *Cry Tuff Dub Encounter Chapter 3* (Cry Tuff/Daddy Kool 1979), *Livity* (Pre 1979), *Cry Tuff Dub Encounter Chapter 4* (Cry Tuff/Trojan 1981), *Voice Of Thunder* (Trojan 1981), *Musical History* (Trojan 1983), *Spear Of The Nation* (Kingdom 1984). With the Suns Of Arqa: *The Musical Revue* (1989, live 1983 recording

- cassette only). Compilations: *Black Man Land* (Front Line 1990), *Dubwise* (Front Line 1991).

Prince Jazzbo

b. Linval Carter, c.1950, Jamaica. Prince Jazzbo is one of the survivors of reggae music. While he has never been as important as other 70s DJs such as U Roy or Big Youth, it is Jazzbo who retains a charismatic personal style and a reasonably healthy following through his label, Ujama, for which he produces and occasionally records. Like many others, Jazzbo first recorded for the Studio One label in the early 70s. Legend has it that Jazzbo had come in from the countryside and was kept waiting in the yard all day by Coxsone Dodd, the studio and label owner, because no one was expecting much from the skinny youth. However, Jazzbo eventually pestered his way into the studio and took the microphone. Dodd ran a backing track at random – Horace Andy's 'Skylarking' – and Jazzbo delivered what was to become a monster hit first-take, 'Crabwalking'. For the next 18 months or so, Jazzbo stuck with Dodd, cutting a string of flawless roots records: 'Crime Don't Pay', 'Pepper Rock', 'School' and 'Imperial I'. However, a much-promised album for Dodd failed to materialize, so Jazzbo, disillusioned, began to record for other producers, Glen Brown and Bunny Lee. A liaison with Lee Perry on the expected one-off single 'Penny Reel' eventually turned into the superb 1976 album *Natty Passing Thru*, AKA *Ital Corner*, for which he was paid a mere $1,000 Jamaican (about £100 at the time). Other albums from this time include *Kick Boy Face* and *Step Forward Youth*, the latter shared with I Roy. By 1977 Jazzbo had launched Ujama, recording as a singer for the label, under the name Johnny Cool. Neither his *alter-ego* or his label worked, sales-wise. Jazzbo reached the start of the 80s and the impending dancehall boom in much the same state as his fellow DJ pioneers I Roy, U Roy and Big Youth: he still had talent but reggae's styles were changing fast. Jazzbo decided that Ujama must become a viable operation, and from around 1983 onwards it has been – even if his idiosyncratic production style and somewhat off-the-wall ideas have held it back in the larger marketplace. Besides offering a shelter for older DJs like U Roy and I Roy, Ujama specialises in finding the sort of reggae acts other producers overlook: Zebra, Manchez and Horace Ferguson. None of them have made it to the status of Jazzbo's most famous ally, Frankie Paul, but that is wholly in keeping with Ujama's symbol of a donkey, because, as Jazzbo never tires of telling people: 'a donkey may not arrive quickly, but it was good enough to carry Jesus and will not suffer a mechanical breakdown on the way'. The cheaply produced sleeves of his albums nearly always feature a cartoon donkey carrying Jazzbo or taking part in a horse race. While Jazzbo is unlikely ever to make it big internationally, his career received an unexpected fillip in 1991 when Studio One finally deigned to release his album, *Choice Of Version*, some 18 years late, to ecstatic reviews and considerable excitement. If it had happened in 1973, Jazzbo might have been in a far stronger position today.

Selected albums: *Kick Boy Face* (Third World 1975), *Natty Passing Thru* aka *Ital Corner* (Black Wax 1976), *Choice Of Version* (Studio One 1990). With I Roy: *Step Forward Youth* (1976). With Jah Stitch: *Straight To Babylon Chest* (1979). With I Roy: *Head To Head Clash* (1990).

Prince Lincoln (The Royal Rasses)

b. Lincoln Thompson. Lincoln Thompson's solo career began at Studio One, where he made three singles in the early 70s which failed to make any impact but established his name amongst the committed following for 'roots' music. He had been involved in the music business in the 60s as a member of the Tartans, and their 'Dance All Night' on Merritone Records was a big rocksteady hit, but they disbanded soon after this early taste of success. 'Live Up To Your Name', 'True

Prince Lincoln

Experience' and 'Daughters Of Zion' are still sought-after records which sell out immediately every time Coxsone Dodd re-presses them. Prince Lincoln left Studio One to establish his own label, God Sent, and released three more singles - this time as the Royal Rasses (Royal Princes) which were effectively solo efforts with harmonies provided by an assortment of back-up singers including Cedric Myton (of Congos fame), Keith Peterkin and Studio One stalwart, Jennifer Lara. 'Love The Way It Should Be', 'Kingston 11' - a musical tour of the ghetto and 'Old Time Friend' were all good sellers both in Jamaica and the UK, and attracted the attention of Ballistic Records who signed them and heavily promoted their debut, *Humanity*. The album contained the three hit singles and songs of the same calibre including 'San Salvador', a hugely in-demand dub plate popularised on Lloydie Coxsone's London-based sound system. The set was issued in a full colour (and very expensive) sleeve with lyric sheet and backed up with a lengthy European tour in 1979. The group were poised on the brink of international stardom and Prince Lincoln's carefully-crafted thoughtful songs and soaring vocals were just right for the time. Sadly, it all went wrong. Although the Royal Rasses were making music that Lincoln defined as 'inter-reg' or crossover music, their follow-up album, *Experience,* failed to scale the heights that *Humanity* had reached and was not particularly popular with either the reggae audience or the pop audience it was aimed at. The third album release, a very brave step and one that brought Lincoln much critical acclaim, but failed to sell in any quantity, was a collaboration with English singer Joe Jackson. The cost of these admirable ventures was borne by Ballistic Records, who went out of business in the process, and Thompson returned to Jamaica in 1981. There was nothing from Prince Lincoln for the rest of the decade but the early 90s have seen a handful of interesting UK releases on God Sent which might signal a return to the business for one of reggae's most gifted singers, songwriters and arrangers. He is one of the few with the vision the music needs.

Albums: *Humanity* (Ballistic 1979), *Experience* (Ballistic 1980), *Ride With The Rasses* (God Sent 1981). With Joe Jackson: *Roots Man Blues* (Ballistic 1981).

Prophet, Michael

b. Michael George Haynes, 1957, Kingston, Jamaica. Prophet's singular crying vocal style was first heard in 1977 when he was discovered by Vivian 'Yabby You' Jackson, who took him to Channel One for his debut, 'Praise You Jah Jah', written some five years earlier. 'Fight It To The Top' was his first hit. With Yabby he made several highly regarded roots albums inevitably featuring the Gladiators in support and mixed by either Scientist or King Tubby, Island releasing *Serious Reasoning* in 1980.

By then Prophet had left for Henry 'Junjo' Lawes, who successfully steered him towards dancehall popularity. 'Gunman', voiced in response to the violent Jamaican elections of that year, becoming his biggest ever hit. After two albums with Lawes he freelanced with varying results; recording *Blood Stain* for Satta Blue and tunes for Don Mais, Al Campbell, Sugar Minott, Winston 'Niney' Holness, Soul Syndicate, Winston Riley and others. All helped maintain his presence throughout the early 80s. By 1986 he was recording for Delroy Wright's Live & Learn label then left Jamaica for Miami, where he briefly voiced for Skengdon. In 1988 he moved to England and within two years had teamed up with former Stur-Mars and Coxsone Outernational DJ, Ricky Tuffy. Their debut single, 'Your Love', was a number 1 hit in 1990 and preceded the best-selling *Get Ready* album for Brixton label Passion a year later. The self-produced *Bull Talk* was released in 1993. Since then Prophet has recorded solo singles with a variety of UK producers including General Saint, Ruff Cutt and Lloydie Crucial. He remains one of the most enduring singers to emerge from the roots era.

Michael Prophet

Selected albums: *Serious Reasoning* (Island 1980), *Righteous Are The Conqueror* (Greensleeves 1980), *Michael Prophet* (Greensleeves 1981), *Love Is An Earthly Thing* (CSA 1983), *Blood Stain* (Satta Blue 1984), *Cease Fire* (Move 1985), *Settle Yu Fe Settle* (Live & Love 1986), *Certify* (Burning Sounds 1988), *Get Ready* (Greensleeves 1991), *Bull Talk* (Greensleeves 1993). With Half Pint: *Joint Favourites* (Greensleeves 1986). Compilation: *Gunman* (Greensleeves 1991; comprises *Righteous Are Conqueror* and *Michael Prophet*).

Pyramids

The Pyramids were a seven-piece, UK-based ska/rocksteady band, although they began their career as a straight 'pop' group, consisting of Josh Roberts, Ray Knight, Roy Barrington, Monty Naismith, Ray Ellis, Mick Thomas and Frank Pitter. A popular live attraction in Britain in the late 60s, they hit with 'Train Tour To Rainbow City', an appropriately chugging piece written and produced by Eddy Grant, which ran through many of the period's most popular records and bore a close resemblance to Prince Buster's 'Train To Girls Town'. As rock steady gave way to reggae, elements of the band, including Ellis, Naismith and Thomas, resurfaced in 1969 as Symarip with 'Skinhead Moon Stomp', based on Derrick Morgan's 'Moon Hop' hit, which was one of the anthems of the skinhead era but which had to wait until its 1980 re-issue to gain a chart placing.

Albums: *Pyramids* (1968). As Symarip: *Skinkead Moon Stomp* (Trojan 1970).

R

Radics, Jack

b. Jordan Bailey, Kingston, Jamaica. As a teenager Radics had become involved with the New World sound system in 1975, responsible for running a little soul selection at their uptown Kingston gigs before trying his hand as a singer. He made one recording, a cover of Kool And The Gang's 'Get Down On It', before moving to London in the early 80s. There he met up with producer Blacker Dread who released 'Easy' (a duet with Debbie Ryvers) and 'Walk On By' in 1985, the year he was signed to Island under his real name. Despite recording an album for them only a handful of tracks ever emerged. When the contract expired in 1988 he returned to Jamaica and promptly scored two local hits with 'Dream Merchant' and 'Conversation'. It was at the Sting '90 festival that he made his reputation for singing in a dramatic and exaggerated baritone which, once harnessed to dancehall rhythms, provided a barrage of releases for a variety of Jamaican producers. 'Set My Heart On Fire' for Shocking Vibes, 'All Of Me' on Freddie McGregor's Big Ship label, 'Good Loving' for boxer Lloyd Honeyghan and 'I'll Be Sweeter' and 'My Love Is On Fire' for Penthouse were all substantial hits in 1991, the year Castro Brown released Radics' debut album, *Jack*.

The following year he repeated the process all over again, increasing his volume of cover versions and also his producers, who by now had grown to include numerous labels in Jamaica, England and America. The list increased throughout 1993 when there was a growing shift towards more self-penned, cultural material, resulting in several fine sides for Star Trail, Shocking Vibes, Bobby Digital and Taxi. That summer the Montego Bay label Top Rank released his second album *Something*, which was followed by his belated Penthouse set, *I'll Be Sweeter,* in October. In December 1993 Sly And Robbie teamed Radics with Chaka Demus And Pliers on a version of 'Twist And Shout' which became an international hit, reaching number 1 on the UK chart in January 1994. Selected albums: *Jack* (New Name 1991), *Something* (Top Rank 1993), *I'll Be Sweeter* (Penthouse 1993).

Raggamuffin/Ragga

It's not often that an entire genre of music can be traced to one record, but Ragga was single-handedly started by one single, Wayne Smith's 'Under Me Sleng Teng' (1985). Legend states that one of the musicians working in Prince Jammy's studio in Waterhouse, Kingston 11, was messing about with a Casio electronic keyboard, and found a pre-set demo rhythm. With the addition of a keyboard bassline, he provided the basis for Wayne Smith to 'voice' it, and the 'digital' era of reggae began. More than 200 other versions of the backing track were recorded, such was its popularity.

Ragga is, therefore, barely distinguishable from the earlier dancehall, other than a slightly more aggressive attitude, and an alignment with the kind of concerns of its youthful audience - one-upmanship, guns, sex - and an all-important, rocking electronic beat. The early years of the genre (1986-89) were dominated by King Jammy's production house, Donovan Germain's Penthouse Studio and a variety of other producers, such as Mixing Lab, Exterminator, Black Scorpio and King Tubby's. Veteran producer Gussie Clarke added a roots edge at his Music Works studio, and released the next biggest watershed record in Gregory Isaacs' 'Rumours'. Leading ragga musicians include Steely & Clevie, Mafia & Fluxy and the Firehouse Crew. Just like dancehall before it, ragga has also created its own set of stars, including Cutty Ranks, General Levy, Tiger, and, the biggest of them all, Shabba Ranks. The music is still 'running t'ings' in Jamaica at the time of writing.

Jack Radics

Selected albums: Various: *Ragga Clash Vol. 1* (Fashion 1990), *Ragga Clash Vol. 2* (Fashion 1990), *Just Ragga Vol. 5* (Charm 1994), *Ragga Ragga Ragga* (Greensleeves 1994). Cutty Ranks: *The Stopper* (Fashion 1990).

Ranglin, Ernest

b. 1932, Manchester, Jamaica. Ranglin had two uncles who played guitar and ukelele, and as a child would pick up their instruments and try to imitate their playing. He was also influenced by the recordings of Charlie Christian, and by Cecil Hawkins, an unrecorded local guitarist. At the age of 15, Ranglin joined his first group, the Val Bennett band, and subsequently played with Eric Deans and Count Boysie. By the early 50s, he had developed into a proficient jazz guitarist, and started to tour overseas. Around 1959, he joined bassist Cluett Johnson in a studio group called Clue J And His Blues Blasters, who recorded several instrumentals for Coxsone Dodd at JBC studio. The first of these recordings, 'Shuffling Jug', is widely regarded as one of the first ska recordings. Ranglin's beautiful, versatile guitar playing ensured that he was in demand as a session musician throughout the ska era, and he provided the musical accompaniment for Millie's world-wide smash, 'My Boy Lollipop'. In the mid-60s he recorded two jazz albums for the Merritone label, *Wranglin* (1964) and *Reflections* (1965). Around this time, Duke Reid employed him as musical director at his Treasure Isle recording studio, where he worked for several years. From the late 60s and all through the 70s he worked as a studio musician and arranger for many of the island's top producers such as Coxsone Dodd, Lee Perry and Clancy Eccles. His most recent albums have been *Ranglin Roots* and *From Kingston JA To Miami USA*. He continues to record, but spends most of his time playing live, both locally and abroad.
Albums: *Wranglin* (Island 1964), *Reflections* (Island 1965), *Ranglin Roots* (Water Lily 1977), *From Kingston JA To Miami USA* (1982).

Ranking Dread

b. Winston Brown, Kingston, Jamaica. Ranking Dread established his reputation as a live DJ for Lloydie Coxsone's London based sound system as yet another in that long line of eccentric, idiosyncratic microphone men associated with reggae music. His particular style of delivery was based around a slurring, almost whining vocal constantly interrupted by comments and interjections, and was definite proof that it was not what you said but how you said it that mattered. His early recordings were inauspicious and failed to make any impact, but *Lots Of Loving* was among the most played records in UK reggae in 1979/1980 where the combination of the Dread's delivery coupled with some of Sly And Robbie's and Sugar Minott's best current rhythms assured his popularity. A number of big selling 12-inch singles followed, a couple of which hovered in the lower reaches of the national charts. He is now believed to be residing in Canada but no longer records or works live.
Album: *Lots Of Loving* (Stand Firm/Freedom Sounds 1980).

Ranks, Cutty

b. Philip Thomas, 12 February 1965, Kingston, Jamaica. Thomas began his working life as a butcher, and it is tempting to state that he continued his DJing career as if he was still working with his cleaver - cutting through rhythms and rivals like so many slices of meat. Off the microphone, Cutty is as friendly and personable a character as you're likely to meet in the reggae business, but his style is strictly no holds barred, and his career during the 90s has progressed from strength to strength due to this uncompromising musical stance.
He first took up the microphone for local sound system Feathertone, and moved on to Stereo Mars, Arrows and Metro Media - all top ranking sounds. He began his recording career for Winston Riley of Techniques Records and then moved to Miami with Skeng Don, learning his craft from Super

Cat and Nicodemus. He then moved on to Patrick Roberts at Shocking Vibes where he made his first - and highly influential - hit, 'The Bomber'. His next move to Donovan Germain's Penthouse set-up further consolidated his popularity, and he hit again with 'Pon Me Nozzle'. His 'rock-stone' ranting attracted the attention of London-based Fashion Records, and his 1990 recording, 'The Stopper', became a huge international reggae hit both in the original and hip hop remix versions. The album of the same name still sells some four years after its release like a new outing, while its catch phrases and hooklines have been endlessly sampled and reworked.

Cutty had arrived and he has now established his position as one of the foremost exponents of the 90s DJing style. He was even able to deal with a falling-off in his popularity on record in 1992 with 'A Who Seh Me Dun', where he dusted out rivals with his customary blend of venom and humour and came out on top again. He's only ever worked with the best producers in the business, such as Sly & Robbie, Roof International and the aforementioned Donovan Germain, Fashion and Shocking Vibes, and has always resisted the ever present temptation for Jamaican DJs to 'voice out' too many tunes for too many producers. It can only be a matter of time before he crosses over in the same way that fellow travellers Buju (Banton) and Shabba (Ranks) have done already, as his 'Limb By Limb', a massive hit in the US in 1993, suggests he will.

Albums: *The Stopper* (Fashion 1991), *Lethal Weapon* (Penthouse 1991), *From Mi Heart* (Shanachie 1992). With Tony Rebel: *Die Hard (Volumes One And Two)* (Penthouse 1991), *20 Man Dead* (Charm 1991).

Video: *Champions Of The Dance* (1992).

Ranks, Shabba

b. Rexton Gordon, 1965, St. Ann's, Jamaica. Although born in a country parish his family moved to Kingston when he was eight; by the age of 12 he was studying DJs like General Echo, Brigadier Jerry, Yellowman and especially Josey Wales, who took him to King Jammys after Shabba had served his apprenticeship on the Roots Melody sound system alongside Admiral Bailey, recording his debut 'Heat Under Sufferers Feet' in 1985. 'Original Fresh' a year later was his first for Jammys. Unable to really establish himself despite an album shared with Chakademus (*Rough And Rugged*) his initial notoriety for 'slackness' came with hits for Wittys ('Needle Eye Punany'), voiced while visiting New York in 1988. Shortly afterwards he left King Jammys for Bobby Digital's new label and Heatwave sound system, scoring immediately with 'Mama Man', 'Peanie Peanie' and then 'Wicked In Bed', which proved highly successful in 1989. Digital, after being engineer with Jammys had known Shabba since he was 15 and this special relationship between the two is still very much in evidence today.

Mike 'Home T' Bennett had also worked for Jammys and first teamed Shabba with Cocoa Tea and his vocal group, Home T4 for 'Who She Love' then 'Stop Spreading Rumours'. They took the formula to Gussie Clarke, who produced a subsequent album, *Holding On*, and big hits like 'Pirate's Anthem', 'Twice My Age' (with Krystal) and 'Mr Loverman' (with Deborahe Glasgow). Later the song would be re-voiced with Chevelle Franklin and become an international success in 1993. Throughout 1989 however, Shabba's presence dominated reggae music, although he recorded for few producers outside of Bobby Digital and Gussie Clarke. His personal appearances in London resulted in riots and, in one tragic case, a shooting. He also attracted the attention of the hip hop fraternity, which had previously forged strong links with reggae before breaking into the mainstream. He was signed to Epic Records in late 1990, the year his duet with Maxi Priest on 'Housecall' became a major crossover hit. The first Epic album, *Raw As Ever*, wisely continued to use the top Jamaican producers and won him a US Grammy in 1991. By now his gruff,

Shabba Ranks

commanding voice had become known world-wide and the follow-up album, *X-tra Naked*, repeated the feat; Shabba becoming the first DJ to win two consecutive Grammy Awards. After releasing a number of commercially successful singles in 1993 he returned to the dancehall arena with a flourish; 'Shine And Criss' and 'Respect' pleasing his still fanatical reggae following immensely.

Selected albums: *Best Baby Father* (John John/Blue Mountain 1989), *Just Reality* (Blue Mountain 1990), *Star Of The 90s* (King Jammys 1990), *Rappin' With The Ladies* (Greensleeves 1990), *As Raw As Ever* (Epic 1991), *Rough & Ready Vol. 1* (Epic 1992), *X-Tra Naked* (Epic 1992), *Rough & Ready Vol. 2* (Epic 1993), *Mr Maximum* (Greensleeves 1992). With Chakademus: *Rough & Rugged* (King Jammys 1988). With Home T4 and Cocoa T: *Holding On* (Greensleeves 1989).

Videos: *Fresh And Wild X Rated* (1992). With Ninjaman: *Reggae Sting Vol. 1* (1992).

Ras Michael And The Sons Of Negus

b. Michael George Henry, c.1943, Kingston, Jamaica. Michael grew up in a Rastafarian community at St. Mary where he learned hand-drumming, eventually becoming a master-drummer. In the early 60s, he formed the Sons Of Negus, a Rastafarian group of drummers and singers. In the mid-60s he founded his own Zion Disc label, and started to release a series of singles including 'Lion Of Judah', 'Ethiopian National Anthem' and 'Salvation'. These recordings, on which the group is usually augmented by guitar and bass, show a remarkable degree of invention and subtlety. Around 1966, he recorded at Studio One as a percussionist, playing with Jackie Mittoo And The Soul Vendors in exchange for studio time. In the early 70s he recorded *Dadawah Peace And Love*, on which his group was augmented by studio musicians, a blend of Rastafarian chant, reggae, Southern soul and psychedelia greatly enhanced by its imaginative arrangements. *Nyahbinghi* was a collection of chants and

hymns in the style of his Zion disc singles. In 1975, he recorded *Rastafari*, on which his group was augmented by several well-known reggae musicians. The album's tight arrangements and excellent songs brought him into the reggae mainstream, but the momentum was lost with 1976's *Tribute To The Emperor* with Jazzboe Abubaka and *Freedom Sounds*. He augmented his group again for 1978's *Kabir Am Lak* (Glory To God) and *Movements*, both of which are strong albums. In 1979, *Rastafari In Dub* was issued, an excellent collection of material culled from *Rastafari* and *Kibir Am Lak*. Further releases included *Promised Land Sounds Live* (1980), *Disarmament* and *Revelation* (1982). His last outstanding album was *Love Thy Neighbour*, whose imaginative production is the work of Lee Perry. During the late 80s Michael spent a great deal of time teaching drumming. He returned to recording with *Zion Train* (1988), a mediocre album made without the Sons Of Negus, followed by *Know How* (1990), a disappointing set which tried to incorporate world music elements.

Albums: *Dadawah Peace And Love* (Trojan 1975), *Nyahbinghi* (1975), *Rastafari* (Grounation 1975), *Freedom Sounds* (Dynamic 1976), *Irations Of Ras Michael* (Top Ranking 1977), *Kibir Am Lak* (Rastafari 1978), *Movements* (Dynamic 1978), *Rastafari In Dub* (Grounation 1979), *Promised Land Sounds Live* (Lions Gate 1980), *Revelation* (Trojan 1982), *Disarmament* (Trojan 1983), *Love Thy Neighbour* (Live & Love 1984), *Rally Round* (Shanachie 1985), *Know How* (Shanachie 1990). With Jazzboe Abubaka: *Tribute To The Emperor* (Trojan 1976). With HR: *Zion Train* (SST 1988).

Rasta Music

By which is meant the 'burru' or 'nyabhingi' drumming, as practised by outfits like Count Ossie & The Mystic Revelation Of Rastafari, and Ras Michael And The Sons Of Negus. There are three drums used in such music, the large bass drum of between two to three feet diameter, played by striking

Ras Michael

with a stick, the end of which is padded. This is used to mark time and keep the pace with a deeply resonant, almost sub-frequency thump. The smaller funde and repeater hand drums lay down the rhythm, with the repeater improvising across the top. These are often complemented by a selection of percussion instruments and home-made bottle horns or saxes. Rasta music derives from the Afro-Jamaican burru and kumina traditions, themselves said to have descended from traditional West African dances. Prior to the late 50s, such music was confined to Rastafarian strongholds at Wareika Hill, Dungle, and other locations. Count Ossie was instrumental in bringing such music to wider public attention, especially when he agreed to provide the backing for Prince Buster's production of the Folks Brothers' 'Oh Carolina'. Count Ossie and his drummers were subsequently used on a number of recordings throughout the next ten years, including 'Babylon Gone' aka 'Going Home' (c.1961), featuring saxophonist Wilton Gatnair, producer Harry Mudie's first record; 'Lumumba' (1961) by Bonny & Skitter, and 'Another Moses' (1961) by the Mellowcats for Coxsone Dodd. 'Cassavubu' (1961) aka 'Chubby' provided another hit for Buster. Other notable releases included 'Ducksoup' (1962) by Drumbago's Orchestra, 'Down The Train Line' (1967) by Stranger Cole & Patsy, and 'Pata Pata Rock Steady' (1967) by Patsy, both for Sonia Pottinger. They managed to cut a few singles under their own steam too, including 'So Long Rastafari Calling' (1971) for Studio One, 'Rasta Reggae' for Arnold Wedderburn's Right On label, 'Whispering Drums' (1969) for Harry Mudie and 'Blacker Black' (1968), wrongly credited to the Ethiopians, and released on Pama's Crab label in the UK in 1968.

In 1973 Count Ossie linked up with Rasta saxophonist Cedric Brooks to record the classic triple set, *Grounation*, released in the UK on the Ashanti label. This remains the essential Rasta music artefact, a compelling *tour de force* of heartbeat drumming, dread

philosophy and free jazz-styled horn playing. Count Ossie died in 1975, crushed when a storm panicked the crowd during a cricket match at Kingston's National Stadium. Cedric Brooks carried out further experimentation with the basic Rasta music structure, with some satisfying results on *United Africa* (1977), and went on to form the Light Of Saba, of whom 'Lambs Bread Collie' (1978) is a fine example. Ras Michael follows much in the tradition of Count Ossie, though his music often fits more easily into the orthodox reggae format. His early albums, *Peace & Love* (1975) and *Freedom Sounds*(1976), remain fairly conventional examples of Rasta music. Later albums such as *Rastafari* (1976) and *Irations Of Ras Michael* (1977) combined burru drumming and standard reggae rhythms to good effect. While Rasta music has never been at the forefront of reggae music itself, it is a uniquely Jamaican aspect that was incorporated into the earliest R&B derived, pre-ska forms. Its influence has been felt in subtle ways ever since.

Albums: Count Ossie: *Grounation* (Ashanti 1973), *Tales Of Mozambique* (Dynamic 1975). Ras Michael & The Sons Of Negus: *Dadawah Peace & Love* (Trojan 1975), *Freedom Sounds* (Dynamic 1976).

Rastafarianism

Rastafari emerged out of the ghettos of Kingston, Jamaica during the 30s. Its rise in popularity among Jamaica's youth in the late 60s and 70s facilitated its worldwide recognition as the driving philosophical force behind the music of prominent reggae artists such as Burning Spear, Culture, Big Youth, Black Uhuru and of course the three main Wailers; Bunny Wailer, Peter Tosh and Bob Marley. So strongly has Rasta been associated with reggae music that for many people the one is unthinkable without the other. But reggae reflects all the aspects and concerns of Jamaican life, whether spiritual, temporal, or purely hedonistic, whatever affects or is held dear by the youth from which it so often springs, and to whom it speaks loudest, is a fit subject for eulogisation in reggae. In this way Rastafarianism was felt most keenly in the 70s, but though it is less crucial to the music's identity nowadays, its reverberations are still felt.

Religion has always played a large part in the lives of Jamaicans. Part of the process of slavery was to ingrain the Bible deeply into the slave psyche in order to provide Holy justification for the superior stance of the slave masters and to reinforce the inevitability of the slaves' bondage and backbreaking toil. The African religions and traditions practised prior to enslavement were severely discouraged, and yet means were found in which they were retained in coded forms, through music, dance and folk tales. These survive in modern Jamaica through such forms as Kumina, and Obeah, and adapted with Christianity, in Pocomania (aka Pukkumina). The majority of the island's population though, adhere to Christian forms such as Anglican, Methodist, Roman Catholic, and The Church of God, as well as a strong following for the Ethiopian Orthodox Church. More than 80 per cent of Jamaica's population is Christian.

The roots of Rasta may be found in the rise of black awareness in Jamaica during the early part of the 20th century. Some African-Jamaicans began to feel increasingly dissatisfied with the Caucasian bias of the Christian churches, and the image of God as a white man. A new interest in African affairs also burgeoned. This new found consciousness was manifested in many ways by as many different individuals and organisations, but in particular in the activities and speeches of Marcus Mosiah Garvey (b. 17 August 1887, St. Ann's Bay, Jamaica, d. 1940). Garvey had established the Universal Negro Improvement Association (UNIA) in Jamaica in 1914 with the aim of providing an impetus for disenfranchised blacks to learn about their history, their African roots, and to make provision for a hopeful future despite their humble present. The limitations of working within the confines of Jamaica soon prompted Garvey's relocation to America where UNIA soon blossomed among the black ghettos and tenements of Harlem and naturally attracted the attention of the authorities. Garvey attempted to launch a steamship company, the Black Star Line, that would hopefully establish a firm business base for the organisation and with which he hoped to provide free passage back to Africa for those African-Americans who wished to return. This eventually proved to be his undoing when he was jailed in Atlanta and deported to Jamaica on trumped-up charges of fraud. Garvey died in obscurity in London in 1940, but when his body was returned to Jamaica for burial he was received as a hero.

Garvey was an important figure in what eventually became the Civil Rights Movement in the US, but his importance to this story lies in certain pronouncements he is said to have made, in particular the famous 'Look to Africa, when a black king shall be crowned, for the day of deliverance is near.' In Jamaica, among his followers (known as Graveyites) this was received literally as prophecy, and when in November 1930 Haile Selassie, the latest in the Ethiopian line of royalty, whose birthright is said to trace back to the Biblical marriage between King Solomon and the Queen of Sheba, was crowned Ras Tafari, King of Kings, Lord of Lords, Conquering Lion of the Tribe of Judah, Emperor of Ethiopia, many Garveyites and sympathisers felt that Garvey's prophecy had been fulfilled.

Another key figure in this story is preacher Leonard P. Howell, who was arrested in 1933 for sedition and blasphemy. Howell had been selling postcards of Emperor Haile Selassie and claiming him to be 'the spirit of our Lord . . . returned'. Howell also claimed that blacks in the west were really Jews, the Biblical lost tribe of Israel. To Howell, Selassie, Ras Tafari, was literally the same man as Jesus, and therefore God made flesh on earth. Citing Selassie's coronation attended by 72 nations paying homage and bearing gifts, Selassie was 'Christ returned to earth to kill Nebuchadnezzar's image'. Other factors and individuals were involved in these early stages, and the Rastafarian movement began to flourish in the ghettos, its followers marked out, in accordance with certain Old Testament passages, by the adoption of dreadlocks, in which the hair is not combed or otherwise teased into submission, but is allowed to grow in wild coils frequently tucked into knitted tams adorned with the colours of the Ethiopian flag; red, green and gold. Frowned upon by the authorities, life was made difficult for the Rastas during these early years. Howell's stronghold in Pinnacle, where hundreds of Rastas lived in quite reflective isolation from the rest of Jamaican society, was raided twice, and finally closed down by police after which the faithful settled in the ghetto districts of Kingston. This was probably the catalyst for the movement's greater influence among Jamaica's poor. By the mid-60s it was established that there were at least 70,000 Rastafarians living in Jamaica.

True Rastafarians are deeply spiritual individuals who hold their faith uppermost in their lives. There are many misconceptions and seemingly mysterious aspects of their faith in terms of behaviour and speech, the headline grabbing use of marijuana (aka ganga, the holy herb), the dreadlocks (though neither ganga smoking or dreadlocks are necessary requirements), the purposeful lack of an organised church and hierarchy (until the inauguration of the Twelve Tribes in the early 70s), the grounations (gatherings where brethren would partake of the herb by way of the chalice, sit and reason, play drums, chant, and sing adapted hymns) (see Rasta Music), the desire for repatriation back to Africa, and the apocalyptic view of the world's present state of affairs. Throughout the 60s interest in Rasta had been growing among Jamaica's youth and this was naturally reflected in the popular music of the day on records such as 'Oh Carolina' by the Folks Brothers which utilised the burru drumming of master Rasta musician Count Ossie and his group, and 'Beardman Ska' (1965) by the Skatalites.

This influence found its fullest flowering in the 70s with Rasta sentiments expressed clearly in popular records such as 'Beat Down Babylon' and 'A Place Called Africa' (both 1971) by Junior Byles, and 'Satta Amassa Gana' (recorded in 1969 but only becoming a hit in 1971) by the Abyssinians.

The movement came to worldwide recognition in the mid-70s with the success of Bob Marley And The Wailers. Marley, like many of his contemporaries, had been interested in the faith since the mid-60s, finally capitulating fully at the turn of the 70s, his guidance coming through Rasta elder Mortimer Planno, the dread who stood on the steps of the plane with the Emperor during his tumultuous visit to Jamaica in 1966. The release of the epochal *Natty Dread* (1976), and the extensive touring Marley undertook subsequently, brought Rasta to the attention of the world's media, and also alerted many in Europe and America to the faith. Rastafarianism's influence waned to some extent during the 80s, many of those attracted to the faith found it hard to adhere to the strict moral, dietary, and philosophical guidelines of fundamental Rastafarianism, and in some cases its practitioners adapted and compromised the faith, to a more easily assimilated lifestyle.

Rastafari still has a struggle to be recognised as a 'proper' religion, and this is probably because many Rastas practise their faith in a personal way rather than adhering to any organisation. Its popularity in the 70s among Jamaica's youth was for many a transitionary phase, later dropped when it became unfashionable. It has also suffered from the bad publicity it has received at the hands of criminals affecting the outward appearance of Rastafarians. It has survived the 'death' of its Godhead Haile Selassie (who never officially recognised, nor denounced, the faith) in 1976 after Ethiopia had endured a communist backed military coup. Nevertheless Rasta has been and still remains a strong and positive influence for many people, of all races, all over the world.

Rebel, Tony

b. Patrick Barrett, Manchester, Jamaica. Rebel is one of the few dreadlocked 'cultural' DJs of the ragga era, but actually started out as a singer, winning local talent competitions as Papa Tony or Tony Ranking on sound systems such as Destiny Outernational, Thunderstorm, Wha Dat and finally Sugar Minott's Youth Promotion. In 1988 he recorded 'Casino' for the MGB label, his first ever release. Sides for Delroy 'Callo' Collins and Shocking Vibes followed, but it was at Penthouse where his true potential began to be realised. 'Fresh Dee-Jay', 'Music Fraternity' and 'Mandella Story' announced his arrival, before he was matched with Cutty Ranks for *Die Hard*. It contained two of his first hit singles, 'The Armour' and 'Instant Death'. Although notable for their combative zeal both revealed an uncompromisingly spiritual approach, and were voiced in a melodic sing-jay fashion that was unique. 'Fresh Vegetable' was the unlikeliest love song of 1990, but proved a sizeable hit; so too 'D.J. Unity' (with Macka B), 'The Herb', 'War And Crime' and 'Hush', the latter voiced for Bobby Digital. Throughout 1991-92 he recorded for a number of different producers, including Exterminator, Redman, Star Trail and the Two Friends label, who teamed him with first Anthony Red Rose ('Gun Talk') and then Judy Mowatt ('Guilty'). Penthouse released his debut album, *Rebel With A Cause,* in 1992 and this was followed by *Rebellious*, a more rootsy set produced by Sky High which included duets with Half Pint and Garnett Silk. 'Chatty Chatty Mouth' continued his winning habits with Penthouse before he recorded the anthemic 'Reggae On Top' for Steely And Clevie. By the end of the year he had signed to Columbia Records for *Vibes Of The Times,* released in 1993. 'Sweet Jamaica', a song voiced for Bobby Digital, was chosen for the soundtrack of the film *Cool Runnings* that November.

Albums: *Rebel With A Cause* (Penthouse 1992), *Rebellious* (RAS 1992), *Vibes Of The Times* (Columbia 1993). With Cutty Ranks: *Die Hard (Vols. 1 & 2)* (Penthouse 1990).

Red Dragon

b. Leroy May, Kingston, Jamaica. One of the most enduring and dependable DJs to emerge from Jamaica, Dragon - or rather Redman as he was then known - learnt his trade on Barrington Hi-Fi in 1981, progressing to Stone Love, Small Axe, Rambo Mango (which he owned) and People's Choice sound systems, before changing his name in 1984 after the popularity of his 'Laughing Dragon' lyric on a dub plate. Fellow DJ Charlie Chaplin had also passed through the ranks of People's Choice and produced his debut tune, 'Computer', in 1985.

The following year Dragon went to Harry J who released 'Nah Get Nutten' and 'Commander' to a welcoming dancehall audience. In 1987 'Hol A Fresh' was a massive hit for Winston Riley, but failed to crossover as predicted owing to poor promotion. Nevertheless its local success ensured a wealth of releases for the late King Tubby ('Canter Mi Horse'), Redman, Vena and King Jammys, where 'Duck Dance' and 'Della Skank' confirmed his ability to define the latest dancehall moves. In 1989 Riley's Techniques label issued an album pairing him with his DJ brother, Flourgon. That same year witnessed the birth of his own Dragon imprint, on which he released tunes by young artists such as John Mouse as well as himself: 'Old', 'Love Unuh' and 'My Anthem' achieving the most recognition. Throughout 1990-91 he recorded very little; concentrating instead on encouraging fresh talent coming up through Rambo Mango and Flourgon's Sweet Love set. Buju Banton and Terry Ganzie both started their careers with Dragon. In 1992 he made a return to the dancehall market with the uncharacteristic *Pum Pum Shorts,* and then several sides for Shang, Steely And Clevie, Mafia & Fluxy and Parrish. The momentum increased during 1993 and there were a proliferation of hits for the likes of Bobby

Digital, Danny Browne, Winston Riley, Fashion and Sly And Robbie's Taxi label, all capturing his deep, rolling vocals and adept rhythm-riding to perfection.

Selected albums: *Red Dragon Vs Flourgon* (Techniques 1989), *Pum Pum Shorts* (Dragon 1992).

Reggae

Although used as the generic title for all Jamaican music, reggae proper first arrived in 1968, with Larry & Alvin's 'Nanny Goat' and the Beltones' 'No More Heartaches' fighting it out for the legendary status of first reggae record. The beat was distinctive from rocksteady in that it dropped any of the pretensions to a smooth, soulful sound which characterised slick American R&B, and instead was perhaps closer in kinship to US southern funk, being heavily dependent on the rhythm section to drive it along. Reggae's great advantage was its almost limitless flexibility: from the early, jerky sound of Lee Perry's 'People Funny Boy' to the uptown sounds of Third World's 'Now That We've Found Love' was an enormous leap through the years and styles, yet both are instantly recognisable as reggae.

Like ska before it, reggae found favour in the UK with the mods' successors, skinheads. They supported the music to a degree that enabled a roll-call of reggae acts to hit the charts between 1968-72, among them Desmond Dekker, Dave & Ansell Collins, Jimmy Cliff and Bob & Marcia. Many similar acts also received a bite of the commercial cherry. By 1970-72 skinheads had begun to tire of the Jamaican sound, which had diversified away from the quirky love songs (Clancy Eccles, Pat Kelly) and the stomping organ instrumentals (Upsetters, Lloyd Charmers) of its early days to embrace Rasta philosophy (Junior Byles, Bob Marley, Abyssinians etc.), DJ music (U Roy, I Roy, Dennis Alcapone) and black rights (Burning Spear, Heptones). Other sub-genres such as skank, dub, rockers, steppers etc. unfolded through the 70s, before all were more or less supplanted by dancehall and ragga for the 80s. Each style, however, remained under the collective banner of reggae, a flag of convenience that never seems to out stay its welcome.

Reggae Philharmonic Orchestra

Formed by original Steel Pulse member Mykaell S. Riley, the Reggae Philharmonic was a noble and bizarre experiment which crossed reggae rhythms with orchestral themes, despite the fact that Riley can neither read nor write music. The idea was to employ the most talented black classical musicians, with Riley adding vocals on top of these arrangements to surprisingly good effect.

Album: *Reggae Philharmonic Orchestra* (Mango/Island 1988), *Time* (Mango/Island 1990).

Reid, Duke

b. c.1915, Jamaica, d. 1974. Perhaps the single biggest influence on reggae music after his close rival, Coxsone Dodd, Duke Reid's marvellous productions were, at their best, reggae at its absolute peak. Reid spent 10 years as a Kingston policeman, a sometimes dangerous profession that enabled him to develop the no-nonsense style he displayed while conducting business negotiations in later life. He and his wife Lucille bought the Treasure Isle Liquor Store in the 50s, and in a sponsorship deal Reid hosted his own radio show, *Treasure Isle Time*, airing US R&B: his theme song was Tab Smith's 'My Mother's Eyes'. Reid also ran his own sound system, Duke Reid The Trojan, for which he visited America to find obscure R&B tunes with which to baffle rivals like Coxsone Dodd's Downbeat sound system. After flirting with the record business for three years, recording tunes such as 'Duke's Cookies', 'What Makes Honey' and 'Joker', he seriously took up record production in 1962, scoring ska hits galore with Stranger Cole, the Techniques, Justin Hinds & the Dominoes and Alton Ellis & the Flames, issuing them on three labels; Treasure Isle, Duke Reid, and Dutchess. Reid didn't exactly dominate

Red Dragon

the music business, but his was a formidable presence: he was notorious for carrying a loaded gun and letting his ammunition belt be clearly visible. However, he was more than mere muscle and had an astute musical sensibility, as the fast approaching rocksteady era would prove beyond doubt.

By 1966 ska was evolving into a slower, more stately beat, and with help from guitarist Ernest Ranglin and the band of sax player Tommy McCook & the Supersonics, Reid's productions at his own Treasure Isle Studio epitomised the absolute peak of the style. Hits such as the Paragons 'Ali Baba' and 'Wear You To the Ball', Alton Ellis' 'Cry Tough', 'Breaking Up', 'Rock Steady' and 'Ain't That Loving You', the Melodians' 'You Don't Need Me', 'I Will Get Along', 'I Caught You' and 'Last Train To Expo '67', the Jamaicans' 'Things You Say You Love' and the Techniques' 'Queen Majesty' were only the tip of an impressive iceberg. All are tasteful, irresistibly danceable, soul-soaked rocksteady classics, released on Reid's own labels in Jamaica and on Trojan (the label was named after his sound) or its imprints (including Treasure Isle and Duke) in the UK. By 1969 rocksteady had died, and Reid was apparently struggling, stuck in a musical revolution he had created. However, in 1970 he did it again, taking a sparsely-recorded toaster named U Roy and single-handedly founded the modern DJ era. At one point U Roy held four out of the top five Jamaican chart positions and both he and Reid were watching them swap places over a period of months: 'Wake The Town', 'Wear You To the Ball', 'Everybody Bawlin'', 'Version Galore': Reid simply dropped the chatter over his old rocksteady hits to start an entire new genre of reggae music. He also had hits with other DJs, such as Dennis Alcapone and Lizzy. Reid's legend in the reggae pantheon was assured. By 1973 Reid's fortunes had again begun to wane, perhaps because he was notorious for not wanting to record rasta lyrics in an era dominated by roots themes, and was considered to be an establishment figure as the senior reggae producer in

Jamaica. He died in 1974, his extensive back catalogue going on to sell thousands of singles and albums through a variety of licensees, his name on a record virtually a guarantee of sheer joy for the duration of its playing time.

Albums: Various: *Golden Hits* (Trojan 1969, covers 1966-69), *The Birth Of Ska* (Trojan 1972, covers 1962-65), *Hottest Hits* (Front Line 1979, covers 1966-69), *Hottest Hits Volume Two* (Front Line 1979, covers 1966-69), *Ba Ba Boom Time* (Trojan 1988, covers 1967-68). The Skatalites: *Tribute To The Skatalites* (1991). Alton Ellis: *Greatest Hits* (1977, covers c.1967-70). Paragons: *On The Beach* (Treasure Isle 1968). Justin Hinds And The Dominoes: *From Jamaica With Reggae* (High Note 1984), *Early Recordings* (Esoldun/Treasure Isle 1991). U Roy: *Version Galore* (Trojan 1971).

Reid, Junior

b. Delroy Reid, 1965, Kingston, Jamaica. Born in the Tower Hill area of Kingston, Junior grew up in the infamous Waterhouse ghetto. He made his first recording in 1979 at the age of 13 for the equally youthful singer Hugh Mundell, entitled 'Speak The Truth', and released through Augustus Pablo's Rockers label. Another Mundell production, 'Know Myself', a version of Dennis Walks' classic, 'Drifter', appeared on Greensleeves in 1981. After Mundell's untimely death – Reid was in the car when he was murdered – he achieved some success as part of the Voice Of Progress group, with a single and album entitled *Mini-Bus Driver* for producer Robert Palmer's Negus Roots label. Recording throughout the rest of the early 80s as a solo artist, Reid scored with tracks like 'Jailhouse', 'Sister Dawn', 'Pallaving Street' and 'Give Thanks & Praise' for Prince Jammy. Other 45s included 'The Original Foreign Mind', which was actually a self-production, for which he adopted a fast delivery similar to that of the new wave of UK DJs like Papa Levi and Smiley Culture, on Sugar Minott's Youth Promotion label. Other notable recordings

Junior Reid

included 'Babylon Release The Chain' for Errol Thompson, 'Chanting' for Delroy Wright and the monster 'Boom Shack A Lack' for Prince Jammy, released in the UK on Greensleeves.

In 1985 Reid's solo career was interrupted when he was enlisted into the ranks of Grammy Award winners Black Uhuru, after lead singer Michael Rose's departure. The first release with Uhuru, 'Fit You A Fe Fit', met with approval from the reggae audience. However, subsequent material, particularly the experimental, rock influenced Arthur Baker production, 'Great Train Robbery', and Grammy-nominated *Brutal* album, made more of an impact on the international market, only serving to alienate the grass roots following he had worked so hard to build up. Aware of this credibility gap, Reid inaugurated his own label, JR Productions, and began to issue roots tunes like 'Pain On The Poor Man's Brain' and 'Nah Get Rich And Switch', credited to Black Uhuru, but far more in the vein of his previous solo material. After recording Uhuru's *Positive* in 1988, Junior left the group to concentrate once more on his own career. Teaming up with English dance outfit Coldcut for 'Stop This Crazy Thing', he reached number 21 in the UK pop chart in September 1988. In 1990, he made another appearance in the singles chart when he joined forces with the indie-dance band the Soup Dragons, for a version of the Rolling Stones' 'I'm Free', hitting number 5 in August of that year.

Back in the reggae world, Reid's return to grass roots favour came in 1989 with the anthemic 'One Blood', followed by the well received album of the same title. Its raw digital rhythms and roughneck ragga production firmly re-established his name at the forefront of the reggae scene. Since then he has issued a flood of tunes on his own label, including 'Married Life', 'Good Man Scarce', 'Can't Tek the Gun Gun', a new version of 'Mini-Bus Driver', 'Friend Enemy', 'Banana Boat Man', 'Strong Survive', and the popular 'All Fruits Ripe', as well as producing other artists like Junior

Demus, Ninjaman, Dennis Brown, and Gregory Isaacs. He has also opened his own studio, one more step towards complete artistic independence. Junior Reid, like that other Waterhouse singer, Yammie Bolo, is an artist who has continued to display his commitment to roots reggae music, and looks set to carry the winning formula on into the millennium.

Albums: *Boom Shack A Lack* (Greensleeves 1983), *Back To Back* (Volcano 1985), *Original Foreign Mind* (Black Roots 1985), *One Blood* (JR Music 1989), *Visa* (Greensleeves 1993). With Voice Of Progress: *Mini Bus Driver* (Negus Roots 1982).

Riley, Winston

Riley started out as a singer, forming the legendary rocksteady outfit the Techniques as a schoolboy in 1962. In 1968 the group broke away from their producer Duke Reid, and Riley, with his brother Buster, borrowed enough money from his mother to form his own label. Their first production, Johnny Osbourne's 'Come Back Darling', was an immediate success followed by an album of the same name. Other early productions include Osbourne's 'See And Blind' and 'Purify Your Heart', Alton Ellis' 'I'll Be Waiting', Lloyd Young's 'High Explosion', Dennis Alcapone's 'Look Into Yourself', Jimmy Riley's 'Prophecy', the Ethiopians' 'Promises', and various Techniques sides. These appeared on a variety of labels in Jamaica; Techniques, Wind, Serpent, Romax and Riley Inc. and a licensing deal with the B&C group resulted in the appearance of many of them on release on the Techniques label in the UK. He scored a number 1 UK hit in May 1971 with 'Double Barrel' by Dave And Ansell Collins, which spawned an album of the same title in 1971. The follow-up, 'Monkey Spanner', reached number 7 in July of the following year.

In 1973 he enjoyed a huge Jamaican hit with his production of Ansell Collins' 'Stalag 17', DJ versions by Big Youth; 'Jim Screechy' and 'All Nations', were also popular. During the mid-70s other fine productions appeared in the then popular roots style, including the Interns' (aka the Viceroys) 'Missions Impossible' and two melodica cuts of the rhythm both entitled 'Black Out', by Augustus Pablo and Ansell Collins, 'Cheer Up Blackman' by former Technique Morvin Brooks, 'Don't Mock Jah' by Donovan Addams and a pair of fine dub albums; *Meditation Dub* and *Concrete Jungle Dub* (both 1976). As the decade drew to a close, Riley was responsible for producing one of the first and most influential of the new breed of dancehall DJs; General Echo, scoring a big reggae hit with 'Arleen' which rode the original 'Staleg' rhythm, and releasing the popular *Ranking Slackness* (1980), which more or less inaugurated the whole trend for lewd lyrics that has prospered since. When quizzed on this in an interview in Canada's *Reggae Quarterly* in 1986, he remarked, with admirable candour; 'Let's face it, that record was a big seller! People would pass by the shop (Techniques Records situated at 2 Chancery Lane, Kingston) and say "You don't have to make a record like that!" But somebody have to do it.' This period also saw numerous sides by Johnny Osbourne including 'Politician', 'Inflation' and a re-cut of 'Purify Your Heart'. In 1982 Riley revived the Techniques with Morvin Brooks and ex-Paragon Tyrone (aka Don) Evans to record an album, *Never Fall In Love*.

In 1985 Riley resurrected the durable 'Stalag' rhythm once more for Tenor Saw's massive dancehall hit, 'Ring The Alarm', which begat the classic one rhythm album, *Stalag 17, 18 And 19* (1985), and brought the rhythm back in a big way. The following year another of his productions; 'Boops' (Jamaican slang for a sugar daddy) by DJ Supercat, went massive, breaking the artist internationally, and starting another trend for records dealing with the same subject. Riley has been among the most successful Jamaican producers of the last 25 years, and many artists have benefited from his expertise including Frankie Paul (*Strange Feeling* 1984), Michael Prophet, Don Evans (*Don Evans* 1983), Admiral Tibet (*Leave People's Business* 1988), Sister Nancy, Red Dragon ('Hol' A Fresh' 1987), Courtney Melody (*Bad Boy* 1988), Ernest Wilson, Gregory Isaacs, Papa San & Lady G ('Legal Rights' 1989), Cutty Ranks, Yammie Bolo, who recorded his debut 'When A Man's In Love' (1985) for Riley, and many others.

Rockers

The name given to the 'militant' double drumming style of reggae that dominated the music from 1975-78. Pioneered by Sly Dunbar, the drummer for Channel One Studio's in house band the Revolutionaries, it became immediately popular and Sly not only worked for Channel One but also laid rhythms for most of Jamaica's other top producers. Sly worked the drum kit like no-one else and made his presence felt on every tune he recorded, but it was not long before every other drummer in reggae had developed his own variation of the Sly Dunbar style. Bunny Lee, Joe Gibbs, Yabby You and ironically Coxsone Dodd (whose original rhythms many of the hit records were based on) all enjoyed success with their versions of the sound. In the ordinary scheme of things all of this would have been of purely parochial interest to reggae fans only, but the rise of Rockers coincided with the first real outside money to ever be invested in Jamaican music - notably from Island Records and Virgin Records. Both were anxious to capitalize on the then current international success of Bob Marley And The Wailers, and the subsequent interest and greater availability of 'roots' reggae meant that the 'Rockers' sound became both well known and influential worldwide. Much of the musical output of the period sounds more dated now than the originals that were being 'updated' but, as always, the best still sounds as fresh and innovative as when it was first released.

Albums: The Revolutionaries: *Vital Dub, Strictly Rockers*. The Mighty Diamonds: *Right Time* (Well Charge/Virgin 1976). Joe Gibbs And The Professionals: *African Dub All Mighty Chapter Three*.

Rocksteady

Rocksteady, among the most elegant and rhythmically pleasing of all pop music forms, grew out of ska, spanning a period circa 1966-68. Ska's furious high-tempo beat had driven dancers into frenzies in Jamaica for five years by then and a new, more confident breed of singers had emerged in Jamaica: the Ethiopians, the Maytals, Ken Boothe, Alton Ellis and the Wailers. Ska offered limited possibilities for a singer: you either fought with it or flowed through it, but the chances of you really stamping your personality on a song, in the same way that American soul stars could, were minimal. As Jamaica's singers began to offer more than just the icing on ska's cake, with the idea of being real songwriters with something to say, so the beat slowed to allow them the time to say it. The bass parts took a distinctive character for the first time, leaving a space in the rhythm that came to characterise all of Jamaican music from this point hence.

It is almost impossible to pinpoint when ska actually became rocksteady in the frantic currents of Jamaican music, though certain records such as Peter Tosh's 'I'm The Toughest', the Wailers' 'Rasta Put It On' and Alton Ellis And The Flames' 'Cry Tough' were rocksteady in all but name before the genre was defined as such. By 1967 the rocksteady era was in full flood, perhaps best epitomised by the sounds emanating from Duke Reid's Treasure Isle Studio in Bond Street, Kingston. Reid's productions were heavily dependent on the arrangements of saxophonist Tommy McCook, and together the pair of them created a pantheon of hits from the likes of Alton Ellis, the Paragons, the Melodians and Joya Landis, that remain unsurpassed today for their sheer melodic strength. Other producers who worked on distinctive rocksteady sides include Coxsone Dodd, Sonia Pottinger and Prince Buster. The shift of emphasis away from costly horn sections meant that more people could now afford to become involved in record production, and many new producers began to make their

mark. The rocksteady bubble burst around 1968, when the new, faster, and more manic style of reggae began to emerge. However, the lines between new and old styles of Jamaican music were blurred, and remain so today - reggae's DJ boom was started by U Roy's use of old rocksteady backing tracks at Treasure Isle; and both dancehall and ragga styles owe plenty to the format.

Selected albums: Various: *Put It On - Its Rocksteady* (Island 1968), *Rocksteady Coxsone Style* (Studio One 1968), *Get Ready Rock Steady* (Studio One 1968), *Hottest Hits (Vols. 1, 2 & 3)* (Treasure Isle 1979), *Rocksteady Years* (Island 1980), *Mojo Rock Steady* (Heartbeat/Studio One 1994). Alton Ellis: *Best Of* (Studio One 1970).

Rodriguez, Rico

b. Emmanuel Rodriguez, 17 October 1934, Kingston, Jamaica. Apart from Don Drummond, Rico aka Reco aka El Reco, was undoubtedly the most gifted trombonist working in the early years of Jamaican music. In the 40s he attended the famous Catholic Alpha Boys School where, by the age of 10, he had learned to play the trombone under the strict tutelage of the Nuns, though he had originally wanted to play the saxophone. In the early 50s he began appearing at and winning local talent contests. He became a Rasta and formed a close musical association with master Rasta drummer Count Ossie at his encampment at Wareika Hill, to the east of Kingston. Rico's first recording session was for Coxsone Dodd, playing on the Jiving Juniors' 'Over The River' and Theophilius Beckford's seminal 'Easy Snappin', and his own 'Stew Peas And Cornflakes'. He went on to work on literally hundreds of sessions for Dodd and most of the top producers of the day including Duke Reid ('Let George Do It'), Leslie Kong, Vincent Chin (Randy's, for whom he cut 'Rico Special'), and Prince Buster, who released a few sides credited to Rico himself including 'Luke Lane Shuffle', 'August 1962', 'This Day', 'Blues From The Hills', and the amazing 'Soul Of Africa'. In an interview with Carl Gayle for *Black Music* magazine in 1977, Rico claimed that some records, issued after he moved to Britain but recorded years earlier ('Let George Do It', 'Salt Lane Shuffle') and credited to his successor Don Drummond, were really by him. In 1966 while resident in the UK, Rico joined Buster when the latter toured the country, and was enlisted to play on 'Barrister Pardon', the follow-up to the infamous 'Judge Dread', during recording sessions in London.

Rico left Jamaica in 1961 and settled in the UK where he continued recording as a session musician for artists such as Laurel Aitken, Georgie Fame, Joe 'Brixton Cat' Mansano and others, and also in his own right with many singles, including the popular 'The Bullet', and a number of albums released on various UK reggae labels throughout the 60s. In March 1964 he experienced a taste of pop chart success with a reworking of Jimmy Cliff's 'King Of Kings' as Ezz Reco And The Launchers, with Boysie Grant on vocals. The record entered the chart one week before Millie's 'My Boy Lollipop' and spent four weeks in the lower reaches of the UK Top 50, but follow-ups 'Little Girl' and 'Please Come Back' failed to sell in any quantity and the band folded. He spent the early 70s in the doldrums, rarely recording, but passing the time by playing live with the Undivided, a band made up of ex-patriot Jamaican musicians. In 1976 he returned to Jamaica to record the well-received *Man From Wareika* utilising many of the key Jamaican session musicians of the day, including Sly And Robbie. With the arrival of 2-Tone in the early 80s Rico enjoyed great success playing on stage and on record with the Specials upon whose label his next album, *That Man Is Forward* (1981) was released. This was followed by *Jama Rico* a year later. Since returning from a protracted stay in Jamaica, where he spent eight years living once more in Wareika, Rico has returned to London and appears regularly on stage with double bassist Gary Crosby's Jazz Jamaica.

Albums: *Reco In Reggae Land* (1969), *Blow Your Horn* (1969), *Brixton Cat* (1969), *Man From Wareika* (1976), *That Man Is Forward* (2-Tone 1981), *Jama Rico* (2-Tone 1982).

Romeo, Max

b. Max Smith, c.1947, Jamaica. It was Romeo who first introduced Britain to the concept of rude reggae with 'Wet Dream', which, despite a total radio ban, reached number 10 in the UK charts. He toured the UK several times in the space of a year and issued two albums: *A Dream* being the best selling. However, despite other similarly-styled singles like 'Mini Skirt Vision', he did not enjoy chart success again. Romeo was, essentially, something of a gospel singer with the ability to convey a revivalist fervour on his records such as 'Let The Power Fall' (a Jamaican political anthem in 1972) and 'Pray For Me'. Furthermore, he had an ability to get the trials, tribulations and amusements of Jamaican life into a song, as evinced by 'Eating Competition', 'Sixpence' and 'Aily And Ailaloo'. In 1972 Romeo began a liason with producers Lee Perry and Winston 'Niney' Holness, and from this point on his records had a musical fire to match his apocalyptical vision and contrasting humour: 'Babylose Burning', 'Three Blind Mice', 'The Coming Of Jah' all maintained his star status in Jamaica between 1972 and 1975. *Revelation Time* was one of the best albums of 1975, and 1976's *War Ina Babylon* was hailed by the rock press as one of the all-time classic reggae albums. However, Perry had much to do with those records' artistic success, and following a much-publicised split between the pair - with Perry recording 'White Belly Rat' about Max, and scrawling 'Judas' over the singer's picture in Perry's studio - Romeo was cast adrift without musical roots. *I Love My Music*, recorded with the help of Keith Richards was a flop, and the stronger *Reconstruction* fared no better. A move to New York's Wackies' label in the early 80s did little to reverse his fortunes, and by the late 80s Max Romeo's name was forgotten in the mainstream reggae market. However, in the spring of 1992, London producer Jah Shaka recorded *Far I Captain Of My Ship* on Jah Shaka Records, an unabashed, Jamaican-recorded roots album generally reckoned to be Romeo's best for over 15 years.

Albums: *A Dream* (1970), *Let The Power Fall* (1972), *Revelation Time* (Tropical Sound Tracs 1975), *War Ina Babylon* (Island 1976), *Reconstruction* (1978), *I Love My Music* (1979), *Rondos* (1980), *Holding Out My Love For You* (Shanachie 1987), *Far I Captain Of My Ship* (Jah Shaka 1992), *On The Beach* (1993).

Roots Radics

Jamaican session band centred around a nucleus of Errol 'Flabba' Holt (bass), Lincoln Valentine 'Style' Scott (drums) and Eric 'Bingy Bunny' Lamont (guitar). Other members at various times included Roy Hamilton (lead guitar), Noel 'Sowell' Bailey (lead guitar), Dwight Pinkney (formerly of the Sharks and Zap Pow, on lead guitar), Carlton 'Santz' Davis (drums), Fish Clarke (drums) and Steely Johnson (later of Steely & Clevie fame, on keyboards). Flabba and Bingy Bunny were previously active as part of Morris 'Blacker' Wellington's Morwells set up, recording such popular tunes as 'Swing & Dine' (1974), 'They Hold Us Down' (1978) and 'Kingston Twelve Tuffy' (1979). Before this Bunny had been teamed with bongo player Bongo Herman, the pair enjoying a big hit, 'Know Far I', in 1971 for producer/singer Derrick Harriott. He had also produced Peter Broggs' *Progressive Youth* LP, and played in the crack Channel One session band the Revolutionaries, whose demise at the end of the 70s was due to Sly & Robbie's production for their Taxi label and live work with Peter Tosh, which had left a vacuum the Radics were only too pleased to fill. Errol Holt was previously noted for his many fine singles during the mid-70s including 'A You Lick Me First', 'Gimme Gimme' and 'Who Have Eyes To See'.

Their initial impact was to slow the beat down a notch from the militant rockers sound of the Revolutionaries. This is perhaps best showcased on an album they worked on for producer Henry 'Junjo' Lawes, the hottest producer of the early 80s. *Bounty Hunter* (1979) was Barrington Levy's debut, as it was for the Radics, and it revolutionised reggae music in the same way that the Mighty Diamond's *Right Time* did five years earlier. The similarities include the revival of old Studio One rhythms central to the success of both groups. The Radics worked on innumerable sessions for as many different producers, including Linval Thompson - it was with their rhythms that Scientist destroyed space invaders and won the World Cup, as the titles of his LPs suggest - and worked for a while as Gregory Isaacs' backing band on tour and record, responsible for the rhythms on his classic *Night Nurse* (1982). They also did sessions for Bunny Wailer and Israel Vibration among many others.

Whilst in the UK on tour with Prince Far I (for whom they recorded under the name the Arabs), the group forged a social and musical friendship with maverick reggae/rock producer Adrian Sherwood, for whom they worked on many sessions as part of the loose conglomerates Creation Rebel and Singers & Players. The Roots Radics came in at the birth of, and were partly responsible for, the dancehall style that dominated in the first half of the 80s. But as their commitments to live work grew, particularly in the States, they were eventually usurped by other outfits. The digital/ragga revolution sparked off by Prince Jammy's production of Wayne Smith's massive hit, 'Under Me Sleng Teng', virtually eradicated the need for live musicians overnight, and the Radics lost their position as Jamaica's number one session band, though they remain in demand for stage shows. Eric Lamont died of prostrate cancer in January 1994.

Albums: *Roots Radics Dub Session* (Solid Groove 1982), *Freelance* (Kingdom 1985), *Forwards Never Backwards* (Heartbeat 1990), *World Peace Three* (Heartbeat 1992). With

Scientist: *Scientist Meets The Space Invaders* (Greensleeves 1981), *Scientist Wins The World Cup* (Greensleeves 1983), *Scientist And Jammy Strike Back* (Trojan 1983).

Rose, Michael

Former Black Uhuru vocalist who left soon after they had earned a Grammy award for *Anthem*. His solo career kicked off with 'Demonstration' on his own Grammy Rose label. 'Bogus Badge', the follow-up, gained strong reviews, but it wasn't until he signed with RCA that he began to attract serious exposure. However, by this time Rose's music had transferred to a pop/soul direction. A cover of Paul Simon's early 70s 'Mother And Child Reunion' cut was indicative of this, being closer to contemporary hip hop than the roots sound which Black Uhuru had peddled. Whatever, it was undeniably effective whichever category critics decided to place it in. His singles for Sly And Robbie's Taxi label heralded a return to roots reggae and 'Monkey Business', 'Visit Them' and 'One A We, Two A We' are already regarded as classics of 90s roots music, with the promise of an album to follow.
Selected albums: *Free Yourself* aka *Proud* (RCA 1990).

Royal Rasses

(see Prince Lincoln)

Royals

Formed by Roy Cousins (b. c.1945, Jamaica) in 1964, alongside Bertram Johnson, Keith Smith and Errol Wilson, though other than Cousins the line-up remained largely fluid. The Royals recorded for Duke Reid and Federal in the mid-60s, and for Coxsone Dodd in 1967, though no releases were forthcoming until 1968 when they cut 'Never See Come See' for producer Joe Gibbs, a dig at the Pioneers. The following year the group recorded 'Never Gonna Give You Up' for Byron Smith, 'Pick Out Me Eye', and, in 1969, '100 Pounds Of Clay' for Lloyd Daley. Though they achieved a

measure of popular, if not fiscal success with these records, Cousins disbanded the group and took a two year sabbatical. He eventually saved enough money from his job in the Jamaican Post Office to finance a self-produced single, 'Down Comes The Rain', issued in Jamaica on his own Tamoki label. In 1973 the Royals again recorded the classic 'Pick Up The Pieces', the success of which prompted Coxsone to release his original version of the song, which had been languishing ignored since the group's stint with him in the late 60s. This too became very popular, particularly the rhythm which has been versioned countless times since.
More self-produced releases followed throughout the decade including 'Promised Land', 'When You Are Wrong', 'Ghetto Man', 'Blacker Black', 'Only For A Time' and 'Sufferer Of The Ghetto', all collected on the essential *Pick Up The Pieces,* which ranks alongside the finest works of contemporaries like the Abyssinians, the Wailing Souls and the Mighty Diamonds. Cousins also produced records by other artists, including 'Jah Jah Children' by the Kingstonians, 'Genuine Way' by Lloyd Ruddock (King Tubby's brother), 'Heart In Pain' by Vinni O'Brien, 'Monkey Fashion' by I Roy and 'Way Of Life' by Gregory Isaacs, many included on the various artists set, *Herb Dust Volume 1* (1983). In 1975, the Royals split yet again, the rest of the group going on to record for Channel One as the Jayes. Roy enlisted two new members with whom he recorded the single, 'Make Believe', followed by two more albums, *Ten Years After* and *Israel Be Wise*, featuring Heptones Barry Llewelyn and Naggo Morris on harmonies. Cousins has been resident in the UK since the early 80s, concentrating mainly on producing other artists for his Wambesi and Dove labels, including the Gaylads, Derrick Pitter, Cornell Campbell, Earl Sixteen (*Julia* and *Crazy Woman*), Prince Far I, Charlie Chaplin (*Diet Rock*) and Don Carlos (*Plantation*).
Albums: *Pick Up The Pieces* (Magnum 1977), *Ten Years After* (Ballistic 1978), *Israel Be Wise*

(Ballistic 1978), *Moving On* (Kingdom 1983).
Compilation: *Royals Collection* (Trojan 1983).

S

Sanchez

b. 28 November 1967, Kingston, Jamaica. In the autumn of 1987, record releases by a singer called Sanchez D first arrived in the reggae shops. His voice was distinctive but untutored. He was not afraid to wail with a roughness that matched the equally gritty dancehall rhythms of the time, and his first hit was 'Lady In Red' for Red Man. By November of that year he was drawing attention with 'Zim Bam Zim', riding a scorching, bizarre Sly And Robbie rhythm. A more traditional 'Tears' followed and almost immediately gave him his debut UK chart appearance, becoming the lead track on *Sanchez* a few months later. By the spring of 1988, Sanchez was the number one singer of love songs in reggae. He became highly popular with a strong female following and 60s-style screaming was *de rigeur* at his concerts. His skinny frame and boyish demeanour and exciting stage act appealed to the ladies. Hit followed hit, including 'Old Friend', 'Green Green Grass Of Home', 'Let It Be Me', 'Impossible', 'Joy', 'Hello Josephine', 'Let Me Love You Now', 'Lonely Won't Leave', 'My Girl' and 'Tell Him I'm Not Home' - in typical reggae style, every producer and label in Jamaica was demanding a piece of the singer. His first UK gigs in the summer of 1988 revealed a massive following there too: Sanchez mania brought screaming to every show. A second album, *Loneliness,* orchestrated by veteran producer Winston Riley, dominated the reggae charts for months and the title cut, 'Loneliness Leave Me Alone', was a massive seller. *Sweetest Girl*, named after yet another hit, was his second 1988 album. Critically dismissed as a cover-singing fad whose own lyrics were slight, Sanchez was merely doing what was practical. When he felt the spirit he turned to writing serious songs such as 'South Africa', which became yet another hit. It was also said that as a singer he was limited, a jibe that he shattered when he recorded a superb version of 'End Of The World' in the spring of 1989, followed by *Wild Sanchez*. Hit singles continued to arrive: 'Me Love Me Girl Bad' with ragga DJ Flourgon; a cover of Bobby Brown's (with whom Sanchez has often been compared) 'My Prerogative', 'Come To Rule' and Tracy Chapman's 'Baby Can I Hold You Tonight' for his original producer Philip 'Fatis' Burrell. *Number One* was released in the UK on Island Records and 1990 saw the release of a 'clash' album with Pinchers *(Meets Pinchers)*, to be followed by two sets with Wayne Wonder.

Albums: *Sanchez* (Vena 1987), *Loneliness* (Techniques 1988), *Sweetest Girl* (Dennis Star 1988), *Wild Sanchez!* (Greensleeves 1988), *Number One* (Mango/Island 1989), *In Fine Style* (Charm 1990), *I Can't Wait* (Blue Mountain 1991), *Bring Back The Love* (World Enterprise 1992), *The One For Me* (1993), *Boom Boom Bye Bye* (Greensleeves 1993). With Pinchers: *Pinchers Meets Sanchez* (Exterminator 1989). With Wayne Wonder: *Penthouse Presents (Volume One & Two)* (Penthouse 1990, 1991).

Scientist

Scientist (real name Overton Brown) burst onto the scene in the early 80s with a reckless mixing style that seemed to outdo even King Tubbys wildest extravaganzas. He began his career as an engineer at Studio One in 1978, mixing the dub to Sugar Minott's 'Oh Mr DC' among others. Shortly after this he became a protegé of King Tubby, and swiftly gained a reputation with his fresh mixing style. In 1980 the UK-based record company Greensleeves began to release the productions of then hot-shot Jamaican producer, Henry 'Junjo' Lawes. Lawes, hitting big with new singing sensation Barrington Levy, used Tubby's studio for his voicing and final mix-downs and offered Greensleeves a couple of dub albums mixed by Tubby's sensational young

Sanchez

engineer. *Scientist v Prince Jammy* (1980), mostly consisting of dub mixes of Barrington Levy tracks, was presented as a 'Big Showdown' between the two dubmasters, the first track mixed by Scientist, the second by Prince Jammy, and so on. The combination of heavyweight Roots Radics rhythms pitted against one another - the cover upping the ante by depicting the two protagonists cartoon style, sitting at their mixing desks in a boxing ring surrounded by a crowd of dreads - made for exciting listening, and gave the dub idiom a much needed shot in the arm.

Greensleeves followed this with an album proclaiming Scientist to be the *Heavyweight Dub Champion*, a similar brew of Roots Radics/Barrington Levy rhythms. Soon, dub albums mixed by Scientist began to appear with bewildering regularity from various sources. Greensleeves in particular continued to issue album after album which, despite their increasingly unlikely sounding titles and garish covers, remain essential listening. Scientist moved from Tubby's four-track studio to Joe Joe Hookim's sixteen-track Channel One studio in 1982, where he also learned to record live. His popularity resurrected dub's fading fortunes for a few years, but the form had lost ground in the Jamaican dancehalls to the new breed of dancehall DJs and vocalists, and by the mid-80s few Jamaican producers felt it prudent to spend money on producing dub albums. He continued as resident engineer at Channel One until the mid-80s when he moved to New York to continue his production career.

Albums: *Introducing* (JB Music/Greensleeves 1979), *Scientist v Prince Jammy* (Greensleeves 1980), *Heavyweight Dub Champion* (Greensleeves 1980), *Scientist Meets The Space Invaders* (Greensleeves 1981), *Dub Landing Vol 1 & 2* (Starlight 1981), *Scientist Rids The World Of The Evil Curse Of The Vampires* (Greensleeves 1981), *Scientist Encounters Pacman* (Greensleeves 1982), *Scientist Wins The World Cup* (Greensleeves 1983), *The People's Choice* (Kingdom 1983), *Dub Duel At King Tubbys* (Kingdom 1983), *High Priest Of Dub* (Kingdom 1983), *In The Kingdom Of Dub* (Kingdom 1983), *King Of Dub* (Kingdom 1987), *1999 Dub* (Heartbeat 1988). Compilation: *Crucial Cuts* (Kingdom 1984).

Scotty

b. c.1950, Jamaica. A singer and DJ, David Scott aka Scotty started out in late 1967 as a member of the Federals vocal group, gaining a massive local hit with 'Penny For Your Song' for producer Derrick Harriott the same year. They also recorded 'By The River' and 'Shocking Love' for Harriott, the original group breaking up after the Jamaican Song Festival in 1969. Scotty then joined the original line-up of the Chosen Few with Noel Brown and Franklin Spence, again at the instigation of Harriott. In July 1970, Scotty recorded his first DJ title, 'Musical Chariot'; this was followed by 'Sesame Street' (1970, Jamaican chart number 3), 'Riddle I This'/'Musical Chariot' (1970, Jamaican chart number 1), 'Jam Rock Style' (1971), later featured in the film *The Harder They Come*, 'Draw Your Brakes'. Scotty and Harriott had followed the trend set by DJs like U Roy and Dennis Alcapone for Duke Reid, combining witty lyrics with classic rocksteady rhythms. He continued recording with Harriott until 1972. He later worked under the supervision of Harry 'J' Johnson. (the original DJ version of 'Breakfast In Bed'), Lloyd Charmers and Sonia Pottinger. Scotty moved to the USA during the mid-70s. During the late 80s, having returned to live in Jamaica, he began recording in a ragga style, with considerable local success.

Albums: *Schooldays* (1972), *Unbelievable Sounds* (Trojan 1988).

Seaton, BB

(see the Gaylads)

Shaggy

Shaggy (b. Orville Richard Burrell, 22 October 1968, Kingston, Jamaica) is, effectively, the man who put New York

Scientist

reggae on the map, thanks to his world-wide hit, 'Oh Carolina'. The same record also helped start the ragga boom of 1993, an explosion that also carried the likes of Shabba Ranks, Chaka Demus & Pliers and Snow to the international pop charts. An amusing vocal stylist who can be as rude as the next man without ever descending into a leer, Shaggy cut his lyrical teeth on Brooklyn's Gibraltar Musik sound system. He'd moved there at 18 with his parents, and at 19 he'd joined the Marines, based at Lejeune, North Carolina. Following active service in the Gulf War, Shaggy began to cut singles for a variety of labels, among them 'Man A Me Yard'/'Bullet Proof Baddie' for Don One, and 'Big Hood'/'Duppy Or Uglyman' for Spiderman. A chance meeting with Sting, a radio DJ at KISS-FM/WNNK, led to Shaggy's first New York reggae chart number 1, 'Mampie', a version of the 'Drum Song' rhythm produced by Sting for New York reggae ruler Phillip Smart's Tan-Yah label.

His next 45, 'Big Up', released on Sting International and recorded in tandem with singer Rayvon, also hit number 1, as would 'Oh Carolina'. A mighty cover of the Folks Brothers classic, replete with samples of the original, the record became a huge hit on import charts wherever reggae was sold. At the time Shaggy was still in the Marines, meaning an 18-hour round trip to Brooklyn for dates and studio sessions. At the end of 1992, Greensleeves picked up 'Oh Carolina' for UK release, and by Spring 1993 Shaggy had scored a pop chart hit all over Europe with the song, reaching number 1 in the UK and several other countries. His next single, the slow, raucous 'Soon Be Done' failed, however, to capitalise on his success. Apparently unruffled by this, a liaison with Maxi Priest for 'One More Chance' led to a Virgin contract, and the *Pure Pleasure* album. A third single from the LP, 'Nice And Lovely', again failed to garner the necessary airplay to repeat the sales of 'Oh Carolina' (which by now had made it on to the soundtrack of Sharon Stone's film, *Sliver*),

but it was a fine, light-hearted record in its own right. The album also contained a version of his earlier 'Duppy Or Uglyman' cut, re-styled as 'Fraid To Ask'. Where Shaggy goes from here is a hard call to make: his *Pure Pleasure* world tour, taking in dates as diverse as Russia and South Africa, was an unqualified success, but Shaggy needs more chart action to maintain his status and to rival his great idol, Sammy Davis Jr.
Album: *Pure Pleasure* (Virgin 1993).

Sherman, Bim

b. Jarrett Tomlinson, 1952, Kingston, Jamaica. His earliest recordings include 'Mighty Ruler' and 'Ever Firm', which appeared on the Love and Ja-Man labels in late 1976/early 1977. Around the same time, a series of singles began appearing on his own Scorpio label. Because of restricted finances, he would often use each rhythm track for two different songs, but his writing skills and plaintive vocals ensured that every record sounded fresh. Several Jah Stone DJ versions of his songs were also issued at this time. In 1978 eight of his Scorpio singles together with 'Mighty Ruler' and 'Ever Firm' were compiled for *Love Forever*, which was released in the UK on the Tribesman label. It is a classic set which he has never equalled. In 1979 he issued *Lovers Leap* which, while not hitting the heights of its predecessor, is a consistently strong collection. A year later he was featured on one side of *Bim Sherman Meets Horace Andy And U Black*, a minor but enjoyable set. Shortly after this he settled in the UK, where he met producer Adrian Sherwood. Sherwood subsequently produced *Across The Red Sea* (1982), but it was not the sensation for which followers of both had hoped. Despite having written some excellent songs, the record loses many of the nuances of the vocals by submerging them in the mix.

In 1984 *Love Forever* was re-released as *Danger,* and he issued his self-produced *Bim Sherman And The Voluntary*, a very disappointing work. This was followed by *Haunting Ground*, an uneven set that boasts

BB Seaton

an excellent Adrian Sherwood-produced title track. Even though his voice could be haunting, he was let down by slight songs and uninspired accompaniments, a trend that continued on *Exploitation* and *Too Hot*. All through the 80s and early 90s he was a featured vocalist on the highly-acclaimed Sherwood produced Singers And Players series of albums. Fragments of his vocals together with some complete songs also appear in works by Fats Comet, Keith LeBlanc and Gary Clail. He remains a very talented artist with enormous potential.

Selected albums: *Love Forever* (Tribesman 1978, reissued as *Danger* Century 1984), *Lovers Leap* (Scorpio 1979), *Across The Red Sea* (On-U-Sound 1982), *Bim Sherman And The Voluntary* (Century 1984), *Haunting Ground* (RDL/Revolver 1986), *Exploitation* (RDL/Revolver 1989), *Too Hot* (Century 1990), *Crazy World* (Century 1992). As The Discoverers: *The Justice League Of Zion* (1994). As Bim Sherman & The Allstars: *African Rubadub* (RDL 1987). With Horace Andy and U Black: *Bim Sherman Meets Horace Andy And U Black* (Yard International 1980). With Dub Syndicate: *Reality* (Century 1992), *Lion Heart Dub* (Century 1993).

Sherwood, Adrian

b. c.1958. A pioneering force in UK reggae, Sherwood's first attempts to set up labels in the late 70s were disastrous, and cost him a small fortune in the process. Despite such misadventures, he couldn't resist having a further try, and set up the On-U-Sound label to house ex-Pop Group singer Mark Stewart's New Age Steppers project. Over a hundred albums and 45s have subsequently been released, including music by Bim Sherman, Dub Syndicate and Mothmen (an embryonic Simply Red). Sherwood styled On-U-Sound after the reggae model of 'house bands' (Revolutionaries, Soul Syndicate etc.). The label/organisation also played out as a sound system, in a similar fashion to its Jamaican counterparts. Among the notable long-term protagonists at On-U-

Sound have been Bonjo (African Head Charge), Bim Sherman and Skip MacDonald, Doug Wimbush and Keith LeBlanc (Tackhead). However, Sherwood is just as well known for his production skills, which he learned at first hand from Prince Far-I and Dr Pablo. The Fall, Depeche Mode and Ministry having been among his notable clients. On-U-Sound came to the attention of the public outside reggae circles when self-styled 'white toaster' Gary Clail entered the charts. However, neither this, nor any other individual release, can be described as representative of the rock-reggae-dance fusion which On-U-Sound have fostered. On-U-Sounds' eclecticism remains rampant, but as Sherwood himself concedes: 'I'm first and foremost a passionate fan of reggae music'.

Selected albums: New Age Steppers: *Vol. 1* (Statik 1979). Dub Syndicate: *Pounding System* (On-U-Sound 1988). Gary Clail & Tackhead: *Tackhead Sound System* (On-U-Sound 1988). African Head Charge: *Songs Of Praise* (On-U-Sound 1984). Various: *On-U-Sound Present Pay It All Back Vol. 4* (On-U-Sound 1993).

Shinehead

b. Edmund Carl Aitken, Kent, England. Although born in the UK, Aitken's family moved to Jamaica when he was two years old, then emigrated to New York in 1976 where he settled permanently. Counting among his influences a diverse array of artists including the Jackson 5 and Otis Redding, together with numerous reggae performers, Shinehead began singing at the age of 19, mixing the Jamaican toasting style with the more urbanized hip-hop which was developing in New York. After studying electrical and computer engineering his first musical activity came with Downbeat International in 1981, with Brigadier Jerry becoming a formative influence. He quickly developed a reputation for an astonishing range of dancehall skills; mimicking, singing, DJing, selecting, rapping and even whistling to great effect over Downbeat's stock-in-

Shaggy

trade Studio One dub plates. It was there he gained his name: by virtue of his distinctive, closely cropped hairstyle.

In late 1983 he joined forces with Claude Evans, who ran the African Love sound system-cum-label in Brooklyn. Evans managed to procure a rhythm track the Wailers had reputedly played for Bob Marley, who had died before using it. In 1984 Shinehead voiced 'Billie Jean'/'Mama Used To Say' over two sides of the rhythm and scored a massive hit for African Love. The debut album, *Rough And Rugged,* which followed in 1986 showcased his remarkably varied talents with a blend of dancehall, ballads, rap and reggae that yielded further hits in the shape of 'Know How Fi Chat', 'Hello Y'All' and 'Who The Cap Fits'. That same year he guested on Sly And Robbie's popular 'Boops' and was signed to Elektra in 1987. Their alliance has proved to be a disappointing one. The second album, *Unity,* was merely the first set re-arranged (some by Run DMC's Jam Master Jay), and contained many of the same tracks, some of which were by then four years old. Increasingly new material was aimed at the US crossover market, and despite the success of 'Strive' with his fading roots audience in 1990, his fortunes have taken a distinctly downward turn. *Sidewalk University* again assembled the services of assorted pop/rap/dance personnel in a bid for commercial reward, with the single 'Jamaican In New York' selling reasonably well. It is a long way removed from the dazzling attributes shown on his earlier work, although he continues to make combative appearances on sound systems both in the US and Jamaica.

Selected albums: *Rough And Rugged* (African Love Music 1986), *Unity* (African Love/Elektra 1988), *The Real Rock* (African Love/Elektra 1990), *Sidewalk University* (African Love/Elektra 1993).

Shirley, Roy

b. c.1948, Kingston, Jamaica. Perhaps one of the most eccentric performers (in a business peopled almost exclusively with eccentric performers), Roy Shirley is known to reggae fans world-wide on the strength of a handful of superb releases and some of the most electrifying stage shows ever. He first recorded for Beverley's in 1964, working in the same territory as luminaries of the ska scene such as Ken Boothe and Joe White. He was also a member of the original Uniques but his breakthrough came one night in 1966 after watching a Salvation Army band parade down Orange Street. Their beat, Roy claims, formed the basis of one of the best known records ever made in Jamaica, and one that many class as the first rocksteady outing - 'Hold Them', produced by Joel 'Joe Gibbs' Gibson - it was his first record too. The record was huge but Roy still feels bitter about the treatment he received from Coxsone Dodd who 'versioned' Roy's tune with Ken Boothe and renamed it 'Feel Good', the sales seriously damaging those of Roy's original.

Undeterred Roy continued his musical career recording in the rock steady and reggae style for Sir JJ, Caltone, Joe Gibbs and most notably Bunny Lee, whose first big hit was 'Music Field' with Roy Shirley. Another big hit followed in 1971 when Roy released 'A Sugar' through Randys. He first toured the UK in 1972 with U Roy and many of the latter's fans were forced to admit that Roy Shirley was a nearly impossible act to follow. Roy has remained in the UK on and off ever since and he set up the All Stars Artistic Federated Union in London in 1976 in order to 'seek promotion and to gain satisfaction for all kinds of artists'. He wanted up-and-coming performers to avoid the pitfalls that had dogged his career, and to put something back into a business that he feels has never really paid him his due rewards. He still possesses the same incredibly intense delivery, and he took 1982's Reggae Sunsplash in Jamaica by storm with his outrageous stage act. His records still promote the virtue of music and living good and despite his setbacks Roy still remains optimistic that, one day, the tide will turn for him.

Bim Sherman

Silk, Garnett

b. Garnett Smith, 1970, Manchester, Jamaica. One of the most significant singer/songwriters to emerge from Jamaica in recent times, Silk began his involvement in music by DJing as Little Bimbo from the tender age of 12. Formative years spent on the Destiny Outernational, Pepper's Disco, Stereophonic and Soul Remembrance sound systems led to his first recording, 'Problem Everywhere', for Delroy 'Callo' Collins in 1987. The following year he moved to Kingston and voiced for Sugar Minott's Youth Promotion label, recording one song, 'No Disrespect'. Next came sessions with the late King Tubby, as well as King Jammy and Penthouse, before he signed a two-year deal with Steely And Clevie. Despite recording an album with them only one track, a duet with Chevelle Franklin on 'We Could Be Together', was released during this period. Disillusioned, he returned to the country parish where he grew up, concentrating instead on writing songs, often in the company of his childhood friend, Anthony Rochester. Tony Rebel then introduced him to Courtney Cole, whose Roof International studio was based in Ocho Rios on Jamaica's north coast.

From there the hits flowed, with 'I Can see Clearly Now' (a duet with dub poet Yasus Afari) and 'Seven Spanish Angels' proving especially popular. During 1992 he voiced the first of his output for Bobby Digital, who was to produce his debut album, *It's Growing,* by the end of the year. It was immediately hailed as a masterpiece of contemporary roots music and revealed a lyricist of rare depth and originality. Given his consistent emphasis on cultural themes - typified by 'I Am Vexed', 'The Rod' and the best-selling title song - and a fluid vocal style which imbues all his work with an almost religious intensity, comparisons were inevitably drawn with the late Bob Marley. By mid-1993 he had signed to Atlantic and seen many of his past recordings either reissued or released for the first time. These included further tracks for Roof, Steely And Clevie, Danny Browne, Black Scorpio, Phillip Smart, Top Rank, Jahmento, Star Trail - for whom 'Hello Africa' made number 1 on the UK reggae charts - and Sly And Robbie.

Selected albums: *It's Growing* (Blue Mountain/VP 1992), *Gold* (Charm 1993), *100% Silk* (VP 1993).

Ska

A generic title for Jamaican music recorded between 1961-67, ska emerged from Jamaican R&B, which itself was largely based on American R&B and doo-wop. The difference being that while the US style smoothed out and became soul, the Jamaican sound, if anything, became wilder and more jerky, in what is commonly assumed to be an exaggeration of the 'jump' beat played on the black radio stations of Miami and New Orleans in the late 50s, and readily heard in Jamaica. Ska was fuelled by the sound systems, the over-amplified mobile discos which were (and still are) Jamaica's preferred method of enjoying music. At first, from the start of the 50s onwards, sound systems used American records. By the mid-to-late 50s competition had become so fierce between rival systems that finding an exclusive record by an American act had become a preoccupation - if you had the right song, your rivals could do little to stop your pre-eminence. Eventually, as the wild beat of the likes of Amos Milburn, Wynonie Harris *et al* began to fade into the past, sound system owners formed an alliance with indigenous Jamaican singers and musicians, which resulted in a hybrid of doo-wop, R&B and jazz that eventually precipitated ska, the jump-up sound where the jump took precedence over everything else.

The sound system bosses became Jamaica's first record producers, and included Sir Coxsone Dodd, Duke Reid and King Edwards: their names reflecting the showmanship and drive for supremacy of the sound systems. The singers numbered Delroy Wilson, Jiving Juniors (see Derrick Harriott), Alton (Ellis) and Eddy, Lord Creator and

Adrian Sherwood

many more. These artists quickly became Jamaica's first stars. The instrumental outings of the bands, under the leadership of talents such as trombonist Don Drummond, tenor saxman Roland Alphonso, and alto sax player Tommy McCook, if anything, outshone the vocal records, with a frequently freewheeling, heavy-jazz philosophy that many have since tried, but failed, to imitate. By 1964 ska had become popular amongst mods in England, where it was known as Blue Beat, the name of the foremost UK licensing label. British acts such as Georgie Fame & The Blue Flames, and The Migil 5 had hits in the ska style, while more authentically Jamaican acts such as Millie, Prince Buster and the Skatalites all scored chart entries. By 1966 ska was beginning to burn out in Jamaica, to be replaced by the more sedate and perhaps more exclusively indigenous sound of rocksteady. However, ska has remained intermittently popular, demonstrated by several 'ska revivals', the most successful of which was the UK 2 Tone movement in the late-70s. It seems that the beat will never truly exhaust itself. At any given time, somewhere in the world from Japan to Germany, a would-be Skatalites can be unearthed, making a nightclub jump to the infectious rhythms of this most animated of musics.

Selected albums: Various: *Ska Authentic* (Studio One), *The History Of Ska* (Bamboo 1969), *Club Ska '67* (Mango/Island 1980), *Intensified Vols 1 & 2* (Mango/Island 1979).

Skatalites

The Skatalites were formed in June 1964, drawing from the ranks of session musicians then recording in the studios of Kingston, Jamaica. The personnel included Don Drummond (trombone), Roland Alphonso (tenor sax), Tommy McCook (tenor sax), Johnny 'Dizzy' Moore (trumpet), Lester Sterling (alto Sax), Jerome 'Jah Jerry Hines (guitar), Jackie Mittoo (piano), Lloyd Brevett (bass), and Lloyd Knibbs (drums). The band name was a Tommy McCook pun on the Soviet space satellite of 1963. The Skatalites'

music, reputedly named after the characteristic 'ska' sound made by the guitar when playing the 'after beat', was a powerful synthesis; combining elements of R&B and swing jazz in arrangements and solos, underpinned by the uniquely Jamaican-stressed 'after beat', as opposed to the 'down beat' of R&B. Many of the musicians had learnt music at Alpha Boys' School in Kingston, then honing their talent in the Jamaican swing bands of the 40s and early 50s, and in numerous 'hotel bands' playing for the tourist trade. Most of the musicians thereby developed recognisable individual styles. Repertoire was drawn from many sources, including adaptations of Latin tunes, movie themes and updated mento, a Jamaican folk song form. Perhaps their most famous and identifiable tune is 'Guns Of Navarone' recorded in 1965 and a big club hit in the UK in the mid-60s. They recorded hundreds of superb instrumentals for various producers, either under the group name or as bands led by the particular musician who had arranged the session. Under the Skatalite name they made important music for Coxsone Dodd and Duke Reid, as well as for Justin and Philip Yap's Top Deck record label. They stayed together for just over two years until August 1965, when a combination of financial, organisational and personal problems caused the break-up of the band after their last gig, a police dance at the Runaway Bay Hotel. Of the main protagonists, Jackie Mittoo and Roland Alphonso were persuaded by Coxsone Dodd to form the Soul Brothers band, who would make many instrumentals and supply backing tracks at Studio One until 1967. Tommy McCook worked principally for Duke Reid, where he formed the studio band known as the Supersonics, and was musical co-director for Reid's Treasure Isle label with alto saxophonist Herman Marques. The tragically wayward Don Drummond suffered from severe depression and died on 6 May 1969 in Bellevue Asylum, Kingston. The Skatalites had backed virtually every singer of note in the studios, at the same time laying the

Garnett Silk

musical foundation for subsequent developments in Jamaican music. They released a reunion album in 1975; not ska, but high quality instrumental reggae. In 1984 the band played the Jamaican and London 'Sunsplash' concerts to rapturous acclaim. The reformed group also toured Japan with vocalists Prince Buster and Lord Tanamo in 1989, recording live and in the studio.

Albums: *Ska Authentic* (Studio One 1967), *Ska Boo Da Ba* (Top Deck/Doctor Bird 60s), *The Skatalites* (Treasure Isle 1975), *Return Of The Big Guns* (Island 1984), *Live At Reggae Sunsplash* (Synergy 1986), *Stretching Out* (ROIR 1987), *Celebration Time* (Studio One 1988). Compilations: *Best Of The Skatalites* (Studio One 1974), *Scattered Lights* (Top Deck 1984).

Sly And Robbie

Sly Dunbar (b. Lowell Charles Dunbar, 10 May 1952, Kingston, Jamaica; drums) and Robbie Shakespeare (b. 27 September 1953, Kingston, Jamaica; bass). Dunbar, nicknamed 'Sly' in honour of his fondness for Sly And The Family Stone, was an established figure in Skin Flesh & Bones when he met Shakespeare. They have probably played on more reggae records than the rest of Jamaica's many session musicians put together. The pair began working together as a team in 1975 and they quickly became Jamaica's leading, and most distinctive, rhythm section. They have played on numerous releases, including those by U Roy, Peter Tosh, Bunny Wailer, Culture while Dunbar also made several solo albums, all of which featured Shakespeare. They have constantly sought to push back the boundaries surrounding the music with their consistently inventive work. Sly drummed his first session for Upsetter Lee Perry as one of the Upsetters; the resulting 'Night Doctor' was a big hit both in Jamaica and the UK. He next moved to Skin, Flesh & Bones, whose variations on the reggae–meets–disco/soul sound gave them lots of session work and a residency at Kingston's Tit for Tat club. Sly was still searching for

more however, and he moved onto another session group in the mid-70s, the Revolutionaries. This move changed the course of reggae music through their work at Joseph 'Joe Joe' Hookim's Channel One Studio and their pioneering rockers sound. It was with the Revolutionaries that he teamed up with bass player Robbie Shakespeare who had gone through a similar apprenticeship with session bands, notably Bunny Lee's Aggrovators. The two formed a friendship that turned into a musical partnership that was to dominate reggae music throughout the remainder of the 70s, 80s and on into the 90s.

Known now simply as Sly And Robbie (and occasionally Drumbar & Basspeare), they not only formed their own label Taxi, which produced many hit records for scores of well known artists but also found time to do session work for just about every important name in reggae. They toured extensively as the powerhouse rhythm section for Black Uhuru and, as their fame spread outside of reggae circles, they worked with Grace Jones, Bob Dylan, Ian Dury, Joan Armatrading and a host of other rock stars. In the early 80s they were among the first to use the burgeoning 'new technology' to musical effect; they demonstrated that it could be used to its full advantage without compromising their musicianship in any way. In a genre controlled by producers and 'this week's star', reggae musicians have never really been given their proper respect, but the accolades heaped on Sly And Robbie have helped to redress the balance. The fact that both have their feet planted firmly on the ground has ensured that they have never left the grass roots of the music behind, either. At the time of writing Taxi's latest beat/sound is tearing up the reggae world again.

Sly And Robbie's mastery of the digital genre coupled with their abiding love and respect for the music's history has placed them at the forefront of Kingston's producers of the 90s, and their 'Murder She Wrote' cut for Chaka Demus & Pliers set the tone for

1992, while 'Tease Mi' for the same duo, built around a sample from the Skatalites 60s hit, 'Ball Of Fire', was another significant UK chart success in 1993. Quite remarkable for a team whose successful career has already spanned three decades, with the promise of yet more to come.

Selected albums: *Disco Dub* (Gorgon 1978), *Gamblers Choice* (Taxi 1980), *Raiders Of The Lost Dub* (Mango/Island 1981), *60s, 70s Into The 80s* (Mango/Island 1981), *Dub Extravaganza* (CSA 1984), *A Dub Experience* (Mango/Island 1985), *Language Barrier* (Mango/Island 1985), *Electro Reggae* (Island 1986), *The Sting* (Taxi 1986), *Rhythm Killers* (4th & Broadway 1987), *Dub Rockers Delight* (Blue Moon 1987), *The Summit* (RAS 1988), *Silent Assassin* (4th & Broadway 1990). Selected compilations: *Reggae Greats* (Mango/Island 1985), *Hits 1987-90* (Sonic Sounds 1991). Productions: Various: *Present Taxi* (Taxi 1981), *Crucial Reggae* (Taxi 1984), *Taxi Wax* (Taxi 1984), *Taxi Gang* (Taxi 1984), *Taxi Connection Live In London* (Taxi 1986), *Taxi Fare* (Taxi 1987), *Two Rhythms Clash* (RAS 1990), *DJ Riot* (Mango/Island 1990), *Sound Of The 90s* (1990), *Carib Soul* (1990), *Present Sound Of Sound* (Musidisc 1994), *Present Ragga Pon Top* (Musidisc 1994). Black Uhuru: *Showcase* (Taxi 1979), *Sinsemilla* (Mango/Island 1980), *Red* (Mango/Island 1981), *Chill Out* (Mango/Island 1982), *Anthem* (Mango/Island 1983). Dennis Brown: *Brown Sugar* (Taxi 1986). Gregory Isaacs *Showcase* (Taxi 1980). Grace Jones: *Warm Leatherette* (Island 1980), *Nightclubbing* (Island 1981), *Livin' My Life* (Island 1982). Ini Kamoze: *Ini Kamoze* (Island 1984), *Statement* (Island 1984), *Pirate* (Island 1986). Sugar Minott: *Sugar And Spice* (Taxi 1986).

Sly And Robbie

Lloyd Brevett of the Skatalites

Smiley Culture

Smart, Leroy

A distinguished vocalist of the hard-working, soulful school, Leroy Smart - the self-styled 'Don' - was orphaned at the age of two and brought up in Kingston's Alpha Catholic Boys School & Home - the first home for many of Jamaica's musical talents. His reputation precedes him as one of Jamaica's most outrageous and colourful characters and he is held in high esteem by the reggae fraternity, to the point where his name is often discussed not only in reverence but in awe. Consquently the stories of his struggles in life have assumed far greater importance over the years than his manifest vocal talents. He began recording in the early 70s and made the usual rounds of Kingston producers achieving success first with Jimmy Radway/Rodway and then with Bunny Lee, Gussie Clarke and Joseph 'Joe Joe' Hookim and many others. His stage shows were truly outrageous and were as famed as much for their acrobatic displays as his vocal pyrotechnics, while his agonised, mannered singing defied categorisation. He achieved classic status on a number of records throughout the 70s, including 'Pride And Ambition', 'Ballistic Affair', 'God Helps The Man' and 'Mr Smart'/'Happiness Is My Desire'. He continued to record in the 80s and on into the 90s too, hitting again with 'She Just A Draw Card' and 'I Am The Don'. His vocal power and forceful personality have always ensured that he is never far from the forefront of reggae music.
Selected albums: *Jah Loves Everyone* (Burning Sounds 1978), *Dread Hot In Africa* (Burning Sounds 1978), *Impressions Of* (Burning Sounds 1978), *She Love It In The Morning* (GG's 1984), *She Just A Draw Card* (Worldwide Success 1985), *Showcase* (Fatman 1985), *Live Up Roots Children* (Striker Lee 1985), *Bank Account* (Powerhouse 1985), *Musical Don* (Skengdon 1988), Propaganda (Burning Sounds 1988), *Talk About Friends* (1993).

Smiley Culture

b. David Emmanuel, c.1960, London, England, of a Jamaican father and South American mother. Smiley gained his nickname at school where his method of chatting up girls was simply to ask for a smile. He served his apprenticeship with a number of local sounds before hitting the big time with south London's Saxon sound system, the home of a formidable amount of British reggae talent including Maxi Priest, Tippa Irie and Phillip 'Papa' Levi. His live reputation attracted the attention of record producers and his first recording for Fashion Records, 'Cockney Translation', featuring Smiley slipping effortlessly from Jamaican patois to a south London accent, touched a nerve and sold an unprecedented 40,000 copies. His follow-up 'Police Officer', again featuring the cockney and 'yardy' voices, did even better and reached the national Top 20 in early 1985. Appearances on BBC television's *Top Of The Pops* followed - a first for a reggae DJ - and Smiley was a 'star'. A major recording deal with Polydor Records followed. As well as hosting his own television show *Club Mix*, Smiley also found the time for a cameo appearance in the film *Absolute Beginners* singing Miles Davis' 'So What'. He continued to record, including some interesting collaborations with American hip hop artists. Smiley's importance is that he was among the first English based reggae artists to challenge the Jamaicans and succeed. The British public also took him to their hearts while the lyrics of 'Cockney Translation' are now used by teachers and lecturers to illustrate the effects and influence of immigration on the 'mother tongue'.
Albums: *The Original* (Top Notch 1986), *Tongue In Cheek* (Polydor 1986).

Smith, Slim

b. Keith Smith, c.1948, Jamaica, d. 1973. Smith first came to prominence as a member of the Victors Youth Band who were highly praised at the 1964 Jamaican Festival. He subsequently became a founding member and lead vocalist of the Techniques who secured a recording contract with Duke

Reid's Treasure Isle label. From 1964-65 they recorded several hits, two of which, 'I Am In Love' and 'Little Did You Know', are included on the Techniques' *Classics* compilation. After leaving the group in 1965, he visited Canada where he recorded his first solo album, *Toronto '66*, which almost instantly sunk into obscurity. On his return to Jamaica, he commenced recording for Prince Buster and Coxsone Dodd's Studio One label, the main rival to Duke Reid. His Studio One recordings brilliantly highlight his passionate, soulful voice, shot through with an almost manic edge, and confirm him to be one of Jamaica's greatest singers. His hits from this period include 'I've Got Your Number', 'Hip Hug' and 'Rougher Yet', many of which were later compiled for *Born To Love*.

In 1967 he formed a new group, the Uniques, and commenced his association with producer Bunny Lee. They topped the Jamaican hit parade with 'Let Me Go Girl', but after recording one album, *Absolutely The Uniques*, Slim left the group, but stayed with Lee to concentrate on a solo career. He had a hit almost immediately with 'Everybody Needs Love'. An album of the same name quickly followed, as did many further hits. By 1972 personal problems led him to be detained at Bellevue sanatorium, and the following year he committed suicide. His death stunned Jamaica. Still widely regarded as one of Jamaica's great vocalists, his lasting popularity has thankfuly resulted in the reissue of the bulk of his work.

Albums: *Toronto '66* (1966), *Everybody Needs Love* (1969, reissued Pama 1989), *Just A Dream* (c.1971, reissued Pama 1989). Compilations: *The Time Has Come* (Pama 1984), *Memorial* (Trojan 1985), *Dance Hall Connection* (Third World 1986), *Born To Love (1966-68)* (Studio One 1979), *20 Super Hits* (Sonic Sounds 1991), *Rain From The Skies* (Trojan 1992).

Snow

b. Darrin O'Brien, 1971, Toronto, Canada. Snow is the most commercially successful white DJ ever, whose debut UK single, 'Informer', reached the UK Top 3 in March 1993. Snow was raised in the Allenbury projects of Toronto and became a frequent visitor to reggae blues parties, where he assimilated the styles of Junior Reid, Eek A Mouse, Tenor Saw and Nitty Gritty. Considered a 'problem child', he spent 18 months in prison on a murder charge at the age of 19, before finally being acquitted; an experience which inspired the lyrics of 'Informer'. Rap mixer DJ Prince introduced him to MC Shan in New York who in turn recommended the East West label. They signed him in late 1992; his debut studio sessions resulting in *12 Inches Of Snow*, released in spring 1993. 'Lonely Monday Morning' subsequently became his first US single. Despite adverse criticism his gift for mimicry is a keen one, and by virtue of 'Informer' he has already entered reggae's record books.

Selected album: *12 Inches Of Snow* (East West 1993).

Soul Syndicate

Yet another of the crack session teams that determined the sound and feel of reggae music at any given time in its evolution, the Soul Syndicate were hugely influential in the early to mid-70s. Their work with Winston 'Niney' Holness, Duke Reid, Keith Hudson and many others was brash and exciting and added a different dimension to the roots sound of the period. The hardcore members were the supremely talented Earl 'Chinna' Smith on guitar, Carlton 'Santa' Davis on drums, George 'Fully' Fullwood on bass, Tony Chin on rhythm guitar and Bernard 'Touter' Harvey, who later joined the Wailers, on keyboards. At one stage their featured vocalist was Freddie McGregor. This nucleus of talent, give or take a few members, also recorded for Bunny Lee as the Aggrovators as the decade wore on. Like so many of the musicians that have actually made reggae music over the years their names and work remain relatively unknown outside of the genre's cogniscenti, but perhaps, one day, their work (and that of so many others) will be given its proper recognition.

Selected album: *Harvest Uptown* (Soul Syndicate 1978).

Sound System

It is impossible to overstate the importance of sound systems to the development of reggae music as just about every record producer, singer and DJ from the 50s onwards has been closely involved with them in one way or another. They were the forerunners of today's mobile disco but the amount and weight of their amplification equipment has always ensured that you felt the sound of the music as much as hearing it. In the 50s, R&B radio stations from southern American cities beamed their music to a responsive Jamaican audience and the popularity of R&B prompted enterprising locals to start their own sound systems. Operators such as Coxsone Dodd 'Sir Coxsone The Down Beat' and Duke Reid 'The Trojan', became stars in Jamaica on the strength of their sounds - both for the records that they played and for the way they presented them. The top outfits would play out in competition against each other and the rivalry was frequently violent and bloody. Records were hunted out in the USA where small fortunes were spent on the right tunes - the label details would be then scratched out to stop their rivals finding out what these top tunes actually were.

The sound system operators started to make their own R&B based recordings as the supply of hard R&B records began to dry up in the late 50s, and the black American audiences moved towards a smoother style of music which the Jamaicans were not interested in. At first these recordings were intended solely for exclusive use (on acetate disc or dub plate) of the sound that made them but they proved so popular that the top 'sounds' began to release these records and ska and the Jamaican recording industry were born. From here on the development of Jamaican music through ska, rocksteady, reggae, rockers, dub, dance hall and ragga has always been inextricably linked with sound systems both as the testing ground for new records but, more importantly, for singers and DJs to test out the crowd's response as they took their turn at the microphone. Their popularity meant the proliferation of sound systems in New York, London and Toronto - at first anywhere with an expatriate Jamaican community - but later their influence was to spread outside and away and the importance of Jamaican Sounds to the development of hip hop and rap in America, for instance, has yet to be fully credited. The Sounds have gone through as many changes in styles and fashion as reggae music and have become a cultural rallying point across the globe. The current fashion is for playing 'specials' - one-off acetate discs recorded exclusively by current big names extolling the virtues of whatever particular sound the 'special' has been voiced for, usually to the tune and rhythm of a popular 'commercial' hit record. DJs' live contributions are kept to a minimum where once they dominated the sound. In many ways the wheel has turned full circle but to hear a top sound system playing out either in the warmth of a Kingston open air dance under the stars or crowded together in a small club in London or New York is to understand fully the strength and power of Jamaican music and to experience its direct and very real influence on its own committed following.

Steel Pulse

Probably the UK's most highly-regarded roots reggae outfit, Steel Pulse originally formed at Handsworth School, Birmingham, and comprised David Hinds (lead vocals, guitar), Basil Gabbidon (lead guitar, vocals) and Ronnie McQueen (bass). However, it is Hinds who, as songwriter, has always been the engine behind Steel Pulse, from their early days establishing themselves in the Birmingham club scene onwards. Formed in 1975, their debut release, 'Kibudu, Mansetta And Abuku', arrived on the small

David Hinds of Steel Pulse

independent label Dip, and linked the plight of urban black youth with the image of a greater African homeland. They followed it with 'Nyah Love' for Anchor. Surprisingly, they were initially refused live dates in Caribbean venues in the Midlands because of their Rastafarian beliefs. Aligning themselves closely with the Rock Against Racism organisation, they chose to tour instead with sympathetic elements of the punk movement, including the Stranglers, XTC etc.: 'Punks had a way of enjoying themselves - throw bottles at you, beer, spit at you, that kind of thing'. Eventually they found a more natural home in support slots for Burning Spear, which brought them to the attention of Island Records.

Their first release for Island was the 'Ku Klux Klan' 45, a considered tilt at the evils of racism, and one often accompanied by a visual parody of the sect on stage. By this time their ranks had swelled to include Selwyn 'Bumbo' Brown (keyboards), Steve 'Grizzly' Nesbitt (drums), Fonso Martin (vocals, percussion) and Michael Riley (vocals). *Handsworth Revolution* was an accomplished long playing debut and one of the major landmarks in the evolution of British reggae. However, despite critical and moderate commercial success over three albums, the relationship with Island had soured by the advent of *Caught You* (released in the US as *Reggae Fever*). They switched to Elektra, and unveiled their most consistent collection of songs since their debut with *True Democracy*, distinguished by the Garvey-eulogising 'Rally Around' cut. A further definitive set arrived in *Earth Crisis*. Unfortunately, Elektra chose to take a leaf out of Island's book in trying to coerce Steel Pulse into a more mainstream vein, asking them to emulate the pop-reggae stance of Eddy Grant. *Babylon Bandit* was consequently weakened, but did contain the anthemic 'Not King James Version', which was a powerful indictment on the omission of black people and history from certain versions of the Bible. Their next move was to MCA for *State Of Emergency*, which

retained some of the synthesized dance elements of its predecessor. Though it was a significantly happier compromise, it still paled before any of their earlier albums. *Centennial* was recorded live at the Elysee Montmarte in Paris, and dedicated to the hundred year anniversary of the birth of Haile Selassie. It was the first recording since the defection of Fonso Martin, leaving the trio of Hinds, Nesbitt and Selwyn. While they still faced inverted snobbery at the hands of British reggae fans, in America their reputation was growing, becoming the first ever reggae band to appear on the *Tonight* television show. Their profile was raised further when, in 1992, Hinds challenged the New York Taxi and Limousine Commission in the Supreme High Court, asserting that their cab drivers discriminated against black people in general and Rastas in particular.

Albums: *Handsworth Revolution* (Island 1978), *Tribute To The Martyrs* (Island 1979), *Caught You/Reggae Fever* (Mango/Island 1980), *True Democracy* (Elektra 1982), *Earth Crisis* (Elektra 1984), *Babylon Bandit* (Elektra 1985), *State Of Emergency* (MCA 1988), *Victims* (MCA 1992), *Rastafari Centennial* (MCA 1992). Compilation: *Reggae Greats* (Mango/Island 1985).

Steely And Clevie

This Jamaican studio 'band' comprises Wycliffe 'Steely' Johnson and Cleveland 'Clevie' Browne. Every five years or so Jamaica produces a rhythm section that dominates reggae. In the 70s it was the Barrett Brothers, who drove the Upsetters and Bob Marley's Wailers. The late 70s/early 80s belonged to Sly And Robbie, but by 1986 reggae required a team fully conversant with computerized music: Steely & Clevie. Wycliffe 'Steely' Johnson first surfaced with Sugar Minott's Youth Promotion organisation, playing keyboards on Sugar's classic *Ghetto-ology* (1978). After a period with the Generation Gap, he joined the Roots Radics, earning a reputation for hard work and innovation. When the Radics became *the* band for the new dancehall music of the early 80s, it gave Steely a perfect understanding of a minimal, raw-basics kind of reggae. Drummer Cleveland 'Clevie' Browne (pronounced *Brown-ie*) began playing as part of the Browne Bunch in the 70s with brothers Dalton and Danny. During the late 70s he played sessions at Studio One, backing Freddie McGregor amongst others. In the early 80s McGregor hired Clevie for his road group, known as the Studio One Band, and on tour Clevie would come into contact with equipment that was not yet *de rigeur* in Jamaican studios and became interested in drum machines, while his fellow-drummers declared them an abomination. Prior to that, Clevie had cut tracks with Bob Marley in 1979 where the singer was using a primitive drum machine in the studio, and Clevie had always kept one ear open for them ever since. In the mid-80s Clevie's brothers Danny & Dalton were the musical pulse of the Bloodfire Posse, the first all-electronic reggae group. By the time 'digital' music arrived, Clevie was ready for it. At some point in the late 70s Steely & Clevie met during sessions for Augustus Pablo at Lee Perry's Black Ark studio, working on Hugh Mundell's *Africa Must Be Free By 1983*. The pair clicked with a kind of yin and yang relationship: Clevie the studious, mild musician, Steely the louder, ragga character. When they took up residence as house 'band' at King Jammy's Studio in 1986, they were clearly on the verge of something big.

Jammy's was the engine of mid-80s reggae; from there Steely & Clevie worked with everyone, cutting 10 singles a week at its peak in 1987 and a stream of albums from various artists such as Cocoa Tea, Dennis Brown, Admiral Bailey and Lieutenant Stitchie. Jammy's had the best ragga sound going and although producer King Jammy got the glory, much of the work was done by Steely & Clevie, engineers Bobby Digital and Squingie Francis, and the arranger, Mikey Bennett. They also gigged for most of the other producers in Jamaica; hence they knew virtually everyone when they began

their own label - Steely & Clevie - in 1988. They immediately hit with a debut release from Johnny P., making the DJ a star. The formula of brash, unusual beats and strong melodies also worked for Foxy Brown, relaunched Tiger's career, scored with Anthony Red Rose, Anthony Malvo and Little Twitch and revived older acts Dillinger and Johnny Osbourne. Sessions for Gussie Clarke helped establish his studio as the major technological force in late-80s' reggae, and Steely & Clevie cut a series of inimitable 'one rhythm' albums on their own label: *Limousine, Bursting Out, Real Rock Style, Can't Do The Work*. Broader attention followed with work for former Soul II Soul singer Caron Wheeler, Maxi Priest, Aswad and J.C. Lodge. While they have not yet been inclined to sign to a major label, it seems that, despite competition from the Firehouse Crew and Mafia & Fluxy, Steely & Clevie will continue their dominance of the reggae studio for the foreseeable future.

Selected albums: Various: *Bursting Out* (S&C 1988), *At The Top* (Black Solidarity 1988), *Can't Do The Work* (S&C 1989), *Limousine* (S&C 989), *Real Rock Style* (S&C/Jet Star 1989), *Godfather* (VP 1990), *Lion Attack* (VP 1990), *More Poco* (VP 1990), *Girl Talk* (VP 1991), *Present Soundboy Clash* (Profile 1991), *Play Studio One Vintage* (Heartbeat 1992).

Studio One
(see Dodd, Coxsone)

Supercat
b. William Maragh, Kingston, Jamaica. Of East Indian extract and the son of a construction worker, Supercat grew up in Sievright Gardens joining Soul Imperial Hi-Fi as a teenage DJ apprentice to Early B. From there he went on to Crystal Blue Flames, Supreme Love, Studio Mix, King Majesty and finally Kilimanjaro. Known as Catarack, he replaced the late Jim Brown as principal DJ in 1980. Two years later he voiced his debut tune, 'Mr Walker', in combination with Bruck Back for Winston Riley. After a break from recording he

Supercat

returned in 1985 with a vengeance, having now been dubbed Supercat. 'Boops' was a massive seller, spawning countless other versions whilst 'Cry Fe De Youth' revealed a more serious side to his nature. Work began on his debut album which was released in 1986. King Jammys, George Phang, Tuff Gong and Ranking Joe had all recorded him by then. That year he left for Miami with the Stur-Mars sound system, being the first artist to voice for their affiliated Skengdon label. They released his second album and the singles 'Vineyard Party', 'Mind Up', 'Sweets For My Sweets' and 'Wild Apache', the latter featuring a prototype ragga/hip hop beat and inspiring the title of his own label.

Resident in Brooklyn from 1988, 'Cabin Stabbin' (with Nicodemus and Junior Demus), 'Nuff Man A Dead', 'Ghetto Red Hot' and his trademark 'Don Dada' all demonstrated his often fiercely militant stance to be undiminished. Further hits with Trevor Sparks ('Dolly My Baby') and Frankie Paul and Heavy D ('Big And Ready') in 1990 eventually led to a deal with Columbia, who released the *Don Dada* album in 1992. That year he produced artists like Private P, Sugar D, Tiger, Papa San, Cutty Ranks and the late Alton Black on his own Wild Apache imprint, as well as guesting on rap duo Kriss Kross' hit, 'Jump Up'. In 1993 'Dolly My Baby' was chosen for the soundtrack of the *Cool Runnings* movie.

Selected albums: *Si Boops Deh* (Techniques 1986), *Sweets For My Sweets* (Skengdon 1986), *Don Dada* (Columbia 1992).

T

Tait, Lynn

Lynn didn't take up the guitar until his fourteenth year – until then he'd been seriously involved in steel pan music. However, he was soon fronting his own band in Trinidad who were booked to play the Independence celebrations in 1962 in Jamaica by Byron Lee. Lynn liked Jamaica so much that he decided to stay there, working his way through the Sheiks, the Cavaliers and the Comets – all 'live' bands that didn't actually make any recordings – although he had recorded with the Skatalites. His next group, Lynn Tait & The Jets, which included Hux Brown, Headley Bennett, Hopeton Lewis, Gladstone Anderson and Winston Wright, were contracted to Federal Records in 1967. Their recording of 'Take It Easy' with Hopeton Lewis as featured vocalist was one of the first rocksteady records – (although many others lay claim to that honour) – and it went straight to number 1. Many see the rocksteady period in Jamaican music as one of the most creative and musically adventurous, and Lynn Tait & The Jets were the rocksteady session band at the eye of the storm. They recorded hit after hit for Federal, Wirl, Derrick Harriott, Bunny Lee & Beverley's, Sonia Pottinger and Duke Reid, sometimes doing up to five sessions a day for different producers. Lynn's modesty about his part in this musical evolution is as gentle as his guitar playing, and he felt that to have the public liking what he did was more than enough, indeed a 'great gift'. All he was interested in was 'creating beautiful music'. Some of his recordings with Johnny Nash, such as 'Cupid' and 'Hold Me Tight', even stole into the UK national charts, and he will always be fondly remembered as a musical giant of the rocksteady era.
Selected album: *Rock Steady Greatest Hits* (Merritone).

Taxi Records
(see Sly And Robbie)

Techniques
Formed by Winston Riley in 1962 while still at school, the Techniques original line-up additionally featured fellow vocalists Slim Smith, Franklyn White and Frederick Waite. Together they performed at future Jamaican prime minister Edward Seaga's club Chocomo Lawn, an important showcase for local talent at the time, appearing alongside Byron Lee, Tommy McCook, Alton Ellis, Marcia Griffiths, the Sensations, who included Riley's brother Buster. The group were spotted by talent scouts from British based Columbia Records, upon which their first single, 'No One', appeared. This was not released in Jamaica however, and it was not until 1965 when singer Stranger Cole introduced them to producer Duke Reid that they recorded their earliest Jamaican releases, 'Don't Leave Me', 'When You Are Wrong', and the popular 'Little Did You Know', featuring the peerless falsetto melisma of Slim Smith. With the advent of rocksteady in 1967 vocal harmony groups specialising in Chicago soul-style love songs really came into their own, and the Techniques, under the Duke's aegis, were perfectly placed to capitalise on the trend. Throughout 1967 the hits poured out of Reid's Treasure Isle studio, situated above his Orange Street liquor store. His classic productions on artists such as Alton Ellis, the Paragons, Phyllis Dillon, the Melodians, Dobby Dobson, and many others, all backed by Tommy McCook And the Supersonics, briefly toppled Coxsone Dodd's dominance as Jamaica's leading hit maker.
In 1966 the group broke up, Smith leaving to pursue a solo career at Studio One, then later with producer Bunny Lee as part of the Uniques vocal trio, and ultimately on to a tragic end. Franklyn White's whereabouts remain obscure, but Frederick Waite migrated to the UK where he managed Musical Youth, whose number included several of his offspring, achieving a UK

number 1 with 'Pass The Dutchie' in 1982. Slim's place was filled by Pat Kelly, who sang lead on some of their most popular records including their big hits 'You Don't Care', versions of Curtis Mayfield's 'You'll Want Me Back' and 'Queen Majesty, the Temptations' 'I Wish It Would Rain' and 'Run Come Celebrate', 'I'm In The Mood', 'There Comes A Time' and the sublime 'It's You I Love'. Other hits from this period featuring different lead singers include 'My Girl', 'Drink Wine', 'Love Is Not A Gamble' and 'Travelling Man'. The Techniques left Treasure Isle in 1968 with Riley going on to set up his own Techniques label, producing other artists and further sides by the group, whose personnel during this period included Jackie Parris, ex-Termite Lloyd Parks, Morvin Brooks and Bruce Ruffin. These included another version of 'Travelling Man', 'Your Love's A Game' and 'Lonely Man' all featuring Dave Barker (Dave And Ansell Collins) on lead vocals, 'What Am I To Do', with Pat Kelly again as lead vocalist, 'What's It All About', and 'Go Find Yourself A Fool'. Riley went on to become one of the most successful producers of the 80s achieving massive hits with General Echo, Tenor Saw, Supercat and others. As a group, the Techniques recorded sporadically in the following years. A re-recording of 'Love Is Not A Gamble', with ex-Paragon Tyrone Evans on lead vocals appeared as a 12-inch in 1982, followed by an album of the same title, since which they have been silent.

Compilations: *Unforgettable Days* (Techniques 1981, covers 1965-72), *I'll Never Fall In Love* (Techniques 1982), *Classics* (Techniques 1991), *Run Come Celebrate - Their Greatest Reggae Hits* (Heartbeat 1993).

Tenor Saw

b. Clive Bright, 1966, Kingston, Jamaica, d. 1988, Houston, Texas, USA. One of the most influential singers of the early digital era, Tenor Saw's eerie, hypnotic wail was stamped with an almost religious fervour. He was raised in the Payne Avenue district of west Kingston; recording his debut 'Roll Call' in 1984 for George Phang's Powerhouse label after an introduction by Nitty Gritty. During 1985 he sang with Sugar Minott's Youth Promotion sound system and label, recording 'Lots Of Sign' and 'Pumpkin Belly' (also versioned for King Jammys). 'Run Come Call Me' and 'Fever' too were sizeable hits. None, however, could compare to 'Ring The Alarm', which Tenor Saw voiced magnificently over Winston Riley's 'Stalag' rhythm for the Techniques label. There was no bigger record that year and it continues to be regarded as an anthem in today's dancehalls. 'Golden Hen' for Uptempo continued the sequence of straight hits into 1986 when Minott released his debut album, *Fever*. Tenor had already left for Miami and the Skengdon crew where 'Dancehall Feeling' and the posthumously released 'Bad Boys' was recorded. After a trip to England and the successful 'Never Work On A Sunday' for Donovan Germain, Tenor journeyed to New York in 1987. There he recorded the epic 'Victory Train' with Freddie McGregor's Studio One Band, and further singles for Witty, Robert Livingston ('Come Me Just A Come'), and Jah Life. His duet with General Doggie on 'Chill Out Chill Out' for Digital English was this most enigmatic of singers' swan song. In August 1988 he was killed by a speeding car in Houston, Texas.

Selected albums: *Fever* (Blue Mountain 1986), *Lives On* (1992). With Cocoa Tea: *Meets Cocoa Tea* (Witty 1987). With Don Angelo: *Clash* (Witty 1985). Various: *Strictly Livestock* (Greensleeves 1986).

Third World

Reggae band blending roots and soul, comprising Michael 'Ibo' Cooper (keyboards), Stephen 'Cat' Coore (guitar/cello), Richard Daley (bass), Willie 'Root' Stewart (drums), Irvin 'Carrot' Jarrett (percussion), William 'Bunny Rugs' Clarke (lead vocal/guitar) and Prilly Hamilton. Coore and Cooper first played together at the end of the 60s, and the early years of the

Third World

band saw the line-up in a state of flux: Coore, Cooper and Daley, plus drummer Carl Barovier (later replaced by Cornell Marshall and Willie Stewart) had all played with Inner Circle, a band that pursued a similar 'uptown reggae' course. By 1975 the line-up had settled to the above, minus Bunny Rugs, who had been pursuing a soul-reggae direction in a series of solo projects, aided by a uniquely spirited voice. Their first album, *Third World*, found them signed to Island and supporting Bob Marley at his breakthrough concerts at London's Lyceum in the summer of 1975. It was a mellow, carefully-crafted debut. *96 Degrees In the Shade* found the band and new singer Clarke in fine form, and delivered a huge international hit in the shape of a cover of the O'Jays/Gamble-Huff song, 'Now That We've Found Love'. The *Journey To Addis* album offered more of the same: a mix of roots and sweet soul. Further hits, 'Cool Meditation' (1979), 'Dancing On The Floor' (1981) and 'Try Jah Love' (1982), the latter two for a new label, CBS, kept their name in the public eye. A lone record for Winston 'Niney' Holness in Jamaica, pretty much summed up their attitude: 'Roots With Quality'. The late-80s saw the band increasingly lauded in America, drawing album contributions from Stevie Wonder, Stetsasonic's Daddy O, the Brecker Brothers and Jamal-ski. Third World still gig regularly, have the wisdom to continue working with their original producer, Geoffrey Chung, from time to time, and remain a name always worth watching out for, even if they haven't yet set the world alight on record.

Selected albums: *Third World* (Island 1976), *96 Degrees In the Shade* (Island 1977), *Journey To Addis* (Island 1978), *Prisoner In The Street* (Island 1980), *Rock The World* (CBS 1985), *Sense Of Purpose* (CBS 1985), *You've Got The Power* (CBS 1987), *Hold On To Love* (CBS 1987). Compilations: *Reggae Ambassadors* (Island 1985).

Thunder, Shelly

One of a rash of female DJs (Lady Patra etc.), native-New Yorker Thunder is at the forefront of a spirited response to the machismo belligerence of dancehall exponents such as Shabba Ranks, Cutty Ranks *et al.* Her first big hit was 1988's 'Kuff', a humorous suggestion that Jamaica's women should give their menfolk a smack around the ears when they get out of line. Other early singles, 'Small Horse Woman' and 'Man Ah Rush Me', continued in a similar vein. She made her major label debut in 1992, but, despite the assertions of a number of critics, it failed to signal her breakthrough into the mainstream.

Selected albums: *Small Horse Woman* (Hawkeye 1986), *Fresh Out The Pack* (Mango/Island 1989), *Backbone Of The Nation* (Mango/Island 1991).

Tiger

b. Norman Jackson, 1960, Kingston, Jamaica. Tiger is perhaps the most entertaining of all Jamaican DJs, his voice a crazy growl one moment and something completely different the next. He recorded his debut, 'Why Can't You Leave Dreadlocks Alone', in 1978 as a singer under the name of Ranking Tiger, following with 'Knock Three Times' and 'Love Line' in 1981. Changing to a DJ he established his reputation on Black Star sound system before releasing 'Bad Boy Stylee' and 'Mi Lover Mi Lover', all the while working out his own material on a tiny electronics keyboard. 'No Wanga Gut' and 'No Puppy Love' were his first real hits in 1985 and two years later Mango issued Tiger's self-produced debut album. By then he was a *bona fide* DJ sensation and embarked upon a remarkable series of songs for producers like Harry J ('Sitting In La La'), Kangal, Kings Crown, Ayeola ('Iron Dumpling') and his own Tiger label. He reappeared the following year with a trio of releases for the Paradise label of which 'Rap Pon Riddim' was his strangest yet. In 1989 he returned to the top with strong tunes for King Jammys, Gussie Clarke, Robert Livingston, Taxi, Steely And Clevie ('Ram Dancehall'), Blacka Dread and

Tiger

Penthouse, recording a duet with US rappers the Fat Boys in 1990 and becoming one of the first ragga DJs to make an impression on the hip hop scene. 1992 was his best year to date. 'When' for Steely And Clevie proved a significant crossover record and helped usher in the new bogle style. Penthouse released the belated *Deadly* album and hits for them ('Crying Fool'), Wild Apache, Exterminator, Shocking Vibes ('Yuh Dead Now') and Tiger's own Hide & Seek label followed. 'Beep Beep Move Over' was voiced in response to the mimicking Zebra. By 1993 Tiger's Chaos production company was signed to Columbia, who released *Claws Of The Cat* that year. In December 1993 Tiger was seriously injured in a Kingston motorcycle accident, but is understood to be making a complete recovery.

Selected albums: *Me Name Tiger* (Mango 1987), *Meets General Trees Live In Concert* (CSA 1987), *Bam Bam* (RAS 1988), *Shocking Colour* (King Jammys 1989), *Ram Dancehall* (Steely & Clevie 1990), *Love Affair* (Rohit 1990), *Touch Is A Move* (Blue Trac 1990), *Tiger A Tiger* (New Name 1991), *Ready Fi Dem* (VP 1991), *Deadly* (Penthouse 1992), *Claws Of The Cat* (Columbia 1993).

Tippa Irie

b. Anthony Henry, 1965, London, England. Raised in a south London community where the sound system business was a way of life. By the age of 13 he was taking the microphone for local sound systems and learning the art of chatting in rhyme by listening to Jamaican DJs on record. At 15 he was a useful MC with King Tubby's sound system (Brixton, not to be confused with the Jamaican dub maestro). Although British MCs were previously held to be inferior to their Jamaican counterparts, when dancehall took a grip on reggae in the early 80s it coincided with the rise of the most talented 'chatters' Britain had ever produced. The live recordings of sound system sessions that swept Jamaica were soon copied in London and Tippa found himself on three live albums in 1983, *Live At DSYC volumes 1-3*, recorded at London's Dick Shepherd Youth Centre. They had an enormous impact: here were British kids proving themselves to be as powerful with a rhyme as their Jamaican counterparts. When Tippa joined Saxon he was alongside the best reggae rappers in Britain: Papa Levi, Peter King, Daddy Rusty, Daddy Colonel, Sandy, and later, Smiley Culture, Asher Senator and singer Maxi Priest. It was the most powerful line-up any UK sound had ever assembled. In 1984 Saxon recorded a live album for Greensleeves, who picked Tippa up for studio recordings. 'Sleng Teng Finish Already' and 'Telephone', and 'It's Good To Have The Feeling You're The Best' all sold well and placed him on television shows such as *Club Mix*. No-one was expecting 'Hello Darling' to plant Tippa on *Top Of The Pops* but the cheeky single was a smash. However, because no-one was expecting it to happen, it took an eternity for Tippa's follow-up to arrive and 'Heartbeat' merely scraped the charts.

A further attempt at chart action came with the appropriately titled 'Panic Panic', with Tippa lost on a dance record. That year's album, *Is It Really Happening To Me?* summed up the pressure he was under. Tippa chose to return to grass roots, and *Two Sides Of...* in 1987 found him more relaxed on album than before: this was Tippa, ragga MC, not chart-climber. In 1988, he teamed with Jamaican ragga star Papa San to record *JA To UK MC Clash*, another fine, low-key album, and in 1989 issued *A Me Dis*, which also earned a debut American release on Miles Copeland's IRS label. He finally quit Saxon in the summer of 1989. Meanwhile the mainstream media kept one eye open for him, he made several television appearances in 1988, including BBC television's current affairs programme *Panorama*, as an anti-crack spokesperson. While he might never recapture the success of 'Hello Darling', Tippa can never be entirely discounted; as long as there is a lyric in his head, he will be working.

Albums: *Coughing Up Fire* (1984), *Is It Really*

Tippa Irie

Happening To Me? (Greensleeves 1985), *Two Sides Of* (GT's 1987), *Ah Me Dis* (GT's 1989), *Original Raggamuffin* (Mango/Island 1990). With Papa San: *JA To UK MC Clash Volume 2* (Fashion 1988). With Peter Hunnigale: *A New Decade* (Mango/Island 1991).

Tosh, Peter

b. Peter McIntosh, 1944, Westmoreland, Jamaica, d. 11 September 1987. Of all the reggae singers from the mid-60s, none 'came on strong' like Peter Tosh, who he declared it so on his anthem, 'I'm The Toughest'. It was he who provided the bite to Bob Marley's bark in the original Wailers, and it was he who appeared most true to the rude boy image that the group fostered during the ska era. Tosh was the first to emerge from the morass of doo-wop wails and chants that constituted the Wailers' early records, recording as Peter Tosh or Peter Touch and The Wailers on 'Hoot Nanny Hoot', 'Shame And Scandal', and 'Maga Dog', the latter another theme for the singer. He also made records without the Wailers and with Rita Anderson, later to become Rita Marley. The Wailers were a loose band by 1966; Bob Marley went to America to look for work, and Peter and Neville 'Bunny Wailer' Livingstone either recorded together or separately. At some point Peter ran into trouble with the law and spent a brief period in prison, probably on ganja charges. When he was not working with the Wailers, he would record solo material ('Maga Dog' again, or 'Leave My Business') with producer Joe Gibbs, once more retaining his ferocious vocal style.

When the Wailers worked with Leslie Kong in 1969 Tosh was at the forefront with 'Soon Come' and 'Stop The Train', but at Lee Perry's Wailers sessions (1970-71) he was often reduced to harmonizing, save for three mighty tracks: '400 Years', an attack on slavery, 'No Sympathy', where Tosh unites rejection in love with the lot of the black ghetto resident, and 'Downpresser', another anti-oppression statement and perhaps his best-ever record. When the Wailers split from Perry and joined Island Records, the writing was on the wall for Tosh; Island apparently preferred Marley's cooler, more sympathetic style, and despite contributing 'Get Up Stand Up' to *Burnin'*, the band's second album for the label, both Tosh and Bunny Wailer quit the group in 1973. Tosh concentrated on work for his own label, Intel Diplo HIM (meaning: Intelligent Diplomat for His Imperial Majesty), and signed to Virgin in 1976. The patronage of Mick Jagger at Rolling Stones Records, which he joined in 1978, nearly gave him a chart hit with a cover of the Temptations 'Don't Look Back'. Reggae fans complained that Jagger's voice was louder than Tosh's in the mix. *Bush Doctor*, his first album for the label, sold well, but *Mystic Man* and *Wanted, Dread & Alive*, did not. He also released three albums with EMI, the last, *No Nuclear War*, his best since *Legalize It*. The record won the first best reggae album Grammy Award in March 1988, but by then Tosh was dead, shot in a robbery on his home in Kingston in September 1987. The tuffest reggae singer of all had finally succumbed to the gun.

Albums: *Legalize It* (Virgin 1976), *Equal Rights* (Virgin 1977), *Bush Doctor* (Rolling Stones 1978), *Mystic Man* (Rolling Stones/EMI 1979), *Wanted, Dread & Alive* (Rolling Stones/Dynamic 1981), *Mama Africa* (Intel Diplo/EMI 1983), *Captured Live* (EMI 1984), *No Nuclear War* (EMI 1987). Compilation: *The Toughest* (Parlophone 1988).

Videos: *Live* (1986), *Downpresser Man* (1988), *Red X* (1993).

Trinity

b. Wade Brammer, 1954, Kingston, Jamaica. After working as a DJ on several local sound systems, Trinity made his recording debut in March 1976 with 'Set Up Yourself' for Joseph 'Joe Joe' Hookim. Shortly after this, he recorded 'Words Of The Prophet' for Yabby You who also released his fine debut album, *Shanty Town Determination* (1976). Heavily influenced by Big Youth, he

Peter Tosh

developed a strong and entertaining style of his own. In late 1976 he joined his neighbourhood friend and fellow DJ Dillinger for an excellent single for Joe Joe Hookim, 'Crank Face', and a rather hurriedly recorded album, *Clash*, for UK producer Clement Bushay. In 1977 he had more than 20 singles released including 'Pumps And Pride' for Winston Riley, 'Smoking Rock' for Tommy Cowan, 'John Saw Them Coming' for Joe Gibbs and 'Peace Conference In A Western Kingston' for Yabby You. His biggest hit that year was 'Three Piece Suit' for Joe Gibbs, on which his excellent delivery, witty lyrics and sheer enthusiasm make it irresistible, and an outstanding album of the same name quickly followed. An answer record to this, Althea And Donna's 'Uptown Top Ranking' (1977), became an even bigger hit, eventually topping the UK pop charts. Trinity recorded his response to that, 'Slim Thing' (1978), but it is a disappointing reply. In 1977 he had another strong album with *Uptown Girl* produced by Bunny Lee, and the following year shared albums with Ranking Trevor, *Three Piece Chicken And Chips*, and appeared on the Mighty Diamonds', *Showcase*. Subsequent recordings met with less success, and in the 80s, he commenced a new singing career as Junior Brammer, with two albums being issued, *Telephone Line* and *Hold Your Corner*.

Selected albums: *Shanty Town Determination* (TR International 1976), *Three Piece Suit* (Joe Gibbs 1977), *Uptown Girl* (Magnum 1977), *Bad Card* (Joe Gibbs 1979), *Rock In The Ghetto* (Trojan 1979), *Full House* (JB Music 1980), *Side Kicks* (Vista Sounds 1983), *Teen Jam* (Kingdom 1983), *Natty Tired To Carry Load* (Burning Sounds 1988), *Big Big Man* (Lagoon 1993). As Junior Brammer: *Telephone Line* (John Dread 1987), *Hold Your Corner* (Live & Learn 1987). With Dillinger: *Clash* (Burning Sounds 1976). With Ranking Trevor: *Three Piece Chicken And Chips* (Cha Cha 1978). With the Mighty Diamonds: *Showcase* (Burning Sounds 1978). Compilation: *Best Of* (Culture Press 1985).

Trojan Records

The most commercially successful of UK reggae labels, Trojan had almost 30 hit singles placed on the UK national charts between 1969 and 1976. 'The Trojan' was the nickname of Jamaican producer Duke Reid (from the truck that was used to transport his sound system) and the label was originally founded to release his Treasure Isle recordings in Britain, yet expanded to license and release the work of nearly every major Jamaican producer. Trojan's directors were Chris Blackwell (of Island Records) and Lee Gopthal, whose Pyramid label had already had chart success in 1967 with Desmond Dekker's '007'. Early success for Trojan came with Jimmy Cliff's 'Wonderful World, Beautiful People' in 1969 and soon the UK charts were full of singles from artists such as John Holt, Ken Boothe, the Pioneers and Nicky Thomas. Sometimes Trojan would 'sweeten' the Jamaican productions by adding strings at London's Chalk Farm studios, and among the biggest-sellers were the pop-reggae of Bob And Marcia and Greyhound. However, the label's only number 1 was a more rootsy record, 'Double Barrel' by Dave And Ansell Collins (1972). Trojan's Big Shot subsidiary enjoyed strong sales with 'Big Six' and other lewd monologues by Judge Dread, and the compilation collections *Tighten Up Volumes* achieved cult status in the UK. Blackwell left the company to concentrate on releasing progressive rock through his Island label but Gopthal stayed on and expanded the Trojan group. In 1975 Trojan's parent company and distributor, B&C, collapsed. The Trojan catalogue was purchased by Marcel Rodd of Saga Records and the label was henceforth devoted to reissues. The policy was continued into the 90s by Trojan's next owner, Colin Newman of Receiver Records.

Selected albums: *The Trojan Story* (Trojan 1971), *The Trojan Story* (Trojan 1988), *20 Reggae Classics Vols 1, 2, 3 & 4* (Trojan 1988), *Tighten Up Box Set Vols 1, 2 & 3* (Trojan 1989).

Norman Grant of the Twinkle Brothers

Twinkle Brothers

This group comprised Norman Grant (vocals/drums), Ralston Grant (vocals/rhythm guitar), Eric Barnard (piano), Karl Hyatt (vocals/percussion) and Albert Green (congas/percussion). All the members were born in Falmouth, Jamaica. Formed in 1962 by the Grant brothers, the Twinkles won various local musical awards and talent competitions before recording their earliest side, 'Somebody Please Help Me', in 1966 for producer Leslie Kong. The group went on to record for other producers such as Duke Reid, Lee Perry, Sid Bucknor, Phill Pratt, Ken Chang and Bunny Lee. In the early 70s they went into self-production, financing their sessions through Norman's employment as a solo artist. Their music embraced calypso, soul, pop and soft reggae which they had performed on Jamaica's north coast hotel circuit. In 1975 an expanded line-up released the celebrated *Rasta Pon Top*, which included such intrinsic Rastafari anthems as 'Give Rasta Praise', 'It Gwine Dreada', 'Beat Them Jah Jah' and the fiery, assertive title track. Over the next few years a number of Norman Grant productions featuring other artists surfaced, including titles by Alla, the Mystics, Phillip Parkinson and DJs Sir Lee and Ili P, as well as further Twinkle Brothers efforts 'Jah Army' and a Rasta version of Jim Reeves' 'Distant Drums'.

In 1977 the group signed to Virgin Records' newly established Frontline label, a move that saw the release of the highly-acclaimned *Love*. This was followed by the patchy *Praise Jah*, and triumphantly, in 1980, by the classic *Countrymen* which featured premier heavy roots items such as 'Never Get Burn, 'Since I Threw The Comb Away' and 'Jah Kingdom Come'. The group were later dropped by Virgin and more or less ceased to be an entity, with Norman Grant settling in the UK to concentrate on a solo career while retaining the Twinkle Brothers epithet. He continues to issue albums and 12-inch singles on his own Twinkle label, and has built himself a large fan base, particularly in Europe where he is an in-demand live attraction. Other recordings, notably the excellent vocal/dub *Right Way*, have emerged through London roots doyen and sound system operator Jah Shaka's imprint.

Albums: *Rasta Pon Top* (Grounation 1975), *Love* (Front Line 1977), *Praise Jah* (Front Line 1979), *Countrymen* (Front Line 1980), *Me No You* (Twinkle 1981), *Underground* (Twinkle 1982), *Dub Massacre Parts 1 - 5* (Twinkle 1982-1990), *Burden Bearer* (Twinkle 1983), *Enter Zion* (Twinkle 1983), *Live From Reggae Sunsplash* (Twinkle 1984), *Right Way* (1985), *Kilimanjaro* (Twinkle 1985), *Anti-Apartheid* (Twinkle 1985), *Respect And Honour* (Twinkle 1987), *Twinkle Love Songs* (Twinkle 1987), *New Songs For Jah* (Twinkle 1989), *Rastafari Chant* (Twinkle 1989), *All Is Well* (Twinkle 1990), *Free Africa* (Front Line 1990), *Live In Warsaw* (Twinkle 1990), *Unification* (Twiinkle 1990), *Wind Of Change* (Twinkle 1990), *Old Cuts (dub)* (1991), *Don't Forget Africa* (Twinkle 1992), *Twinkle Love Songs Vol. 2* (Twinkle 1992), *Dub With Strings* (Twinkle 1992), *Babylon Rise Again* (Twinkle 1992), *Higher Heights (Twinkle Inna Polish Stylee)* (1993). Compilations: *Crucial Cuts* (Virgin 1983), *All The Hits From 1970-88* (Twinkle 1988).

U

U Roy

b. Ewart Beckford, 1942, Kingston, Jamaica. U Roy, began as a sound system DJ in 1961, spinning records for the Doctor Dickies set, later known as Dickies Dynamic, in such well-known Jamaican venues as Victoria Pier, Foresters Hall and Emmett Park. His inspiration was the DJ Winston 'Count' Machuki, who worked for Coxsone Dodd and subsequently on Prince Buster's Voice Of The People sound system. By the mid-60s he was DJ for Sir George The Atomic, based around Maxfield Avenue in Kingston. Around 1967 he began to work with King Tubby as DJ for his Home Town Hi-Fi. From this association developed the whole modern DJ style; Tubby's work at Duke Reid's studio, where he was disc-cutter, led him to discover dub. He found that by dropping out the vocal track and remixing the remaining rhythm tracks he created new 'versions' of much-loved tunes. He began to record a series of special acetate recordings or dub plates for exclusive use on his sound system. The space left by the absent vocal tracks enabled U Roy to improvise his own jive-talk raps or toasts when the sound system played dances. The effect in the dancehall was immediate and electrifying. In 1969 U Roy was invited to play for Dodd's Down Beat sound system, playing the number 2 set; the number 1 set had King Stitt as DJ. U Roy became dissatisfied with playing the latest Coxsone music only after Stitt had first exposed it to dance patrons, and returned to Tubby's. He then began his recording career in full, recording two discs for Lee Perry, 'Earth's Rightful Ruler' and 'OK Corral', before moving to producer Keith Hudson, for whom he made the outstanding 'Dynamic Fashion Way'. U Roy then began recording for Duke Reid, using as backing tracks Reid's rocksteady hits from 1966-67; their success was unprecedented. His first record for Reid, 'Wake The Town', which used Alton Ellis' 'Girl I've Got A Date' as backing, immediately soared to the top of both Jamaican radio charts. His next two releases, 'Rule The Nation' and 'Wear You To The Ball', soon joined it. These three releases held the top three positions in the Jamaican charts for 12 weeks during early 1970. Other sound system DJs were quick to follow U Roy, including Dennis Alcapone and Scotty. The radio stations refused to play DJ music just to give singers a chance, so big was the demand. U Roy recorded 32 tracks for Reid, in the process versioning almost every rocksteady hit issued on the label and releasing two albums. By 1973 he was recording for other producers, including Alvin Ranglin, Bunny Lee, Glen Brown and Lloyd Charmers as well as self-productions. However, the rise of the next DJ generation including Big Youth signalled the partial eclipse of U Roy.

In 1975 he made a series of albums for producer Prince Tony Robinson which were leased to Virgin Records in the UK, wherein the DJ revisited Reid's earlier hits in the then prevalent rockers style. He appeared at the London Lyceum in August 1976, backed by a band featuring Channel One stalwarts Sly Dunbar (bass) and Ansell Collins (organ). He operated his own sound system, Stur-Gav, featuring Ranking Joe and selector Jah Screw. When they left after the sound system was broken up during the turbulent 1980 Jamaican election, it was rebuilt with new DJs Charlie Chaplin and Josey Wales, and Inspector Willie as selector.

U Roy continued to record sporadically throughout the 80s, recording 'Hustling', a single for Gussie Clarke, in 1984, and two excellent albums for DJs turned producers Tapper Zukie and Prince Jazzbo, in 1986 and 1987 respectively. In 1991 he played a successful 'revival' concert at the Hammersmith Palais, London. U Roy is the man who is responsible for putting the DJ on the map, both as a recording artist in Jamaica

U Roy

and as a major, indirect influence on the US rap movement. As such his importance is immense.

Selected albums: *Version Galore* (Trojan 1971), *U Roy* (Attack/Trojan 1974), *Dread Inna Babylon* (Virgin 1975), *Natty Rebel* (Virgin 1976), *Dread In A Africa* (1976), *U Roy Meet King Attorney* (1977), *Rasta Ambassador* (Virgin 1977), *Jah Son Of Africa* (Front Line 1978), *With Words Of Wisdom* (Front Line 1979), *Love Is Not A Gamble* (Stateline 1980), *Crucial Cuts* (Virgin 1983), *Line Up And Come* (Tappa 1987), *Music Addict* (RAS 1987), *True Born African* (Ariwa 1991). As U Roy & Friends: *With A Flick Of My Musical Wrist* (Trojan 1988, rec. 1970-73). With Josey Wales: *Teacher Meets The Student* (Sonic Sounds 1992). Selected compilations: *The Best Of U Roy* (Live & Love 1977), *Version Of Wisdom* (Front Line 1990), *Natty Rebel - Extra Version* (Virgin 1991), *U Roy CD Box Set* (Virgin 1991, CD box set), *Super Boss* (Esoldun/Treasure Isle 1992).

UB40

Named after the form issued to unemployed people in Britain to receive benefit, UB40 are the most long-lasting proponents of crossover reggae in the UK. The multi-racial band was formed around the brothers Robin (b. 25 December 1954, Birmingham, England; lead guitar) and Ali Campbell (b. 15 February 1959, Birmingham, England; lead vocals/guitar), the sons of Birmingham folk club singers Lorna and Ian Campbell. Other founder members included Earl Falconer (b. 23 January 1957, Birmingham, England; bass), Mickey Virtue (b. 19 January 1957, Birmingham, England; keyboards), Brian Travers (b. 7 February 1959; saxophone), Jim Brown (b. 21 November 1957; drums), and Norman Hassan (b. 26 January 1958, Birmingham, England; percussion). Reggae toaster Astro (b. Terence Wilson, 24 June 1957) joined UB40 to record 'Food For Thought' with local producer Bob Lamb (former drummer with Locomotive and the Steve Gibbons band).

'King' (coupled with 'Food For Thought') was a tribute to Martin Luther King. The debut *Signing Off*, boasted an album sleeve with a 12-inch square replica of the notorious, bright yellow unemployment card. This image attracted a large contingent of disaffected youth as well as proving popular with followers of the 2-Tone/ska scene. The following year the group formed their own label DEP International on which they released 'One In Ten', an impassioned protest about unemployment. *Labour Of Love*, a collection of cover versions, signalled a return to the reggae mainstream and it brought UB40's first number 1 in 'Red Red Wine' (1983). Originally written by Neil Diamond, it had been a big reggae hit for Tony Tribe in 1969. The album contained further hit singles in Jimmy Cliff's 'Many Rivers To Cross' (1983) and Eric Donaldson's 'Cherry Oh Baby' (1984). The follow-up, *Geoffrey Morgan*, a UK number 3 album, supplied the group with the Top 10 hit 'If It Happens Again'. 'I Got You Babe' (1986) was a different kind of cover version as Ali Campbell and Chrissie Hynde of the Pretenders duetted on the Sonny And Cher hit.

The same team had a further hit in 1988 with a revival of Lorna Bennett's 1969 reggae song 'Breakfast In Bed'. *Rat In Mi Kitchen* included the African liberation anthem 'Sing Our Own Song' with Herb Alpert on trumpet. After performing 'Red Red Wine' at the 1988 Nelson Mandela, Wembley concert, re-promotion in the USA resulted in the single reaching the number 1 spot. The group had further single success with the Chi-lites' 'Homely Girl' (1989) and Lord Creator's 'Kingston Town' (1990), both of which would appear on a second volume of cover versions, *Labour Of Love II*, (which has subsequently sold 5 million copies worldwide). In 1990, the group had separate Top 10 hits in the UK and USA as a Campbell/Robert Palmer duet on Bob Dylan's 'I'll Be Your Baby Tonight' charted in Britain and a revival of the Temptations' 'The Way You Do The Things You Do' was

UB40

a hit in America. Throughout the 80s, the group toured frequently in Europe and North America and played in Russia in 1986, filming the tour for video release. Following a quiet period they returned in 1993 with a version of 'I Can't Help Falling In Love With You' which reached number 1 in the UK, also fostering the career of new pop-reggae star Bitty McClean. Unkindly described by some critics as 'cod-reggae', UB40 have loyally stuck to their chosen musical path, for which they have been amply rewarded.

Albums: *Signing Off* (Graduate 1980), *Present Arms* (DEP 1981), *Present Arms In Dub* (DEP 1981), *UB44* (DEP 1982), *UB40 Live* (DEP 1983), *Labour Of Love* (DEP 1983), *Geffrey Morgan* (DEP 1984), *Baggariddim* (DEP 1985), *Rat In Mi Kitchen* (DEP 1986), *UB40* (DEP 1988), *Labour Of Love II* (DEP 1989), *Promises And Lies* (DEP 1993). Compilations: *The Singles Album* (Graduate 1982), *The UB40 File* (DEP 1985, double album), *The Best Of UB40, Volume I* (DEP 1987), *UB40 Box Set* (Virgin 1991).

Videos: *Labour Of Love* (1984), *Best Of* (1987), *Live* (1988), *Dance With The Devil* (1988), *Labour Of Love II* (1990), *CCCP* (1991), *A Family Affair Live In Concert* (1991)

UK MCs

By the early 80s UK reggae fans (DJ fans in particular) felt that they had assimilated enough of Jamaica's musical output, and demanded a voice of their own. lovers rock in the mid-70s had been a particularly English phenomenon, which started as a reaction against the dominant rasta/roots music of the time, and the rise of the UK MCs (not DJs) mirrored it in many ways. The increasing availability of live sound system tapes from Jamaica from the late 70s onwards meant that DJs in the UK were able to actually study their Jamaican counterparts at work on the set, as opposed to their finished work on record, and for a while many DJs simply 'pirated' the lyrics they had heard on tape. The better ones soon realised that this was simply not good enough, and Saxon Sound were at the forefront of this revolution, with English DJs - now MCs - riding rhythms in a very English way, that was to have repercussions throughout the reggae world, and on into US rap music too. Phillip 'Papa' Levi was Saxon's number one mic. man, and the first to record, but standing right behind him were Peter King - the 'fast style' originator Smiley Culture, Asher Senator, Tippa Irie, Daddy Colonel

UK MCs: Tippa Irie and Peter Hunnigale

and Rusty. Saxon Sound were unassailable and many memorable sound system 'battles' were fought at such exotic venues as Lewisham Boys Club, as Saxon proved again and again that they were the best. The Midlands too had their own home grown stars and Macka B and Pato Banton came to the fore - Macka B in particular was incomparable, and not afraid to show his musical influences either - one of his party turns was set to the melody of Shirley Bassey's 'Hey Big Spender'.

DJs had recorded in the UK before - Papa Face and Laurel & Hardy had both made very strong records which were very popular - but the release of Phillip 'Papa' Levi's 'Mi God, Mi King' in 1984 changed everything when, towards the end of the record, he dropped into the UK 'fast style'. Asher Senator gives a rundown on record on the origins of the fast style, and there is no doubt that Peter King was the originator (humble origins too - Peter stated that his girlfriend wasn't too keen on his constantly practising lyrics, so he did them double time to get it over with quickly!) but Levi was the first to put the style on record. 'Mi God, Mi King' was quickly released in Jamaica where it went straight to number 1 and stayed there - the first English DJ record to ever top the Jamaican charts, and Levi was promptly signed up by Island Records.

Smiley Culture's Fashion release, 'Cockney Translation', stayed at the top of the UK reggae charts for weeks in 1984 and the follow-up, 'Police Officer', went straight into the UK national charts in early 1985. Jamaican and American DJs desperately tried to catch up with the UK style which concentrated on lyrics that actually told a story, often in a humorous way, with repeated punch or hooklines. The subjects were usually themselves and their experiences, without having to pretend, as they once had, that they'd been raised in Western Kingston. No longer would English DJs be regarded as second best and many classic records have been made in the UK in the ensuing years. Tippa Irie has made a

long-standing commitment to UK reggae music, Macka B has produced some of the genre's most incisive lyrics such as 'Invasion' and 'Don't Judge Me' - two all time classics. Levi continues to record without any apologies or concessions to anyone - his '84 Tion' was arguably the best ever account of a second generation black English upbringing, while Top Cat's version to an updated 'Lock Jaw' rhythm track, proved one of the most popular records in the UK during the latter part of 1993. The UK MC is definitely here to stay.

Selected albums: Various: *Great British M.C.'s* (Fashion 1985), *Coughing Up Fire - Saxon Studio Live* (Greensleeves 1985). *JA To UK MC Clash - Asher Senator Meets Johnny Ringo* (Fashion 1984), *JA To UK MC Clash Pt 2 - Tippa Irie Meets Papa San* (Fashion 1988), *JA To UK MC Clash Pt 3 - Top Cat Meets Poison Chang* (Fashion 1993). Asher Senator: *Born To Chat* Fashion 1986). Smiley Culture: *The Original* (Top Notch/Fashion 1986). Macka B: *Sign Of The Times* (Ariwa 1986). General Levy: *The Wickeder General* (Fashion 1993).

UK Reggae

Far too easily derided as being a mere derivative of the original Jamaican article, UK Reggae has long since cast off the charges of imitation, and has become a vibrant, exciting reggae form in its own right. Inevitably, early British reggae music was chiefly built on the input of Jamaicans resident in the UK. Ernest Ranglin arrived in Britain in 1963 at the request of Island Records boss Chris Blackwell, and working as musical director cut a huge hit for Millie, 'My Boy Lollipop', in 1964. Other British ska efforts, however, were less laudable, and it wasn't until 1968-69 that producers such as Clancy Collins and Laurel Aitken began to make British reggae - albeit the work of Caribbean expatriates - worthy of its name. Another early mover in the field was Eddie Grant, who made one classic with the Pyramids, 'Train Tour To Rainbow City' in 1969. Reggae soon became hugely popular in the UK, chiefly thanks to the efforts of two labels, Trojan and Pama, both dealing principally with Jamaican-recorded product. By 1970-71 British reggae bands like the Cimarons and the Undivided could be regularly found on the club circuit, either in their own right or backing visiting Jamaican artists. By 1974 the Cimarons had developed their own style, slightly more subdued than the Jamaican version, and wholly recognisable as their own. Their *On The Rock* set remains under-rated to this day. The lovers rock scene, a blend of soul and rub-a-dub rhythms, threw up a heap of popular, chiefly female acts: 15,16,17, Brown Sugar (featuring future Soul II Soul diva Caron Wheeler), Carroll Thompson and Janet Kay among them. The mid-70s saw a vast number of new reggae bands and artists emerge in the UK: Steel Pulse, the first UK reggae band to be taken seriously by the rock world; a youthful Aswad, whose 'Warrior Charge' is a stepper's classic; Matumbi, mixing lovers grooves and roots with ease, resulting in a top 40 hit, 'Point Of View' in 1979, and Linton Kwesi Johnson, the pioneering dub poet, backed by Matumbi member Dennis Bovell's Dub Band.

Inevitably studios specialising in reggae emerged in the UK, including London's Mark Angelos and Easy Street, and at the turn of the 80s, two label-owning studio complexes arrived, Ariwa and Fashion, the former, under the aegis of producer-owner Neil Fraser, specialising in lovers and dub, the latter tackling more or less anything that took its fancy. The 80s saw Aswad rise to chart success with the number 1 'Don't Turn Around', and the emergence of uniquely British-sounding artists like Smiley Culture and the internationally successful Maxi Priest, whose style crossed lovers rock with dancehall and soul. Meanwhile Britain's MC culture, built on the success of the likes of Saxon and Jah Tubby's sound systems in the mid-80s, had unleashed a volley of unique DJs, including Tippa Irie, Phillip 'Papa' Levi and Macka B. Jamaican acts such as Barrington Levy, Dennis Brown and Pat

Kelly even came to Britain to record, an idea that might have seemed laughable in the 60s. Meanwhile Trojan had a successor at last in the shape of Greensleeves, a label that could be relied upon for releasing chiefly Jamaican product. By the early 90s, British reggae was no longer a term that meant anything: the music had proved its world-wide appeal, with its hybrids, such as bhangramuffin, a fusion of Asian and ragga styles, sounding truly 'international'. From here on in, there's only reggae, not British reggae.

Uniques

The original line-up of this vocal harmony group consisted of Slim Smith (b. Keith Smith, Kingston, Jamaica), Roy Shirley and Franklyn White. The formative years of the Uniques overlap confusingly with the Techniques. In an interview appearing in the Canadian based magazine *Reggae Quarterly* in the early 80s, Roy Shirley states that he formed the group with Slim Smith and Franklyn White, when the latter pair left the Techniques. They made their first recording, 'The Journey', for Ken Lack's Caltone label. Other early ska sides included 'Do Me Good'; and 'Evil Love' for JJ Johnson in 1966, the same year as the Techniques earliest records, just prior to Smith's sabbatical at Studio One and Shirley's successful resumption of his solo career. White's subsequent whereabouts remain obscured. Towards the end of 1967 Smith left Coxsone and formed the Uniques Mk. 2, teaming up with Martin Riley (aka Jimmy Riley), brother of Technique Winston Riley, and Lloyd Charmers (b Lloyd Tyrell, 1947, Kingston, Jamaica), former member of the Charmers, with whom he had recently enjoyed some success with 'Time After Time' for Prince Buster. He had previously recorded as a solo singer for Coxsone Dodd in 1964. Cornell Campbell was another who featured around this time.

The group borrowed some money from one Winston Lowe and recorded their debut, 'Watch This Sound', a version of the Stephen Stills/Buffalo Springfield protest song, and the achingly soulful 'Out Of Love'. These were a success, as were such subsequent recordings as 'People Rock Steady', 'Never Let Me Go', 'Gypsy Woman', 'Let Me Go Girl', 'Speak No Evil', 'Girl Of My Dreams', 'My Womans Love', 'Love & Devotion', 'Girls Like Dirt', 'The Beatitude' (aka 'Blessed Are The Meek') and the classic 'My Conversation', which producer Bunny Lee gave to Rupie Edwards, who built an entire LP around it. This was the first one-rhythm album, predating the vogue for such discs by several years. These were all produced by Bunny Lee, though some carry a credit for Winston Lowe. They also recorded the wonderful 'Secretly' (1969) for Lloyd Daley, though this seems to have been a one-off. These records were issued in the UK on a variety of Trojan and Pama labels, some acknowledged as the work of the Uniques, some allowing Slim Smith the sole credit. Trojan issued *Absolutely The Uniques* in 1969. The group folded during that same year, the members fragmenting to pursue solo careers. Smith, until his untimely demise, with Bunny Lee; Charmers moving deeper into production work.

Album: *Absolutely The Uniques* (Trojan 1969).

Upsetters

This was a collective tag for whatever group reggae producer Lee Perry had in his studio at the time of recording, or for his sporadic live dates. The name was drawn from his massive 1967 Jamaican smash, 'The Upsetter', and had previously been used by saxophonist Roland Alphonso, who in turn drew it from Little Richard's stage band. The Upsetters secured a UK Top 5 hit in 1969 with the hugely influential 'Return Of Django'. Among those who passed through Perry's Upsetters were Glen Adams, Winston Wright, (organ), Aston 'Familyman' Barrett, Boris Gardiner (bass), Carlton Barrett, Lloyd 'Tinleg' Adams, Mikey 'Boo' Richards, Sly Dunbar, Clevie Browne (drums), Hux Brown (guitar) and innumerable others. Perry was dictatorial with his bands, and hence always achieved a totally different sound from the other producers using the same musicians in the hothouse music business of Jamaica.

Selected albums: *Return Of Django* (1969), *The Upsetter* (1969), *Scratch The Upsetter Again* (1970). Compilation: *Upsetter Collection* (1981).

V

Viceroys

Formed in Jamaica c.1966. The group was formed by lead vocalist and songwriter Wesley Tinglin (b. c.1947, Jamaica). They recorded, initially as the Voiceroys, for Coxsone Dodd's Studio One label, with early recordings including 'Love And Unity' (1967), 'Fat Fish' (1968) and 'Ya Ho' (1968). Again in 1968 they recorded 'Lip And Tongue' and 'Send Requests' for the Morgan's label. In the early 70s they joined Winston Riley as the Inturns, seeing success with 'Mission Impossible', and in the mid-70s returned to Studio One to record as the Voiceroys with 'The Struggle' and 'Slogan On The Wall'. In 1978 they took the name the Interns, and recorded *Detour* for Phill Pratt, which was largely ignored at the time. Shortly after this, they adopted the name the Viceroys, and the line-up stabilised with Wesley Tinglin being supported by harmony singers Neville Ingram and Norris Reid. Reid had already had a handful of singles released under his own name, and continued to further his solo career while remaining a full-time member of the group. They had a big hit with 'Heart Made Of Stone' (1980), a Sly And Robbie production, and followed it with the self-produced 'Shaddai Children' (1981).

In 1982 they recorded *We Must Unite*, on which the combination of their rural, rootsy harmonies and Linval Thompson's heavy duty production attracted a lot of attention. They then repeated the formula for *Brethren And Sistren* (1983), which was their biggest selling record, and *Detour* was re-released later that year in response to public interest in the group. Shortly after this, Norris Reid left the group to concentrate on his solo career with Augustus Pablo, and was replaced by Chris Wayne, who had made a name for himself singing on Sugar Minott's Youth Promotion sound system. The group's *Chancery Lane* (1984) was recorded for Winston Riley, but was a rather low-key outing which did not enjoy the popularity of their previous albums. They commenced recording a new album, but it was never released, and nothing further has been heard from them. Chris Wayne left the group in 1985 and has since recorded an album for Wackies, *Freedom Street* (1988), and two for Sugar Minott; *Progress* (1989) and *Talk About Love* (1991). Norris Reid has continued to record for Augustus Pablo, and his first album, *Root And Vine*, was issued in 1988.
Albums: As the Interns: *Detour* (1979). As the Viceroys: *We Must Unite* (Trojan 1982), *Brethren And Sistren* (CSA 1983), *Chancery Lane* (Greensleeves 1984), *Ya Ho* (Burning Sounds 1985).

W

Wailer, Bunny

b. Neville O'Riley Livingston, 10 April 1947, Kingston, Jamaica. Bunny Wailer's relationship with Bob Marley and Peter Tosh, the two other principal members of the Wailers in the 60s and early 70s, stretches back to his childhood, when Marley and Wailer lived under the same roof in Trench Town. As teenagers, Peter, Bob and Bunny would spend their evenings practising harmonies tutored by Joe Higgs of Higgs & Wilson fame. In the early 60s, as the nascent Jamaican recording industry began to gather strength, the trio formed the Wailers, recruiting other friends like Junior Braithwaite, Beverley Kelso and Cherry Smith into the fold. Possessed of a high tenor, rather in the style of American soul singers of the Curtis Mayfield school, Bunny's role in the Wailers was principally that of harmony singer. But on occasions his voice was featured as lead on songs like 'Dancing Shoes', 'He Who Feels It Knows It' and the beautiful 'Sunday Morning', recorded in the early 60s for the group's first producer, Coxsone Dodd. Bunny spent part of 1967 in prison on charges of marijuana possession. It was this experience that prompted him to write the song 'Battering Down Sentence', which later appeared on his solo debut, *Blackheart Man*.

The Wailers spent a couple of years recording for other producers, most notably Leslie Kong and Lee Perry, as well as issuing their own self-produced efforts on their Wail 'N' Soul 'M' and Tuff Gong labels. During this period Bunny contributed lead vocals on 'This Train', 'Riding High', 'Brain Washing' and 'Dreamland'. In 1972 the Wailers signed to Island Records. With founder Chris Blackwell's understanding of contemporary rock markets, and the emphasis on albums and live shows, the Wailers brought the sound of roots reggae to an international audience with *Catch A Fire* (1973) and *Burnin'* (1973), the latter featuring two fine songs from Bunny, 'Hallelujah Time' and 'Pass It On'. These albums broke the Wailers outside of Jamaica and its expatriate environs in the US and Europe, gaining a new worldwide respect and focus for reggae music. However, this success had taken its toll on the group. Peter Tosh resented the way in which Marley appeared to be promoted as leader of the group, and Bunny, for largely unspecified reasons, seemed reluctant to take part in the endless globetrotting necessary to consolidate success in Europe and America. By 1974, just prior to the release of *Natty Dread*, both Peter and Bunny left the group to concentrate on their solo careers.

Bunny inaugurated his own Solomonic label upon which all his recordings have since appeared in Jamaica. His first solo record, 'Searching For Love' had emerged in limited quantities in the early 70s, concurrent with his involvement with the Wailers. His other Solomonic releases, 'Life Line', 'Bide Up', 'Pass It On' (different to the version on the *Burnin'* album) and 'Arabs Oil Weapon', credited to the Wailers, came out in 1975. A year later Island released *Blackheart Man* to immediate and unanimous acclaim from the world's music press. With tracks like 'Rastaman', 'Reincarnated Souls', 'Bide Up', 'Fig Tree', 'Amagideon (sic)' and the title track, *Blackheart Man* is still regarded as Bunny's masterpiece. Wailer's subsequent albums continued with varying degrees of success, in much the same vein, until he adapted to incorporate aspects of the burgeoning dancehall style, hitting big with records like 'Riding', an adaptation of the Perry produced 'Riding High' track, 'Crucial', 'Cool Runnings', 'Rock And Groove' and the rootsy 'Rise And Shine'. An album of Wailers' covers, *Bunny Wailer Sings The Wailers*, garnered further critical plaudits, followed by a similar collection entitled *Tribute To The Hon. Robert Nesta Marley*, in honour of the passing of his old spar. However, as the decade wore on

Bunny Wailer

Junior Marvin of the Wailers

Wailer, like many of the old school Rasta artists, seemed increasingly out of step with the digital ragga that had taken over in 1986, and he has since relied mainly on the loyalty of existing fans outside of Jamaica. Recent albums have made little impact upon the reggae scene at a grass roots level, despite the acclaim heaped upon the lushly packaged *Liberation*, seen by many critics as a return to the roots militancy of yore.

Albums: *Blackheart Man* (Island 1976), *Protest* (Island 1977), *Struggle* (Island 1978), *In I Fathers House* (Solomonic 1980), *Bunny Wailer Sings The Wailers* (Island 1981), *Tribute To The Hon. Nesta Marley* (Solomonic 1981), *Rock 'n' Groove* (Solomonic 1981), *Hook Line & Sinker* (Solomonic 1982), *Roots Radics Rockers Reggae* (Shanachie 1984), *Marketplace* (Solomonic 1986), *Bunny Wailer Live* (Solomonic 1986), *Roots Man Skanking* (Shanachie 1987), *Rule Dancehall* (Solomonic 1987), *Liberation* (Solomonic 1989), *Gumption* (Solomonic 1991).
Video: *Blackheart Man* (1990).

Wailers

(see Marley, Bob, And The Wailers)

Wailing Souls

Originally named the Renegades, the group first consisted of Lloyd 'Bread' McDonald and George 'Buddy' Haye, with Winston 'Pipe' Matthews as lead vocalist. This line-up recorded backing vocals for an Ernest Ranglin album before breaking up in 1968. Matthews and McDonald then teamed up with Oswald Downer and Norman Davis, recording 'Gold Digger' for Lloyd 'Matador' Daley. Their next move was to Coxsone Dodd at Studio One where, like so many other Jamaican artists, they recorded some of their finest work often credited to the Classics, but they became Pipe And The Pipers when they recorded two classic singles, 'Harbour Shark' and 'Back Biter', for Bob Marley's Tuff Gong label in the early 70s. Their vocals had a raw edge neatly counterpointed by their harmonies and their early work set the pattern for their entire

careers. Put simply their vocal prowess and ability to write songs almost to order meant that for the next 20 years they were never far from the limelight, recording in whatever the current musical fashion was yet still making fine music of lasting quality. In 1974 Davis and Downes left and Hill rejoined. Joe Higgs also entered the group's ranks for a short while, but left to tour the USA with Jimmy Cliff. Their next producer Joe Joe Hookim put them firmly in the hit parade with a succession of local hits for Channel One notably "Things And Time', 'Joy Within Your Heart' and 'Very Well'. In 1976 Garth Dennis (of Black Uhuru) joined the group.

Their next move was towards more artistic and financial independence with the formation of their own label Massive and their first two releases, 'Bredda Gravalicious' and 'Feel The Spirit', were massive hits in 1977/78. They moved on to Sly And Robbie's Taxi label in the early 80s for two more monster records, 'Old Broom' and 'Sugar Plum Plum'. Their next release for current hit producer, Henry 'Junjo' Lawes, 'Fire House Rock', was one of their most popular records ever. Somehow they found time (and energy) to make some beautiful records for Linval Thompson during this both artistically and commercially successful period. Throughout the 80s they continued to make superbly crafted conscious records, which although out-of-step with the times still sold well to discerning listeners worldwide. They proved they could still do it in the dancehalls as well, with some serious tunes for King Jammys towards the end of the decade. The 90s saw them signed to Sony and the big time now beckons one of Jamaica's finest ever vocal groups.

Albums: *The Wailing Souls* (Studio One 1976), *Wild Suspense* (Massive/Island 1979), *Fire House Rock* (Greensleeves 1980), *Wailing* (Jah Guidance 1981), *Inch Pinchers* (Greensleeves 1983), *On The Rocks* (Greensleeves 1983), *Soul & Power* (Studio One 1984), *Stranded* (Greensleeves 1984), *Lay It On The Line* (Live & Learn 1986),

Willie Williams

Kingston 14 (Live & Learn 1987), *Kingston 14* (Live & Learn 1987), *Stormy Night* (Rohit 1990), *All Over The World* (1992). Compilations: *Best Of* (Empire 1984), *Very Best Of* (Greensleeves 1987).

Wales, Josey

b. Joseph Sterling, Kingston, Jamaica. Raised in West Kingston, he began DJing in 1977 with Roots Unlimited sound system, alongside Buru Banton, taking his name from a popular Clint Eastwood movie. The next three and a half years were spent on U Roy's King Sturgav Hi-Fi where he enjoyed a successful partnership with Charlie Chaplin. By 1982 his gruff, reality-laced lyrics could be heard on live dancehall albums for Bunny Roots' Kris Disk label. He then joined Volcano, which under the auspices of owner, promoter and producer Henry 'Junjo' Lawes had become the leading sound system on the island. Junjo produced Josey's first hit; 'Leggo Mi Hand', later that same year, and work began on a debut album, *The Outlaw Josey Wales,* which confirmed his status as a serious rival to Yellowman when released in 1983. *Two Giant Clash* witnessed them both sharing the same Roots Radics rhythms but the follow-up set, *No Way Better Than Yard,* in 1984, was produced by Wales himself and Mickey Pep from Cornerstone, with no discernable drop in quality. Wales took his talents to King Jammys and the hits continued to flow. 'Na Lef Jamaica', 'Water Come A Mi Eye', 'It's Raining', 'Culture A Lick' and 'My Special Prayer' showed his feel for plain speaking and cultural ghetto truths was undiminished. The following three years reaped several fine albums, including one for George Phang (*Undercover Lover*) and then Black Solidarity (*Ruling*). He introduced both Admiral Bailey and Shabba Ranks to the Jammys camp.

By 1988 Wales could be heard voicing for Gussie Clarke, Exterminator and even Jimmy Cliff. Relocating to America he briefly recorded for Count Shelly before going into semi-retirement, occasionally guesting on stage shows and sound systems. In 1993 he made a successful comeback, topping the UK reggae charts with 'Hey Girl', a duet with Beres Hammond. Further tunes with Hammond and then for Tapper Zukie, Exterminator, Gussie Clarke, Bobby Digital and King Jammys quickly followed, with Wales often reworking his former lyrics to renewed effect. A good example of this is *Cowboy Style*, which King Jammys released in 1994.

Selected albums: *The Outlaw Josey Wales* (Greensleeves 1983), *No Way Better Than Yard* (Greensleeves 1984), *Rulin'* (Black Solidarity 1986), *Na Lef Jamaica* (Mango/Island 1986), *Ha Fi Say So* (Jammys 1988), *Undercover Lover* (Powerhouse 1989), *Special Prayer* (VP 1990), *Code Of Conduct* (Powerhouse 1991), *Cowboy Style* (Jammys/Greensleeves 1994). With Yellowman: *Two Giants Clash* (Greensleeves 1984). With Early B: *Josey Wales Meets Early B* (Sonic Sounds 1987).

Williams, Willie

b. St Ann's, Jamaica. Best known for his huge 'Armagideon Time' hit for Coxsone Dodd in 1979, one of the records that heralded the dancehall era where old Studio One rhythms were revitalised and garnished with new lyrics. In this case the original Sound Dimension instrumental, 'Real Rock', was dusted down for Willie to sing his portentous lyric over. The Clash were sufficiently impressed to try their hand at the song. The rhythm has always been popular and there are still innumerable versions doing the rounds in the mid-90s. Williams started in the business at the age of 14, recording 'Calling' for Coxsone, and going on to run his own sound system, Tripletone, at the end of the decade. In the early 70s he ran his own label, Soul Sounds, producing the likes of Delroy Wilson and the Versatiles. He also sang alongside Freddie McGregor with the Generation Gap. Dodd issued a number of follow-up singles including 'Addis Adaba' and 'Jah Righteous Plan', though they failed to make as much of an impression. He also recorded for Yabby You, cutting a variation on his big hit entitled 'Armagideon Man', but further success eluded him. In the 80s he has continued to make records. Some, like 'Sweet Home' for Black Victory records, were extremely good, but he is still looking for the record to re-establish his name in the market-place.

Albums: *Messenger Man* (Jah Muzik 1980), *Armagideon Time* (Studio One 1982), *Unity* (Blackstar 1987), *Natty With A Cause* (Jah Shaka 1992), *See Me* (Jah Shaka 1993).

Wilson, Delroy

Like Dennis Brown and Freddie McGregor, Delroy Wilson (b. 1948, Kingston, Jamaica) was barely out of short pants when he cut his debut single for Coxsone Dodd's Studio One label. His first hit, 'Joe Liges' (1963), was written by Lee Perry, then working as a talent spotter/songwriter/singer for Dodd, and was a lyrical attack on former Coxsone employee and now rival, Prince Buster. ('One hand wash the other, but you don't remember your brother, Joe Liges, Joe Liges, stop criticise') set to a rollicking early ska rhythm. The record was so popular that his follow-up, 'Spirit In The Sky', another Perry penned barb aimed at the Prince, was actually credited to Joe Liges when it was released in the UK on the Bluebeat and Black Swan labels. Delroy went on to cut numerous records in the same vein for Dodd, including 'One Two Three', 'I Shall Not Remove', a duet with Slim Smith entitled 'Look Who Is Back Again', and the anti-Buster 'Prince Pharoah', notable for being the only occasion in which Coxsone himself is heard on record, admonishing Buster in a coded, spoken outburst.

Delroy's voice broke just in time for the emergence of rocksteady in 1966, and his version of the Tams' 'Dancing Mood' of that year, one of the first rocksteady records, became a monstrous hit, alerting music fans to a new soul-styled crooner to match Alton Ellis. Throughout the rest of the decade Delroy, still recording mainly for Studio One, increased his popularity with titles like

'Riding For A Fall', another Tams cover, 'Once Upon A Time', 'Run Run', 'Won't You Come Home', 'Never Conquer', 'True Believer', 'One One', 'I'm Not A King', 'Rain From The Skies' and 'Feel Good All Over', as well as covering the Temptations' 'Get Ready'. Leaving Studio One in 1969, Delroy sojourned briefly at Bunny Lee's camp, which resulted in a popular reading of the Isley Brothers' 'This Old Heart Of Mine' (1969), before he drew his brakes at Sonia Pottinger's Tip Top Records, where he cut the excellent 'It Hurts' and a version of the Elgins' 'Put Yourself In My Place' (both 1969).

He teamed up once more with Bunny Lee to score a huge Jamaican hit with the anthemic 'Better Must Come' (1971), which was so popular it was adopted as a theme song by Michael Manley's PNP to increase their vote amongst 'sufferers', during that year's election campaign. In 1972 his success continued with 'Cool Operator', again for Lee, and throughout the next few years he maintained his position as one of reggae's best loved singers, with songs such as 'Mash Up Illiteracy' and 'Pretty Girl' for Joe Gibbs, 'Love' for Gussie Clarke, 'Rascal Man' for Winston 'Niney' Holness, a cover of the Four Tops' 'Ask The Lonely' for Harry J Johnson, 'It's A Shame' (a version of the Detroit Spinners' song for Joe Joe Hookim), 'Have Some Mercy' for A. Folder, 'Keep On Running' for Prince Tony. In 1976 his career took a further step forward when he recorded a hugely popular version of Bob Marley's 'I'm Still Waiting' for Lloyd Charmers LTD label, later followed by the well-received *Sarge*, still regarded by most aficionados as his best set. The misnomered Greatest Hits was also issued by Prince Tony during this period.

Further recordings towards the end of the decade, including 'All In This Thing Together', 'Halfway Up The Stairs' and 'Come In Heaven' for Gussie Clarke, did well, but Delroy's career floundered somewhat during the early part of the 80s, apart from a few sporadic sides, including the

Delroy Wilson

popular 'Let's Get Married', for London's Fashion Records. The digital age, however, saw him back in the running with the massive 'Don't Put The Blame On Me'/'Stop Acting Strange' for King Jammy in 1987, and 'Ease Up', a cut of the famous 'Rumours' rhythm for Bunny Lee, as well as albums like *Looking For Love* for Phil Pratt and *Which Way Is Up*, produced by Flabba Holt (see Roots Radics) for Blue Mountain, since when he has once again drifted into semi-retirement. Despite being one of the best singers Jamaica has ever produced, Delroy has rarely been able to meaningfully consolidate the success that has come his way, but he remains a much-loved and respected, but sorely under-used and, outside reggae circles, underrated performer.

Albums: *I Shall Not Remove* (Studio One c.1966), *Best Of Delroy Wilson* (aka *Original 12*, c.1969), *Good All Over* (1969), *Songs For I* (1974), *Greatest Hits* (1976), *Sarge* (1976), *Looking For Love* (1986), *Which Way Is Up* (Blue Mountain 1987). Compilation: *Collection* (Striker Lee 1985).

Wright, Winston

b. 1944, d. 1993. A name largely unknown outside the committed reggae fraternity, but the sound of Winston Wright's organ playing is familiar to anyone who has ever had more than a passing acquaintance with the music. Winston came onto the Kingston music scene in the mid-60s and began playing sessions in the rocksteady era, initially for Duke Reid but, as his work became better known, he was in constant demand from many other top producers. His mastery of, and feel for, the Hammond organ gained him an integral role in Tommy McCook's Supersonics - Duke Reid's house band. He later hit the UK charts in 1969 as one of Harry J's All Stars with 'Liquidator' and also made some of his finest recordings that same year with Clancy Eccles' Dynamites. Throughout the 70s he worked as part of the Dynamic Sounds nucleus of musicians and from 1975 onwards became one of Toots & The Maytals touring band. He still continued

his session work for Kingston's producers when he was back home 'resting', and his contribution to many classic 70s recordings was as uncredited and anonymous as his 60s output. More recently he returned to Dynamic Sounds where he acted as arranger, mixer and keyboard player. His tragic and untimely death in 1993 robbed the reggae world of one of its greatest unsung talents.

Selected albums: *Grass Roots* (Third World 1976), *Jump The Fence* (Third World 1976). With the Harry J All Stars: *Liquidator* (Trojan 1970). With the Dynamites: *Fire Corner* (Trojan/Clandisc 1969), *Herbsman* (Trojan/Clandsic 1970).

Y

Yabby You

b. Vivian Jackson, Kingston, Jamaica. Yabby acquired his nickname from the drawn out, chanting refrain on his 1972 debut 45, 'Conquering Lion': 'Be You, Yabby Yabby You'. Despite courting controversy in his repudiation of Rastafarian godhead Haile Selassie, in favour of a personalised form of Christianity, his output throughout the 70s and early 80s has nonetheless rarely deviated far from the orthodox Rastafarianism typically expressed at the time. As leader of the Prophets (additional personnel at various times included Alrick Forbes, Dada Smith, Bobby Melody and the Ralph Brothers) Yabby cut a remarkable series of roots reggae classics, including 'Jah Vengeance', 'Run Come Rally', 'Love Thy Neighbours', 'Valley Of Jehosaphat', 'Judgement On The Land', 'Fire In Kingston', 'Chant Down Babylon' and many others, mostly appearing on his own Vivian Jackson and Prophets labels in Jamaica.

With the release of *Ramadam* in 1975, the UK variation of the Jamaican-issued *Conquering Lion* (one or two tracks were different), Yabby swiftly acquired cult status in the UK: his name synonymous with reggae music of a particularly deep, spiritual nature. He also gained a reputation as a producer of other artists, including DJs Trinity, Jah Stitch, Dillinger, Prince Pompado, Tapper Zukie and Clint Eastwood, and singers Wayne Wade, Junior Brown, Willie Williams, Patrick Andy, Tony Tuff, and Michael Prophet. The 80s saw him retreat from the music business as his health deteriorated, though he made something of a comeback in the early 90s with some new productions and the re-appearance of many of his classic 45s and albums, re-pressed off the original stampers to cater for the large European collectors' market.

Selected albums: *Conquering Lion/Ramadam* (Prophet 1975), *Ram A Dam* (Eve 1976), *King Tubby's Prophecy Of Dub* (1976), *Deliver Me From My Enemies* (Prophet 1977), *Chant Down Babylon* (Ital 1978), *Beware Dub* (Grove Music 1978), *Jah Jah Way* (Island 1980), *One Love, One Heart* (Shanachie 1983), *Fleeing From The City* (Shanachie 1988). Compilation: *Yabby You Collection* (Greensleeves 1984).

Yard tapes

Also known as 'Sound Tapes', yard tapes are simply live recordings of reggae sound systems in action. They first became popular circa 1981, as dancehall began to exert a huge influence over the reggae audience: yard tapes offered the chance to hear the top Jamaican sounds in action, with reggae stars performing live over dub plates, often showcasing material that would not be available on record for months, if ever. Sometimes suffering from poor sound quality, this is more than compensated for by the sense of occasion and the sheer excitement of hearing what is, after all, reggae in its natural habitat: the dancehall. The name Yard, incidentally, means home in Jamaican slang, ie Jamaica. Yard Tapes remain a unique, perennially popular, and exclusively reggae phenomenon to this day.

Yellowman

b. Winston Foster, Jamaica. Yellowman was the deejaying sensation of the early 80s and he achieved this status with a fair amount of talent and inventive and amusing lyrics. He mainly built his early career around the fact that he was an albino and his success has to be seen within its initial Jamaican context. The albino or 'dundus' is virtually an outcast in Jamaican society and Foster's early years were more difficult than anyone outside of Jamaica could possibly imagine. Against the odds he used this background to his advantage and, like King Stitt who had previously traded on his physical deformities, Foster paraded himself in the Kingston dance halls as 'Yellowman', the DJ with endless lyrics about how sexy, attractive and appealing he was to the opposite sex. Within a matter of months he went from social pariah to headlining act on Jamaican stage shows and his popularity rocketed. Obviously the irony of his act was not lost on his audiences. His records were both witty and relevant - 'Soldier Take Over' being a fine example - and he was the first to release a live album - not of a stage show but actually recorded live on a sound system - *Live At Aces,* which proved hugely successful and was widely imitated. It captured him at the height of his powers and in full control of his 'fans' None of the excitement is lost in the transition from dancehall to record.

Yellowman's records sold well and he toured the USA and UK to ecstatic crowds - his first sell-out London shows caused traffic jams and road blocks around the venue. He could do no wrong and even his version of 'I'm Getting Married In The Morning' sold well. He was soon signed for a major deal to CBS and was 'King Yellow' to everyone in the reggae business. This did not last and by the mid-80s it had become difficult to sell his records to the fickle reggae market. By this time, however, he had been adopted by 'pop' audiences all over the world as a novelty act and while he has never become a major star he is still very popular and his records sell in vast quantities in many countries. He has released more records than a great many other reggae acts - no mean feat in a business dominated by excess. Made both rich and successful through his DJing work, it is mainly his ability to laugh at himself and encourage others to share the joke which has endeared him to so many. It should be immediately apparent to all who has had the last laugh.

Selected albums: *Them A Mad Over Me* (J&L 1981), *Bad Boy Skanking* (Greensleeves 1982), *Mr Yellowman* (Greensleeves 1982), *Live At Sunsplash* (Sunsplash 1982), *The Yellow, The Purple, And The Nancy* (Greensleeves 1983), *Divorced* (Burning Sounds 1983), *Zungguzungguguzungguen g* (Greensleeves 1983), *King Yellowman* (CBS 1984), *Nobody Move, Nobody Get Hurt* (Greensleeves 1984), *Galong Galong Galong* (Greensleeves 1985), *Going To The Chapel* (Greensleeves 1986), *Rambo* (Moving Target 1986), *Yellow Like Cheese* (RAS 1987), *Don't Burn It Down* (Shanachie/Greensleeves 1987), *Blueberry Hill* (Greensleeves/Rohit 1987), *King Of The Dancehall* (Rohit 1988), *Sings The Blues* (Rohit 1988), *Rides Again* (RAS 1988), *One In A Million* (Shanachie 1988), *Badness* (La/Unicorn 1990), *Thief* (Mixing Lab 1990), *Party* (RAS 1991), *Reggae On The Move* (RAS 1992), *Live In England* (Greensleeves 1992), *In Bed With Yellowman* (1993). With General Trees: *A Reggae Calypso Encounter* (Rohit 1987). With Josey Wales: *Two Giants Clash* (Greensleeves 1984). With Charlie Chaplin: *The Negril Chill* (ROIR 1988). Compilations: *20 Super Hits* (Sonic Sounds 1990).

Video: *Raw And Rough (Live At Dollars Lawn)* (1989).

Yabby You

Z

Zukie, Tapper

b. David Sinclair, Jamaica. Tapper began as a DJ in his early teens, influenced by U Roy and Dennis Alcapone. In order to curb his youthful proclivity for getting into trouble, his mother sent him to England in 1973, where producer Bunny Lee organised some live shows and recording sessions under the aegis of UK based entrepreneur Larry Lawrence, for whom he cut his debut, 'Jump And Twist'. He also recorded material for Clem Bushay which later emerged as *Man A Warrior*. On his return to Jamaica he again worked for Bunny Lee, though Tapper's ambitions to be as famous as U Roy led him to record 'Judge I Oh Lord' for Lloydie Slim, and 'Natty Dread Don't Cry' for Lee. Zukie's frustration at Bunny Lee's indifference manifested itself in an altercation with the producer. The police were called, but their differences were settled when Bunny gave him some rhythms to DJ on for himself. These, and others he obtained from Joe Joe Hookim, were DJ'd in a spare hour at King Tubby's studio, and eventually issued as *MPLA* in 1976.

In 1975 he returned to the UK to find that he had acquired something of a cult following due to the belated popularity of *Man A Warrior*. An arrangement with Klik Records saw the release of 'MPLA' as a single, which met with immediate success and persuaded Zukie to let them release the whole album, which finally established his name amongst the higher echelons of DJdom. Other recordings dating from the same period included a batch of 45s for Yabby You including 'Don't Get Crazy' and 'Natty Dread On The Mountain Top'. Whilst in the UK he appeared alongside new wave heroine Patti Smith after she had met with him and told him how inspiring his *Man A Warrior* had been to her. The album was later re-issued on Smith and partner Lenny Kaye's Mer label. Smith would later contribute sleeve notes to *Man From Bosrah*. Zukie also produced a number of artists during this period for his own Stars label, including Junior Ross and The Spear ('Babylon Fall', 'Judgement Time'), Prince Alla ('Bosrah', 'Daniel' and 'Heaven Is My Roof') and one all-time classic for Horace Andy, 'Natty Dread A Weh She Want'. In addition he released two dub albums, *Escape From Hell* and *Tapper Zukie In Dub*. His protégés, Knowledge, were signed to A&M but subsequently dropped. His fortunes improved further with the release of *Peace In The Ghetto* and *Tapper Roots*, as well as popular singles like 'She Want A Phensic' and his first big Jamaican hit, 'Oh Lord'. Returning to Jamaica, Zukie became active again in his local community. Largely silent during the late 80s, he has returned with a vengeance in the 90s producing huge hits for stars such as Dennis Brown and Beres Hammond, opening his own compact disc centre on Eastwood Park Road in Kingston in 1994.

Albums: *Man A Warrior* (Klik 1975), *MPLA* (Klik 1976), *Man From Bosrah* (Stars 1977), *Escape From Hell* (Stars 1977), *In Dub* (Stars 1977), *Peace In The Ghetto* (Stars 1978), *Tapper Roots* (Stars/Front Line 1978), *People Are You Ready?* (Stars 1983), *Raggamuffin* (World Enterprise 1986).

RECOMMENDED LISTENING

Abyssinians	*Forward On To Zion*
Abyssinians	*Satta Massa Gana*
Alcapone, Dennis	*Forever Version*
Alcapone, Dennis	*My Voice Is Insured For Half A Million Dollars*
Alphonso, Roland	*Best Of*
Alphonso, Roland	*King Of Sax*
Andy, Bob	*Song Book*
Andy, Horace	*Skylarking*
Big Youth	*Everyday Skank*
Big Youth	*Natty Cultural Dread*
Big Youth	*Screaming Target*
Black Uhuru	*Showcase*
Black Uhuru	*Sinsemilla*
Black Uhuru	*Vital Selection*
Brooks, Cedric 'Im'	*Flash Forward*
Brown, Dennis	*Brown Sugar*
Brown, Dennis	*Just Dennis*
Brown, Dennis	*Love Has Found Its Way*
Brown, Dennis	*Money In My Pocket*
Brown, Dennis	*Wolf And Leopards*
Brown, Glen, And Others	*Boat To Progress*
Brown, Glen, And Others	*Check The Winner*
Brown, Glen, And Others	*Dubble Attack*
Burning Spear	*Hail H.I.M.*
Burning Spear	*Marcus Children* aka *Social Living*
Burning Spear	*Marcus Garvey*
Burning Spear	*Rocking Time*
Burning Spear	*Studio One Presents*
Carlton And His Shoes	*Love Me Forever*
Chin-Loy, Herman	*Aquarius Dub*
Clarendonians	*Best Of*
Congos	*Heart Of The Congos*
Count Ossie & The Mystic Revelation Of Rastafari	*Grounation*
Daley, Lloyd 'Matador' (Collection)	*Scandal*
Daley, Lloyd 'Matador' (Collection)	*Way Back When*
Dekker, Desmond	*The Original Reggae Hit Sound*
Dekker, Desmond	*This Is Desmond Dekker*
Dillinger	*CB 200*
Dodd, Coxsone (Studio One Collection)	*All Star Top Hits*
Dodd, Coxsone (Studio One Collection)	*Pirates Choice*

Marley, Bob, And The Wailers	*Soul Revolution 1 & 2*
Marley, Bob, And The Wailers	*Survival*
Marley, Bob, And The Wailers	*Upsetter Record Shop Part 2*
Marley, Bob, And The Wailers	*Wailing Wailers*
Maytals	*Do The Reggae*
Maytals	*From The Roots*
McGregor, Freddie	*Bobby Babylon*
McKay, Freddie	*Picture On The Wall*
Mighty Diamonds	*Changes*
Mighty Diamonds	*Right Time/I Need A Roof*
Minott, Sugar	*Back Roots*
Minott, Sugar	*Live Loving*
Minott, Sugar	*Showcase*
Mittoo, Jackie	*Macka Fat*
Mutabaruka	*Check It*
Niney And Friends	*Blood And Fire*
Observer All Stars	*Dubbing With The Observer*
Osbourne, Johnny	*Truths & Rights*
Pablo, Augustus (Rockers Collection)	*Classic Rockers 2*
Pablo, Augustus (Rockers Collection)	*Original Rockers*
Pablo, Augustus	*East Of The River Nile*
Pablo, Augustus	*King Tubby Meets Rockers Uptown*
Pablo, Augustus	*This Is*
Paragons	*On The Beach*
Paul, Frankie	*Sara*
Prince Buster	*Fabulous Greatest Hits*
Prince Jazzbo	*Choice Of Version*
Radway, Jimmy	*Micron Dub*
Reid, Duke (Treasure Isle Collection)	*Hottest Hits Vols. 1 & 2*
Revolutionaries	*Vital Dub Well Charge*
Royal Rasses	*Humanity*
Royals	*Pick Up The Pieces*
Scientist	*Scientist Meets The Space Invaders*
Sherman, Bim	*Love Forever/Danger*
Skatalites	*Ska Authentic*
Smith, Slim	*Early Days*
Techniques	*Classics*
Tetrack	*Let's Get Started*
U Roy	*Version Galore - Sound Of Now*
Uniques	*Early Days*
Upsetter And Friends	*Excaliburman*
Upsetter And Friends	*Open The Gate*
Upsetter And Friends	*Public Jestering*
Upsetter And Friends	*The Upsetter Collection*
Upsetters	*Blackboard Jungle Dub*
Upsetters	*Megaton Dub 2*
Upsetters	*Super Ape*
Various (Ska)	*Intensified*
Various (Ska)	*More Intensified*
Various (Ska)	*Scattered Lights*

Various (Ska)	*Ska Boo Da Ba*
Various (Ska)	*Ska Strictly For You*
Various	*A DeeJay Explosion Inna Dance Hall Style*
Various	*King Tubby Soundclash*
Various	*Knotty Vision*
Various	*Monkey Business*
Various	*Rebel Music*
Various	*Reggae Hits Vols. 1 -14*
Various	*Tougher Than Tough*
Wailer, Bunny	*Blackheart Man*
Wailer, Bunny	*Dub D'sco*
Wailing Souls	*Presenting*
Wailing Souls	*Wild Suspense*
Wilson, Delroy	*Feel Good All Over*
Wilson, Delroy	*Original 12 (The Best Of)*
Yabby You And The Prophets	*Conquering Lion*
Yabby You And The Prophets	*King Tubbys Prophecy Of Dub*

Compiled from lists drawn up by Harry Hawke, Paul Cooteur and Lol Bell-Brown.

BIBLIOGRAPHY/SOURCES

Books

General Reference

Black Music in Britain - Essays On The Afro-Asian Contribution To Popular Music, ed. Paul Oliver (Open University Press 1990).

Deep Roots Music, Howard Johnson & Jim Pines (Proteus/Channel Four 1982).
The book to accompany Channel Four's ground breaking *Deep Roots Music* series.

Jah Music - The Evolution Of The Popular Jamaican Song, Sebastian Clarke (Heinemann Educational Books 1980).
An in-depth analysis of the music and artists following on from reggae's big overground break in the 70s.

The Pop Process, Richard Mabey (Hutchinson Educational 1969).
Mainly concerns pop music but there is some particularly perceptive analysis on the influence of ska on pop music and dance in the UK.

Reggae, A People's Music, Rolston Kallyndyr & Henderson Dalrymple (Carib Arawak Publications 1976).
The first (slim) book ever written about the music.

Reggae Bloodlines - In Search Of The Music & Culture Of Jamaica, Stephen Davis & Peter Simon (Anchor Press Doubleday 1977).
Excellent pictures but the text is often misleading and misrepresentative.

Reggae International, Stephen Davis & Peter Simon (Thames & Hudson 1983).
A much-improved update of *Reggae Bloodlines* with contributions from writers such as Carl Gayle. The presentation is faultless.

Reggae Island - Jamaican Music In The Digital Age, Brian Jahn & Tom Weber (Kingston Publishers Ltd. 1992).
A strictly up to date look at the 90s music scene in Jamaica with fine photographs and interviews with most of the current top performers.

Rock File, Charlie Gillett (First Pictorial Presentations New English Library 1972).
Interesting for 'Skins Rule' by Pete Fowler and the confused (and confusing) 'Johnny Cool &

The Isle of Sirens' by one Johnny Copasetic, two early looks at the phenomenon.

Rock File 2, Charlie Gillett (Panther 1974).
Worthy of inclusion for 'Are You ready For Rude & Rough Reggae' by Carl Gayle.

The Rock Primer, ed. John Collis (Penguin 1980).
Well worthwhile for the 'reggae' section by Nick Kimberley - essential singles and albums.

Biographies

Bob Marley

Inevitably Bob Marley has had more books written about his career than the rest of reggae's musicians put together (which is hardly his fault) and, because of the very nature of his talent and fame, many are very, very good. How could they fail with the subject matter?

Bob Marley - The Roots of Reggae, Cathy McKnight & John Tobler (Star 1977).
A slim paperback which makes up with enthusiasm what it lacks in knowledge and background: 'Reggae is power and Marley knows it!'

Bob Marley - Soul Rebel - Natural Mystic, Adrian Boot & Vivien Goldman (Eel Pie/Hutchinson 1981).
Lovely photographs and an interesting text.

Catch A Fire - The Life of Bob Marley, Timothy White (Elmtree Books 1983). Revised and updated as: *Catch A Fire - The Life of Bob Marley*, Timothy White (Omnibus Press 1991).
Highly entertaining account concentrating on the early years of Bob Marley's career.

Bob Marley, Stephen Davis (Arthur Baker 1983). Revised and updated as: *Bob Marley - Conquering Lion of Reggae*, Stephen Davis (Plexus 1993).
A more objective overview of Bob Marley's career.

Bob Marley - Rebel With A Cause, Dennis Morris (DMMP Publications 1986).
Large format picture book. The photographs are beautiful.

Bob Marley - Reggae King Of The World, Malika Lee Whitney & Dermot Hussey (Plexus/Kingston Publishers Ltd 1984).
Large format with superb rare photographs. Written from a Jamaican point of view.

Bob Marley - The Illustrated Discography/Biography, Observer Station (Omnibus Press 1985).
A run down on some of the vast recorded output of Bob Marley & The Wailers.

Bob Marley in His Own Words, Ian McCann (Omnibus Press 1993).
Exactly what it says - a selection of quotes (painstakingly compiled) from Bob Marley on a wide range of subjects.

Bob Marley: Songs Of Freedom - An Illustrated Song Book, (Hal Leonard/Polygram Music Publishing 1992).

Specialist Publishers

Black Star & Muzik Tree have put together some of the best books ever written about reggae music, researched and written by fans of the music for fans of the music. Sometimes a bit too esoteric for the man in the street, more often 100% essential.

Rhythm Wise, Ray Hurford (Muzik Tree/Black Star 1989).
Rhythm Wise Two, Jean Scrivener (Black Star 1990).
Rhythm Wise Three, Jean Scrivener (Black Star 1991).
Details of many of the rhythms (or backing tracks) that reggae musicians endlessly recycle and update - the backbone of the music.

More Axe, Ray Hurford, Geoff Sullivan, Dave Hendley & Colin Moore (Muzik Tree/Black Star 1987).

More Axe 7, Ray Hurford, Ian McCann, David Katz, Ardella Jones & Tero Kaski (Muzik Tree/Black Star 1989).
Interviews and articles taken from the long running 'Small Axe' fanzine.

Reggae Inna Dancehall Style, Tero Kaski & Pekka Vuorinen (Black Star 1984).
Excellent, in-depth look at Volcano Hi Power Sound System and all its major stars. Fascinating enough at the time, but becoming more and more absorbing as time goes by.

King Jammy's, Beth Lesser (Muzik Tree/Black Star 1989).
One of the best reggae books ever - mainly about Jammy's digital revolution of reggae music, but packed full of insight and anecdotes. Essential.

Discographies

Studio One has dominated the Jamaican music scene since its inception and there are two discographies documenting Coxsone Dodd's recorded works.

Downbeat Special - Studio One Album Discography, Rob Chapman (Self-published, 1985).
An illustrated discography detailing Studio One's vast long playing output.

Never Grow Old - Studio One Singles Listing & Rhythm Directory, Rob Chapman (Self-published 1989).
A very brave attempt to make some kind of sense of Studio One's vast recorded output. A bit like painting the Forth Bridge but fascinating nevertheless. Second edition revised and updated in 1992.

Reggae Discography, Hermann Moter (Minotaurus Projekt 1983).
A good try. Needs to be updated urgently.

Background Reading

The Rastafarians - The Dreadlocks of Jamaica, Leonard E Barrett (Heinemann/Sangsters 1977).

Dread - The Rastafarians of Jamaica, Joseph Owens (Sangsters 1976).

Rastaman - The Rastafarian Movement In England, Ernest Cashmore (Allen & Unwin 1979).

Rastafari & Reggae - A Dictionary Source Book, Rebekah Michelle (Mulvaney/Greenwood Press 1991).
Jamaica - Babylon On A Thin Wire, Adrian Boot & Michael Thomas (Thames & Hudson 1976).

Jah Revenge - Babylon Revisited, Michael Thomas & Adrian Boot (Eel Pie Publishing 1982).

The Harder They Come, Michael Thelwell (Pluto Press 1980).
A 'novelisation' of the film of the same name which actually takes on a life of its own.

The Children Of Sisyphus, Orlando Patterson (Houghton Mifflin 1965).
Another novel which fills in many of the gaps in the music's background.

Beats Of The Heart - Popular Music Of The World, Jeremy Marre & Hannah Charlton (Pluto Press 1985).
Some revealing insights on the making of 'Roots Rock Reggae'.

The How To Be Jamaican Handbook - The Jamrite Cultural Dissemination Committee, Kim Robinson, Harclyde Walcott & Trevor Fearon (Jamrite Publications 1987).
Irreverent, hilarious look at Jamaica & Jamaicans.

The Illustrated Encyclopedia Of Black Music, Various authors (Salamander 1982).
One of the first music encyclopedias that actually took reggae music into account with some very detailed biographies and potted histories.

Sociology/Anthropology

Reggae has been picked over by sociologists for some time now and there are a growing number of books about what the music means (as opposed to the music itself) and its influence on youth subcultures.

Subculture - The Meaning Of Style, Dick Hebdige (New Accents 1979).

Cut 'N' Mix - Culture, Identity & Caribbean Music, Dick Hebdige (Comedia 1987).

Black Culture From JA To UK - The Reggae Trading From JA To UK, Simon Jones (Macmillan 1988).

Noises In The Blood - Orality Gender & The 'Vulgar' Body Of Jamaican Popular Culture, Carolyn Cooper (Warwick University Caribbean Studies/Macmillan 1993).

Resistance Through Rituals - Youth Subcultures In Post-War Britain, ed. Stuart Hall & Tony Jefferson (Hutchinson 1975).

Magazines

Swing Magazine
Pioneering late 60s/early 70s Jamaican magazine with extensive musical coverage.

Blues & Soul Magazine
In the 70s (for a time) carried a reggae feature every issue - initially by Chris Lane and then by Dave Hendley. These offered the first insights into a neglected and ignored musical form. The best of these were collected in *The Best Of Rebel Music* fanzine. The Blues & Soul features were seminal in that they represented the first time that the music was taken seriously in print.

Black Music Magazine
Also in the 70s, this contained some superb articles by Carl Gayle and some in-depth Jamaican reports.

Reggae Quarterly
The only magazine to cover the dancehall phenomenon of the 80s - put together by Beth Lesser & Dave Kingston from Canada.

Black Echoes (now Echoes)
This newspaper's weekly format offers little scope for in-depth analysis, but its review sections and occasional articles are still well worth reading.

Some reggae fanzines have been worthwhile - such as *Pressure Drop* - although it only ran to two issues in the mid 70s, the second issue still stands the test of time. *Small Axe*, the most committed and longest serving fanzine, is now in temporary retirement after the release of the innovative *Small Axe Files* series. *Boom Shacka Lacka* was issued in direct response to the lack of roots music coverage in the late 80s and with the current upsurge of interest in said music, now seems somewhat redundant. There have been more over the years but a couple of the most interesting (and visually appealing) have been in Finnish - *Cool Runnings* and Japanese - *Riddim* and *Reggae Magazine*. I'm unqualified to comment further on them.

Roger Dalke's long running series of UK label discographies make up in hard information what they lack in grammar and punctuation. Lists of catalogue numbers and record titles rarely appeal to anyone other than seriously involved followers of the music. Currently available (Spring 1994) are; *Record Selector 15, Record Selector 16, Record Selector 17*

Films

A number of reggae films have appeared over the years – the first, Horace Ove's *Reggae,* documented the shows at Wembley in 1970, while *The Harder They Come,* starring Jimmy Cliff, was the catalyst – in many instances even more so than the success of Bob Marley – that started the overground interest in the music. *Rockers, Babylon, Country Man* and *Smile Orange* are all well worth catching up with and there is now a vast catalogue of live shows and sound systems available on home video.

Television too has come up with some interesting programmes. *Reggae From The Edinburgh Festival* has never been repeated since it was first shown in the early 70s. *Deep Roots Music* was a brave attempt to bring across just what the music was all about, and featured some spellbinding footage. It followed in the footsteps of *Roots Rock Reggae* which, even though it was accused of being a promotional exercise for recent Virgin signings, was also marvellous in parts and went places no film crew had ever even thought about before. The director of *Roots Rock Reggae,* Jeremy Marre, also made a film on British Reggae for LWT's *Aquarius* series. His experiences (detailed in the *Beats Of The Heart* book) show just what the music and its followers were up against.

Videos

Bob Marley, inevitably, has had many videos made about his life and music:

Bob Marley - Live At Santa Monica
Bob Marley - One Love Peace Concert – The momentous Kingston concert in 1978.
Legend - The Best Of Bob Marley & The Wailers
Caribbean Nights – A Documentary on the life of Bob Marley
Bob Marley & The Wailers Live At The Rainbow 1977
Time Will Tell – A beautiful cinematic biography

Peter Tosh was the subject of the recent (1993) *Stepping Razor (Red X)* documentary.

One other notable video:

Various Artists: *This Is Ska.*
Recorded live at Kingston's Sombrero Club in the early 60s, featuring Prince Buster, Jimmy Cliff, The Maytals, The Charmers and Stranger Cole.

INDEX

The Guinness Encyclopedia of Popular Music

Compiled and Edited by Colin Larkin

' A landmark work. As much as the history of popular music deserves. ★★★★★' *Q Magazine*

'This is an absolutely invaluable addition to any musicologist's shelf.' *Vox*

'This is musical history in the making.' *Rolling Stone*

'(A) work of almost frightening completeness' *The Times*

'A remarkable achievement by any standards. . .The detail is stunning – and extraordinary.' *Today*

The most comprehensive and authoritative guide to popular music that has ever been published, *The Guinness Encyclopedia of Popular Music* covers every important artist, band, genre, group, event, instrument, publisher, promoter, record company and musical style from the world of popular music in four 832-page volumes in a slipcase. Price £225.00

The product of over four years of intensive labour by an international group of more than 100 skilled writers, musicologists and advisors, its scope is truly global. Compiled in an A-Z format, it covers all forms of popular music from 1990 to 1992 and contains almost 10,000 entries varying in length from 100 to 5,000 words.

A bibliography of over 4,000 entries is included along with a full index of artists' names.

For further details of this essential reference work, please write to:
Section D,
The Marketing Department,
Guinness Publishing,
33 London Road,
Enfield,

The Guinness Who's Who of Blues

General Editor: Colin Larkin

From the publishers of *The Guinness Encyclopedia of Popular Music* comes the definitive guide to the Blues. The return of Eric Clapton and Gary Moore to their blues roots has coincided with the rise of musicians such as Robert Cray and Jeff Healey. This, together with the phenominal revival of John Lee Hooker's career with *The Healer* and *Boom Boom* puts us in the midst of the biggest blues boom since the 60s.

Collected in this volume are the artists who shaped the blues, which in turn greatly influenced the development of popular music in the 20th century. Included are, Elmore James, Robert Johnson, Muddy Waters, B.B. King, Lighnin' Hopkins, Leadbelly, Buddy Guy and Albert Collin s; the great singers Bessie Smith, Victoria Spivey, Billie Holiday, Big Joe Turner and Koko Taylor and the legion of white musician's who have popularized the blues since the 60s, such as Alexis Korner, Paul Butterfield, Mike Bloomfield, Roy Buchanan, John Mayall, Johnny Winter, Peter Green and Stevie Ray Vaughan.

This book is available from all good bookshops and from selected record stores. For information on this or on forthcoming titles in the series, please write to:

Section D,
The Marketing Department,
Guinness Publishing,
33 London Road,
Enfield,
Middlesex,
EN2 6DJ,
England.

The Guinness Who's Who of Sixties Music

General Editor: Colin Larkin

From the publishers of *The Guinness Encyclopedia of Popular Music* comes the definitive guide to the groups and artists who created the music of the 60s. From the early years of Del Shannon, Bobby Darin, Ricky Nelson, and Cliff Richard; the Beach Boys, Jan and Dean and the Shangri-Las to the beat-boom with the Beatles and the Rolling Stones; the 'swinging London' era of the Who and the Kinks, and the explosion of sound from California's west coast with the Byrds, Doors, Jefferson Airplane and Grateful Dead. Folk protest, the blues boom, psychedelia, soul, jazz, ska, Merseybeat, pirate radio plus the impact on a whole generation by Bob Dylan - it's all told here with information on the musicians, songwriters and personalities.

From those who survived to those lost in the mists of time, everything you'd ever want to know is included in this complete and accurate record of the music and major artists of the decade. With hundreds of entries written by some of today's leading rock writers, this is the definative guide to the movers and shakers of 60s music.

This book is available from all good bookshops and from selected record stores. For information on this or on forthcoming titles in the series, please write to:

Section D,
The Marketing Department,
Guinnesss Publishing,
33 London Road,
Enfield,
Middlesex EN2 6DJ,
England

The Guinness Who's Who of Indie and New Wave Music

General Editor: Colin Larkin

From the publishers of *The Guinness Encyclopedia of Popular Music* comes the definitive guide to the groups and artists who have moulded the shape of popular music in the 70s, 80s and 90s. From the beginnings of punk in the late 70s with the Sex Pistols, Clash, Damned, X-Ray Spex and the Buzzcocks in the UK, and Television, Talking Heads, Blondie and the Ramones in the US, modern popular music was shaken to its foundations. These bands paved the way in the ensuing years for many new and varied forms of exciting music including Siouxsie And The Banshees, Joy Division/New Order, the Cure, Smiths, Cocteau Twins, Birthday Party, Jesus And Mary Chain, Happy Mondays, Stone Roses, James and R.E.M.

This book contains entries on all these bands plus many others on groups and artists who are usually, and unjustifiably, ignored in lesser encyclopedias. In all, there are hundreds of entries including contributions by some of the leading pop and indie writers today plus an introduction by Johnny Rogan.

This book is available from all good bookshops and from selected record stores. For information on this or on forthcoming titles in the series, please write to:

Section D,
The Marketing Department,
Guinnesss Publishing,
33 London Road,
Enfield,
Middlesex EN2 6DJ,
England